Advanced Word Processing

Microsoft® Word 2016

D1712730

Lessons 56–110

20e

Susie H. VanHuss
Ph.D., Distinguished Professor Emeritus,
University of South Carolina

Connie M. Forde
Ph.D., Mississippi State University

Donna L. Woo
Cypress College, California

Vicki R. Robertson
Southwest Tennessee Community College

COLLEGE
KEYBOARDING

CENGAGE
Learning®

Australia • Brazil • Japan • Korea • Mexico • Singapore • Spain • United Kingdom • United States

CENGAGE Learning

College Keyboarding: Advanced Word Processing, Lessons 56-110, Twentieth Edition
Susie H. VanHuss, Connie M. Forde,
Donna L. Woo, Vicki R. Robertson

General Manager, Science, Technology, Math:
Balraj Kalsi

Product Director: Kathleen McMahon

Product Manager: Amanda Lyons

Product Development Manager: Leigh Hefferon

Senior Content Developer: Anne Orgren

Product Assistant: Cara Suriyamongkol

Vice President, Marketing Services: Jennifer
Ann Baker

Marketing Director: Michele McTighe

Production Director: Patty Stephan

Senior Content Project Manager: Stacey Lamodi

Senior Designer: Diana Graham

Cover image(s): en-owai/Shutterstock.com

For product information and technology assistance, contact us at
Cengage Learning Customer & Sales Support, 1-800-354-9706
For permission to use material from this text or product,
submit all requests online at **www.cengage.com/permissions**
Further permissions questions can be e-mailed to
permissionrequest@cengage.com

Library of Congress Control Number: 2016938331

ISBN: 978-1-337-10326-8

Cengage Learning
20 Channel Center Street
Boston, MA 02210
USA

Cengage Learning is a leading provider of customized learning solutions with employees residing in nearly 40 different countries and sales in more than 125 countries around the world. Find your local representative at **www.cengage.com.**

Cengage Learning products are represented in Canada by Nelson Education, Ltd.

To learn more about Cengage Learning, visit **www.cengage.com**

Purchase any of our products at your local college store or at our preferred online store **www.cengagebrain.com**

Notice to the Reader

Publisher does not warrant or guarantee any of the products described herein or perform any independent analysis in connection with any of the product information contained herein. Publisher does not assume, and expressly disclaims, any obligation to obtain and include information other than that provided to it by the manufacturer. The reader is expressly warned to consider and adopt all safety precautions that might be indicated by the activities described herein and to avoid all potential hazards. By following the instructions contained herein, the reader willingly assumes all risks in connection with such instructions. The publisher makes no representations or warranties of any kind, including but not limited to, the warranties of fitness for particular purpose or merchantability, nor are any such representations implied with respect to the material set forth herein, and the publisher takes no responsibility with respect to such material. The publisher shall not be liable for any special, consequential, or exemplary damages resulting, in whole or part, from the readers' use of, or reliance upon, this material.

Printed in the United States of America
Print Number:06 Print Year: 2021

Contents

The Power of Word 2016...Starts Here!

LEARN . . . DISCOVER

Word 2016

Document Design

Communication Skills

Projects

Co-Authoring in Real Time

Windows 10 Basics

Discover the power of *College Keyboarding, 20th edition* print and digital solutions for *Microsoft Word 2016*.

College Keyboarding, 20e, L56–110 combines easy-to-use tools with a proven track record of ensuring classroom and workplace success.

Keyboarding in Skills Assessment Skills Manager (SAM) provides the tools to master document skills for use in school, career, and personal situations.

NEW to This Edition

- Coverage of *Windows 10*
- Coverage of *Word 2016*
- Correlation with the web-based *Skills Assessment Manager (SAM)* to build, apply, and assess skills
- New letterhead and memo forms throughout the text, removing clip art and providing better images for documents
- New themes and updated document elements, such as page numbers, headers, footers, SmartArt, and tables, in many documents.
- Updated Hess Pet Center project including modified setting, updated pictures, and new letterhead and other forms.
- Communication exercise topics are tied to rules in the Reference Guide (Appendix C)
- Communication Pretests and Post-Tests were moved to instructor resources
- In Module 15, all comments and tracked changes were updated
- Module 20 has been completely rewritten to provide instruction and applications on new *Windows 10* and *Word 2016* features including Save to Cloud, Share, and co-authoring in real time

Meet SAM (Skills Assessment Manager)

SAM's online learning environments enable students to learn *Microsoft Office* and computer concepts essential to academic and career success. Students observe and practice, then apply their skills in the live application. Auto-graded assignments save time and energy.

For the 20th edition of *College Keyboarding*, SAM replaces KPDO as an optional digital companion to the print text. With SAM, the keying drills, timed writings, skill buildings, and other activities can be completed and submitted online. If your course is using SAM, visit www.sam.cengage.com to find out more about how to use SAM with this textbook.

Accelerate Learning—Integrate Document Formatting and Word 2016

Follow the path **(Tab/Group/Command)** and illustrated step-by-step directions to make learning new commands easy.

Each new command is immediately applied within a short drill and then reinforced in **Apply It.**

Data files provide immediate opportunities to practice the new command quickly.

Learn and Reinforce New Commands with Drills and Apply It

Present concept, path, and step-by-step illustrated directions

Apply immediately; use data file to shorten keying time

Ensure Success with QuickChecks, Discover, and Tips

Quick Check shows a suggested solution

Discover teaches additional functions or a simple new command

Tip provides additional information

Document Design

Learn, Apply, and Reinforce Document Designs with Deliberate Learning Approach

Learn document designs with brief instructional narrative with illustrated examples

Key first document from a full-page model document with callouts on letterhead

Reinforce document design in authentic learning activity with unarranged copy and limited instructions

Projects

Timed writing for training or assessment provided

All 11 projects in this textbook are located in Hess Office Park

Same company setting used for Modules 14 and 19 to provide continuity and realism in the work environment

Productivity, working independently, using SOPs, and communication skills are emphasized

Powerful Tools . . . Working for You

College Keyboarding 20e provides the tools students need to develop expertise in keyboarding, document formatting, and essential word processing skills using *Microsoft Word 2016*.

ISBN 9781337103251

ISBN 9781337103022

ISBN 9781337103268

ISBN 9781337103275

Supplemental Resources

Instructor Companion Site

A robust instructor companion website provides the materials you need to teach this course, including an instructor's manual; tests; solutions files; syllabus; Communication Skills pretests, post-tests, and references; and more. To access the instructor companion site, sign in to http://login.cengage.com and add this text to your instructor dashboard.

Student Companion Site

The data files needed to complete this text's activities are found on the free student companion website for this text. To access the student companion site, visit http://login.cengage.com and search for this text.

Keyboarding in Skills Assessment Manager (SAM)

For the 20th edition of *College Keyboarding*, SAM replaces KPDO as an optional digital companion to the print text. With SAM, the keying drills, timed writings, skill buildings, and other activities can be completed and submitted online. Most Drills, Apply-Its, and end-of-module projects have been converted into computer-graded SAM tasks and projects.

Instructors may teach the course using the print book only, the print book plus SAM, or SAM only. If your course is using SAM, visit http://sam.cengage.com to find out more about how to use SAM with this textbook.

To purchase SAM with a print textbook, speak to your Cengage Learning Consultant.

Commands by Module

Lesson	Commands
Module 10 Advanced Business Correspondence	
56	Template, Quick Parts
57	Review Envelope, Review Left Tab
59	Header, Review Date
Module 11 Documents with Tables and Graphics	
61	Review Table Tools
62	Change Text Direction, Distribute Rows or Columns, Repeat Header Row/Page Orientation
63	Decimal Tabs in Tables, Formulas in Tables, Sort in Tables
64	Format Pictures, WordArt, SmartArt
65	Page and Paragraph Borders, Drop Cap, Picture Styles, Online Video
66	Watermarks, Page Color, Text Boxes
67	Columns
Module 12 Business Reports	
70	Multi-level List, Review Footnotes, Document Themes, and Page Numbers
71	Header/Footer, Cover Page, Section Breaks, Page Number Format, Review Insert File
72	Table of Contents
73	Captions, Table of Figures
74	GoTo, Splitting Panes, Document Formatting Style set

Lesson	Commands
Module 13 Mail Merge	
76	Mail Merge Wizard
77	Edit Data Source, Sort and Filter Source
78	Merge Envelopes and Labels
Module 15 Meeting, Travel, and News Documents	
84	Comments
85	Track Changes
86	Change User Name, Track Changes Options
Module 17 Medical Documents	
96	Underline Tab
Module 18 Legal Documents	
101	Bookmark
Module 20 Real-Time Co-Authoring	
108	Share, Invite Authors, Open in Word, Edit in Real Time

See Appendix D, Command Summary, for a detailed list of commands, the path, and button for each command.

OVERVIEW

One search using a popular search engine and *digital citizenship* as keywords produced over three million results. A quick survey of the list of documents indicated that digital citizenship is a popular, if not required, topic in the curricula of K–12 schools. Many of the documents focused on digital citizenship research by Dr. Mike Ribble, on the framework developed by the Partnership for 21st Century Skills, and on the International Society for Technology in Education Standards for Students. A relatively small percentage of the documents listed referred to collegiate education or business and industry.

This article focuses on effective digital citizenship from four perspectives that can affect your career.

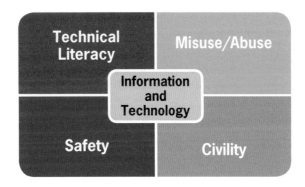

TECHNICAL LITERACY

Understanding how the Internet, social media applications, and other digital tools work enables you to use these tools creatively, responsibly, and safely. Technology is constantly evolving; things learned today can be outdated in a very short time. Therefore, continual learning is the only way to keep up with technology. Protecting your (or your company's) computer, network, and information from unauthorized access is critical. Many students and young employees who have grown up using all types of technology may be more technically savvy than their instructors or their managers. However, they often do not have the social skills and business savvy to be effective in using digital tools.

MISUSE/ABUSE

The Internet is a vast collection of information that can be accessed easily and at little or no cost. However, just because information has been posted on the Internet does not mean that it is accurate or valid.

Information Verification. Information should be analyzed carefully to determine the credibility of the writer, the source of the information, the accuracy of details, knowledge of the literature, and the currency of the information before relying on that information.

Plagiarism. Copyright laws protect material from unauthorized use. Request permission before using copyrighted materials. It is not acceptable to copy information from the Internet without properly documenting the source of the information and giving the writer proper credit. Software is available to check a paper and quickly determine if it has been plagiarized.

Piracy. Downloading of music, games, and movies and making copies of software without permission are illegal.

SAFETY

Privacy. Protecting private information and company proprietary information are key safety concerns. Protect your information and/or your company's information by using up-to-date antivirus software, antispyware, and firewalls.

Identity theft. Unauthorized persons may obtain information such as your Social Security number or credit card information and use it for criminal purposes. Posting private information on social networks can have serious negative consequences as shown in the following examples.

- Posting pictures of vacation sites and travel information alerted criminals that the family was away and their home was robbed.
- Posting pictures of children on the Internet and address information in other locations attracted predators to the home.
- Unprofessional information and pictures on a social network were viewed by a potential employer, causing the person not to be hired. Many employers check out potential employees on social networks before hiring them.
- Negative information posted about a person's supervisor and company was viewed by company executives.

CIVILITY

Courtesy and good manners when posting information, sending emails, participating in a chat room, blogging, or posting on a social media site are always appropriate. The following tips are examples of good *netiquette*.

Monkey Business Images/Shutterstock.com

- Consider anything you post to be public information. Many people use technology to deliver messages that they would never send in a face-to-face situation.
- Use appropriate, non-offensive language and be sensitive to cultural issues.
- Avoid inflammatory messages and messages keyed in all capital letters.
- Be helpful to people who have less technical expertise than you do. They may have great ideas even though they are not technically savvy.
- Avoid texting and checking and sending emails, and place cell phones on vibrate during meetings and dining.

Beyond the Essentials— Formatting Advanced Documents

Learning Outcomes

Document Design Skills

+ Design and prepare attractive documents.

+ Organize content effectively in tables and graphics.

+ Enhance report formats with design elements that add structure, provide a consistent image, and increase readability.

+ Create merged documents with envelopes and labels.

Word Processing Skills

+ Review and apply basic *Word 2016* commands.

+ Learn and apply *Word 2016* commands to create and format effective documents.

Communication Skills

+ Review and improve basic communication skills.

+ Produce error-free documents and apply language arts skills.

Keyboarding

+ Improve keyboarding speed and accuracy.

110-d3

Compose Memo

hess memo

Mr. Patrick Hess asked you to compose a memo to **All Hess Office Park Tenants** from him. Use **Short-Term Rental Facilities** as the Subject. Use the rough notes shown below. Add other information that you think would be appropriate. Save it as *110-d3* and upload it to your OneDrive Module 20 folder. (*110-d3*)

- Indicate that the completion of the two new buildings and the renovation of the existing short-term rental conference and office facilities have more than doubled short-term rental facilities now available.

- Thank the Short-Term Tenant Advisory Committee for working with him to survey and determine the needs of regular and occasional users. Point out that current Hess Office Park tenants represented approximately two-thirds of the past usage of these facilities.

- Tell them that next week they will receive an invitation to tour the facilities and a link to the new *Profile of Services* and detailed *Price List for Short-Term Rental Facilities*, which is currently being finalized.

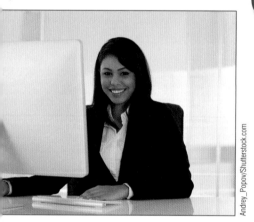

! WORKPLACE SUCCESS

Employee Empowerment

Employee empowerment refers to allowing employees to participate actively in decision making relative to their jobs. Employees cannot truly be empowered unless they have the knowledge, skills, and ability to make good decisions that affect their jobs. Empowerment requires training and experience as well as a desire on the part of the individual employee to make contributions and decisions relative to the job being performed.

Skill Builder 4

Skill Building *Improve Techniques*

DRILL 15

Keystroking Patterns

Key each line once for fluency; DS between groups.

3rd row
1 it we or us opo pop you rut rip wit pea lea wet pit were quiet
2 pew tie toe per rep hope pour quip rope your pout tore rip quirk

Home row
3 ha has kid lad led last wash lash gaff jade fads half sash haggle
4 as dad had add leg jug lads hall lass fast deal fall leafs dashes

1st row
5 ax ban man zinc clan bank calm lamb vain amaze bronze back buzzer
6 ax sax can bam zag cab mad fax vans buzz caves knack waxen banana

Timed Writings

1. Take a 1' writing on each paragraph.
2. Take one 3' writing on both paragraphs.

A | ALL LETTERS

Writing 28

	gwam 1'	3'

Who is a professional? The word can be defined in many | 11 | 4 | 53
ways. Some think of a professional as someone who is in an | 22 | 7 | 56
exempt job category in an organization. To others the word can | 35 | 12 | 61
denote something quite different; being a professional denotes an | 48 | 16 | 65
attitude that requires thinking of your position as a career, not | 61 | 20 | 69
just a job. A professional exerts influence over her or his job | 73 | 24 | 73
and takes pride in the work accomplished. | 82 | 27 | 76

Many individuals who remain in the same positions for a long | 12 | 31 | 80
time categorize themselves as being in dead-end positions. | 24 | 35 | 84
Others who remain in the same position for a long time consider | 36 | 39 | 88
themselves to be in a profession. A profession is a career to which | 50 | 44 | 93
you are willing to devote a lifetime. How you view your profession | 63 | 48 | 97
is up to you. | 65 | 49 | 98

```
1' |  1  |  2  |  3  |  4  |  5  |  6  |  7  |  8  |  9  | 10  | 11  | 12  |
3'       1           2           3           4
```

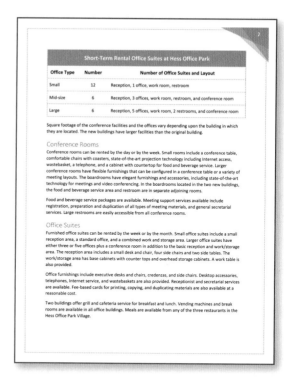

Profile of Services

Conference Rooms and Offices

Hess Office Park has more than doubled its short-term rental conference rooms and office suites by building new upscale facilities and renovating all of its previously existing short-term rental conference rooms and offices. All of these facilities now feature state-of-the-art technology. These changes were made based on a survey of both regular and occasional users of short-term facilities. Many of the regular users are companies of all sizes that have offices in Hess Office Park, but have short-term needs for additional facilities, such as a large boardroom, conference room, or training room. As soon as they schedule board meetings or executive staff meetings for the year, they reserve the facilities needed for each meeting during the year. A number of nonprofits also schedule all of their board meetings in our rental facilities. Some Hess Office Park companies rent office suites for special projects, visiting executives, or investors.

All conference rooms and office suites offered on a rental basis are furnished and include all utilities and janitorial service. The upscale furnishings and services provided depend on the size, type of the facility rented, and the specific needs of the client beyond the basic package that is part of the rental fee.

Short-Term Rental Facilities

Currently, Hess Office Park has 16 short-term rental conference facilities and 24 office suites. These facilities vary in style and size to accommodate special needs of clients. The first table provides size and style information about conference facilities.

Short-Term Rental Conference Facilities at Hess Office Park			
Type of Room	Number	Capacity	Layout
Boardrooms	4	24	Fixed board style
Small conference rooms	6	12	Fixed board style
Large conference rooms	4	50	Flexible
Training rooms	2	30	Fixed classroom style

The second table provides information about the number and layout of office suites that are available for short-term rental.

Short-Term Rental Office Suites at Hess Office Park		
Office Type	Number	Number of Office Suites and Layout
Small	12	Reception, 1 office, work room, restroom
Mid-size	6	Reception, 3 offices, work room, restroom, and conference room
Large	6	Reception, 5 offices, work room, 2 restrooms, and conference room

Square footage of the conference facilities and the offices vary depending upon the building in which they are located. The new buildings have larger facilities than the original building.

Conference Rooms

Conference rooms can be rented by the day or by the week. Small rooms include a conference table, comfortable chairs with coasters, state-of-the-art projection technology including Internet access, wastebasket, a telephone, and a cabinet with countertop for food and beverage service. Larger conference rooms have flexible furnishings that can be configured in a conference table or a variety of meeting layouts. The boardrooms have elegant furnishings and accessories, including state-of-the-art technology for meetings and video conferencing. In the boardrooms located in the two new buildings, the food and beverage service area and restroom are in separate adjoining rooms.

Food and beverage service packages are available. Meeting support services available include registration, preparation and duplication of all types of meeting materials, and general secretarial services. Large restrooms are easily accessible from all conference rooms.

Office Suites

Furnished office suites can be rented by the week or by the month. Small office suites include a small reception area, a standard office, and a combined work and storage area. Larger office suites have either three or five offices plus a conference room in addition to the basic reception and work/storage area. The reception area includes a small desk and chair, four side chairs and two side tables. The work/storage area has base cabinets with counter tops and overhead storage cabinets. A work table is also provided.

Office furnishings include executive desks and chairs, credenzas, and side chairs. Desktop accessories, telephones, Internet service, and wastebaskets are also provided. Receptionist and secretarial services are available. Fee-based cards for printing, copying, and duplicating materials are also available at a reasonable cost.

Two buildings offer grill and cafeteria service for breakfast and lunch. Vending machines and break rooms are available in all office buildings. Meals are available from any of the three restaurants in the Hess Office Park Village.

110-d2

Invitation

 hess letterhead

Mr. Hess has asked you to format an invitation to all employees of Hess Office Park. Once Mr. Hess approves the invitation, it will be uploaded to OneDrive and shared with the employees of Hess Office Park.

Directions for Invitation

1. Format the invitation on Hess Office Park letterhead.
2. Tap ENTER twice and key the invitation shown below. Center each line; use 2.5 line spacing.
3. Apply 16-point Lucida Calligraphy font and bold to the first line.
4. Apply 14-point Lucida Calligraphy font to the remaining lines.
5. Save and close. (110-d2)

New Facilities Tour and Reception
You are cordially invited to a tour of the
Hess Office Park New Conference Facilities and
Short-Term Rental Offices on
Wednesday, May 15 at 5:15 p.m.
Tour Begins in our Headquarters Building in the
Newly Renovated Conference Center
Enjoy Refreshments at Each Facility

Skill Building *Improve Techniques*

DRILL 16

Keyboarding Technique

Key each line once for fluency; DS between groups.

1st
1 Zam and six lazy men visited Cecil and Bunn at a bank convention.
2 Zane, much to the concern of Bev and six men, visited their zone.

2nd
3 Jill said she wished that she had fed Dale's dog a lot less food.
4 Jake Hall sold the glass flask at a Dallas "half-off" glass sale.

3rd
5 Did either Peter or Trey quip that reporters were out to get you?
6 Either Trey or Peter tried to work with a top-quality pewter toy.

4th
7 18465 97354 12093 87541 09378 34579 74629 45834 28174 11221 27211
8 02574 29765 39821 07623 17659 20495 39481 10374 32765 77545 22213

Timed Writings

A ALL LETTERS

1. Take three 1' writings on each paragraph.
2. Take two 3' writings. Proofread; circle errors; determine *gwam*.

Writing 29

gwam 1' | 3'

 Students for decades have secured part-time jobs to help 11 | 4
pay for college expenses. Today, more students are gainfully 23 | 8
employed while they are in college than ever before. Many of 35 | 12
them are employed because their financial situation requires that 48 | 16
they earn money. Earnings from jobs go to pay tuition, books, living 62 | 21
costs, and other necessities. Some work so that they can 73 | 24
own cars or buy luxury items; others seek jobs to gain skills or 86 | 29
to build their vitas. These students are aware that many 97 | 32
organizations prefer to hire a person who has had some type of 109 | 36
work experience than one who has had none. <u>118</u> | 39

 Students often ask if the work experience has to be in 11 | 43
exactly the same field. Obviously, the more closely related the 23 | 47
experience, the better it is. However, the old adage, anything 36 | 51
beats nothing, applies. Regardless of the types of jobs students 49 | 55
have, they can demonstrate that they get to work regularly and on 62 | 60
time, they have good human relations skills, they are organized 74 | 64
and can manage time effectively, and they produce good results. 87 | 68
All of these factors are very critical to employers. The bottom 99 | 72
line is that employers like to use what you have done in the past 112 | 77
as a predictor of what you will do in the future. <u>122</u> | 80

1' | 1 | 2 | 3 | 4 | 5 | 6 | 7 | 8 | 9 | 10 | 11 | 12 |
3' | 1 | 2 | 3 | 4 |

Instructions for Author 2 (Author 1 see instructions beginning on page 4-136.)

1. Key the following information after the second paragraph in the data file.
2. Insert a 4-column, 6-row table.
3. Size column widths:
 a. Column A 1.8″
 b. B, C, and D. 1.5″

Short-Term Rental Facilities

Currently, Hess Office Park has 16 short-term rental conference facilities and 24 office suites. These facilities vary in style and size to accommodate special needs of clients. The first table provides size and style information about conference facilities.

Short-Term Rental Conference Facilities at Hess Office Park			
Type of Room	Number	Capacity	Layout
Boardrooms	4	24	Fixed board style
Small conference rooms	6	12	Fixed board style
Large conference rooms	4	50	Flexible
Training rooms	2	30	Fixed classroom style

The second table provides information about the number and layout of office suites that are available for short-term rental.

4. Review the material that both authors added to the document and correct any keying errors that may have been made.
5. Format the table you keyed as follows:
 a. Increase top row height to 0.5″ and all other rows to 0.4″.
 b. Merge the cells in the top row and apply List Table 3 – Accent 1. Deselect First Column in the Table Style Options.
 c. Use 14-point font and apply Align Center to row 1. Apply 12-point bold font and Align Center to row 2.
 d. For remaining rows, apply Left Align to columns A and D and Align Center to columns B and C.
 e. Center the table.
6. In the paragraph under the heading *Conference Rooms*, make the following edits:
 a. Replace *overhead projector and screen* with **state-of-the-art projection technology including Internet access**.
 b. At the end of the second-to-last sentence, add: and **video conferencing**. Then add this as the last sentence: **In the boardrooms located in the two new buildings, the food and beverage service area and restroom are in separate adjoining rooms.**
7. Add a Facet Odd Page heard; suppress the number on the first page.
8. Compare your solution to the Quick Check below. Correct any errors.
9. Save the document as *110-d1* in your Module 20 folder.
10. Close the document and exit the editing session.

DRILL 17

Number Reaches

Key each line once at a comfortable rate; practice difficult lines.

1 My staff of 11 worked 11 hours a day from May 11 to June 11.
2 Her flight, PW 222, lands at 2:22 p.m. on Thursday, June 22.
3 We 3, part of the 333rd Corps, marched 33 miles on August 3.
4 Car 444 took Route 4 east to Route 44, then 4 miles to Aden.
5 The 55 wagons traveled 555 miles in '55; only 5 had trouble.
6 Put 6 beside 66; result 666, and add another 6 to get 6,666.
7 She sold 7,777 copies of Record 77, Schubert's 7th Symphony.
8 In '88, it took 8 men and 8 women 8 days to travel 88 miles.
9 The 9 teams, 9 girls and 9 boys, depart on Bus 999 at 9 a.m.
10 Billion has nine zeros; as 000,000,000. Ten has but one 0.

Timed Writings

A **ALL LETTERS**

1. Take two 3' writings on all paragraphs.

2. Take one 5' writing on all paragraphs. Proofread; circle errors; determine *gwam*.

Writing 30

gwam 3' | 5'

	3'	5'

Planning, organizing, and controlling are three of the 4 | 2
functions that are familiar to all sorts of firms. Because these 8 | 5
functions are basic to the managerial practices of a business, 12 | 7
they form the very core of its daily operations. Good managerial 16 | 10
procedures, of course, do not just occur by accident. They must 20 | 12
be set into motion by people. Thus, a person who plans to enter 25 | 15
the job market, especially in an office position, should study 29 | 17
all of the elements of good management in order to apply those 33 | 20
principles to her or his work. 35 | 21

Leadership is another very important skill for a person 39 | 23
to develop. Leaders are needed at all levels in a business to 43 | 26
plan, organize, and control the operations of the firm. A person 47 | 28
who is in a key position of leadership usually is expected to 51 | 31
initiate ideas as well as to carry out the goals of a business. 55 | 33
Office workers who have developed the qualities of leadership are 60 | 36
more apt to be promoted than those without such skills. While 64 | 38
leadership may come naturally for some people, it can be learned 68 | 41
as well as be improved with practice. 70 | 42

Attitude is an extremely important personality trait that 74 | 44
is a big contributor to success in one's day-to-day activities. 78 | 47
Usually a person with a good attitude is open-minded to the ideas 83 | 50
of others and is able to relate with others because he or she has 87 | 52
an interest in people. Thus, one's attitude on the job often 91 | 55
makes a great difference in whether work gets done and done 95 | 57
right. Because teamwork is a part of many jobs, developing a 99 | 59
good attitude toward work, people, and life seems logical. 103 | 62

3' | 1 | 2 | 3 | 4 |
5' | 1 | 2 |

2. Above the *Conference Rooms* heading in the data file, insert a 4-column, 5-row table and key the paragraph shown below.

3. Position the table at the left margin and size the column widths as follows:

 a. Columns A and B 1″

 b. Column C 4.5″

Short-Term Rental Office Suites at Hess Office Park			
Office Type	Number	Number of Offices and Layout	
Small	12	Reception, 1 office, work room, and restroom	
Mid-size	6	Reception, 3 offices, work room, restroom, and conference room	
Large	6	Reception, 5 offices, work room, 2 restrooms, and conference room	

Square footage of the conference facilities and the offices vary depending upon the building in which they are located. The new buildings have larger facilities than the original building.

4. Review the material that both authors added to the document and correct any keying errors that may have been made.

5. Then edit the next paragraph (first paragraph of the data file) as follows:

 a. In the second sentence, change *The furnishings* to **The upscale furnishings**.

 b. Delete the last sentence of the paragraph.

6. Format the table you keyed as follows:

 a. Increase top row height to 0.5″ and all other rows to 0.4″.

 b. Merge the cells in the top row and apply List Table 3 – Accent 1. Deselect First Column in the Table Style Options.

 c. Use 14-point font and apply Align Center to row 1. Apply 12-point bold font and Align Center to row 2.

 d. For remaining rows, apply Left Align to columns A and D and Align Center to column B.

 e. Center the table.

7. Apply Title format to the title and Subtitle format to the subtitle. Then apply Heading 1 style to all headings.

8. Add this sentence to the end of the document: **Meals are available from any of the three restaurants in the Hess Office Park Village.**

9. Add a Box Page Border; apply Orange, Accent 1 color to all of the document.

10. Compare your solution to the Quick Check below. Correct any errors.

11. Save the file as *110-d1* in your Module 20 folder.

12. After you receive notification that Author 2 has exited, close the document to exit the editing session.

Skill Building *Improve Techniques*

DRILL 18

Improve Response Patterns

Key each line once; DS between 4-line groups; work at a controlled rate; repeat drill.

direct reaches: reaches with the same finger; keep hands quiet

1 brand much cent numb cease bright music brief jump special carved
2 create mumps zany mystic curve mummy any checks brag brunch after
3 Bradley broke his left thumb after lunch on a great hunting trip.
4 After having mumps, Cecil once saw June excel in a funny musical.

adjacent reaches: keep fingers curved and upright

5 were junior sad yuletide trees polo very join safe property tweed
6 tree trio trickle tripod quit excess was free easy million option
7 Gwen and Sumio are going to be quite popular at the Western Club.
8 Fred said we were going to join the guys for polo this afternoon.

double letters: strike keys rapidly

9 dill seem pool attic miss carry dragged kidded layoff lapped buzz
10 commend accuse inner rubber cheer commission football jazz popper
11 Tammy called to see if she can borrow my accounting book at noon.
12 Lynnette will meet with the bookseller soon to discuss the issue.

Timed Writing

A ALL LETTERS

1. Take three 1' writings on each paragraph.

2. Take one 3' writing on all paragraphs. Proofread; circle errors; determine *gwam.*

Writing 31

gwam 1' 3'

	1'	3'
Working at home is not exactly a new phenomenon, but the	11 4	76
concept is growing quite rapidly. For many years, people have worked	25 8	81
at home. In most instances, they were self-employed and operated	38 13	85
a business from their homes. Today, the people who work at home	50 17	89
fit into a variety of categories. Some own their own businesses;	63 21	94
others bring extra work home after the workday ends. A key change	76 25	98
is the large group of people who are employed by huge organizations	89 30	102
but who work out of home offices. These employees are in jobs that	103 34	107
include sales, creative, technical, and a host of other categories.	116 39	111
The real change that has occurred is not so much the numbers	12 43	115
of people who are working at home and the variety of jobs, but the	25 47	120
complex tools that are now available for doing the job. Technology	38 51	124
has truly made the difference. In many cases, clients and customers	52 56	129
are not even aware that they are dealing with individuals working	65 60	133
at home. Computers, printers, fax machines, telephone systems,	77 64	137
and other office equipment enable the worker in the home to function	91 69	142
in the same way as workers in a typical business office.	102 73	145

1' | 1 | 2 | 3 | 4 | 5 | 6 | 7 | 8 | 9 | 10 | 11 | 12 | 13 |
3' | 1 | 2 | 3 | 4 |

Lesson 110 Hess Office Park

Learning Outcomes

- Share and edit documents in real time.
- Work independently with few specific instructions.

Project Setting

HESS OFFICE PARK

In this project, you continue to work with the management team of the Hess Office Park. Your work will focus on real-time co-authoring on OneDrive. OneDrive was selected because it gives you the ability to work remotely with two types of tenants—small entrepreneurial businesses and short-term tenants who rent the offices and/or conference rooms on a daily, weekly, or monthly rental plan. The renovation of the initial conference rooms and rental offices has been completed, new offices and conference rooms are online, and state-of-the-art technology is now available.

110-d1

Profile of Services

 services

Your first task is to update the profile of services that Hess offers to tenants on the short-term rental plan. The initial profile of services (contained in the *services* data file) was developed several years ago. Your team will update the Profile of Services and share it with the Short-Term Tenant Advisory Committee for input.

1. Each student must be paired with a second student to form a co-authoring team. Assign one student as Author 1 and a second student as Author 2. Instructions are labeled as instructions for Author 1 and Author 2.

2. Author 1 will save the data file *services* to OneDrive and share it with Author 2. Author 2 will access the document and both will begin editing in real time. The first thing each author must do is key additional information from the last meeting this is shown below. Directions will be provided for editing after it is keyed.

Instructions for Author 1 (Author 2 see instructions on page 4-138.)

1. Key the paragraph shown below between the subtitle and the first paragraph in the data file.

Hess Office Park has more than doubled its short-term rental conference rooms and office suites by building new upscale facilities and renovating all of its previously existing short-term rental conference rooms and office suites. All of these facilities now feature state-of-the-art technology. These changes were made based on a survey of both regular and occasional users of short-term facilities. Many of the regular users are companies of all sizes that have offices in Hess Office Park but have short-term needs for additional facilities, such as a large boardroom, conference room, or training room. As soon as they schedule board meetings or executive staff meetings for the year, they reserve the facilities needed for each meeting during the year. A number of nonprofits also schedule all of their board meetings in our rental facilities. Some Hess Office Park companies rent office suites for special projects, visiting executives, or investors.

(continue)

Timed Writing

1. Take two 3' writings on all paragraphs.

2. Take one 5' writing on all paragraphs. Proofread; circle errors; determine gwam.

Writing 32

gwam 3' | 5'

Many small businesses fail. Surprisingly, though, many 4 | 2 | 57
people are still willing to take a chance on starting one of 8 | 5 | 60
their own. A person who is willing to take the risks necessary 12 | 7 | 62
to manage a business in order to receive the potential rewards is 16 | 10 | 65
called an entrepreneur. In a sense, such individuals are pioneers 20 | 12 | 67
who enjoy each step on the way to achieving objectives that 24 | 15 | 70
they have determined to be important. This type of person has 28 | 17 | 72
had a profound impact on shaping our economy and our quality of 33 | 20 | 75
life. 33 | 20 | 75

What does it take to start a business venture, and what 37 | 22 | 77
kinds of people make it work? Obviously, the desire to make 41 | 24 | 79
money and to be one's own boss are two basic incentives, but 45 | 27 | 82
these alone are not enough to guarantee success. Two qualifications 49 | 29 | 84
common to most successful entrepreneurs, whatever field 53 | 32 | 87
they are in, are an attentiveness to detail and a knack for 57 | 34 | 89
solving day-to-day problems without losing sight of long-range 61 | 36 | 91
goals. 61 | 37 | 92

While there is a high risk in organizing any new business, 65 | 39 | 94
the entrepreneur who is successful is seldom someone who could be 69 | 42 | 97
considered a gambler. Most gamblers expect to have the odds 73 | 44 | 99
against them. On the other hand, a clever businessperson sees to 78 | 47 | 102
it that the odds are as good as possible by getting all of the 82 | 49 | 104
facts and planning carefully before going ahead. Luck helps, to 86 | 52 | 107
be sure, but a new business enterprise depends far more on good 90 | 54 | 109
ideas and detailed plans. 92 | 55 | 110

3' | 1 | 2 | 3 | 4 |
5' | 1 | 2 |

QUICK ✓

Business Plan
Pommery Limo Service

Pommery Limo Service (Pommery), since it was founded as a Delaware corporation in 2008, has operated as a niche player in the limousine service industry. Headquarters for Pommery are located in Chicago, Illinois.

Industry
Three distinct segments comprise the limousine service industry:

- Small local limousine service companies that provide individual services by reservation or on demand.
- Large companies with licenses in virtually every state that provide a full range of services.
- Niche markets that target specific types of clientele.

Pommery operates in the third industry segment, focusing primarily on business executive services and event services. It also provides some miscellaneous services to individuals requesting service. The overall industry is highly competitive. The most intensive competition exists in the first two segments of the industry. Pommery's Board of Directors and management agree that Pommery cannot and should not try to compete with the major national companies for numerous reasons. They also agree that Pommery cannot compete with the small, local services because of the cost structure involved in providing a fleet of luxury cars and stretch limos.

Services
The mix of Pommery Limo Services is composed of business executive services, major event services, and general limo services. The primary services are those provided for business executives. Business executive services include an array of services depending on the needs of the client. Services for business and client needs are provided to executives of the company and to guests who visit the company.

Event Services
These services are called event services because they exist to transport passengers to attend specific events that are occurring. The range of events spans from those that occur one time or rarely to regularly scheduled events.

Seasonal events are those that occur regularly during a specified period of time. Weddings, athletic events, proms, and graduation events are the most popular events. These events often include requests for other services from out-of-town clients.

BUSINESS PLAN

Contract Business Services
Contract business services sometimes overlap with event services. The primary difference is that the contracts are with specific business organizations for all of their ground transportation needs for their own executives and for clients who visit their organizations.

Requests for services in markets not covered by Pommery are handled by cooperative arrangements with a national organization that offers a significantly reduced rate to Pommery for its clients.

General Limo Services
Pommery provides service by reservation or on demand from individuals or companies without a contract. In larger markets, many companies begin with general services and later convert to contract services. In smaller markets, these services help to increase the vehicle utilization rates.[1]

Market Analysis
Pommery is headquartered in Chicago, Illinois with its main office located at 1340 N. Astor Street. Pommery Limo Service provides services in 18 cities in 12 states located in the Midwest, Southwest, and Atlantic Coast regions. The first regional office was established in the Southwest region. The regional office in Houston serves other cities in Texas, Louisiana, Oklahoma, Colorado, and Arizona.

Emerging Markets
The focus on market growth is on cities in the Midwest, Southwest, and Atlantic Coast regions. It is advantageous to serve mid-size cities within 125 miles of a large city served by Pommery. The larger city can provide support for large events in the mid-sized cities.

Competition
National companies (licensed in most states) compete in all of the markets in which Pommery operates. Pommery has some advantages because of its local presence and relationships with the business community.

Market Expansion
The real challenge is to increase the number of markets Pommery serves. Business can be increased through promotional activities and strategic alliances with travel partners. Pilot projects have produced promising results and are being evaluated as part of the growth strategy. However, the challenge is to attract investors (and chauffeur investors) who can support the costs associated with a significant increase in the number of vehicles in the fleet.

[1] The vehicle utilization rate in large cities is 32 percent higher than in mid-size cities.

Page 2 of 3

BUSINESS PLAN

Pro Formas
Pro formas for each year since inception as well as projections for the next three years are provided in a separate financial package. The data are presented in both printed format and electronic format that also includes interactive models for "What if" scenarios.

Ownership
Three million shares of common stock have been authorized. Of the authorized shares, 750,000 shares have been issued. Common stock ownership is diverse, as noted in the five groupings—founders, business community, senior officers, outside directors, and employees.

Strategy
Pommery Limo Service strives to become the dominant limo service in the cities it serves. Pommery also plans to expand its geographic area over the next three years. Pommery's core competencies involve providing safe, high-quality, luxury services that are cost effective. All other services provided are designed to facilitate and enhance the continual development of the core competencies.

To implement this strategy, Pommery Limo Service must expand its service in the cities it currently serves as well as expand into other areas. Expansion will require a major increase in vehicle fleet size.[2]

[2] The fleet currently consists of 192 stretch limos and 450 executive cars.

Page 3 of 3

Skill Building *Improve Techniques*

DRILL 19

Opposite Hand Reaches

Key at a controlled rate;
concentrate on the reaches.

1 yj my say may yes rye yarn eye lye yap any relay young berry

y/t 2 tf at it let the vat tap item town toast right little attire

3 Yesterday a young youth typed a cat story on the typewriter.

4 bf but job fibs orb bow able bear habit boast rabbit brother

b/n 5 nj not and one now fun next pony month notice runner quicken

6 A number of neighbors banked on bunking in the brown cabins.

7 gag go gee god rig gun log gong cog gig agog gage going gang

g/h 8 huh oh hen the hex ash her hash ah hush shah hutch hand ache

9 Hush; Gregg hears rough sounds. Has Hugh laughed or coughed?

10 row or rid air rap par rye rear ark jar rip nor are right or

r/u 11 cut us auk out tutu sun husk but fun cub gun nut mud tug hug

12 Ryan is sure you should pour your food from an urn or cruet.

Timed Writing

A ALL LETTERS

1. Take two 3' timed writings on both paragraphs.

2. Take one 5' writing on both paragraphs.

Writing 33

gwam 3' | 5'

Most people think traveling is fun because they associate 4 | 2 | 46
travel with exciting vacations. People who have to travel as 8 | 5 | 48
part of their jobs have a very different view of travel. They 12 | 7 | 51
are more prone to view business travel as a hassle than a pleasure. 16 | 10 | 53
Business travelers often have to work under less than 20 | 12 | 56
ideal circumstances. While they are away from the office, regular 24 | 15 | 58
work tends to pile up; and they often return to find stacks 28 | 17 | 61
of work waiting for them. Many business travelers learn to utilize 33 | 20 | 63
wisely the waiting time that is a part of most travel. 36 | 22 | 65

A successful business trip requires careful planning. The 40 | 24 | 68
typical business traveler tends to think of a trip as a success 44 | 26 | 70
if two conditions are met. The business goals must be achieved, 48 | 29 | 73
and the trip must be totally free of headaches. The person making 53 | 32 | 75
the trip has to worry about achieving the business goals, but 57 | 34 | 78
a good travel agent can relieve the traveler of many of the worries 61 | 37 | 80
of making travel arrangements. A good checklist can help to 65 | 39 | 83
ensure that all the personal items as well as business items 69 | 41 | 85
needed for the trip will be handy when they are needed. 73 | 44 | 87

3' | 1 | 2 | 3 | 4
5' | 1 | 2

109-d2

Business Plan

 business plan

The student who was Author 1 of the first document should be Author 2 for this document.

The student who was Author 2 should be Author 1 for this document.

Instructions for Author 1

1. Upload the business plan data file to your OneDrive and share it with Author 2.

2. Open the file and review the document before beginning to edit it.

3. Edit the second line of the first paragraph as follows:

 ...has **operated as a niche** player....and add **Illinois** after *Chicago*.

4. Add Orange, Accent 2, Darker 25 % Square bullets to the three industry segments.

5. Edit the second bulleted item as follows:

 ...licenses in **virtually** every state.

6. Insert Footnote 2 as noted in blue in parentheses. Then delete the directions. Footnote 2:

 The fleet currently consists of 192 stretch limos and 450 executive cars.

7. On the third page after the Ownership paragraph, insert a basic SmartArt graphic (Cycle) and add two shapes after the last one. Key and bold the text in each slice:

 a. **Founders 28.68%** in the exploded slice, then moving to the right
 b. **Business Community 24.25%**
 c. **Senior Officers 16.75%**
 d. **Outside Directors 15.67%**
 e. **Employees 14.65%**

8. Change the colors to Accent 1 Gradient Range – Accent 1.

9. Insert a Semaphore footer to add page numbers. Do not show on first page.

10. Compare your document to the 109-d2 Quick Check.

11. After you receive notification that Author 2 is no longer editing the document, save it as *109-d2* in your Module 20 folder and close.

Instructions for Author 2

1. Access the file Author 1 shared with you. Make sure you open the document in *Word*.

2. Open the file and review the document before beginning to edit it.

3. Apply Wisp theme with Casual document formatting.

4. Tap ENTER three times and apply the headings in blue throughout the report. Then delete the blue directions only for the headings in parentheses.

5. In the first line of the second paragraph, edit as follows:

 Three **distinct** segments....

6. Edit the second paragraph below the *industry* heading as follows:

 ...Pommery **cannot and should not try to** compete with the **major** national companies....

7. In the last sentence under the *Services* heading, edit as follows:

 Services for business and client needs....

8. Insert Footnotes 1 where noted in blue in parentheses. Then delete the directions. Footnote 1:

 The vehicle utilization rate in large cities is 32 percent higher than in mid-size cities.

9. Add a Retrospect header to the document with Business Plan as the title and pick the current date. Do not show on first page.

10. Compare your document to the 109-d2 Quick Check.

11. Save to your Module 20 folder. (*109-d2*)

12. Close and exit from the editing session.

Advanced Business Correspondence

LEARNING OUTCOMES

- Format memo and use templates.
- Format block and modified block business letters with special features.
- Format two-page memos and letters.
- Create envelopes with special notations.
- Improve keying speed and accuracy.

Lesson 56 Memos and Productivity Tools

New Commands
- Templates
- Quick Parts

Warmup *Lesson 56a Warmup*

lesson 56a warmup

Skill Building

56b Timed Writing

1. Key a 1' timing on each paragraph; work to increase speed.
2. Key a 3' timing on all paragraphs.

	gwam	1'	3'
Good plans typically are required to execute most tasks		11	4
successfully. If a task is worth doing, it is worth investing the time		25	8
that is necessary to plan it effectively. Many people are anxious to get		39	13
started on a task and just begin before they have thought about the		53	18
best way to organize it. In the long run, they frequently end up wasting		67	22
time that could be spent more profitably on important projects that		81	27
they might prefer to tackle.		86	29
A task plan may or may not include organizational steps. The		12	33
better a plan is organized, the more likely the execution of the plan		26	37
will be successful. The way you plan and organize a task generally will		40	42
depend on how frequently it has to be done. For tasks that are done		53	47
occasionally, determine the quickest and the easiest way to complete		67	51
the job. For repetitive tasks, try to automate them to save future time.		81	56
The importance of the job is another factor that should be considered.		95	61

1'	1	2	3	4	5	6	7	8	9	10	11	12
3'		1			2			3			4	

7. In the second sentence of the appliances paragraph, place a period after *confirmed* and delete the remainder of the sentence.

8. Key **Final Painting and Inspection** above the last paragraph and apply Heading 1 style. Then add the following sentence at the end of the paragraph: **The final project schedule is shown in the table at the right.**

9. Add Facet (odd page) header to the document. Suppress the header on the first page.

10. Add a Box Page Border to the document. Apply Dark Red, Accent 2, Lighter 60% color.

11. Save a copy of the document in your Module 20 folder (*109-d1*) and exit the editing session after you are notified that Author 2 has exited the session.

9. Edit and format the table at the end of the plan.

 a. Insert a row between Wallboard repair and Install flooring. In column A, key **Install crown moulding** and in column B, key **May 10**.

 b. Apply Grid Table 7 Colorful – Accent 1 table design.

 c. In the Table Style Options group, Check First Column; Header row and Banded Rows should also have checks.

 d. Apply Align Center Right position to column A and the title. Apply Align Center to column B.

 e. Apply Right Alignment to the table and position it as shown in the Quick Check.

10. Save a copy of the document in your Module 20 folder (*109-d1*) and exit the editing session.

TEMPLATES

Templates are preformatted documents that can be used to create multiple documents with the same formats. Featured templates are placed on the hard drive during installation, and online templates are available from office.com. Suggested searches for templates include letters, resume, fax, labels, cards, calendar, and blank. After a template is opened, it can be customized with the user's specific information and saved as a custom office template.

DOWNLOAD TEMPLATE AND CREATE A TEMPLATE
File/New

1. Click one of the suggested searches ❶ or click in the Search for online templates box ❷ and key a descriptive keyword. Click the Start searching arrow or tap ENTER.

2. Click the desired template and click Create.

3. Customize the template by adding a company name, addresses, or other template elements.

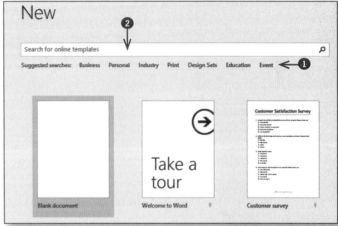

To save as a new template:
File/Save As

1. Click File, Save As, This PC, and then Browse. Key a name such as **vanhuss memo** in the File name box. Change the Save as type to Word Template ❸ and click Save. Note that the template is saved in the Custom Word Templates folder.

2. Click File, New, and then Personal. Click on the custom template you just created.

Lesson 109 Real-Time Co-Authoring II

This lesson is designed to give you experience in co-authoring different types of documents. If necessary, review the directions and illustrations in Lesson 108 on how to share documents and use real-time co-authoring.

Apply It

109-d1

Report

 renovation final plan

To get started on this application:

1. Each student must be paired with a second student to form a co-authoring team.

2. One student must be assigned as Author 1, and a second student must be assigned as Author 2. For the second application (*109-d2*), students reverse roles. Author 1 becomes Author 2 and Author 2 becomes Author 1.

3. Instructions are labeled for Author 1 and Author 2.

4. Establish the time that both of you will work on this activity. It may be during class, lab, or any other time that is convenient. Students must have each other's email address and a Microsoft account and access to their own OneDrive.

Instructions for Author 1

1. Upload the *renovation final plan* data file to your OneDrive and share it with Author 2.

2. Open the file and review the document before beginning to edit it.

3. In the first paragraph, delete the last sentence and replace it with: **The costs are summarized in the table at the right.**

4. Format and edit the Confirmed Quotations table.

 a. Apply Grid Table 7 Colorful – Accent 1 table design.

 b. In the Table Style Options group, Check First Column; Header row and Banded Rows should also have checks.

 c. Apply Align Center Right position to both columns including the title.

 d. Apply Right Alignment to the table and position it as shown in the Quick Check.

 e. Increase the Labor Amount to $2,300 and the Materials Amount to 1,450. Sum the column.

5. Key **Cabinetry** above the paragraph about Cabinetry and apply Heading 1 style.

6. Key **Appliances** above the paragraph about appliances and apply Heading 1 style.

Instructions for Author 2

1. Access the file Author 1 shared with you. Make sure you open the document in *Word*.

2. Open the file and review the document before beginning to edit it.

3. Apply Title and Subtitle styles to the Title and Subtitle.

4. Key **Demolition** above the second paragraph and apply Heading 1 style.

5. Insert **crown** before the word *mouldings* in the first sentence. Delete *Then an assessment can be made* and replace it with **The original plan called for an assessment to be made during the demolition**...

6. Add these two sentences to finish the paragraph: **A small test area has been removed, and it was determined that new flooring and crown moulding must be installed in the entire area. The estimated cost increased $825 in materials and labor.**

7. Key **Electrical Work** before the next paragraph and apply Heading 1 style.

8. In the first sentence, make these edits: appropriately **positioned** receptacles...

(continued)

To create a new document with the template:
File/New

1. Click Personal to display the templates you have created.
2. Select the new template and click OK.
3. Key the new document and save it.

DRILL 1 CREATE NEW TEMPLATE

1. Click File, New, and then key **Memo** in the Search for online templates box.

2. Tap ENTER. Select Interoffice Memo (Professional Design) and download it.

3. Key **VanHuss & VanHuss, Inc.** in the Company Name box.

4. Delete the text below the horizontal line. Change font to Arial 10 point.

5. Save the template as **vanhuss memo** and close it.

6. Open the *vanhuss memo* template you just created and key the memo shown below.

7. Save and close. (*56-drill1*)

To: Pat VanHuss | From: Susie VanHuss | cc: Connie Forde | Date: Current Date | Re: Customized Template for VanHuss & VanHuss

This template was downloaded from online templates by searching for memos in the Search for online templates box.

Note that the template was customized with our company name. Having our name stored with the template makes us more productive as we prepare memos. | xx

QUICK ✓ Check your document against the illustration below.

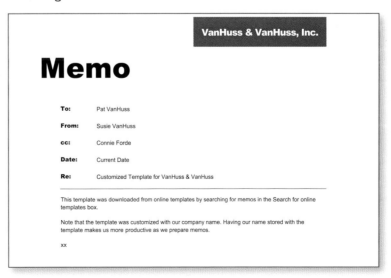

Apply It

Module 108-d1

 trails

1. Prepare for a co-authoring session in real time.

 a. Begin with a team of two students. One student will be listed as Author 1 and the other will be listed as Author 2. Determine who will be Author 1.

 b. Both authors must be signed in to a OneDrive account and use *Word 2016* for all documents in this Module. Authors must have each other's email address.

 c. Review the information on the previous three pages carefully and refer to it as needed.

 d. Read the trails document that you will edit carefully to become familiar with it.

 e. Set up a time that you both are available to edit the document.

 f. The remaining instructions are divided into two sections—Author 1 and Author 2.

2. Get started. Follow the instructions for your role—either as Author 1 or Author 2.

Instructions for Author 1

1. Open *trails* from your data files and click Share. Then click Save to Cloud.

2. Select OneDrive and create a new folder named **Module 20**. Save and name the document **108-d1**.

3. In the Invite people text box, key the email address of Author 2.

4. Make sure the Automatically share changes box is either on Ask me or Always. If you click Always, sharing will take place automatically.

5. You are now ready to begin editing. Make the edits listed for Author 1 below.

 a. Apply Title style to the title and tap ENTER.

 b. At the end of the first paragraph under the *Healthy Heart Study* heading, change 55 to **65**.

 c. Select the SmartArt graphic and click the Design tab; in the Change Colors section, apply Simple Fill.

 d. Insert Plain Number page numbers at the top of the page. Suppress the page number on the first page.

 e. Add a Box Page Border to the whole document. Apply Red from Standard Colors and ½ pt. width.

6. Check to ensure that all changes have been made for both authors. Compare the document to the 108-d1 Quick Check.

7. After you are notified that Author 2 is no long editing, save and close. (*108-d1*)

Instructions for Author 2

1. Check your email and follow the link sent to you by Author 1. If the document opens in *Word Online*, click OPEN IN WORD.

2. Click Yes in the Automatically share changes pane that opens.

3. When you click in the document to edit it, a colored flag will appear at the insertion point. You should also be able to see a flag where Author 1 is editing.

4. You are now ready to begin editing. Make the edits listed for Author 2 below.

 a. Apply Heading 1 style to *Healthy Heart Study* and *Trail Cost and Timeframe* heading.

 b. Apply Heading 3 style to the remaining headings.

 c. Select the table, click the Design tab, and apply List Table 4 – Accent 1.

 d. Add a row at the bottom of the table and key in column A: **Total Project**; in column B: **All**; and in column C sum the column; then verify that the total is $658,500.

 e. Delete the comment attached to the table.

 f. In the paragraph under *The Bike Trail* heading, change 125 to **100**.

5. Check to ensure that all changes have been made for both authors. Compare the document to the 108-d1 Quick Check.

6. Use Save as to save a copy of the document for your files in a folder named **Module 20**. (*108-d1*)

7. Close and exit from the real-time editing session.

BUILDING BLOCKS OVERVIEW

Documents can be segmented into parts called building blocks. Building blocks consist of formatted text, images, or other objects that can be saved and reused in other documents, such as a memo heading or closing lines of a letter.

CREATE QUICK PARTS

The Quick Part Gallery is one of the galleries of building blocks. A Quick Part is created by selecting a segment of formatted text or an image and saving it in the Quick Part Gallery for reuse in other documents. The text and format can be used in new letters or memos without rekeying them. When you create the building block, save the following information about the new building block.

Name	Key a unique name that suggests the content of the building block.
Gallery	Click the down arrow to view all the galleries.
Category	General is a broad category to use, or create your own category name.
Description	Key a brief description of the building block.
Save in	Name of an open template. Typically, you will use Building Blocks.
Options	The options include: Insert content only, Insert content in its own paragraph, or Insert content in its own page.

To create a content building block that can be used in other documents:
Insert/Text/Quick Parts

1. Select the text you want to save as a building block. Make sure the text is formatted in the way you plan to use it.

2. Follow the path and click Save Selection to Quick Part Gallery ❶ to display the Create New Building Block dialog box. Note the options in the Create New Building Block dialog box that are described above.

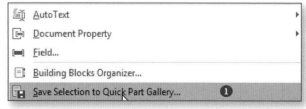

3. Key the name of the building block (if you want to change the default name that displays) and the description. For now, use the other options that are filled in—Quick Part Gallery, General Category, Save in Building Blocks, and Insert content only. Click OK.

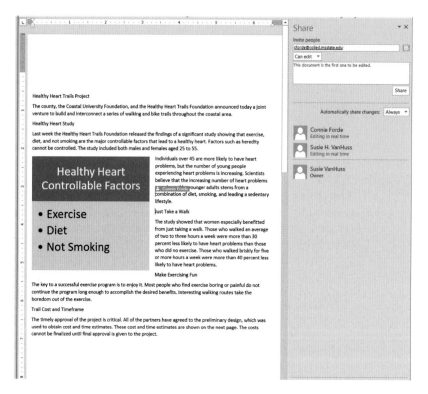

Note the draft file is shown above with the authors beginning editing. The final document with the extensive edits the authors made in real-time editing is shown in the Quick Check below.

QUICK ✓

TIP

Key the name or part of the name of the Quick Part and tap F3 to enter the Quick Part.

To add Quick Parts to a document:
Insert/Text/Quick Parts

1. Position the insertion point where you wish to insert the Quick Part in the document.

2. Follow the path and view the list of Quick Parts you have added.

3. Click the Quick Part you wish to insert. Repeat these steps for each Quick Part you want to add to the document.

DRILL 2 — CREATE QUICK PART

heading

1. Open *heading* from the data files, and select the entire document (CTRL + A).

2. Save the selection as a Quick Part.

3. Key the name and description **memo heading**; then click OK.

4. Save and close. (*56-drill2*)

DRILL 3 — USE QUICK PART

1. In a new blank document, insert the building block *memo heading* that was created in Drill 2.

2. Complete the memo heading with **Julia Fortenberry** as the recipient of the memo and **Stephen Dill** as the sender.

3. Use the current date. The subject is **Memo Heading Inserted as Building Block**.

4. Save and close. (*56-drill3*)

QUICK ✔

Check your document against the illustration below.

TO:	Julia Fortenberry
FROM:	Stephen Dill
DATE:	Current date
SUBJECT:	Memo Heading Inserted as Building Block

2. Each author must agree to automatic sharing by selecting Yes unless they have already checked Always in the Automatically share changes box. When authors begin working on your document, colored flags will appear at the location each author is working. All authors can see each other's work. Note in the first illustration that Author 1 (Susie) can see what Connie edits each time she makes an edit. In the second illustration Author 2 (Connie) can see what Susie is editing each time she makes an edit.

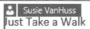

> d the findings of a significant study showing that exercise,
> rs that lead to a healthy he Connie Forde h as heredity
> ınd females aged 25 to 55.
>
> ▮ Individuals over 45 are more likely to have heart

> 👤 Susie VanHuss
> Just Take a Walk
>
> The study showed that women especially benefitted from just taking a walk. Those who walked an average of two to three hours a week were more than 30 percent less likely to have heart problems than those who did no exercise. Those who walked briskly for five or more hours a week were more than 40 percent less likely to have heart problems.
>
> Make Exercising Fun

Authors Editing in Real Time

The illustration on the left shows both authors editing in real time. The illustrations on the right show the Share button for each author.

When an author exits, others are notified.

> **CONNIE FORDE IS NO LONGER EDITING THIS DOCUMENT.** ✕
> Click the Share button to see who's still here.

The memo is the most formal type of informal message and may be preferred over email when a somewhat formal communication with company employees is demanded, such as the announcement of a new policy or participation in a mandatory training program. While a memo may be printed and distributed internally, often this formal memo is attached to an email and distributed to all employees. Memos and letters may be also distributed to individuals or groups by using the Share command in *Word*.

Study the formatting guidelines below and refer to the full model on the next page.

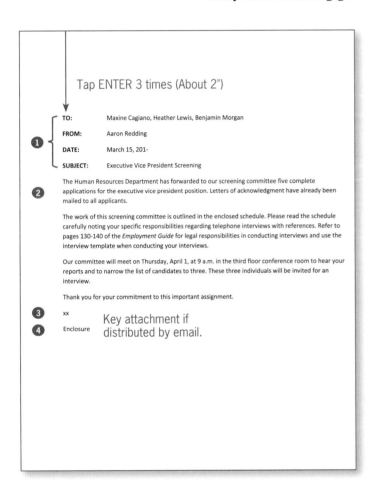

Tap ENTER 3 times (About 2")

TO: Maxine Cagiano, Heather Lewis, Benjamin Morgan

FROM: Aaron Redding

DATE: March 15, 201-

SUBJECT: Executive Vice President Screening

The Human Resources Department has forwarded to our screening committee five complete applications for the executive vice president position. Letters of acknowledgment have already been mailed to all applicants.

The work of this screening committee is outlined in the enclosed schedule. Please read the schedule carefully noting your specific responsibilities regarding telephone interviews with references. Refer to pages 130-140 of the *Employment Guide* for legal responsibilities in conducting interviews and use the interview template when conducting your interviews.

Our committee will meet on Thursday, April 1, at 9 a.m. in the third floor conference room to hear your reports and to narrow the list of candidates to three. These three individuals will be invited for an interview.

Thank you for your commitment to this important assignment.

xx

Enclosure Key attachment if distributed by email.

Heading: ❶

- Tap ENTER 3 times (about 2" from the top of the page) to begin the memo.
- Format the memo heading in bold and uppercase.
- Tap TAB once or twice after each heading to align the text that follows each item. You may also set a left tab at 1" and tap TAB once.
- Tap the ENTER key once after each line of the heading.

Body: ❷

- Use the 1.08" default line spacing. Tap ENTER once after each paragraph.

Notations:

- Reference initials ❸: Tap ENTER once after the body.
- Enclosure or attachment notation ❹: Key one line below the reference initials. Use *Enclosure* when items are enclosed in an envelope and *Attachment* if items are attached with the memo to an email.
- Key the copy notation one line below the enclosure notation or one line below the reference initials if no enclosure notation is needed.

Distribution lists:

When memos are sent to more than one person, key the names after the word TO and separate them with commas, or key them in a list. Generally, names should be in alphabetical order by last name or listed in order of rank.

TO: Maxine Cagiano, Heather Lewis, Benjamin Morgan or TO: Maxine Cagiano
 Heather Lewis
 Benjamin Morgan

REAL-TIME CO-AUTHORING

In previous modules in this text, you have saved documents to your OneDrive. This is the first step to begin the process of co-authoring.

Getting Started—Author 1

Begin by having one author save a document to OneDrive and invite others to work on it.

1. Open an existing *Word 2016* document and click Share ❶ and then Save to Cloud ❷.

2. Select OneDrive and select a folder or create and name a new folder, then click Save.

Invite Authors

3. In the Invite people text box, key the email addresses of the authors you want to invite.

4. Make sure the Automatically share changes box is either on Ask me or Always, and set the permission to Can edit; otherwise the author will only be able to view the document. If you click Always ❸, sharing will take place automatically. See the illustration below. Then click Share.

5. Start editing your document. If you have not already agreed to let others see your changes, select Yes to automatic sharing.

Getting Started—Author 2 (or more)

1. When your co-author follows the link you sent, your document will open in his or her *Word 2016*. If it opens in *Office Online*, click OPEN IN WORD as shown below.

Tap ENTER 3 times (about 2")

TO: Maxine Cagiano, Heather Lewis, Benjamin Morgan ↓1

FROM: Aaron Redding ↓1

DATE: March 15, 201- ↓1

SUBJECT: Executive Vice President Screening ↓1

The Human Resources Department has forwarded to our screening committee five complete applications for the executive vice president position. Letters of acknowledgment have already been mailed to all applicants. ↓1

The work of this screening committee is outlined in the enclosed schedule. Please read the schedule carefully noting your specific responsibilities regarding telephone interviews with references. Refer to pages 130-140 of the *Employment Guide* for legal responsibilities in conducting interviews and use the interview template when conducting your interviews.

Our committee will meet on Thursday, April 1, at 9 a.m. in the third floor conference room to hear your reports and to narrow the list of candidates to three. These three individuals will be invited for an interview.

Thank you for your commitment to this important assignment. ↓1

Typist's
first and
last initials

xx ↓1

Enclosure

Key **Enclosure** if item distributed with memo is in an envelope; key **Attachment** when memo and items are distributed by email.

Memo

Real-Time Co-Authoring

LEARNING OUTCOMES

- Share documents on OneDrive.
- *Editing documents using real-time co-authoring.*
- Work effectively on team writing projects.

Lesson 108 Real-Time Co-Authoring I

REAL-TIME CO-AUTHORING OVERVIEW

In today's business environment, much of the work that is project-based is completed by teams working collaboratively rather than by individuals. Often team members working on a project represent different departments or divisions of an organization and may be in remote locations. Teams are often required to produce a variety of different documents, such as proposals, procedures, reports of various types, and business plans.

The combination of OneDrive and a new productivity feature of *Word 2016*, real-time co-authoring enhances and facilitates team writing. Multiple team members can work simultaneously to create and/or edit a document. Generally, teams can be more productive by having various team members create a rough draft or at least an outline of the section for which they are responsible. Then the document can be shared and edited simultaneously by team members.

Two students are required to work together to edit the documents in this module. Your instructor will help you form a team to get started. Both team members can work remotely as long as both are available at the same time for editing. Students will be referred to as authors during the editing session, and the first author will be shown as the owner of the document.

56-d1 Memo

1. In a new blank document, key the memo on page 3-14.
2. Save and close. (*56-d1*)

56-d2

Create Quick Part

memo letterhead

1. Open *memo letterhead* from the data files, and select the entire document by pressing CTRL + A. Create a Quick Part named **sanchez memo letterhead**.
2. Key the description **sanchez memo letterhead**. Click OK.
3. You will use the Quick Part in the next document.

56-d3

Use Memo Quick Part

1. In a new blank document, insert the Quick Part *sanchez memo letterhead* created in *56-d2*. Key the memo shown below.
2. Key your reference initials and the attachment notation.
3. Save and close. (*56-d3*)

> To: New Sales Representatives | Date: Current date | Subject: Focus on Recycling and Reusing
>
> As you talk with potential clients, please remember to emphasize recycling and reusing. Before meeting with clients, review their business operations and have specific recommendations for both recycling and reusing. Here are a few examples you might share.
>
> 1. Recycling: Purchase products that can be recycled and that have minimal packaging. Set up special recycle boxes that are easy and convenient for everyone to use.
>
> 2. Reusing: Make double-side copies, reuse office supplies (such as file folders and hanging files), use the back of used paper for scratch paper, reuse interoffice envelopes, save to a hard drive or server to avoid printing, and use ceramic mugs instead of disposable cups.
>
> Please refer to the attached newsletter that highlights unique and effective ways that our current clients are cutting costs while sustaining our world.

56-d4

New Template from Existing Template

1. In a new blank document, download the Fax cover sheet template.
2. In the open document (*vanhuss fax*), key **VanHuss & VanHuss, Inc.** in the company Name Box. Key the contact information: **120 East Main Street | Ada, OK 74820-5602 | Phone: 580.555.0188 | Fax: 580.555.0143 | www.vanhuss&vanhuss.com** and **From: Susie VanHuss**
3. Save as a *Word* template named **vanhuss fax**. The template will be saved to Custom Office Templates unless your instructor directs you otherwise. Close the template.
4. Save and close. (*56-d4*)

Writing 53

gwam 1' | 3'

We are living in a wonderful period of history. This is a 11 | 4

time when historians are recording many exciting changes in our 24 | 8

world. The past two decades have shown that all inhabitants of 36 | 12

this planet must learn to exist together. We no longer are able 49 | 16

to isolate ourselves from other countries. The action of one 61 | 20

nation has a direct effect on nearly every other nation in the 73 | 24

world. We must quickly recognize and adjust to peaceful solutions. <u>87</u> | 29

Writing 54

gwam 1' | 3'

Traffic jams, deadlines, problems at work, and squabbles at 12 | 4 | 84

home are several ways in which tension is created. When our 24 | 8 | 88

tension is about to reach the boiling point, what do people usually 37 | 12 | 93

tell us? In most cases, they urge us to relax. But relaxing is not 50 | 17 | 97

always easy to accomplish. We frequently think we cannot find 62 | 21 | 101

the time for this important part of our daily activity. <u>73</u> | 24 | 105

To understand how relaxation works for us, we must realize 12 | 28 | 109

how the stress of contemporary existence works against us. 23 | 32 | 112

Developed for survival in a challenging world, the human body reacts 37 | 37 | 117

to a crisis by getting ready for action. Whether we are preparing for 51 | 41 | 122

a timed writing or for an encounter in a dark street, our muscles 64 | 46 | 126

tighten and our blood pressure goes up. After years of this type 76 | 50 | 130

of response, we often find it difficult to relax when needed. <u>89</u> | 54 | 134

Now think about the feeling which is the opposite of this 11 | 58 | 138

turmoil. The pulse slows down, the breath comes slowly and 23 | 62 | 142

calmly, and the tension leaves the body. This is total relaxation. 36 | 66 | 146

And if it seems good, consider how good it must actually feel. Our 49 | 70 | 151

bodies are already prepared to relax; it is an ability all 61 | 74 | 155

individuals have within themselves. What we have to practice is 74 | 79 | 159

how to use this response. <u>79</u> | 80 | 160

Lesson 57 Letter Review

Skill Building

57b Improve Techniques

Key each line once, concentrating on using good keying techniques.

adjacent reaches

1 Sand castles are fun to build but are poor shelter in a downpour.

2 The Hoosiers scored three points in the fourth to avoid an upset.

3 Her articles are going to be reported in an edition of the paper.

4 Fewer people attend West Point to play polo than to join a choir.

5 A dazed beggar scattered after a red car swerved on a wet street.

one hand

6 Mimi feasts on milky eggs at noon after I feed Kipp plum dessert.

7 Mo started ragweed tests in a vacated garage after greeting Dave.

8 You debate Phil after I defeat John; rest up, you brave braggart!

9 Handiwork is busy work, but it's also a memento of a rich entity.

10 The hairy ape bit the fish, but the apricot and corn lay dormant.

balanced hand

11 Henry may dismantle an authentic antique auto for Zoe's sorority.

12 An Irish auditor quit work at the city and ambled to the fields.

Communication

57c

1. Review the *Use a Comma* subsection of the "Punctuation" section of Appendix C.

2. For each group of sentences, select the sentence that has applied the use of commas correctly. Key the sentence number and then key the letter that corresponds to the correct sentence, e.g., (1a).

3. Save and close. (57c)

1a. The legislators voted on Policy #2083 on May 23, 2010, at 5 p.m.

1b. The legislators voted on Policy #2,083 on May 23, 2010 at 5 p.m.

2a. To view Michelle's entire social networking site I need her permission.

2b. To view Michelle's entire social networking site, I need her permission.

3a. The parents volunteered to bring coffee, juice, milk, and pastries.

3b. The parents volunteered to bring coffee juice milk and pastries.

4a. Several club members designed an attractive logo, and the fundraising committee created an online store for selling merchandise.

4b. Several club members designed an attractive logo and the fundraising committee created an online store for selling merchandise.

5a. Mr. Rankin explained "Monday is the deadline for our class blog."

5b. Mr. Rankin explained, "Monday is the deadline for our class blog."

6a. The independent film festival will be held in Baton Rouge, Louisiana, on May 11-15.

6b. The independent film festival will be held in Baton Rouge Louisiana on May 11-15.

7a. Chef Nate I appreciate your answering my questions about organic gardening on your blog.

7b. Chef Nate, I appreciate your answering my questions about organic gardening on your blog.

Timed Writings
Key with fluency and control.

Writing 51

gwam 1' | 3'

Educated people realize that they can find important 10 | 3
details just through the simple act of listening. The secret, 23 | 8
however, as is well known, is to listen with discretion. Our 35 | 12
usual ability to hear forces us to hear many thousands of noises, 48 | 16
while our amazing listening ability lets us select only what we 60 | 20
think is important from what is minutiae. Often our only input 73 | 24
is a question; and if our listening area is an exciting TV show, 85 | 28
we are not required to reply. 91 | 30

1' | 1 | 2 | 3 | 4 | 5 | 6 | 7 | 8 | 9 | 10 | 11 | 12 |
3' | 1 | 2 | 3 | 4 |

Writing 52

gwam 1' | 3'

People spend far more time listening than they spend 10 | 3
communicating in any other way, but only a very few people have 23 | 8
developed good listening skills. There is a big difference between 36 | 12
hearing and listening. Hearing does not require major effort, but 49 | 16
listening is hard work. One of the problems with listening is that 62 | 21
we can listen about three times faster than most people speak. 75 | 25
We are able to hear what the speaker is saying and still have 87 | 29
extra time for our minds to wander to other things. 97 | 32

An active listener utilizes the difference between the 11 | 36
listening and the speaking rates to make mental summaries of 23 | 40
the conversation. One way to listen actively is to anticipate 35 | 44
the next point that the individual will make. It is also 46 | 48
important to clarify in your own mind what is being said. Generally, 60 | 52
people try to assume too much. A good listener will let the 72 | 56
person explain in her or his words exactly what he or she would 84 | 60
like to say. Paraphrasing is a good way to confirm that the message 98 | 65
is understood. 100 | 66

A person who has developed good listening skills will not 11 | 70
interrupt the person who is speaking. The problem is that more 24 | 74
people prefer to speak than to listen. Sometimes it takes a 36 | 78
considerable amount of effort to give the person an opportunity 48 | 82
to get the message across. Showing that you are interested in 60 | 86
what is being said helps to put the speaker at ease. It is not enough 74 | 91
just to listen; you also have to look like you are listening. The 87 | 95
effective use of body language enhances listening. 97 | 98

1' | 1 | 2 | 3 | 4 | 5 | 6 | 7 | 8 | 9 | 10 | 11 | 12 |
3' | 1 | 2 | 3 | 4 |

BUSINESS LETTER REVIEW

The block letter style and modified block letter style are the typical business letter formats used. The two punctuation styles include open and mixed punctuation.

Block letter style: All letter parts are keyed at the left margin.

Modified block style: Date, complimentary closing, writer's name, and title are keyed at the center of the page.

Open punctuation: Does not include punctuation after the salutation or after the complimentary closing.

Mixed punctuation: Includes a colon after the salutation and comma after complimentary closing.

Compare the illustrations below to understand each letter style and punctuation style. Full-page models are shown on pages 3-19 and 3-20.

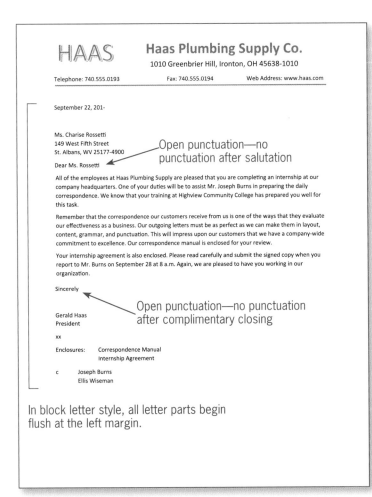

Block Letter Style with Open Punctuation

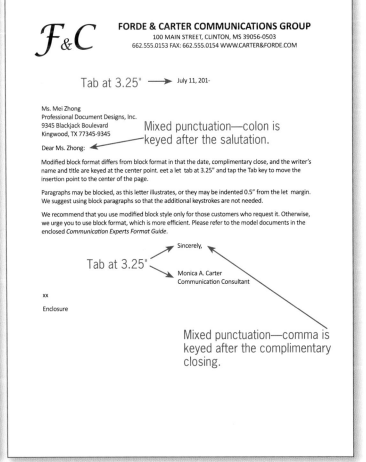

Modified Block Letter Style with Mixed Punctuation

Skill Building *Technique Builder*

DRILL 27

Number Review

Key each line once at a comfortable rate; practice difficult lines.

1 On June 11 and July 11, 11 men and 11 women worked 11 hours each.
2 Al received Invoice 22RC22 on May 22 and paid $225.22 on June 22.
3 The 33 boys visited 3 girls at 3:30 p.m. on May 3 at 33 Oak Road.
4 The 44 men found 44 sections of 4' pipe required before 4:44 p.m.
5 On June 15, 55 women ran over 25 miles in 2 hours and 55 minutes.
6 The 66 players shot 6,666 free throws in 66 minutes and made 666.
7 The 7 rooms were 17' 7" wide and 7' 7" long with 17' 7" ceilings.
8 Those 8 coaches made 88 trips averaging 88 miles each in 88 days.
9 The 9 boys packed 9 boxes weighing 99 pounds in 9 hours on May 9.
10 Was the value listed at $10,000,000 or $20,000,000 on October 20?

Timed Writings

A ALL LETTERS

Writing 50

gwam 1' | 3'

The kinds of leisure activities you choose constitute 11 | 4
your life style and, to a great extent, reflect your personality. 24 | 8
For example, if your daily activities are people oriented, you 36 | 12
may balance this by spending your free time alone. On the other 49 | 16
hand, if you would rather be with people most of the time, your 61 | 20
socialization needs may be very high. At the other end of the 73 | 24
scale are people who are engaged in machine-oriented work and 86 | 29
also enjoy spending leisure time alone. These people tend to be 98 | 33
rather quiet and reserved. 103 | 34

Every individual needs a certain amount of relaxation to 11 | 38
remain physically and mentally alert. However, what one person 24 | 42
finds relaxing may be just the opposite for another person. For 36 | 47
example, one person may like to read a good book; another may 48 | 51
find that reading causes nervousness and fatigue. The same holds 61 | 55
true for the person who enjoys sports. Studies have shown that 74 | 59
jogging may be quite good for a person who enjoys it but may be 86 | 63
detrimental to another person who does not enjoy it. 97 | 67

Experts have noted that the proper balance of leisure, 11 | 70
relaxation, and recreation is almost essential for individuals 23 | 74
who live and work in a highly automated world. This balance is 36 | 79
necessary if each person is to be productive in handling the 48 | 83
everyday pressure and stress of life. Because every person has 60 | 87
unique needs that are met in a variety of ways, one must properly 73 | 91
assess all of the day's activities if the maximum benefit is to 86 | 95
be gained from each day of life. 92 | 97

1' | 1 | 2 | 3 | 4 | 5 | 6 | 7 | 8 | 9 | 10 | 11 | 12 |
3' | 1 | 2 | 3 | 4 |

LETTER PARTS

Letterhead: Preprinted or electronically stored stationery that includes information such as the company or individual's name, logo, address, telephone number, email address, or web address.

Dateline: Date the letter is prepared. To position the date on plain paper, tap ENTER three times (about 2"); on electronically stored letterhead, click below the letterhead (about .05") to position it.

Letter address: Complete address of letter recipient. Tap ENTER two times after the date. Generally includes receiver's name, company name, street address, city, state (one space after the state), and ZIP Code. Include personal title (Mr., Ms., Dr.). Capitalize the first letter of each word. Remove the added space between the lines of the letter address.

Salutation (or greeting): Tap ENTER one time after the letter address. Include a courtesy title with the name, e.g., Dear Mr. Nibert. Use *Ladies and Gentlemen* when addressing a company.

Body: Message of the letter. Tap ENTER one time after the salutation. Use the 1.08" default line spacing; tap ENTER once between paragraphs.

Complimentary closing: Formal goodbye. Tap ENTER one time after the body. Capitalize only the first letter of the first word of the closing.

Writer's name and title: Tap ENTER two times after the complimentary closing. Include a personal title (Mr., Ms.) only if it is not apparent to the reader if the person is male or female (Jan, Pat, Chris). Key the name and title on either one or two lines, whichever gives better balance. Use a comma to separate name and title if on one line. If two lines are used, remove the added space between the two lines.

HAAS

Haas Plumbing Supply Co.

1010 Greenbrier Hill, Ironton, OH 45638-1010

Telephone: 740.555.0193 Fax: 740.555.0194 Web Address: www.haas.com

September 22, 201- Date

Letterhead

Ms. Charise Rossetti Letter address
149 West Fifth Street
St. Albans, WV 25177-4900

Dear Ms. Rossetti Salutation

All of the employees at Haas Plumbing Supply are pleased that you are completing an internship at our company headquarters. One of your duties will be to assist Mr. Joseph Burns in preparing the daily correspondence. We know that your training at Highview Community College has prepared you well for this task.

Remember that the correspondence our customers receive from us is one of the ways that they evaluate our effectiveness as a business. Our outgoing letters must be as perfect as we can make them in layout, content, grammar, and punctuation. This will impress upon our customers that we have a company-wide commitment to excellence. Our correspondence manual is enclosed for your review.

Body

Your internship agreement is also enclosed. Please read carefully and submit the signed copy when you report to Mr. Burns on September 28 at 8 a.m. Again, we are pleased to have you working in our organization.

Sincerely Complimentary closing

Gerald Haas Writer's name and title
President

xx Reference initials

Enclosures: Correspondence Manual Enclosure notation
 Internship Agreement

c Joseph Burns
 Ellis Wiseman Copy notation

Block Letter with Open Punctuation

Reference initials: Tap ENTER one time after the writer's name and title. Replace *xx* with your initials. Include no spaces or periods.

Enclosure notation: Tap ENTER one time after the reference initials. If multiple enclosures are listed, set a tab at 1" and remove added space between lines.

Copy notation: Tap ENTER one time after the reference initials or enclosure notation if an enclosure notation is included. If multiple copies are listed, set a tab at 0.5" to align and remove added space between lines.

Skill Building *Technique Builder*

DRILL 26

Response Pattern

Key each line once.

 TIP

Use top speed for easy words and phrases and lower speed for words that are more difficult to key. Key phrases marked with a line as a unit.

1 it to the us me you so go now we my he two in can her by of do no

2 it is | it is the | is it | is it you | he can | can he | he can go | can he go

3 who is | who is it | is it you | you can go | can you go | you can go to it

4 car mail two you may just can lake ask sail sign his form her who

5 who can sail | you can sail | you may sign | can you sign | sign his form

6 sign the form | mail the form | sign and mail | sign and mail that form

7 it was | was it so | if she can go to | can he go to the | can she go to the

8 she can | she may not | she may not go | can you go to the | so we may go

9 sign the | sign the form | they may sign that | they may sign that form

Timed Writings

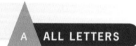 **A ALL LETTERS**

Writing 49

	gwam 1'	3'

An essential part of analyzing a career option is to 10 | 3
determine the type and extent of education that are required for 23 | 8
a selected career. A main factor to consider about an education 36 | 12
is how long it will take to get the skills that are needed to 48 | 16
compete successfully for a job. This factor includes any other 60 | 20
training that may be essential at the outset of employment. 72 | 24
Because jobs change, also assess how an educational program is 85 | 28
structured to meet work changes. <u>91</u> | 30

Many people choose a career without considering how well 11 | 34
they may be suited for it. For example, a person who is outgoing 24 | 38
and enjoys being around people probably should not select a 36 | 42
career that requires spending long hours working alone. A job 48 | 46
that requires quick, forceful action to be taken probably should 61 | 51
not be pursued by a person who is shy and contemplative. Just 73 | 55
because one has an aptitude for a specific job does not mean he 86 | 59
or she will be successful in that job. Thus, be sure to consider 98 | 63
individual personality traits before making a final career 110 | 67
choice. <u>111</u> | 67

Money and inner satisfaction are the two leading reasons 11 | 71
why most people work. For most persons, the need for money 23 | 75
translates into food, shelter, and clothing. Once the basic 35 | 79
needs of a person are met, satisfaction is the greatest motivator 48 | 83
for working. To the average person, a job is satisfying if he or 60 | 88
she enjoys the work, likes the people associated with the work, 73 | 92
and feels a sense of pride in a job well done. Because you may 85 | 96
not be the average person, analyze yourself to discover what will 98 | 100
provide job satisfaction. <u>103</u> | 102

1'	1	2	3	4	5	6	7	8	9	10	11	12	
3'		1		2			3			4			

Haas Plumbing Supply Co.
1010 Greenbrier Hill, Ironton, OH 45638-1010

Telephone: 740.555.0193 Fax: 740.555.0194 Web Address: www.haas.com

September 22, 201- ↓ 2

Ms. Charise Rossetti } Press SHIFT + ENTER
149 West Fifth Street }
St. Albans, WV 25177-4900 ↓ 1

Open Punctuation → Dear Ms. Rossetti

All of the employees at Haas Plumbing Supply are pleased that you are completing an internship at our company headquarters. One of your duties will be to assist Mr. Joseph Burns in preparing the daily correspondence. We know that your training at Highview Community College has prepared you well for this task.

Remember that the correspondence our customers receive from us is one of the ways that they evaluate our effectiveness as a business. Our outgoing letters must be as perfect as we can make them in layout, content, grammar, and punctuation. This will impress upon our customers that we have a company-wide commitment to excellence. Our correspondence manual is enclosed for your review.

Your internship agreement is also enclosed. Please read carefully and submit the signed copy when you report to Mr. Burns on September 28 at 8 a.m. Again, we are pleased to have you working in our organization.

Open Punctuation → Sincerely ↓ 2

Gerald Haas } Press SHIFT + ENTER
President
 Align enclosures at 1"
xx ↓ 1 ↓

Enclosures: Correspondence Manual } Press SHIFT + ENTER
 Internship Agreement

c Joseph Burns } Press SHIFT + ENTER
 Ellis Wiseman
 ↑
Align copy notations at 0.5"

Block Letter with Open Punctuation

Skill Building *Technique Builder*

DRILL 25

Direct Reach Combinations

Key each line once.

 TIP

Key fluently, without rushing.

br/rb
1 break barb brawn orbit brain carbon brakes barbecue brazen barber
2 Barbara Brady brought us a new brand of barbecue to eat at break.

ce/ec
3 cease decide cent collect cell direct cedar check center peck ice
4 Cecil recently received a check for his special barbecue recipes.

mu/um
5 mull dumb must human mud lumber mulch lump mumps slump music fume
6 Bum Muse must have dumped too much muddy mulch on the bumpy lawn.

nu/un
7 nut sun fun nurse gun sinus number punch nuzzle pound lunch until
8 Uncle Gunta, a nurse, was uneasy about numerous units unionizing.

gr/rg
9 grade merge grand purge great large grab organ green margins gray
10 Margo, our great grandmother, regrets merging those large groups.

ny/yn
11 Wayne any shyness many agony balcony Jayne lynx penny larynx myna
12 Wayne and Jayne fed many skinny myna birds on that sunny balcony.

Timed Writings

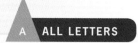

Writing 48

	gwam	1'	3'

The job market today is quite different than it was a few 11 | 4
years ago. The fast track to management no longer exists. 23 | 8
Entry-level managers find that it is much more difficult to 35 | 12
obtain a promotion to a higher-level position in management than 47 | 16
it was just a few years ago. People who are in the market for 60 | 20
new jobs find very few management positions available. In fact, 72 | 24
many managers at all levels have a difficult time keeping their 85 | 28
current management positions. Two factors seem to contribute 97 | 32
heavily to the problem. The first factor is the trend toward 109 | 36
self-managed teams. The second factor is that as companies 120 | 40
downsize they often remove entire layers of management or an 132 | 44
entire division. <u>136</u> | 45

Layoffs are not new; but, what is new is that layoffs are 11 | 49
affecting white-collar workers as well as blue-collar workers. 24 | 53
Coping with job loss is a new and frustrating experience for many 37 | 57
managers. A person who has just lost a job will have concerns 49 | 62
about personal security and welfare, and the concerns are 60 | 65
compounded when families are involved. The problem, however, 72 | 69
is more than just an economic one. Job loss often damages an 84 | 73
individual's sense of self-worth. An individual who does not have 97 | 78
a good self-concept will have a very hard time selling himself 110 | 82
or herself to a potential employer. <u>117</u> | 84

1'	1	2	3	4	5	6	7	8	9	10	11	12
3'		1			2			3			4	

FORDE & CARTER COMMUNICATIONS GROUP
100 MAIN STREET, CLINTON, MS 39056-0503
662.555.0153 FAX: 662.555.0154 WWW.CARTER&FORDE.COM

Tab 3.25" ⟶ July 11, 201-

Ms. Mei Zhong
Professional Document Designs, Inc.
9345 Blackjack Boulevard
Kingwood, TX 77345-9345

Dear Ms. Zhong: Mixed Punctuation

Modified block format differs from block format in that the date, complimentary close, and the writer's name and title are keyed at the center point. Set a left tab at 3.25" and tap the Tab key to move the insertion point to the center of the page.

Paragraphs may be blocked, as this letter illustrates, or they may be indented 0.5" from the left margin. We suggest using block paragraphs so that the additional keystrokes are not needed.

We recommend that you use modified block style only for those customers who request it. Otherwise, we urge you to use block format, which is more efficient. Please refer to the model documents in the enclosed *Communication Experts Format Guide*.

Sincerely, Mixed Punctuation

Tab 3.25"

Monica A. Carter
Communication Consultant

xx

Enclosure

Modified Block Letter with Mixed Punctuation

Skill Building *Technique Builder*

Specific Rows

Key each line once; DS between groups.

Reach to the first and third rows with a minimum of hand movement; keep hands quiet; don't bounce on the keys.

Rows 3, 2, 1

1 you we quip try pot peer your wire put quit wet trip power toy to
2 salad fad glad lass lag has gall lash gas lad had shall flag half
3 comb zone exam man carve bun oxen bank came next vent zoo van cab

4 we try to; you were; put up your; put it there; you quit; wipe it
5 Gail asked Sissy; what was said; had Jake left; Dana sold a flag
6 Zam came back; can Max fix my van? a brave man, Ben came in a cab

7 Peter or I will try to wire our popular reports to Porter or you.
8 Ada Glass said she is glad she had half a kale salad with Dallas.
9 Zack drove a van to minimize expenses; Ben and Max came in a cab.

Timed Writings

A | ALL LETTERS

Take two 3' or one 5' writing; key with fluency and control.

Writing 47

gwam 3' | 5'

	3'	5'
Sports are very big business today; that is, those sports	4	2
competitions in which men participate are very big business. What	8	5
about sports for women? At the professional level, women have made	13	8
real progress in golf and tennis; they, as well as their sponsors, can	17	10
make big money in both of these events. The other sports for women	22	13
still are not considered to be major revenue sports. The future	26	15
may be much better, however, because sports for women at all levels	30	18
are gaining in popularity. Programs that are designed to help	34	21
young girls develop their athletic skills and interest are having	39	23
an impact. The result is that girls now expect to play for organized	43	26
clubs as well as in school programs just as boys do. Club	47	28
sports often will lead to varsity teams.	50	30
Many people question how much impact the current emphasis	53	32
on gender equity will have on sports at the college level. Most	58	35
people agree that this new emphasis is very positive for women.	62	37
Some people feel, though, that it either has had or could have a	66	40
negative impact on sports for men. They believe that resources	70	42
that would have been spent on sports such as football, basketball,	75	45
and baseball for men are now being spent on the Olympic sports for	79	47
women. Overall, most people believe that both men and women who	83	50
have the ability to excel in an athletic event as well as in the	88	53
classroom should have the opportunity and should be encouraged to	92	55
do so. Success for both women and men is better than success for	96	58
either.	97	58

3' | 1 | 2 | 3 | 4 |
5' | | 1 | | 2 |

Apply It

57-d1

Create Quick Part

 closing

1. Open *closing* from the data files, and select the closing lines used by Gerald Haas (complimentary closing through reference initials) and create a Quick Part named **Gerald Closing Lines**.

2. Key the description **Gerald Closing lines**.

3. You will use the Quick Part in the next document.

57-d2

Block Letter

 haas letterhead

1. Open *haas letterhead* from the data files, and key the block letter on page 3-19 with open punctuation. Begin the date at about 2".

2. Insert the Quick Part *Gerald Closing lines*, created in *57-d1* above.

3. Align the enclosure notations at the default tab set at 1".

4. Send a copy to **Joseph Burns** and **Ellis Wiseman**; align the names at the default 0.5" tab.

5. Press SHIFT + ENTER to remove the added space between the letter address, writer's name and title, enclosures, and individuals receiving copies of this letter.

6. Add an envelope to the letter. (Mailings/Create/Envelope)

7. Save and close. (*57-d2*)

57-d3

Modified Block Letter

 f & c letterhead

1. Open *f & c letterhead* from the data files, and key the modified block letter on page 3-20 with mixed punctuation.

2. Click below the letterhead and set a left tab at 3.25" for keying the date, complimentary close, writer's name, and title. *Hint:* To set a left tab, check the tab selector to be sure the left tab is selected. Then, click the Horizontal Ruler where you want to set the left tab.

 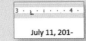

3. Add an envelope to the letter.

4. Save and close. (*57-d3*)

57-d4

Block Letter

 puppies

1. Open the *puppies* data file, and add the letter parts that are missing and format the letter as a block letter with open punctuation. Here is information you will need.

Date: **Use current date**

Letter recipient: **Ms. Sarah Atkinson, 1234 Elm Lane, Bronx, NY 10466-1234**

Sender of letter: **Andrew Rogers | Kennel Manager**

Salutation: **Dear Ms. Atkinson**

Complimentary closing: **Sincerely**

Copy: **Daniel Foster**

Attachment notation is needed as letter and picture are being attached to email.

2. Add an envelope to the letter.

3. Save and close. (*57-d4*)

DRILL 23

Specific Fingers

Key each line once;
DS between groups.

1st
1 fun gray vent guy hunt brunt buy brunch much gun huge humor vying
2 buy them brunch; a hunting gun; Guy hunts for fun; try it for fun

2nd
3 cite decide kick cider creed kidded keen keep kit idea ice icicle
4 keen idea; kick it back; ice breaker; decide the issue; sip cider

3rd
5 low slow lax solo wax sold swell swollen wood wool load logs doll
6 wooden dolls; wax the floor; a slow boat; saw logs; pull the wool

4th
7 quip zap Zane zip pepper pay quiz zipper quizzes pad map nap jazz
8 zip the zipper; jazz at the plaza; Zane quipped; La Paz jazz band

Timed Writings

1. Take three 1' writings on each paragraph.
2. Take two 3' writings.

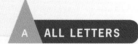 A ALL LETTERS

Writing 46

gwam 1' | 3'

	1'	3'	
How much power is needed? Is more power always better than	12	4	81

How much power is needed? Is more power always better than — 12 | 4 | 81
less power? People often raise the question in many different — 24 | 8 | 85
instances. Regardless of the situation, most people seem to seek — 37 | 12 | 89
more power. In jobs, power is often related to rank in an — 48 | 16 | 93
organization, to the number of people reporting to a person, and — 61 | 20 | 97
to the ability to spend money without having to ask someone with — 74 | 25 | 101
more power. Most experts indicate that the power a person has — 86 | 29 | 105
should closely match the responsibilities (not just duties and — 98 | 33 | 110
tasks) for which he or she can be held accountable. — 108 | 36 | 113

Questions about power are not limited to jobs and people. — 11 | 40 | 117
Many people ask the question in reference to the amount of power — 24 | 44 | 121
or speed a computer should have. Again, the response usually — 36 | 48 | 125
implies that more is better. A better approach is to analyze how — 49 | 52 | 129
the computer is to be used and then try to match power needs to — 62 | 57 | 134
the types of applications. Most people are surprised to learn that — 75 | 61 | 138
home computer buyers tend to buy more power than buyers in — 86 | 65 | 142
offices. The primary reason is that the computers are used to — 99 | 69 | 146
play games with extensive graphics, sound, and other media — 110 | 73 | 150
applications. Matching the needs of the software is the key. — 122 | 77 | 154

1' | 1 | 2 | 3 | 4 | 5 | 6 | 7 | 8 | 9 | 10 | 11 | 12 |
3' | | 1 | | 2 | | 3 | | 4 |

Lesson 58 Special Letter Parts

Skill Building

58b Timed Writing

1. Key a 1' timing on each paragraph; work to increase speed.
2. Key a 3' timing on all paragraphs.

gwam 1' | 3'

	1'	3'
You may be familiar with the expression that we live in an	12	4
information age now. People interpret this expression in a host of	25	8
diverse ways, but most people agree on two key things. The first thing	39	13
is that a huge amount of information exists today; some even think we	53	18
suffer from information overload. The second thing is that technology	66	22
has changed the way we access these large pools of data.	78	26
Some people are quick to point out that a large difference exists	13	30
between the quantity and the quality of information. It is very critical	27	35
to recognize that anyone who has access can simply post information	41	39
on the Internet. No test exists to screen for junk before something is	55	44
posted. Some of the data may be helpful and accurate. However, much	68	49
of it must be analyzed quite carefully to judge if it is valid.	81	53
Just how do you ascertain if the data accessed is valid? Some of	13	57
the similar techniques that can be used with print media can be applied	27	62
with electronic media. An effective way to assess material is to examine	41	67
its source carefully. What do you know about the people who provided	55	71
this information? If you cannot unearth the answer to this question,	69	76
you should be wary of trusting it.	75	78

1' | 1 | 2 | 3 | 4 | 5 | 6 | 7 | 8 | 9 | 10 | 11 | 12 | 13 |
3' | 1 | 2 | 3 | 4 |

SPECIAL LETTER PARTS TRENDS

Communicating Today ▶

Special letter parts include mailing notations, reference line, attention line, subject line, enclosure/attachment notations, and copy notations. They provide information from the writer to the recipient that is generally not included in the body of the letter. Notations may be provided on the letter, in the email heading, and/or at the bottom of the email.

Today, businesses distribute letters in a variety of ways. Frequently, technology is used to replace services previously provided by the postal service. The majority of letters are distributed either by email or by sharing the document using cloud-based services, eliminating the need for most mailing notations. Airmail for international mail is the primary mailing notation used frequently on the envelope. However, many letters with international destinations are distributed by email or shared by a cloud-based system.

Personal and confidential notations may be included on the letter and the envelope if the letter is mailed, and in the subject line or at the bottom of an email. Copies are noted on the bottom of the letter and in the email heading. Blind copies are typically sent by email in the bcc heading. With email, attachment notations replace enclosure notations because they are attached to the email.

DRILL 20

Adjacent Keys

Key each line once; repeat entire drill. DS between groups.

Goal: To eliminate persistent errors on side-by-side keys.

as/sa
1 has sale fast salt was saw vast essay easy say past vast mast sap
2 We saw Sam; Sal was sad; Susan has a cast; as Sam said; as I said

er/re
3 were there tree deer great three other her free red here pert are
4 we were there; here we are; there were three; here are three deer

io/oi
5 point axiom prior choir lion boil toil billion soil action adjoin
6 join a choir; prior to that action; millions in a nation rejoiced

op/po
7 polo drop loop post hope pole port rope slope power top pony stop
8 rope the pony; drop the pole; power at the top; hope for the poor

rt/tr
9 trail alert train hurt tree shirt trap smart trim start tray dirt
10 trim the tree; start the train; dirt on the shirt; alert the trio

ew/we
11 few we stew were pew went dew web sew wept crew wear brew wet new
12 we were weak; few were weeping; the crew went west; we knew a few

gh/ui
13 sight quit laugh suit might ruin ghost guide ghastly guilt ghetto
14 a ghastly suit; quit laughing; recruit the ghost; might be guilty

DRILL 21

Outside Reaches

Key each line once.
DS between groups.

Goal: To key with a maximum of one error per line. (Letters are often omitted in outside reaches—concentrate.)

a/p
1 tapioca actual against casual areas facial equally aware parallel
2 impower purpose people opposed compute pimple papyrus pope puppet
3 Perhaps part of the chapter page openers can appear on red paper.

s/w
4 class sash steps essential skills business discuss desks insisted
5 wow wayworn away awkward wrong awaits wildwood waterworks wayward
6 The snow white swan swayed as the waves swept the swelling shore.

z/l
7 hazard zip zero zeolite freezer zoom zealous z-axis zodiac sizing
8 likely indelibly, laurel finally leaflet regularly eloquently lily
9 A New Zealand zoologist was amazed as a zebra guzzled the zinnias.

x/?
10 fax oxford exert excite examples xylan exercise oxygen exact taxi
11 When? Where? Which? For her? How much? What color? To whom?
12 After examining the x-rays, why did Dr. Ax exempt an exploratory?

DRILL 22

Alphabetic Sentences

Key each line once with good rhythm. Keep fingers curved and upright over the keys. DS between groups.

1 Judge McQuoy will have prizes for their next big track meet.
2 Jack may provide some extra quiz problems for the new group.

3 Gary Quazet mended six copies of books and journals we have.
4 Jack quibbled with a garrulous expert on Zoave family names.

5 Jake will study sixty chapters on vitamins for the big quiz.
6 Max asked Quin to provide a jewel box for the glossy zircon.

7 This judge may quiz the Iowa clerks about extensive profits.
8 Meg Keys packed and flew to Venezia to acquire her next job.

SPECIAL LETTER PARTS

Special letter parts may often be added to a business letter. When adding special letter parts causes the letter to move too far down on the page, adjust the date higher than the standard 2". However, letterhead typically determines the position of the date. Always preview letters to determine the most attractive appearance. With today's technology, virtually all businesses use letterhead, and most individuals use electronically created and stored letterhead for personal business letters. Letterhead creates a better impression than a plain sheet of paper. Special letter parts are explained below and illustrated on a full-page model on page 3-25.

An **attention line** is used to direct a letter to a position or department within an organization. The attention line is keyed on the second line below the company name. Whenever an attention line is used to direct a letter to a department, division, or company, the correct salutation is *Ladies and Gentlemen*. If it is used for a specific position title, then the salutation would be Dear (position title), such as *Dear Office Manager*.

> Chou and Chou Furniture Company
> Attention Accounting Department
> 189 First Avenue Olympia,
> WA 99504-6480
>
> Ladies and Gentlemen:

A **reference line** is used to direct the reader to source documents or to files. Tap ENTER one time after the letter address.

> Ms. Allison Raymond
> P.O. Box 3100
> Natchez, MS 39120-2030
>
> Re: Order No. R1084
>
> Dear Ms. Raymond:

A **subject line** provides the reader with a short description of the purpose of the letter. Tap ENTER one time after the salutation. Key the subject line using initial caps; do not key the word *Subject*.

> Dear Mr. Jones:
>
> Projected Sales Figures
>
> The sales figures for the first quarter have been released.

Writing 43: *85 gwam*

	gwam	1'	3'

Business letters can be defined by their goals; for example, a letter of inquiry, a reply letter, a promotion letter, a credit letter, or other specialized letter. While you learn to compose these letters, just keep each letter's individual goals always in front of you. If you fix in your mind a theme, a pattern, an idea for your writing, composing good business letters may emerge as one of the best tricks in your bag.

	12	4	59
	25	8	64
	38	13	68
	51	17	72
	63	21	76
	74	25	80
	83	28	83

Competent business writers know what they want to say—and they say it with simplicity and clarity. Words are the utensils they use to convey ideas or to convince others to accomplish some action. The simple word and the short sentence usually are more effective than the big word and the involved sentence. But don't be afraid of the long or unusual word if it means exactly what you intend to say in your business letter.

	11	32	87
	24	36	91
	37	40	96
	50	44	100
	62	49	104
	75	53	108
	83	55	111

Writing 44: *90 gwam*

	gwam	1'	3'

Although many of us are basically comfortable with sameness and appear to dislike change, we actually prize variation. We believe that we are each unique individuals, yet we know that we are really only a little different; and we struggle to find "sense of self" in how we think and act. Our cars, too, built on assembly lines are basically identical; yet when we purchase one, we choose the model, color, size, and style which suits us individually.

	12	4	63
	24	8	67
	37	12	71
	49	16	75
	61	20	79
	73	24	83
	86	29	88
	89	30	88

Also many people expect to create security by buying things that are in keeping with society's "image" and "status." But what we think of as "status" always changes. The wise buyer will buy those items that give most in utility, comfort, and satisfaction. Status should just be a thing we create in ourselves, not a thing created for us. Common sense should guide us in making good decisions—and if our "status" is increased thereby, well, why not?

	12	33	92
	24	37	96
	36	41	100
	48	45	104
	61	50	109
	74	54	113
	87	58	117
	88	59	118

Writing 45: *95 gwam*

	gwam	1'	3'

Normally, customers just do not abandon a firm because of a mistake. All firms will make mistakes at one time or another. The way aproblem is resolved is far more crucial than the fact that a problem existed. More customers leave a firm and take their business to a competitor because they get upset with an employee than for any other reason. The key qualifications for a customer service employee are superb human relations skills and product and service knowledge.

	12	4	35
	25	8	39
	38	13	43
	50	17	47
	62	21	51
	75	25	56
	88	29	60
	92	31	61

A **blind copy notation** (bc) indicates that others are receiving a copy of the letter without the addressee's knowledge. Tap ENTER one time after the reference initials, enclosure notation, or copy notation (if any). The blind copy notation appears on copies but not on the original. Align multiple recipients at the 0.5" tab. **Note:** When email is used to distribute a letter with blind copies, the Bcc letter box in the email heading is used.

John Mastrangelo, President

xx

Enclosure

bc Norman Elswick
 Sheila Solari

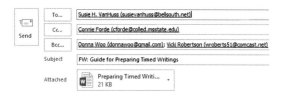

A **mailing notation** such as AIRMAIL, OVERNIGHT, or SPECIAL DELIVERY provides a record of how the letter was sent. Other notations such as CONFIDENTIAL or PERSONAL indicate how the recipient should treat the letter.

Key special notations in UPPERCASE at the left margin one line below the date. On the envelope, key notations that affect postage right-aligned below the stamp (1.2"). Key envelope notations that pertain to the recipient below the return address (1").

December 14, 201-

CONFIDENTIAL

Mr. Joshua Clinard
Clinard Security Services
207 Hollyhill Avenue
Downers Grove, IL 60515-0935

Dear Mr. Clinard

To add notations to an envelope:

1. Click the Add to Document button.
2. Position the insertion point on the line below the return address and tap ENTER twice (at 1"). Key the recipient's notation, e.g., CONFIDENTIAL, at the left margin.
3. Position the insertion point one line below the recipient's notation and tap ENTER one time (1.2") or one line below the return address if a recipient's notation is not used and tap ENTER three times (1.2"). Click the Align Right button. Key the mailing notation, e.g., AIRMAIL.

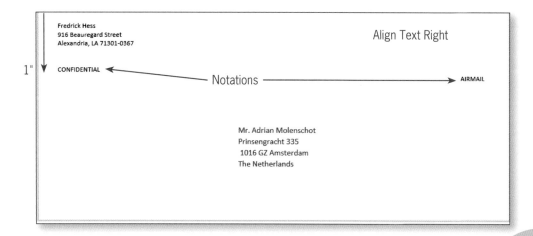

Writing 40: 70 *gwam*

	gwam	1'	3'

Foreign study and travel take extra time and effort, but these two activities quickly help us to understand people. Much can be learned from other cultures. Today, business must think globally. Learning about the culture of others is not a luxury. Even the owner of a very small business realizes that he or she cannot just focus on the domestic scene.

11	4	50
24	8	54
36	12	58
49	16	62
61	20	67
69	23	69

Many examples can be used to show how a local business may be influenced by global competition. A hair stylist may be required to learn European styles because customers may want to try a style just like they saw on their travels. Or salons may want to offer additional services such as facials that people have tried while they were traveling abroad.

11	27	73
23	31	77
36	35	81
49	40	86
63	44	90
69	46	92

1' | 1 | 2 | 3 | 4 | 5 | 6 | 7 | 8 | 9 | 10 | 11 | 12 | 13 |
3' | 1 | | 2 | | 3 | | 4 |

Writing 41: 75 *gwam*

	gwam	1'	3'

Getting a job interview is certainly a triumph for a job seeker. Yet anxiety quickly sets in as the applicant becomes aware of the competition. The same attention to details that you used in writing the successful resume should be used for the interview. Experts often say that the first four or five minutes are the most important in making a strong impact on the interviewers.

11	4	53
23	8	57
36	12	61
48	16	65
62	21	70
75	25	74

First, people focus on what they see. Posture, eye contact, facial expression, and gestures make up over half of the message. Next, people focus on what they hear; enthusiasm, delivery, pace, volume, and clarity are as vital as what is said. Finally, people get to the actual words that are said. You can make a good impression. But, realize, you may have just four minutes.

12	29	78
25	33	83
38	37	87
49	41	91
61	45	95
74	49	99

1' | 1 | 2 | 3 | 4 | 5 | 6 | 7 | 8 | 9 | 10 | 11 | 12 | 13 |
3' | 1 | | 2 | | 3 | | 4 |

Writing 42: 80 *gwam*

	gwam	1'	3'

Would a pitcher go to the mound without warming up? Would a speaker go to the podium without practice? Of course not! These experts have spent many long hours striving to do their best. Similarly, the performance of business employees is rated. The manager's evaluation will include a record of actual performance and a list of new goals. A good mark in any of these areas will demand much hard work.

11	4	56
24	8	61
37	12	65
49	16	69
62	21	73
74	25	77
79	26	79

Many work factors can be practiced to help one succeed on the job. Class attendance and punctuality can be perfected by students. Because work is expected to be correct, managers do not assign zeros. Thus, students must learn to proofread their own work. A project must also be completed quickly. Students can learn to organize work and time well and to find ways to do their work smarter and faster.

11	30	83
24	34	87
36	38	91
48	42	95
60	46	99
73	51	103
79	53	105

1' | 1 | 2 | 3 | 4 | 5 | 6 | 7 | 8 | 9 | 10 | 11 | 12 |
3' | 1 | | 2 | | 3 | | 4 |

Hill University

Cultural Center Erin Bland, Coordinator
Box 910
Charleston, WV 25301-0910 | 304.555.0167 | www.hillculturalcenter.edu

May 25, 201-

SPECIAL DELIVERY Mailing notation

Redmon Publishers
Attention Order Department
5280 Circle Point
Long Beach, CA 90840-0792

Re: Purchase Order W1029 ◄───── Reference line

Ladies and Gentlemen

Summary Workshop ◄───── Subject line

The Cultural Center at Hill University is hosting a summer workshop entitled "Women of the Mountains." Elizabeth is our keynote speaker, and we know our attendees will be clamoring for her exciting book, *The Legacy of Mountain Women*.

A purchase order with shipping instructions for 100 copies of Ms. Gainwright's book is enclosed. These books must be delivered to the Massey Convention Center during the first week in June where they will be stored until the seminar on June 15.

If you have questions regarding this order, please call me at 10 a.m. or 2 p.m. on either Thursday or Friday. We appreciate your assisting us with this order and special delivery.

Sincerely

Erin Bland, Coordinator

xx

Enclosure

bc John Connor Blind copy notation (Not printed on the addressee's copy)
 Angela Ward

Special Letter Parts

Writing 37: 55 *gwam*

<table>
<tr><td></td><td>*gwam*</td><td>1'</td><td>3'</td></tr>
</table>

A crucial life skill is being able to put things in proper | 12 | 4 | 39
perspective. Individuals often fail to realize that many things | 24 | 8 | 44
are just not worth fighting about. An effective way to learn quickly | 38 | 13 | 48
whether an issue is worth fighting for is to view it from a long-term | 52 | 17 | 53
perspective. | 54 | 18 | 54

If you will care five or six years from now that you defended | 12 | 22 | 58
an issue, it is a principle worth defending. However, if you will | 25 | 26 | 62
not remember, the situation does not justify the effort required | 38 | 31 | 66
for defending it. Consider your odds of winning. Why fight a | 50 | 35 | 70
losing battle? | 53 | 36 | 71

```
1' | 1 | 2 | 3 | 4 | 5 | 6 | 7 | 8 | 9 | 10 | 11 | 12 | 13 |
3' |       1       |       2       |       3       |       4       |
```

Writing 38: 60 *gwam*

<table>
<tr><td></td><td>*gwam*</td><td>1'</td><td>3'</td></tr>
</table>

Why do we remember some things and forget others? Often, | 11 | 4 | 43
we associate loss of memory with aging or an illness such as | 23 | 8 | 47
Alzheimer's disease. However, the crux of the matter is that we | 36 | 12 | 51
all forget various things that we prefer to remember. We tend to | 49 | 16 | 56
remember things that mean something special to us. | 59 | 20 | 59

For many people, recalling dates is a difficult task; yet | 11 | 23 | 63
they manage to remember dates of special occasions, such as | 23 | 27 | 67
birthdays. Processing information requires one not only to hear | 36 | 31 | 71
but to ponder and to understand what you heard. We recall | 47 | 35 | 75
things that we say and do longer than things we hear and see. | 59 | 39 | 79

```
1' | 1 | 2 | 3 | 4 | 5 | 6 | 7 | 8 | 9 | 10 | 11 | 12 |
3' |       1       |       2       |       3       |       4       |
```

Writing 39: 65 *gwam*

<table>
<tr><td></td><td>*gwam*</td><td>1'</td><td>3'</td></tr>
</table>

Humor is very important in our professional and our personal | 12 | 4 | 47
lives. Fortunately, we realize that many things can and do go | 24 | 8 | 51
wrong. If we can learn to laugh at ourselves and with other | 36 | 12 | 55
people, we will get through the terrible times. Adding a little | 49 | 16 | 59
extra laughter can help put the situation in proper perspective | 61 | 20 | 63
much quicker. | 64 | 21 | 64

Maintaining our sense of humor lets us enjoy our positions | 12 | 25 | 68
to a greater degree. No one is perfect, and we cannot expect | 24 | 29 | 72
perfection from ourselves. However, the quality of our | 34 | 33 | 75
performance is greater when we do the things we like. We realize | 47 | 37 | 80
our prime time is devoted to work. Thus, enjoying the time at | 59 | 41 | 84
work is very important. | 64 | 43 | 85

```
1' | 1 | 2 | 3 | 4 | 5 | 6 | 7 | 8 | 9 | 10 | 11 | 12 |
3' |       1       |       2       |       3       |       4       |
```

Apply It

1. Open *hill univ letterhead* from the data files, and key the letter with special letter parts on page 3-25. **Note:** Most letters do not include this many special letter parts.

2. Save and close. (*58-d1*)

1. Create an envelope for John Conner, one of the recipients of a blind copy in *58-d1*. The address is **Mr. John Conner, 209 Sweet Acre Drive, Decatur, AL 35601-4892**.

2. Key the mailing notation **CONFIDENTIAL** below the date. At 1.2", right-aligned, key the mailing notation **SPECIAL DELIVERY**.

3. Save and close. (*58-d2*)

1. Open *fair* from the data files, and format the letter as a modified block letter with mixed punctuation.

2. In the correct position, key the attention line **Attention Order Department**.

3. In the correct position, key the subject line **Annual Craft Fair Booth**.

4. Save and close. (*58-d3*)

TIP

Do not key reference initials since you are the writer of this letter.

1. In a new blank document, compose a letter of appreciation to a person who has recently done something for you. Examples may include served as a job reference, directed you to a resource, introduced you to a potential employer, or spoke to your class.

2. Key all the letter parts for a block letter with open punctuation. Be sure to check for accurate mailing information for the letter address.

3. Key **Thank You** as the subject of the letter.

4. In the body of the letter, first thank the person for the specific action or gift that was given to you. Next explain specific reasons why you are grateful and how you have benefited from this kindness (e.g., after the introduction to Mr. Jones you now have an interview scheduled next week).

5. Send a blind copy to your instructor.

6. Save and close. (*58-d4*)

Skill Builder 5

Timed Writings

1. Key a 1' writing on each paragraph.
2. Practice each ¶ in a set until you can complete it in 1' with no more than one error.
3. Take a 3' writing; strive to maintain your 1' rate.
4. Move onto the next set. Notice that each set progresses by 5 words.

Writing 34: 40 *gwam*

	gwam	1'	3'

"An ounce of prevention is worth a pound of cure" is really 12 | 4 | 30
based on fact; still, many people comprehend this statement more 25 | 8 | 35
for its quality as literature than on a practical, common-sense 37 | 12 | 39
philosophy. <u>39</u> | 13 | 39

Just take health, for example. We agonize over stiff costs 12 | 17 | 43
we pay to recover from illnesses; but, on the other hand, we give 25 | 21 | 48
little or no attention to health requirements for diet, exercise, 38 | 26 | 52
and sleep. <u>40</u> | 26 | 53

```
1' |  1  |  2  |  3  |  4  |  5  |  6  |  7  |  8  |  9  | 10  | 11  | 12  | 13  |
3' |        1        |        2        |        3        |        4        |
```

Writing 35: 45 *gwam*

	gwam	1'	3'

Problems with our environment show an odd lack of foresight. 12 | 4 | 33
We just expect that whatever we may need to support life will be 25 | 8 | 38
available. We rarely question our comforts, even though they may 38 | 13 | 42
abuse our earth, water, and air. <u>44</u> | 15 | 44

Optimism is an excellent virtue. It is comforting to think 12 | 19 | 48
that, eventually, everything can be fixed. So why should we worry? 25 | 23 | 52
A better idea, certainly, is to realize that we don't have to fix 38 | 27 | 57
anything we have not yet broken. <u>44</u> | 29 | 59

```
1' |  1  |  2  |  3  |  4  |  5  |  6  |  7  |  8  |  9  | 10  | 11  | 12  | 13  |
3' |        1        |        2        |        3        |        4        |
```

Writing 36: 50 *gwam*

	gwam	1'	3'

Recently, a friend of mine grumbled about how quickly papers 12 | 4 | 37
accumulated on her desk; she never seemed able to reduce them to 25 | 8 | 41
zero. She said some law seemed to be working that expanded the 37 | 12 | 45
stack today by precisely the amount she reduced it yesterday. <u>49</u> | 16 | 49

She should organize her papers and tend to them daily. Any 12 | 20 | 53
paper that needs a look, a decision, and speedy, final action 24 | 24 | 57
gets just that; any that needs closer attention is subject to a 36 | 29 | 61
fixed completion schedule. Self-discipline is the key to order. <u>49</u> | 33 | 66

```
1' |  1  |  2  |  3  |  4  |  5  |  6  |  7  |  8  |  9  | 10  | 11  | 12  |
3' |        1        |        2        |        3        |        4        |
```

Lesson 59 Multiple-Page Documents

New Commands • Header

New Commands

59b

HEADER

A header contains text that is keyed in the top margin of the page. Generally the header is suppressed on the first page. In this module you will prepare a header for a two-page memo and letter.

To insert a header for a multiple-page letter or memo:
Insert/Header & Footer/Header

1. Display the Built-in gallery of Header styles. Click the Blank style.
2. Key the name of the recipient and tap ENTER.
3. Key **Page** followed by a space.
4. From the Header & Footer group, click the Page Number drop-list arrow and choose Current Position. Choose the Plain Number style. Tap ENTER.
5. In the Insert group, click Date & Time. Select the month, day, and year format (October 10, 201-). Tap ENTER to leave a blank space between the header and the first line of the text.
6. In the Options group, select Different First Page to suppress the header on the first page.

To edit a header:
Insert/Header & Footer/Header

To edit a header, click Edit Header. An alternate method is to double-click in the header section of the document. To move to the text of the document, double-click in the document—not the header.

To remove a header, click Remove Header.

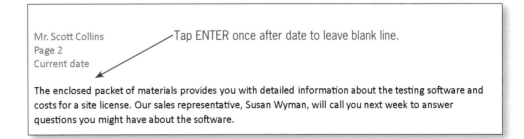

Mr. Scott Collins
Page 2
Current date
— Tap ENTER once after date to leave blank line.

The enclosed packet of materials provides you with detailed information about the testing software and costs for a site license. Our sales representative, Susan Wyman, will call you next week to answer questions you might have about the software.

a. *sadie*: size 1.8" high; flip the image horizontally; apply a bevel rectangle picture style.

b. *halle 2*: size 1.5" high; apply a reflected perspective right picture style.

c. *andy couch*: size 1.7" high; adjust corrections: brightness: +20% contrast: +20%; apply a drop shadow rectangle picture style.

d. *henry and choo*: size 2.25" high; adjust corrections: brightness: +40% contrast: 0% (normal); apply a soft edge oval picture style.

e. *wally 2*: size 2.6" high; adjust apply a snip diagonal corner, white picture style.

f. *coco 2*: size 2.3" high; apply a bevel rectangle picture style.

9. Insert the Integral footer; show the footer on both pages. Key the address in the left placeholder rather than the author's name: **186 Hess Boulevard, Austin, TX 78712-2149**

10. Preview the document. Check to see that it is a two-page document and that the pictures are placed and sized appropriately.

11. Save and close. (*19-d11*)

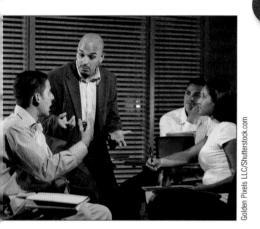

Golden Pixels LLC/Shutterstock.com

! WORKPLACE SUCCESS

Influencing Others

Effective leaders can influence others to do things even though they have no authority over them. The ability to influence others is a valuable career skill for upward job mobility.

There is no one right or wrong way to go about influencing others. However, effective leaders tend to use techniques that have common characteristics. Some examples are:

- They approach the situation from the perspective of the other person rather than from their own. They have learned how to use empathy effectively.

- They make the effort to show the benefits to the other person.

- They try to get agreement on the big concepts before getting into the details that bog people down.

- They use good human relations skills and make it easy for the other person to grant requests.

Participating in meetings with individuals from different departments provides an excellent opportunity to learn how to influence other people. A good way to get started is to observe leaders who are able to bring a group to a consensus even though the discussion might have begun with very diverse positions. Meetings provide an opportunity to demonstrate good communication skills, leadership skills, and good time management and organization skills as well as good negotiation skills.

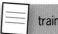
Insert/Header & Footer/Header

1. Open *training* from the data files, and create a header for the second page of the memo. Include the recipient's name, page number, and date.

2. If necessary, tap ENTER one time to leave one blank line between the header and the body of the document. Suppress the header on the first page.

3. Save and close. (*59-drill1*)

Document Design ▸ TWO-PAGE LETTERS AND MEMOS

Letters and memos that are more than one page in length require special layout considerations. For letters, use letterhead paper for the first page only, and for additional pages, use plain paper that matches the letterhead in quality and color. Be sure that there are at least two lines of text from the final paragraph of the body on the last page with the closing lines. Study the full-page model on pages 3-29 and 3-30.

To format multipage letters and memos:

1. Click below the letterhead to position the date on the first page below the letter-head 2" from the top of the page.

2. Begin the text on the second and succeeding pages one blank line below the date in the header.

3. Create a header ❶ that includes the recipient's name, page number, and date on separate lines, and suppress the header on the first page.

Page 1

Page 2

Hess Pet Center News and Views

Hess Pet Center now provides full-service, luxury pet care. Our services are now offered to owners of both dogs and cats. Our survey to all of our current clients strongly endorsed broadening our services to include cats.

Grand Opening—Huge Success

Thanks to all of you who turned out for the Grand Opening ceremony. The attendance far exceeded our expectations and was a fun event for both owners and pets. Many clients enjoyed the tour of the new cat facility and meeting the new veterinarian who specializes in medical services for cats. Sadie was the first to use these new facilities.

Picture-Taking Sessions

We encourage all clients to have pictures taken of their pets. The schedule is posted in the main office and on our website. Your written permission is required to feature the pets in our publications and on the website. The form is provided at the picture taking sessions. Halle was the first to have her picture *taken*.

Suites

Andy laid first claim to reservations in one of the luxury suites and tried out the new leather couch that arrived this week. Three levels of luxury suites are available in addition to the standard units. Luxury suites feature all of the comforts of home—couches, comfortable beds, rugs, toys, windows, climate control, premium food, a play yard, and a homey atmosphere.

Multiple Pets Per Unit

Standard units can accommodate two or three small or medium-size dogs or cats. All three levels of luxury suites are large enough to accommodate any size pet. Henry and Choo were happy that they can stay together in one of the luxury suites with comfortable furniture and a climbing tree.

186 HESS BOULEVARD, AUSTIN, TX 78712-2149 1

Grooming and Spa

Professional groomers pamper your pet with all natural products at the grooming salon and spa. Standard grooming services include:

- Bathing
- Trimming
- Scissor finishing
- Nail trimming
- Ear cleaning
- Teeth brushing

Molly particularly likes the sumptuous spa treatments including whirlpool and massage therapy. Massage therapy increases circulation, relaxes muscles, and stimulates the skin. Grooming and spa services are available by special appointment, while your pet is boarding, or in Doggy Day Camp.

Hess Pet Center Boutique

The Boutique provides one-stop shopping to meet all of your cat or dog's needs.

- Scientifically prepared food
- Treats
- Beds
- Carriers
- Bowls and dishes
- Collars, harnesses, and leashes
- Natural grooming products
- Coats, raincoats, and sweaters
- Toys
- Pet staircases
- Grooming tools

Doggie Day Camp

Day camp is a wonderful experience for daytime pet accommodations. Day camp includes supervised play, games, exercises, treats, and socialization with other pets. Coco does not like to be left behind when the family

goes on trips, but she is a regular at day camp and particularly enjoys playing with other campers in the outdoor play area. A 500-square-foot indoor pet romping room is available during inclement weather. Coco prefers the outdoor area, but enjoys the indoor facilities too. Both facilities are supervised by trained staff.

Total Professional Care

Board-certified veterinarians and highly trained technicians provide the highest level of pet care using state-of-the-art technology. Medical services for both dogs and cats include:

- Comprehensive physical exams
- Immunizations
- Preventive medicine
- Microchip database
- All areas of internal medicine
- Surgical services
- Radiology
- Dental care
- Nutritional specialists
- Pharmacy
- Pain management
- Hospice service

186 HESS BOULEVARD, AUSTIN, TX 78712-2149 2

1. In a new document, apply Narrow margins.

2. Tap ENTER once and insert the *hpc logo* data file; apply Tight Text Wrapping.

3. Key **HPC News and Views**; tap ENTER twice. Select the text and apply 24-point, Dark Red, Accent 1 font and bold to the title. Insert 18-point space before the title.

4. Move your insertion point down one space (do not tap ENTER again). The font should be Normal, 11-point, Automatic color. With the Insertion point at the first ¶ marker below the title, insert a Continuous section break.

5. On the line below the section break, insert the *hpc newsletter* data file. With the insertion point at the beginning of the inserted text, format into two columns.

6. Format all headings using Intense Emphasis and apply bold. Make sure headings stay with the text that follows. Insert column breaks or use Keep lines together, if necessary.

7. Change the bullets by using the bullet (◈) from the Wingdings 2 font. Use Decrease Indent to position the bullets at the left edge of the column.

8. Insert the pet pictures from the data files in the order indicated and apply the formats specified for each photo. Crop each picture close to the image of the pet, as shown in the illustration above. Compress all pictures and apply Tight Text Wrapping.

(continued)

Brown-Mayfield Corporate Development

203 East Ridge Road, Bangor, ME 04401
Telephone: 207.555.0132 Fax: 207.555.0133

Current date

Mr. Dylan Franz
Human Resources Department
Covin Industries
23891 Magnolia Street
Birmingham, AL 35244-9730

Dear Mr. Franz

Automated Test Development and Generation System Subject line

Recently, we decided to upgrade our system and market it as a system rather than as a complete testing service provided by our staff. The system automates all phases of assessment: generating tests, taking tests, and scoring tests. It enables an organization such as yours to incorporate quality testing in the selecting and training of employees.

Users have identified numerous advantages of our automated test development and generation system. The test generation component enables you to maintain a large database of all standard types of test items, including the following:

True/False	Modified true/false
Multiple choice	Multiple answer
Fill in the blank	Matching
Numeric response	Short answer
Essay	Problem
Case	Bimodal
Yes/no	Ordering

Validated items enable you to generate a test automatically that meets high standards. These items are stored with complex competency identifiers, answer keys, critiques of answers, and a variety of item statistics.

The test administration component enables your employees to take the test in an online testing setting. At the conclusion of the tests, the results with feedback can be viewed by the employee.

The scoring component enables you to produce score reports and itemize analysis statistics. These statistics can then be added to the item database to be used in future test generation purposes. In addition to individual score reports, reports for groups and a variety of subgroups can be prepared automatically.

Two-Page Letter, Page 1

19-d10

Itinerary

itinerary form

To use the Quick Parts itinerary created in *19-d9* do the following:

1. Open *19-d9*. Change to Narrow margins and the Ion theme.
2. Insert the HPC Itinerary Quick Part and prepare an itinerary for Mr. Schmidt using the information below.

(**Note:** If you are using another computer, use the itinerary form data file.)

3. Preview and save and close. (*19-d10*)

Trip: Chicago, Illinois Tuesday, March 12 - Thursday, March 14, 2018

Destination/Purpose: Meet in Chicago with potential suppliers of upscale merchandise for the Pet Boutique

Departure: March 12; Midtown Airlines; depart on Flight 2846 at 5:45 p.m.

Flight connections: One stop in Atlanta; same aircraft; arrive 7:45 p.m.

Ground transportation: Picked up by Executive Cars; Confirmation #OH493802; 312.555.0121

Hotel: Chicago Levernoir, 725 N. Michigan Avenue; Confirmation #87B0376519

Return: March 14; Midtown Airlines; Flight 8937 at 7:45 a.m.

Flight connections: Direct, nonstop flight; arrives 9:43 a.m.

Wednesday, March 13 Breakfast: 7:15 | Hotel Lobby
8:30 | Roger Demus, Elegant Puppy Mart, 312.555.0136 | 34 E. Division Street

10:30 | Mark Lane, Chicago Pet Spa Supplies, 312.555.0196 | 17 E. Scott Street

Lunch: 12:15 | Lynn Marcus, Marcus Pet Boutique Supplies, 312.555.0137 | Hotel Levernoir Bistro

2:00 | Martin Walker, Anna Metz, and Leslie Walker, Walker Furniture, 312.555.0186 | 2408 S. State Street

4:00 | Leon Ranson and Jan Anders, Pet Boutique Specialties, 312.555.0147 | Meet in hotel lobby; drive to Pet Boutique Specialties

Dinner: 8:30 | Elaine Beswick, President, and Rae LaFevre, Design Director, Pet Boutique Specialties | Charlie Truluck Restaurant

Comments: Reservations for lunch and dinner are in your name.

19-d11

Newsletter

hpc logo
hpc newsletter
sadie
halle 2
andy couch
henry and choo
wally 2
coco 2

Hess Pet Center will use the newsletter you design as the standard style for all newsletters in the future. The body of the newsletter has already been keyed; you will insert the text and format it. Before you begin, review the illustrations on the next page. Pay particular attention to the following items:

• Placement of logo and text for the banner heading.
• Placement of the pictures of pets that are featured throughout the newsletter.
• Type and position of the bullets used.
• Format of the headings.

(continued)

Header Mr. Dylan Franz
Page 2
Current date

The enclosed packet of materials provides you with detailed information about the testing system, training, and costs for a site license.

Sincerely

Vikram Yadama
Sales Manager

xx

Enclosure

c Susan Wyman

Two-Page Letter, Page 2

Mr. Schmidt travels frequently to visit with suppliers for Hess Pet Center. Create a form using a table for these types of trips. You will use this form to prepare an itinerary for Mr. Schmidt's trip.

1. In a new blank document, use Narrow margins. Tap ENTER once and insert a 2-column, 18-row table; apply List Table 3 – Accent 1 style. Place brackets around the variable information that will be selected and replaced.

2. Merge and format the first row as follows: change cell height to 1.2"; apply 20-point font to the first line and 16-point font to the next three lines. Apply Align Center to text.

3. Format the remaining rows 0.4" high and apply Align Center Left to all text.

4. Key the table as shown below. Adjust column widths as indicated.

5. After completing the travel information section, merge the cells in row 9 and leave it blank. Make sure all borders are still showing on row 9.

6. Split each of the columns in the remaining rows and format them as shown.

7. Apply Bold to the headings in row 10. Make sure all items in column A are still bold.

8. In the last row (*Other Activities or Comments*), merge cells B, C, and D.

9. Use Select All and save as a Quick Part with the name and description: **HPC Itinerary**. Select the option Insert content in its own page.

10. Save and close. (*19-d9*)

59-d1

Two-Page Letter

brown-mayfield ltrhd
testing

1. Open *brown-mayfield ltrhd* from the data files, and key just through the first paragraph of the two-page letter shown on pages 3-29 and 3-30.

2. Insert the data file *testing* below the first paragraph (Insert/Object/Text from File), which is the remaining text of the two-page letter. **Note:** Be sure to position the insertion point where you want the text to appear before inserting the file.

3. Create a header to include the three required items of a multiple-page header.

4. Tap ENTER once after the date to leave one blank line between the header and the letter. Suppress the header on the first page.

5. Add a copy notation to **Susan Wyman**.

6. Save and close. (59-d1)

59-d2

Two-Page Letter

application

▶ REVIEW

Date

Insert/Text/Date & Time

1. Open *application* from the data files, and format as a modified block letter with mixed punctuation.

2. Add the mailing notation **Confidential**.

3. Add the reference line **Re: Position #1839**.

4. Create a header to include the three required items of a multiple-page header. Insert the Date command and choose to update automatically.

5. Tap ENTER once after the date to leave one blank line between the header and the letter. Suppress the header on the first page.

6. Delete the reference initials since this is a personal business letter prepared by the sender.

7. Create an envelope and add to the document; key the mailing notation **Confidential** below the return address.

8. Save and close. (59-d2)

! WORKPLACE SUCCESS

Pressmaster/Shutterstock.com

Letters should be carefully planned. List all the points that need to be covered and make sure they relate to the main purpose of the letter. Letters need to be accurate and written in a timely manner. Business letters often have financial implications, so check to make sure that all stated facts are accurate.

Letters are a more formal means of communicating than are emails, text messages, or memos. Letters should be formal and factual, and at the same time be reader friendly. If the letter is part of a package, limit the cover letter to one page and relegate technical details to enclosed documents. Avoid language that is specific to gender, race, or religion in all business correspondence. For example, use words such as workforce rather than manpower and chairperson rather than chairman.

The hpc Wellness Plan (Title style)

For Healthy and Happy Pets (Subtitle style)

Many families that own pets think of those pets as part of their family. Today, families express more concern about wellness for their families than was the case some years ago. And, not surprisingly, that concern also applies to the wellness of their pets. Many clients have asked hpc to provide them with sound information in a non-technical manner about wellness for pets. This report is designed to address issues of wellness for pets and to announce the new hpc Wellness Plan.

Wellness for Pets (Heading 1 style)

When you ask people what they think should be included in a successful wellness program for their families, most people will provide a list of items such as the one that follows:

- Good nutrition
- Exercise to improve fitness
- Drink a substantial amount of water
- Weight control
- Preventive health care
- Preventive dental care
- Effective medical care when needed
- Avoidance of bad habits
- Effective social interaction
- Safety awareness—avoiding hazardous situations

Interestingly, the list provided was developed by a leading authority on preventive health care for pets, Dr. Monica C. Bradford. While many differences exist in the health-care needs of pets compared to the needs of their owners, many similarities also exist. Dr. Bradford says that common sense is the key to wellness for pets.

hpc Wellness Plan (Heading 1 style)

In response to the many requests from clients, eaf interviewed a young veterinarian (Guidice), who is a former student of Dr. Bradford's, and whose research focuses on the components of effective pet wellness programs. As a result of that interview, Dr. Guidice was hired to develop the hpc Wellness Program. Dr. Guidice currently serves as the director of the program. In addition to the standard components listed above, the program utilizes highly trained technicians to monitor pet health and wellness.

(Insert *wellness report* data file here.)

Lesson 60 Hess Office Park

Skill Building

60b Timed Writing

1. Key a 1' timing on each paragraph; work to increase speed.
2. Key a 3' timing on all paragraphs.

A ALL LETTERS

	gwam	1'	3'
If you wish to advance in your career, you must learn how to		12	4
make good decisions. You can develop decision-making skills by		24	8
learning to follow six basic steps. The first three steps help you to see		39	13
the problem. They are identifying the problem, analyzing the problem		53	18
to find causes and consequences, and making sure you define the goals		66	22
that your solution must meet.		72	24
Now you are ready to solve the problem using the last three		12	28
steps. They include finding alternative solutions to the problem,		25	32
analyzing each of the alternatives carefully to locate the best solution, and		40	37
putting the best solution into action. Once you have implemented a plan		54	42
of action, check to make sure that it meets all of your objectives. If it does		70	47
not, then determine if the problem is with the solution or with the way		84	52
it is being implemented. Always keep all options open.		95	56

1' | 1 | 2 | 3 | 4 | 5 | 6 | 7 | 8 | 9 | 10 | 11 | 12 | 13 |
3' | 1 | 2 | 3 | 4 |

Project Setting

HESS OFFICE PARK

At the end of each module in this book, you will work as an assistant to Patrick J. Hess, manager of Hess Office Park, a 500-acre office park managed by Hess Property Enterprises. You will apply the keying, formatting, and word processing skills that you have developed in the module.

You will learn to apply **standard operating procedures** (SOPs). These procedures enable you to work independently without extensive directions. Pay particular attention to the SOPs and the documents you prepare in this lesson because they will provide you with information that you will use each time you work with Hess Office Park. The logo and contact information are shown below.

Hess Office Park
100 Hess Boulevard, Austin, TX 78712-2149
Phone 512.555.0157 | Fax 512.555.0158
www.hesspropertyenterprises.com

Standard operating procedures for the project:

1. Use block letter style with open punctuation and the Hess Office Park letterhead from the data files. Include an appropriate salutation and use Sincerely as the complimentary closing. Place the date at 2". Use **Patrick J. Hess | Manager** as the writer's name and title.
2. Prepare all documents using Retrospect document theme.
3. Create envelopes for letters only when directed, as many letters are attached to emails.
4. The data files also contain a Hess Office Park memo form. Use an appropriate subject line if a subject line is not provided.
5. Add your reference initials and other notations as appropriate.

Join your friends and their families

for the

Grand Opening of the expanded facilities

located in Hess Office Park

Refreshments, tours, and seminars

Sunday, April 14, 3:30 p.m.

at the

Hess Pet Center

186 Hess Boulevard

Austin

Sample document ©Cengage Learning. Embedded images, from left to right: "Maggie" © Cengage Learning, courtesy of Susie VanHuss. "Coco" © Cengage Learning, courtesy of Vicki Robertson. "Halle" courtesy of Shelley Vescovo. "Andy" © Cengage Learning, courtesy of Susie VanHuss. "Wally" courtesy of Susan Brooks.

19-d8

Unbound Report

wellness report
hpc cover page

⭐ **TIP**

Remember to break the link between the sections for both the header and the footer. Set the number on the first page of the report to 1. The pages should be in the following order: cover page, table of contents, page 1 of report, page 2 of report (which should be the only page with a page number).

The veterinary staff has drafted the information for a report to distribute to clients. They have asked you to prepare the report.

1. Key the report on the next page as an unbound report.
2. Apply custom dog bullets for the items that are bulleted.
3. Insert the *wellness report* data file where noted. Apply the formats noted in the comments; then delete all comments.
4. Insert a Next Page break at the beginning of the document and insert the *hpc cover page* data file. Fill in the placeholder information and add a ½-pt Dark Red, Accent 1 Box border to the cover page only.
5. Number the pages using Rounded Rectangle 3 at the top of the page. Do not show the page number on the cover page or first page of the report.
6. Insert another Next Page break on the first page of the report and generate a table of contents using Automatic Table 2 style. Apply the Title style to Table of Contents and a blank line after.
7. Preview to ensure that the format is correct and that pages are numbered correctly. If necessary, update the table of contents.
8. Save and close. (*19-d8*)

(continued)

You have worked for only one day and have observed that you are constantly keying a list of services for insertion in various office documents. To save keying time, key the bulleted list below and save as a Quick Part named **services**.

After keying the list, proofread carefully and save as a Quick Part. You will use the Quick Part in the next document.

- A fee-based print and copy service center that is used by most of the small businesses managed by our company.

- Conference rooms that can be rented for the day or week and offices that can be rented by the month.

- A fee-based health and fitness center that is open 24 hours a day and 7 days a week. Personal trainers are available to outline the best possible fitness plan for each client.

- Three food service facilities that are managed by the company. These facilities are conveniently located and offer numerous dining options, including gluten-free and vegetarian.

- A fee-based child care center that is convenient for parents and managed by the company. The child care center opens at 6 a.m. and closes at 8 p.m.

- A fee-based pet center that offers two full-time veterinarians as well as grooming and boarding services.

Open *hess letterhead* from the data files, and key the two-page letter for **Mr. Hess** to **Mr. Aiden Madison**, a prospective tenant he met at the Chamber of Commerce meeting today. You are to add all the letter parts and format the letter. Mr. Madison's address is **1289 Maple Street, San Antonio, TX 78201-1289**.

1. Insert the Quick Part created in *60-d1* as directed in the text below.
2. Insert the second-page heading and suppress the heading on the first page.
3. Send a copy to **Jayden Mason**.
4. Create an envelope and add to the document.
5. Save and close. (*60-d2*)

It was a pleasure meeting you today at the local Chamber of Commerce meeting. I know John Forde very well and appreciate his inviting you to our meeting and introducing you to me. I am pleased that you will be locating your business in Austin and am happy to share some information with you about the property and services available at Hess Office Park.

(continued)

Ann Taylor	Technician, Internal Medicine
David P. Guidice, DVM	Director, Wellness Program
Lynn West	Technician, Wellness Program
Retail and Service Operations	
dcs	Managing Partner
mm	Office Manager
Jan Cotter	Intern
Lynn Babcock	Manager, Grooming and Spa
Mark Jones	Assistant Manager, Grooming and Spa
Aaron Barr	Manager, Boutique
JoAnn Jameson	Assistant Manager, Boutique
Lisa Owens	Manager, Boarding and Pet Care
Jan Marcus	Assistant Manager, Boarding and Pet Care

19-d7

Invitation

maggie
coco
halle
andy
wally

★ TIP

Remember to undo automatic capitalization, as necessary.

1. In a new document, change the top margin to 0.5" and apply a ½-point Dark Red, Accent 1 Box border to the page. Use the Page Color Fill Effects and apply the Parchment texture.

2. Insert the five pictures from the data files in the order listed. Crop the pictures close to each dog, as shown in the illustration on the next page; apply Square Text Wrapping. Size each picture 2" high. Position the pictures against the top border and within the side borders. Make the following picture corrections:

 a. *Maggie*: Sharpen: 25%; Brightness: 0% Contrast: +20%.

 b. *Coco*: Sharpen: 25%; Brightness: +20% Contrast: +20%.

 c. *Halle*: Sharpen: 25%; Brightness: +20% Contrast: +20%.

 d. *Andy*: Sharpen: 25%; Brightness: +20% Contrast: +20%.

 e. *Wally*: Sharpen: 25%; Brightness: +20% Contrast: –20%. Flip the picture horizontally.

3. Draw a text box directly below the pictures; size it 0.3" high and extend it from side border to side border.

 a. Apply Dark Red, Accent 1 Shape Outline.

 b. Click in the text box and apply Shape Fill, No Fill.

 c. Set left-align tabs at 0.25", 2", 3.5", 5.25", and 6.75".

 d. Key the names of the dogs in the order shown above at each of the tab stops; apply Dark Red, Accent 1 font color and bold italic.

4. Tap ENTER five times after the text box and key the text for the invitation; center the text. Apply Lucida Calligraphy, 18-point, Dark Red, Accent 1 font.

5. Save and close. (*19-d7*)

(continued)

Hess Office Park is located at 100 Hess Boulevard and is home to 125 businesses that either own or lease offices located on 500 acres of beautiful wooded property that is conveniently located to downtown. Hess Office Park is managed by Hess Property Enterprises with a board of directors representing owners and investors of the office park. In addition to selling or leasing office space, we offer a number of other services that you may find beneficial. These services include the following:

Insert Quick Part named *services* created in *60-d1.*

As a tenant in Hess Office Park, you are automatically a member of the Owners and Tenants Association that meets the first Monday of each month at 7 p.m. at a hosting owner/tenant's office. In addition to the excellent programs initiated by the association, members also partner with the local community to sponsor award-winning programs that are enhancing our communities.

A map of the office park is attached with available office space highlighted including detailed space specifications. Additional brochures and fact sheets about Hess Office Park are also enclosed for your review.

I do look forward to meeting with you to discuss your leasing office space with us.

60-d3

Memo

 hess memo

Open *hess memo* from the data files, and prepare the memo below for Mr. Hess to the **Owners and Tenants Association** informing them of the upcoming energy efficiency inspection.

1. Date the memo **November 14** and key the subject **Energy Efficiency Evaluation Scheduled for January**.
2. Save and close. (*60-d3*)

As a result of action taken at the October meeting of the Owners and Tenants Association, I have contracted with Lehman-Bass Energy Services to complete an energy efficiency evaluation of all office space in our property. Inga Koch, senior engineer assigned to our contract, will attend our December meeting and explain the details of the energy efficiency evaluation and provide checklists for our preparation prior to the inspections.

Ms. Koch has already scheduled our inspections for January. You will be notified of your specific day and time at the December meeting.

If you have any questions, please call or email me.

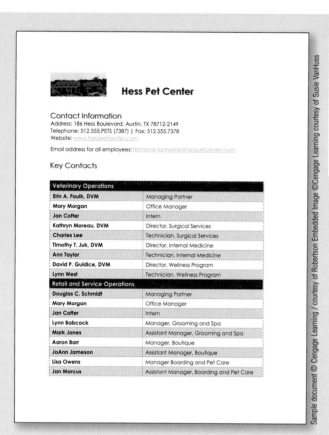

Contact Information
Address: 186 Hess Boulevard, Austin, TX 78712-2149
Telephone: 512.555.PETS (7387) | Fax: 512.555.7378
Website: www.hesspetcenter.com

Email address for all employees: firstname.lastname@hesspetcenter.com

Key Contacts

Veterinary Operations	
Erin A. Faulk, DVM	Managing Partner
Mary Morgan	Office Manager
Jan Cotter	Intern
Kathryn Moreau, DVM	Director, Surgical Services
Charles Lee	Technician, Surgical Services
Timothy T. Juk, DVM	Director, Internal Medicine
Ann Taylor	Technician, Internal Medicine
David P. Guldice, DVM	Director, Wellness Program
Lynn West	Technician, Wellness Program
Retail and Service Operations	
Douglas C. Schmidt	Managing Partner
Mary Morgan	Office Manager
Jan Cotter	Intern
Lynn Babcock	Manager, Grooming and Spa
Mark Jones	Assistant Manager, Grooming and Spa
Aaron Barr	Manager, Boutique
JoAnn Jameson	Assistant Manager, Boutique
Lisa Owens	Manager Boarding and Pet Care
Jan Marcus	Assistant Manager, Boarding and Pet Care

Sample document © Cengage Learning / courtesy of Robertson Embedded Image ©Cengage Learning courtesy of Susie VanHuss

Address: 186 Hess Boulevard, Austin, TX 78712-2149

Telephone: 512.555.PETS (7387) | Fax: 512.555.7378

Website: www.hesspetcenter.com

Email address for all employees:

firstname.lastname@hesspetcenter.com

6. Insert a 2-column, 20-row table; key the table below and format as follows:

 a. Apply Grid Table 2 – Accent 1 style. Size all rows 0.27" high; apply Align Center Left text alignment.

 b. Adjust the width of the first column to 2.7" and the second column to 3.5".

 c. Merge the cells in both the *Veterinary Operations* and the *Retail and Service Operations* rows. Format both rows as follows: change the Shading to Dark Red, Accent 1; change the font color to white and the font size to 12 point.

7. Use Select All and save as a Quick Part with the name and description: **HPC Contact List**. Select the option Insert content in its own page.

8. Save and close. (*19-d6*)

Veterinary Operations	
eaf	Managing Partner
mm	Office Manager
Jan Cotter	Intern
Kathryn Moreau, DVM	Director, Surgical Services
Charles Lee	Technician, Surgical Services
Timothy T. Juk, DVM	Director, Internal Medicine

(continued)

60-d4

Letter

hess letterhead

Key a letter to **Mr. Robert Kaczynski, President | East Central Education Foundation**, with details about their fun run/walk that will be held on the Hess Office Park property. The mailing address is **30032 Johnson Street, Austin, TX 78712-0388**.

1. Date the letter **November 14, 201-**.
2. Use an attachment notation since this letter is being emailed to Mr. Kaczynski.
3. Save and close. (*60-d4*)

We are pleased to confirm that you will be hosting your annual 5K Scholarship Fun Run/Walk on our property Saturday, April 10, 201-. As we discussed at our initial meeting, parking will be available in the south parking lot all day Saturday. We will also have several spaces designated for you and your staff Friday beginning at noon.

We will have the entire boulevard around the office park blocked from 6 a.m. to 2 p.m. on Saturday starting at the intersection of Elm Street and Hess Boulevard. The run will start at 9 a.m. in front of the Hess Office Building and end at the same location. Tables and chairs will be set up along the race route for your volunteers to distribute drinks and snacks.

Security and police assistance will be provided at the main intersection of Hess Boulevard and Elm Street. Space will also be provided for your vendors near the entrance to the office park. Please provide all vendors with the attached traffic rules and map to our complex.

A wrap-up meeting is needed to finalize the remaining details. Please call or email me so we can schedule the meeting. We are pleased to assist you in this worthwhile event.

60-d5

Compose Memo

hess memo

Mr. Hess has asked you to compose a memo for him to send to the **Owners and Tenants Association** informing the members of the change of date for the December meeting.

1. In the first paragraph, explain that the December meeting was originally scheduled for Monday, December 1, at the offices of Schniepp Enterprises but has been changed to Tuesday, December 2. Explain that the reason for the change was to allow members to participate in the Christmas Parade scheduled for December 1.
2. In the last paragraph, remind members that the January meeting will return to the first Monday of the month.
3. Date the memo **November 15, 201-**. Supply an appropriate subject line that alerts the member to the date change.
4. Save and close. (*60-d5*)

Overview (Heading 1)

mm reported that Mr. Schmidt and Dr. Faulk requested that the team plan an event to mark the completion of the hpc facilities expansion. hpc has been so successful in the Hess Office Park location that expansion was needed. The new facilities will give us twice the space to expand our veterinary and boarding services. All work has been completed, and the furnishings will be in place in approximately two to three weeks.

Date and Time (Heading 1)

The team discussed the advantages and disadvantages of a weekday event versus a weekend event, and an afternoon versus an evening event. The group agreed that a Sunday afternoon would probably attract the largest crowd and selected April 14 at 3:30 p.m. as the date and time.

Type of Function (Heading 1)

Mark reported that the management team wanted the function to appeal to families and to be pet friendly. JoAnn and Jan agreed to work with Mark on appropriate food and beverages to serve. Pet treats will be provided as well. The team agreed that small group tours should be hosted by a staff member in each area to showcase the state-of-the-art facilities and equipment. The veterinary staff should conduct a brief seminar on the latest trends in pet medical care.

(Insert *minutes* data file here.)

19-d6

Contact List

 hpc logo

Mr. Schmidt has asked you to prepare a company contact sheet that could be handed out or emailed to clients and potential clients.

1. In a new blank document, insert *hpc logo* and apply Square Text Wrapping; position as shown in the illustration on the next page. Depress tab.
2. Key **Hess Pet Center** on the first line in bold, 24-point font. Apply Dark Red, Accent 1, Darker 25% font color; add 18-point spacing before the title. Tap ENTER and apply Normal style to remove formats.
3. Tap ENTER and key **Contact Information**; apply Heading 1 style.
4. Key the contact information shown on the next page. Remove the space after each paragraph except the last one. Apply Dark Red, Accent 1, Darker 25% font color to the vertical bar in the telephone line.
5. Key: **Key Contacts**; apply Heading 1 style.

(continued)

Documents with Tables and Graphics

LEARNING OUTCOMES

- Create and format tables.
- Change table structure.
- Use table functions.
- Insert and format graphics, pictures, and online videos.
- Use WordArt and SmartArt.
- Create documents with columns and graphics.
- Build keying speed and accuracy.

Lesson 61 Table Tools

Warmup *Lesson 61a Warmup*

lesson 61a warmup

Skill Building

61b Timed Writing

1. Key a 1' timing on each paragraph; work to increase speed.
2. Key a 3' timing on all paragraphs; work for control.

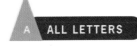
A ALL LETTERS

	gwam	1'	3'	
Beginning college students are very eager about beginning the		12	4	58
next step in the journey after high school. Going away to college offers		27	9	63
many opportunities and challenges to these young students. Choosing		40	13	68
what time to attend classes, when to go to bed, when to get up, what		54	18	72
to eat each day, and how to spend their money seems fantastic at		66	22	76
an initial glance. But, wait, are these students adequately prepared		80	27	81
for the hard choices that come with these freedoms?		90	30	84
One major area in which students need help is in making good		12	34	88
food selections. Pizza, pasta, and macaroni and cheese do not make		25	38	93
a wise choice even if these foods are easy to make and affordable.		38	43	97
Be sure to have five fruits and vegetables each day and add some		51	47	101
physical activity in the schedule. Remember nutritious meals and		64	51	106
exercise are important to success in college.		73	54	109

```
1' |  1  |  2  |  3  |  4  |  5  |  6  |  7  |  8  |  9  | 10  | 11  | 12  | 13  |
3' |       1       |         2         |        3        |        4        |
```

The expansion of the facility and the new construction has been completed. Your next task is to prepare an agenda for a meeting of the Grand Opening Planning Team.

1. In a new blank document, use a 2" top margin and key the agenda below. Apply Title style to the title, Heading 1 style to the meeting title, and Subtitle style to the location, time, and date information; center all three lines. Tap ENTER twice after the subtitle.

2. Before keying the body of the agenda, set tabs as follows: set a left tab at 1" and a right dot leader tab at 6.5".

3. Tap ENTER twice after keying the agenda and add this note: **Note: Bring Facilities Master Plan to the meeting.**

4. Add a Draft 1 watermark to the document. Participants will be given an opportunity to make additions to the agenda.

5. Save and close. (*19-d4*)

Agenda

Grand Opening Planning Session

Vet Conference Room	10:30 a.m.	March 5, 2018
10:30	Overview	mm
10:35	Date and Time of Opening	Team
10:40	Type of Function	Mark Jones
10:50	Invitation List	Lynn Babcock
11:00	Promotion Options	Aaron Barr
11:15	Budget	mm
11:30	Wrap Up	mm

19-d5

Minutes

 minutes

Prepare minutes from the the grand opening planning session.

1. In a new blank document, key the minutes shown below. Insert the data file *minutes* at the end of the keyed document. Use Show/Hide to remove extra spaces that are not needed.

2. Format as suggested in the comments; then remove the comments.

3. Insert Top of Page, Plain Number 3 page number. Do not show the page number on the first page.

4. Save and close. (*19-d5*)

Grand Opening Planning Session (Title style)

Minutes—March 5, 2018 (Subtitle style)

The Grand Opening Planning Team met on March 5, 2018 at 10:30 a.m. in the Vet Conference Room. Team members present were Lynn Babcock, Aaron Barr, Mark Jones, JoAnn Jameson, Jan Marcus, Mary Todd, and mm.

(continued)

Review Commands

61c

TABLE TOOLS

Table tools are used to design and format tables. To display the Table Tools, click in the table and select either the Design or Layout tab.

LAYOUT TAB

Commands in the Rows & Columns group and the Merge group can change the table structure and enhance its readability.

To insert and delete rows and columns:
Table Tools Layout/Rows & Columns

1. Click in the row or column to insert or delete.
2. Click the desired Insert option or click the Delete drop-list arrow and select the appropriate command.

—or—

1. Position the mouse on the left edge or above the table.
2. Click the plus symbol to insert a new row or column.

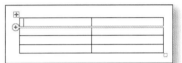

To merge and split cells:
Table Tools Layout/Merge/Merge Cells or Split Cells

Merge joins cells horizontally or vertically. A common use of this command is to combine the cells in the first row for the heading of the table. Use Split Cells to create multiple columns below a single cell for a heading that spans multiple columns.

1. To merge cells, select the cells and click Merge Cells.
2. To split cells, click in the cell to be divided, or select multiple cells to divide, and then click the Split Cells command. Key the number of columns or rows into which the selected cell(s) will be divided.

DRILL 1 MERGE AND SPLIT CELLS

1. In a new blank document, create a 2-column, 5-row table.

2. Select cells B2–B5 and split them into two columns and four rows. Merge cells A1 and A2.

3. Key the table below. Bold and center column heads. Align Right the cells that include pricing.

4. Save and close. (61-drill1)

Hotel	Room Rates (per night)	
	Sunday–Thursday	Friday–Saturday
Bellflower Gardens	$139.00	$99.00
House of Five Gables	$265.00	$180.00
Ramona Beach House	$250.00	$325.00

19-d2

Memo

hpc memo form

1. Open *hpc memo form* from the data files and key the memo shown below to **All Employees** from **Doug Schmidt** (use *dcs* and AutoCorrect will spell it out).
2. List the attachment as: **Attachment: HPC #1 Document Processing Standards.**
3. Do not spell out HPC where shown in uppercase.
4. Save and close. (*19-d2*)

SUBJECT: Standard Operating Procedures

Our management team has worked with most of you to develop standard operating procedures for all phases of our operations. Procedures will be reviewed and revised on a continual basis. All employees are encouraged to review procedures and suggest ways to improve hpc operations.

The office manager has been designated as the person responsible for keeping all procedures up-to-date. The procedures will be stored on the shared drive. Please note that the attached procedure is labeled HPC #1 Document Processing Standards. The HPC #1 label indicates that the procedures outlined in this document apply to all hpc documents that are prepared for internal and external use. Procedures that apply only to the Veterinary Operations are labeled HPC-VO, and those that apply only to the Retail and Service Operations are labeled HPC-RSO.

19-d3

Letter

hpc letterhead

1. Open *hpc letterhead* from the data files and prepare the following letter for your own signature. Be sure to key **mm** for your name and add your title on a separate line.
2. Send Mr. Schmidt a copy of the letter; use his name and title: **dcs, Managing Partner | Retail and Service Operations**
3. Save and close. (*19-d3*)

> ★ TIP
>
> Do not include your initials since this letter has your signature. To enhance your productivity, save your closing lines as a Quick Part.

Mr. Mark Anderson | Placement Director | Austin Technical College | 2044 55th Street | Austin, TX 78710-8711

Last year you assisted me in obtaining an internship at hpc. The internship was a very valuable experience for me. My internship not only gave me an opportunity to apply the knowledge and skills I acquired in the business program at Austin Technical College, it also was a great learning experience that led to a permanent position.

I have recently been named the office manager of hpc. As you might remember, hpc is a thriving new business that resulted from a joint venture between Dr. eaf and Mr. dcs, an entrepreneur. The new business integrates a veterinary clinic with a full-service luxury pet boarding, grooming, and boutique center.

We would like to hire an intern who is academically successful, has leadership skills, and can work without close supervision. A job description listing the specific skills required is enclosed. Would you please recommend some of your outstanding junior or senior students for this position?

To adjust column width and row height:
Table Tools Layout/Cell Size

Column width can be adjusted by dragging column borders. Leave approximately 0.5" between the longest line and the border. Row height can be adjusted by dragging the row border until the row is the desired height.

For more precision, use the commands in the Cell Size group. Click in a cell, or select multiple cells, then use the spin arrows to increase or decrease column width or row height.

To change text alignment:
Table Tools Layout/Alignment

The options in the Alignment group offer combinations of vertical and horizontal alignment that allow you to position text at the top, middle, or bottom of a table cell, as well as at the left, center, or right side of a cell.

To change table alignment:
Table Tools Layout/Table/Properties

A table that is not full-page width is usually centered horizontally on the page. Use the Center Alignment command in the Table Properties dialog box to center the table horizontally.

The Table Properties dialog box can also be used to set table width. Place a check mark in the Preferred width checkbox and then key the desired table width in the box, or use the spin arrows to set the width.

DRILL 2 **INSERT ROW, ADJUST COLUMN WIDTH, ROW HEIGHT, AND ALIGNMENT**

1. Open *61-drill1* that you saved in Drill 1, insert a row above row 1, and merge the cells.

2. Key **VOLARO NATIONAL PARK** in bold, 14-point font. Change the height of row 1 to 0.4". Align Center the text.

3. Change the height of rows 2–6 to 0.25". Align all text vertically in the cells.

4. Align Center all column heads.

5. Adjust column widths and center table horizontally.

6. Save and close. (*61-drill2*)

19-d1

Procedures

TIP

Remember to proofread and preview each document as an SOP. You will not be reminded to do this.

Mr. Schmidt reviewed with you the standard operating procedures shown above. He and Dr. Faulk asked you to work with them to standardize a format for the procedures that have been developed for all areas of Hess Pet Center. The procedures will be stored electronically. Each procedure will begin with an explanatory paragraph followed by bulleted or numbered procedural steps.

1. In a new document, key the procedures shown below.
2. Apply the Ion theme and Casual document formatting.
3. Tap ENTER three times and key the title **Standard Operating Procedures** and subtitle **HPC #1: Document Processing Standards**; apply Title and Subtitle styles as appropriate. Do not spell out HPC in the subtitle.
4. Apply square bullets to the list of procedures that follow the introductory paragraph.
5. Add a Blank footer and key: **Last revised on (Current date).**
6. Save and close. (*19-d1*)

hpc has developed standard operating procedures for all phases of its operation. Document processing standards apply to all employees in both the veterinary and the retail operations. Documents are a key part of our image and branding. Therefore, the logo, colors, fonts, and document styles must be used consistently throughout hpc. Accurate documents are critical; errors not only create a bad impression, but they could also create medical problems and liability issues.

Proofread and preview each document you prepare.

Use the standardized guide for naming and saving all files. Save a copy of each document on the shared drive if it will be accessed by others.

Use the Ion theme for each document you prepare.

Use Casual Document Formatting for reports and other documents with titles.

Create a Quick Parts building block based on the hpc letterhead so that you can insert it in documents when needed.

Spell out hpc in all documents; do not abbreviate the name unless instructed to do so.

Prepare all letters using the hpc letterhead.

Prepare all memos using the hpc memo form.

Use complete names in the closing lines of letters you prepare for the managing partners; they will sign first names on letters to individuals they know well.

Apply a draft watermark on documents that are still in draft form.

Use software features to automate as many processes as possible.

Share tips with other employees to enhance productivity.

DESIGN TAB

The Table Styles group is located on the Table Tools Design tab. Styles contain font attributes, color, shading, and borders to enhance the appearance of a table.

Display additional styles by clicking the More button to show the entire style gallery. Three groups of table styles display: Plain, Grid, and List. Each style is given a name that indicates its group and the row in which it displays. For example, Grid Table 5 Dark – Accent 2 indicates that the style is located in the fifth row in the Grid Tables group. The table colors are labeled Accents 1 – 6 from left to right.

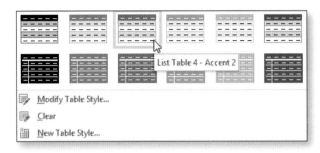

Move the mouse over each style to see your table formatted in that style. The name of the style will be displayed.

To add, change, or remove a table style:
Table Tools Design/Table Styles

1. Click in the table where the style is to be applied and select the desired table style.
2. To see the entire style gallery, click the More button.
3. To change to another style, click in the table and choose a different style.
4. To remove a style, click the table and then click the More button. Below the gallery of styles, click Clear.
5. To make a change to the style, click in the table and then click the option you wish to change in the Table Style Options group.

☑ Header Row	☑ First Column
☐ Total Row	☐ Last Column
☑ Banded Rows	☐ Banded Columns

Table Style Options

DRILL 3　　　　**APPLY STYLE AND TABLE STYLE OPTIONS**

1. Open *61-drill2* that you saved in Drill 2 and display the entire style gallery. In the first row of the style gallery, choose Plain Table 1 style.

2. Move the mouse to the fourth row below Grid Tables; all styles in this row have the name *Grid Table 4*. The color of each table is labeled with Accent 1 – Accent 6. Move the mouse to the right to select Grid Table 4 – Accent 4 style.

3. Scroll down to display List Tables. Select List Table 6 Colorful – Accent 3 style (sixth row below List Tables).

4. Select Grid Table 5 Dark – Accent 6 style. In Table Style Options, deselect First Column. Reapply bold to the title row, if necessary.

5. Align all text vertically in the cells.

6. Center the table horizontally.

7. Save and close. (*61-drill3*)

HESS PET CENTER

Hess Pet Center

186 Hess Boulevard, Austin, TX 78712-2149

Telephone 512.555.PETS (7387) | Fax 512.555.7378 I www.hesspetcenter.com

House image ©Cengage Learning, courtesy of Susie VanHuss.

As Mary Morgan you worked as an intern with Dr. Erin A. Faulk and Mr. Douglas C. Schmidt at Hess Pet Center, a veterinary clinic and luxury pet spa. Hess Pet Center is located in Hess Office Park, which is managed by Hess Property Enterprises, and has become a very successful business. Because of your excellent work as an intern, you have been hired as the office manager.

Hess Pet Center has recently made changes to enhance its corporate image and to develop a strong brand. Your focus in Hess Pet Center II is to ensure that all documents enhance that image and that productivity tools are used effectively to improve your efficiency.

Prepare all documents using the Ion document theme and Casual document formatting. Letterhead and memo forms are provided in the data files, but you will need the theme for reports, newsletters, and other documents that you prepare.

TIP

Remember to add other AutoCorrect Options for names or phrases that you key repeatedly to be more efficient.

PRODUCTIVITY TOOLS

To create AutoCorrect entries:
File/Options/Proofing/AutoCorrect Options

hpc	Replace with: **Hess Pet Center**
eaf	Replace with: **Erin A. Faulk, DVM**
dcs	Replace with: **Douglas C. Schmidt**
mm	Replace with: **Mary Morgan**

TIP

It is acceptable to use *hpc* in themes, file names, and similar applications.

Hess Pet Center
- Change back to "hpc"
- Stop Automatically Correcting "hpc"
- Control AutoCorrect Options...

To reverse an AutoCorrect action such as retaining HPC as initials, press CTRL + Z or click the AutoCorrect down arrow, and select the desired option.

STANDARD OPERATING PROCEDURES (SOPs)

1. Proofread and preview each document you prepare.
2. Use the Ion theme for all documents.
3. Use the Hess Pet Center letterhead and memo data files for letters and memos.
4. Spell out *hpc* as Hess Pet Center, *eaf* as Erin A. Faulk, DVM, and *dcs* as Douglas C. Schmidt each time they appear in documents using AutoCorrect.
5. Use block letter style with open punctuation for all letters.
6. Use *Dear* + the title and last name as the salutation on all letters unless directed to use the individual's first name.
7. Add enclosure or attachment notations and copy notations when they are referenced in a letter or memo.
8. Use the current date on all documents unless directed otherwise. Use standard formatting for reports and meeting documents. (Apply Title style and position title at 2".)
9. Use the standard cover page with the logo for multiple-page reports.

Apply It

61-d1

Create Table

1. In a new blank document, create the table below; adjust column widths and center the table horizontally.
2. Center column B; right-align columns C and D. Bold and center column heads.
3. Save and close. (61-d1)

> ⭐ **TIP**
>
> Text is keyed left-aligned. Numerical amounts are right-aligned.

Employee	I.D.	Hardware	Software
Alexander, J.	R492	$105,134,384	$1,868,553
Courtenay, W.	R856	79,364,091	1,384,219
Holsonback, E.	C845	27,386,427	1,098,237
Rajeh, C.	M451	82,665,900	1,052,564

61-d2

Merge and Split Cells

1. In a new blank document, insert a 3-column, 7-row table at 2".
2. Merge rows 1 and 2 in column A; select rows 2–7 in column B and split them into two columns. Do the same for column C.
3. Key the table below; right-align all numbers. Adjust column widths.
4. Insert a row above the table and merge the cells. Center **WEXMARK COLLEGE** in 14-point, all caps. Tap ENTER and key **201- Enrollments** in 12-point font.
5. Apply Grid Table 1 Light – Accent 2 style.
6. Change the height of rows 2–8 to 0.25". Center the copy vertically in the cells.
7. Change the height of row 1 to 0.6". Bold and Align Center all headings.
8. Center the table horizontally on the page.
9. Save and close. (61-d2)

College	Semester		Division	
	Fall	Spring	Upper	Lower
Business Administration	1,296	677	395	1,586
Computer Science	945	322	124	1,143
Allied Health Sciences	3,925	2,650	4,500	7,125
Arts and Sciences	98	76	29	108
Engineering Technology	179	156	32	96

Hess Pet Center II

Lessons 105–107 *Hess Pet Center II*

LEARNING OUTCOMES

- Apply keying, formatting, and word processing skills.
- Create a variety of documents.
- Follow standard operating procedures.
- Work independently and with few specific instructions.

Warmup *Lesson 105a Warmup*

lesson 105a warmup

Skill Building

105b Timed Writing

1. Key one 3' timed writing on each paragraph; key at your control rate.
2. Key one 5' timed writing; key at your control rate.

ALL LETTERS

	gwam	3'	5'
Most people find it amazing that mobile telephones can create a	4	3	59
number of etiquette and safety problems. The use of hand-held mobile	9	5	62
telephones has increased dramatically in the past few years. Just	13	8	65
because a mobile telephone can be taken almost anywhere does not	17	10	67
mean that it is appropriate to use it in any place that it can be carried.	22	13	70
Common sense and good manners seem to have been forgotten when it	27	16	73
comes to using a mobile telephone.	29	17	74
The major safety hazard of using a hand-held telephone results	4	20	77
from its use in moving automobiles. A significant percentage of all	9	22	79
accidents is the result of drivers being distracted. Of all the distractions	14	26	82
reported, the most frequent are those that occur while a driver is	18	28	85
holding a telephone in one hand and trying to drive at the same time.	23	31	88
A hands-free telephone is not as dangerous, but it can still cause a	27	34	91
driver to be distracted.	29	35	92
The etiquette problem is the result of a person speaking on a	4	37	94
telephone in a place that disturbs another person. Either the individual	9	40	97
doing this just does not care or does not realize how rude he or she is	14	43	100
being to another individual. It is not unusual to see signs that prohibit	18	46	103
the use of a mobile telephone in meeting rooms, restaurants, movie	23	48	105
theaters, concert halls, and a number of other places. What is most	27	51	108
shocking is that these signs are necessary. Except in rare cases, a	32	54	111
telephone should not be used in these places. What has happened to	36	56	113
basic courtesy?	37	57	114

```
3' |  1  |  2  |  3  |  4  |  5  |  6  |  7  |  8  |  9  |  10 |  11 |  12 |  13 |
5' |       1       |       2       |       3       |       4       |
```

61-d3
Insert and Delete Columns and Rows

1. Open *61-d1* that you saved in Apply It 61-d1 and insert a column between columns B and C. Key the following information in the new column and left-align.

 Department | Public Relations | Maintenance | Accounting | Engineering

2. Delete the row containing *Holsonback*.

3. Insert two additional rows and key the names and accompanying information below in correct alphabetical order. Adjust column widths as necessary.

Baxter, L.	**K511**	**Accounting**	**44,296,101**	**971,360**
Talbert, S.	**P053**	**CFO**	**82,091,433**	**985,201**

4. Insert a row above row 1. Merge the cells and key **LAUREL CANYON ENTERPRISES** using 14-point font, all caps.

5. Apply List Table 4 – Accent 5 style. Bold and center all headings. Adjust column widths to make the table more attractive.

6. Save and close. (*61-d3*)

Communication

61d

SEMICOLONS

1. In a new blank document, create the table shown below. Adjust the width of column A to 2.25". Review the "Use a Semicolon" subsection of the Punctuation section in Appendix C.

2. Review the rules in the left column and the examples in the right column. Apply the rule and key a corrected copy of the sentence labeled *Application*.

3. Insert a row above the table and merge the cells. Key **Use a Semicolon** in 16-point font and change the row height to 0.5". Change the height of row 2 to 0.3".

4. Apply Grid Table 4 – Accent 3 style. Align Center and apply bold to all headings. Center the table horizontally.

5. Save and close. (*61d*)

Rule	Example and Application
To separate independent clauses in a compound sentence when the conjunction is omitted.	**Example:** Please review the information; give me a report by Tuesday. **Application:** The citizens voted to recall the mayor an election will be held in November.
To separate independent clauses when they are joined by conjunctive adverbs (however, nevertheless, consequently, etc.).	**Example:** The traffic was heavy; consequently, I was late. **Application:** Mr. Smith refused to increase our travel expense budget furthermore he suggested that we decrease it by 10 percent.
To separate a series of elements that contain commas.	**Example:** The new officers are Fran Pena, President; Harry Wong, Treasurer; and Muriel Williams, Secretary. **Application:** We will be driving this summer to Las Vegas Nevada Phoenix Arizona Austin Texas and Chicago Illinois.

State of Tennessee

County of (Bookmark:COUNTY)

On (Bookmark:DATE), before me (Bookmark:NOTARY), personally appeared (Bookmark:CLIENT), proven to me on the basis of satisfactory evidence to be the person whose name is subscribed to the within instrument and acknowledged to me that she executed the same in her authorized capacity and that by her signature on the instrument the person, or the entity upon behalf of which the person acted, executed the instrument.

WITNESS my hand and official seal.

Signature _____ (Seal)

104-d4 and 105-d5

Complete Notary Forms

1. Open document *104-d3* and key the information for each bookmark for Document 104-d4.
2. Save and close. (*104-d4*)
3. Repeat the steps, inserting the information for Document 104-d5.
4. Save and close. (*104-d5*)

Bookmark	Document 104-d4	Document 104-d5
COUNTY	Shelby	Tipton
DATE	May 2, 2018	May 20, 2018
NOTARY	Patrick Plunk, Vice President, Orion Federal Credit Union	Susan Pickens, Notary, Bank of Bartlett
CLIENT	Janice Marie Bennett	Dennis Lee Morris

Lesson 62 Table Commands

New Commands
- Text Direction
- Distribute Rows or Columns
- Repeat Header Rows
- Page Orientation

lesson 62a warmup

Skill Building

62b Textbook Keying

Key each line once, concentrating on using good keying techniques.

az
1 Zen and Ozzie zealously played the anthem in the Aztec Jazz band.
2 Batz went to Phoenix, Arizona, to take a math quiz he had missed.

by
3 Boyd drove by the Blue Bayou to bypass the roadblocks at the Bay.
4 By daybreak, Mary will stop by to bake a birthday cake for Jayne.

cx
5 Please carry the X-ray from exit C to exit X for Cece and Xavier.
6 Carol can meet Xian at the exit doors following the movie Exodus.

dw
7 Don walked the dog at dawn when he dwelled in his downtown condo.
8 Did Dwight drive Wendy to the new drive-in or the new drive-thru?

figures
9 The 12 teams spent $3,489.00 on groceries for the 567 boy scouts.
10 Judy's 13 puzzles had 60,789 pieces, but 524 pieces were missing.

New Commands

62c

TEXT DIRECTION

Text Direction

Occasionally it is preferable to display text vertically in a cell, such as when a number of narrow columns are included in a table. The Text Direction button rotates text in a cell 90 degrees each time you click the button. Rotated text will be easier to read if it is centered in the table cell.

To change text direction:
Table Tools Layout/Alignment/Text Direction

1. Click in the cell where the text will be rotated.
2. Click the Text Direction button to rotate the text. Continue clicking Text Direction until the text displays in the desired direction.
3. Use Align Center to center the text in the cell.

PLEASE TAKE FURTHER NOTICE that the Defendant Susan Reckless is to vacate the premises within five (5) days of this written notice. Failure to do so will result in a default judgment for the Plaintiff Donald Hurt. As stipulated in the rental agreement, all past due rent and monetary fees and court costs incurred by Plaintiff Donald Hurt will be due from the Defendant Susan Reckless.

Dated this 19th of June, 2018.

JAMES W. LEE
Attorney for Plaintiff

104-d2

SOAP Note

 SOAP notes

1. Open *SOAP notes* from the data files. Use the information below to complete the SOAP note form.

2. Fill in the form with the following information:

 Lucas, Steve

 Patient No. **22653**; Age: **42**

 Allergies: **None known**

 Meds: **Esomeprazole Magnesium**

 T: **99.0**; P: **80**; R: **15**; B/P: **118/76**

 C/O: **Pain in left elbow**; Date: **4-10-2018**

S	Patient complains of pain in his left elbow. Patient fell yesterday.
O	Elbow is tender to the touch. No inflammation. X-ray shows a hairline fracture.
A	Hairline fracture in medial epicondyle.
P	Arm in cast. Recheck in two weeks. 500 mg of Ibuprofen taken every 4 hours as needed for pain.

3. Center the text vertically in the cells.

4. Save and close. (*104-d2*)

104-d3

Notary Form

1. In a new blank document, key the notary form using default margins. Replace the text in parentheses with bookmarks.

2. Tap ENTER twice to the signature. Set a right underline tab at 3.5" to create the signature line; tap TAB to key **(SEAL)**.

3. Save and close. (*104-d3*)

(continued)

DISTRIBUTE ROWS OR COLUMNS

When a table has many columns or rows, it is difficult to set each column width or height the same dimension. The Distribute Rows and Distribute Columns commands will distribute the columns and rows evenly for you.

To distribute rows or columns:
Table Tools Layout/Cell Size/Distribute Rows or Columns

1. Select the rows or columns that are to be distributed evenly.
2. Click Distribute Rows or Distribute Columns.

REPEAT HEADER ROWS

When a table is divided between pages, repeat the header row (column heads) at the top of each page so the reader understands the data that displays in each column. More than one header row can be repeated by first selecting the rows and then applying the command.

To repeat header row(s):
Table Tools Layout/Data/Repeat Header Rows

1. Select the row or rows that are to be repeated.
2. Click Repeat Header Rows.

DRILL 1 | **TEXT DIRECTION, DISTRIBUTE COLUMNS, REPEAT HEADER ROW** | text direction

1. Open *text direction* from the data files and select cells B1–F1.

2. Click Text Direction until the text reads from bottom to top.

3. Increase the row height by clicking the Height up arrow until the column heads in columns B–D display on two lines.

4. Bold and Align Center the column heads.

5. Change the width of column A to 2.5″.

6. Select columns B–F and click Distribute Columns.

7. Select rows 2–13. Click the Insert Below command three times to add more rows to the table.

8. Click the cursor in row 1. Click the Repeat Header Rows command. Scroll to verify that column heads display at the top of the next page.

9. Center the table horizontally on the page.

10. Save and close. (*62-drill1*)

PAGE ORIENTATION

A page may be displayed in either portrait (8 ½" × 11") or landscape (11" × 8 ½") orientation. Use landscape orientation when a table is extremely wide.

To change page orientation:
Layout/Page Setup/Orientation/Landscape

Warmup *Lesson 104a Warmup*

 lesson 104a warmup

Apply It

104-d1

Notice of Eviction

legal pleadings
28 lines

1. Open *legal pleadings 28 lines* from the data files and key the eviction notice. Click the bracketed text (Placeholders) and key the new text. Align your text with the line numbers shown at the left. (Option: See *100-d1*, pages 4-81 through 4-83.) Use uppercase as shown. Use the fonts of the template.

2. Save and close. (*104-d1*)

LEE & DURAND, LLP
ATTORNEYS AT LAW
James W. Lee, Esquire
State Bar Number 202256
8578 Main Street, Suite 202
Huntington Beach, CA 92646-1801

Telephone: 714.555.0174

Attorneys for Plaintiffs

SUPERIOR COURT OF THE STATE OF CALIFORNIA
FOR THE COUNTY OF ORANGE

DONALD HURT, et. al., Case No.: 01 CC05144

 Plaintiff NOTICE OF EVICTION

vs.

SUSAN RECKLESS, et. al.,

 Defendant

TO: ALL PARTIES AND THEIR ATTORNEYS OF RECORD

PLEASE TAKE NOTICE that the Plaintiff has submitted a notice to vacate the premises located at 3500 Civic Center Drive, Suite 250, Santa Ana, CA 92701-3821. The Defendant Susan Reckless has violated the rental agreement. The breach of lease is based on the nonpayment of rent on the part of the Defendant for the past sixty (60) days.

(continued)

DRILL 2 — PAGE ORIENTATION

1. Open *landscape* from the data files and change the page orientation to landscape.

2. Insert a column on the right side of the table.

3. Key in cell C1: **120,000 square feet of office space available for lease.**

4. Key in cell C3: **58,000 square feet on first floor available for lease.**

5. Align Center the text in columns B and C.

6. Save and close. (*62-drill2*)

Apply It

62-d1

1. In a new blank document, create a 7-column, 7-row table. Key the following text in row 1.

Name of College	Bachelor of Science Degree	Associate of Science Degree	Certificate	Classroom	Online	Hybrid

2. Change the Text Direction of the column heads in columns B–G so that the text reads bottom to top.

3. Increase the height of row 1 to 1.5" so that all column heads fit on one line.

4. Change the page orientation to Landscape.

5. Add a column to the right of the table and key **Financial Aid** as the column head.

6. Change the width of column A to 3.0". Make column H narrower so that the right border of column H is at approximately 9" on the Ruler.

7. Select columns B–H and click the Distribute Columns command.

8. Apply Grid Table 4 – Accent 3 style.

9. Insert a row above row 1; merge the cells. Change the row height to 0.75".

10. Key **COLLEGE COMPARISON CHART** in row 1. Apply 16-point bold font; Align Center the title.

11. Apply bold and Align Center to all column heads.

12. Change the height of rows 3–8 to 0.4".

13. Use the Quick Check below to compare your table.

14. Save and close. (*62-d1*)

QUICK ✓

Check your document against the illustration below.

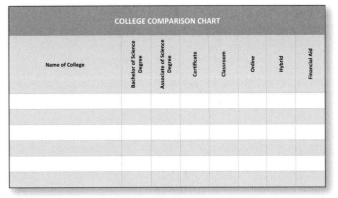

Indent paragraph ⟶ **IN TESTIMONY WHEREOF**, the above named Lessor and the above named Lessee have executed this instrument the _____ day of _____, 2018. ↓ 4

Lessee
↓ 4

Lessor

103–d3 and 103–d4

Complete Commercial Lease Agreement

1. Open document *103-d2* and key the information for each bookmark for Document 103-d3. In the paragraph beginning *TO HAVE AND TO HOLD*, insert the current year and then the subsequent year for 201-.
2. Proofread and check; click Next Activity. (*103-d3*)
3. Repeat the steps, inserting the information for Document 103-d4.
4. Save and close. (*103-d4*)

Bookmark	Document 103-d3	Document 103-d4
LESSEE	Hutcherson Home Builders	Tune Accounting Services
BEGIN_DAY	1st	15th
BEGIN_MONTH	November	December
END_DAY	31st	14th
END_MONTH	October	November
SUM	$36,000.00	$33,000.00
MONTHLY	$600.00	$550.00

103–d5

Compose

 hess memo

1. Compose a memo to Mr. William Wright from you.
2. Inform him you have created the two lease agreements for him to review. Verify that the amounts and dates are correct for each company. Find out if he wants you to email the lease agreements.
3. Attach the lease agreements. Save and close. (*103-d5*)

1. In a new blank document, key the following memo according to memo formatting guides.

2. Insert the table after the first paragraph; adjust column widths and center the table horizontally.

3. Apply List Table 4 – Accent 2 table style.

4. Center the dollar amounts in each column.

5. Save and close. (62-d2)

TIP

Insert space between a table and the following paragraph by clicking in the paragraph below the table and choosing Add Space Before Paragraph (Home/Paragraph/Line and Paragraph Spacing).

TO: Parents | FROM: Lynn Marshall | DATE: May 15, 201- | SUBJECT: Tuition Increase

The Board of Directors has reviewed our financial statements, the proposed budget for next year, and our current tuition plan. Although we have tried to maintain tuition at the current rate, it is not possible to do so. Our costs for utilities, food, supplies, and gasoline for the buses have increased substantially. Therefore, we have applied a 2.5% increase in tuition for next year. The following table summarizes our new weekly rates.

Age Group	Single-Child Rate	Multi-Child Rate	Half-Day Rate
Infant/Toddler	$368	$345	$195
Preschool 2	$363	$333	$185
Preschool 3	$340	$330	$175
Preschool 4	$337	$328	$173
Preschool 5	$335	$325	$173

The new rates take effect on July 1 and will be guaranteed not to change for one full year. The Children's Center will continue to accept credit cards and personal checks. Tuition may be paid weekly, monthly, or annually. If you have questions about tuition or other financial issues, please check with our business manager at the Children's Center.

We look forward to seeing all of you at the annual picnic next week.

Delivery at End of Lease:

And on the expiration of the term of this lease to deliver unto the Lessor the possession of said building, lot and premises, cleared of all persons, goods not properly belonging to the same, and in good condition as the same were received, destruction or damages by fire, storm or other casualty and ordinary wear and tear excepted;

Attorney Fees:

Lessee agrees to pay all costs of collection, including reasonable attorney fees, if all or any of the rent or utility charges reserved herein is collected after maturity with the aid of an attorney; also to pay reasonable attorney fees in the event it becomes necessary for the Lessor to employ an attorney to force the Lessee to comply with any of the covenants, obligations, or conditions imposed by this lease;

Indemnification:

Lessor not be liable to Lessee's employee's agents, invitees, licensees or visitors, or to any other person, for any injury to person or damage to property on or about the leased premises, whether caused by the negligence or misconduct of Lessee, its agents, servants or employees, or of any person entering upon the leased premises under express or implied invitation of Lessee, or caused by the Project and improvements located thereon becoming out of repair, or caused by leakage of gas, oil, water or steam or by electricity emanating from the leased premises. Lessee agrees to indemnify and hold harmless Lessor from any loss, attorney's fees, expenses or claims arising out of such damage or injury, such indemnification to survive the termination of this lease. Any liability insurance which may be carried by Lessor with respect to the Project shall be for Lessor's sole benefit and under its sole control.

Lessee further agrees to indemnify and hold Hess Office Park harmless from any liability which may be imposed upon Lessor and costs including attorney fees incurred as a result of any claim made against Lessor from injury arising out of machinery, caused or contributed by Lessee's or user's failure to provide safety equipment, instructions, and/or warnings necessary to operate this machinery safely. Lessee further agrees to indemnify and hold harmless Hess Office Park for any liability which may be imposed upon Lessor and any costs, including attorney fees, incurred as a result of any claim made against seller for injury arising out of use of this machinery, caused or contributed to by any actions or inactions of Lessee;

(continued)

Lesson 63 Table Functions

New Commands
- Decimal Tabs
- Formulas
- Sort in Tables

Skill Building

63b Timed Writing

1. Key a 1' timing on each paragraph; work to increase speed.
2. Key a 3' timing on all paragraphs; work for control.

A ALL LETTERS

	gwam	1'	3'

What is a college education worth today? If you asked that 12 4
question to a random sample of people, you would get a wide range of 25 8
responses. Many would respond that you cannot quantify the worth of 39 13
a bachelor's degree. They quickly stress that many factors other than 52 17
wages enhance the quality of life. They tend to focus on the benefits 66 22
of sciences and liberal arts and the appreciation they develop for 79 26
things that they would never have been exposed to if they had not 92 31
attended college. 96 32

Research shows, though, that you can place a value on a college 13 36
education in respect to wages earned. Less than twenty years ago, a 26 41
high school graduate earned only about fifty percent of what a college 40 45
graduate earned. Today, that number is quite different. The difference 54 50
between the wages of a college graduate and the wages of a high school 68 55
graduate has more than doubled in the last twenty years. 79 58

The key factor in economic success is education. The new jobs that 13 63
pay high wages require more skills and a college degree. Fortunately, 27 67
many high school students do recognize the value of getting a degree. 41 72
Far more high school graduates are going to college than ever before. 55 77
They know that the best jobs are jobs for knowledge workers and 67 81
those jobs require a high level of skill. 75 83

fixtures, and all other fixtures erected or put in place upon the premises by or through the Lessee or other occupants for the payment of rent and also for the satisfaction of any causes of action which may accrue to the Lessor by the Provisions of this instrument;

Lawful & Moral Uses:

That the premises and all buildings and improvements thereon shall, during the term of this lease, be used exclusively for lawful and moral purposes, and no part of the premises or improvements shall be used for any purpose in violation of the laws of the United States, the State of Texas, or the ordinances and laws of the City of Austin that are enforced;

Alterations:

Not to make any changes, alterations, or additions about the said building or premises without first obtaining the written consent of the Lessor and in no event to do anything that shall weaken the building or structure now on or that may hereafter be erected on the premises;

Protection from Violations:

To save and hold the Lessor harmless from violations of the laws of the United States, of the State of Texas, and the ordinances and laws of the City of Austin;

Invalidation of Insurance:

Not to suffer anything to be or remain upon the premises which will invalidate any policy of insurance which Lessor may now or hereafter have upon said building;

Damages, Accidents, Etc.:

To hold Lessor harmless against all damages, accidents, and injuries to persons or property caused by or in connection with any power plant, machinery, elevator, elevator shaft, stairway, signs, awnings, glass, brick, or other building material, hatch, coal chute or other openings, flag pole, and other parts of said premises in or pertaining to or upon the premises during the term of this lease or while the Lessee is occupying the premises;

Insolvency, Etc. of Lessee:

That in the event of the insolvency or bankruptcy of the Lessee, or the filing of any petition under the bankruptcy statute voluntarily or involuntarily and whether or not resulting in an adjudication in bankruptcy, or in the event of a partial or general assignment for the benefit of a creditor, the Lessor shall have the right to terminate this lease upon giving written notice thirty days in advance;

(continued)

New Commands

63c

DECIMAL TABS

 Decimal tabs are used to align numbers containing decimals in a column or to right-align numbers in a column. You have already used the Align Text Right command to right-align numbers in a column. Setting a decimal tab keeps the numbers right-aligned and makes them appear centered in the column. If the tab for the column needs to be moved, select all the numbers in the column before moving the tab, or the change will only occur in the cell where the insertion point is positioned.

To set a decimal tab:

1. Key the table with the numbers left-aligned in each column. Select the column or the cells in the column where the decimal tab will be used.

2. Click the tab selector at the left edge of the Ruler until the decimal tab displays.

3. Click the Horizontal Ruler where you want to set the tab. The numbers immediately align to the decimal tab.

4. If you need to move the decimal tab, first select the column or the necessary cells before moving the tab marker on the Ruler.

Numbers with Decimals	Align Right	Decimal Tab
2.1	56	56
10.75	100	100
325.333	1,050	2,050

DRILL 1 — DECIMAL TAB AND COLUMN WIDTH

1. In a new blank document, create the table shown above. Apply Grid Table 4 – Accent 5. Center the column headings. Uncheck First Column in the Table Style Options group.

2. Change the width of column A to 1.9″, column B to 1.2″, and column C to 1.3″.

3. Center the table horizontally on the page.

4. Select cells A2–A4 and set a decimal tab at 1″ on the Horizontal Ruler. The numbers automatically align with the decimal tab.

5. Select cells B2–B4 and click the Align Right button.

6. Select cells C2–C4 and set a decimal tab at 3.5″.

7. Select cells C2–C4; move the decimal tab on the Ruler to 4″.

8. Save and close. (63-drill1)

FORMULAS

fx Formula When numbers are keyed in a table, *Word* can perform basic mathematical calculations such as addition, subtraction, multiplication, and division. SUM (addition) is the default formula that appears if you click in a cell below a column of numbers or to the right of a row of numbers.

If a change is made to one of the numbers that is part of the calculation, *Word* can recalculate the answer. Fields can be updated by right-clicking in a field and then clicking Update Field or by clicking in the field and then tapping F9.

103-d2

Commerical Lease Agreement

1. Open a new blank document and use default margins. Key the title and tap ENTER twice; apply Title Style, Underline, and Center. Single-space the text and remove spacing after paragraphs. Bold and capitalize as indicated.

2. Insert the bookmark command where indicated. Name the bookmarks in ALL CAPS. For example, the first bookmark will be for LESSEE. If you make a mistake on the location of the bookmark, delete the bookmark and re-enter it. Check spacing.

3. For the date lines in the last paragraph, key 10 underlines.

4. Tap ENTER four times before each signature line; set a right underline tab at 3.0".

5. Save and close. (103-d2)

<div align="center">

LEASE

↓ 2

</div>

Parties:

THIS LEASE between, Hess Office Park party of the first part hereby called Lessor, and (Bookmark:LESSEE), party of the second part, hereinafter called Lessee,

Consideration:

WITNESSETH: That each of the aforesaid parties acknowledges the receipt of a valuable consideration from the other, and they and each of them act in further consideration of the engagements of the other as herein stated.

Premises:

That Lessor has and does hereby grant, demise, and lease unto Lessee the following described premises situated in the City of Austin, State of Texas; namely, a portion of the building located at 100 Hess Boulevard.

Term:

TO HAVE AND TO HOLD the above described premises unto the Lessee for the period of five (5) years commencing on the (Bookmark:BEGIN_DAY) day of (Bookmark:BEGIN_MONTH), 2018 and ending on the (Bookmark:END_DAY) day of (Bookmark:END_MONTH) 2019.

Insert the current year and then the subsequent year for 201-

Rental:

Lessee hereby covenants and agrees to pay Lessor as rent for the aforesaid premises the sum of (Bookmark:SUM) payable in advance in monthly installments as follows: (Bookmark:MONTHLY) due on the first of each and every month until paid in full.

Lien on Leasehold, Etc.:

A first lien is hereby expressly reserved by the Lessor and granted by the Lessee upon the terms of this lease and upon all interest of the Lessee in this leasehold for the payment of rent and for the satisfaction of any cause of action which may accrue to the Lessor by the provisions of this instrument. A first lien is also expressly reserved by the Lessor and granted by the Lessee upon all buildings, improvements, store fixtures, water fixtures, and gas

(continued)

To total a column or row of numbers:
Table Tools Layout/Data/Formula

1. Position the insertion point in the empty cell that is to contain the answer.

2. In the Formula dialog box, the SUM formula appears with either ABOVE or LEFT depending if you clicked below a column or at the end of a row.

3. Select the number format desired and click OK.

The SUM feature only works with adjacent cells. To add nonadjacent cells, key the formula in the Formula box (=b3 +b7+b9).

To recalculate a column or row of numbers:

1. Right-click in the cell where the new total is to appear, then click Update Field.

–or–

2. Highlight the cell where the new total is to appear and tap F9.

| DRILL 2 | SUM FUNCTION | sum |

Table Tools Layout/Data/Formula

1. Open *sum* from the data files and position the insertion point in the last cell and tap TAB to add a row at the bottom.

2. Key **TOTAL** in cell A8.

3. Insert the total for column C in cell C8. Insert the total for column D in cell D8. Verify the number format is the same as the numbers in the column.

4. Insert a column at the right of the table.

5. Key **Total per Employee** in cell E1; it will wrap to a second line. Align Center the column head.

6. Add the numbers in columns C and D (=C2+D2, etc.) and place the total for each row in column E; you do not need to insert a sum for the total row. If the formula displays as =SUM(ABOVE), replace the word *ABOVE* with **LEFT**. Center the numbers vertically in the cells to match the other columns.

7. Save and close. (*63-drill2*)

| DRILL 3 | RECALCULATE |

1. Open *63-drill2* that you saved in Drill 2 and position the insertion point in cell D5 (Palombo/Software).

2. Change the number to **950,225**.

3. Click the insertion point in cell E5, then tap F9 to recalculate the total.

4. Click the insertion point in cell D8 and tap F9 to recalculate the total.

5. Change the amount in cell C7 to **85,150,000**.

6. Recalculate the totals in cells E7 and C8, then recalculate E8.

7. Save and close. (*63-drill3*)

103-d1

Mail Merge Letter

hess letterhead

1. Open *hess letterhead* from the data files and prepare two letters for Mr. Wright.
2. Create the data source using the field names in the table (*103-d1data*).
3. Merge the data source and the main document (*103-d1main*).
4. Remove the extra spacing between the lines of the letter address. Refer to Lesson 76 for help with mail merge if necessary.
5. Remove the hyperlink to the URL and the email address. Add closing lines, your initials, and closing notations.
6. Save and close. (*103-d1*)

	Letter 1	Letter 2
Title	Mr.	Mrs.
First Name	Nolen	Michelle
Last Name	Hutcherson	Tune
Company Name	Hutcherson Home Builders	Tune Accounting Services
Address	1500 Broad Street	3250 Walker Avenue
City	San Antonio	Austin
State	TX	TX
ZIP Code	78260	78724

Insert Date

«AddressBlock»

«GreetingLine»

We are pleased that «Company_Name» is considering leasing office space in Hess Office Park. Our offices have a prestigious business address for your client meetings, mail, business cards, and website.

A variety of office layouts and amenities are available to accommodate your needs. You will have 24/7 access to fully furnished executive office suites, conference rooms, as well as other shared office space.

Please review the enclosed brochure that outlines the services, prices, and other a la carte amenities that we provide. You may obtain additional information and take a virtual tour by going to our website at www.hesspropertyenterprises.com.

Once you have reviewed the enclosed brochure, please let me know if you have any questions. My direct telephone number is 512.555.0130 or my email address is william.wright@hessofficepark.com.

I look forward to assisting you with your office needs.

SORT IN TABLES

Data can be sorted in three ways:

- **Text sort.** Text is sorted alphabetically. Numbers sorted in a text sort are based only on the first digit. If the numbers 1, 7, and 100 are sorted, the resulting list will be in this order: 1, 100, 7.

- **Number sort.** Numbers are sorted numerically. For example, a list of 1, 100, 7 would be sorted as 1, 7, 100.

- **Date sort.** When dates are involved, text is sorted chronologically.

To sort data in a table:
Table Tools Layout/Data/Sort

1. Click in the table; then display the Sort dialog box.

2. When row 1 contains column headings, it is called the *header row*. Click the appropriate button indicating whether the table contains a header row.

3. Click the drop-list arrow next to *Sort by*. (**Note:** Sort by tells *Word* how to arrange the information.)

4. Select Ascending to sort the list from A to Z. Descending sorts from Z to A.

5. If the first-level sort cannot establish the sort order (this will be true if several cells are identical in the first column), then you will need to establish a second-level sort in the first *Then by* section. You can also enter a third-level sort in the subsequent *Then by* section.

DRILL 4 **SORT TABLE** 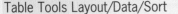 sort

Table Tools Layout/Data/Sort

1. Open *sort* from the data files and sort the table by Dish in ascending order. (Sort by Dish; Ascending.)

2. Sort the table by Cost in descending order. (Sort by Cost; Number; Descending.)

3. Sort the table by Nationality in ascending order and then by Dish in descending order. (Sort by Nationality; Text; Ascending; Then by Dish; Text; Descending.)

4. Your sorted table should look like the one at the right.

5. Save and close. (*63-drill4*)

Dish	Nationality	Cost
Hamburger	American	6.50
Sweet and Sour Pork	Chinese	8.95
Hong Kong Steak	Chinese	15.95
Veal Marsala	Italian	18.75
Shrimp Tempura	Japanese	11.50
Fish Burrito	Mexican	6.96

Lesson 103 Hess Office Park

Skill Building

103b Timed Writing

Key a 3' timing on both paragraphs; work at your control rate.

	gwam	3'

Today, a huge number of white-collar workers use computers in · 4 | 105
their daily work. Most of these workers also have access to the Internet. · 9 | 110
Using the Internet for work purposes is becoming more and more · 13 | 114
common and, most of the time, is quite effective. Some organizations · 18 | 119
are finding, though, that a number of their workers do abuse the · 22 | 123
Internet. The abuse tends to occur in two forms. · 25 | 126

The first type of abuse they find is that a large number of employees · 30 | 131
visit sites that are not related in any way to their work. Some of the · 34 | 135
sites that workers visit contain material that is very offensive to others. · 39 | 140
The problem becomes more serious when offensive emails or materials · 44 | 145
from websites are sent to other employees. In some cases, the courts · 48 | 149
have found that these materials create a hostile work environment. The · 53 | 154
second type of abuse is the waste of work time. Employees who spend · 57 | 159
excessive amounts of time surfing the Internet simply are not doing the · 62 | 163
work they are paid to do. · 64 | 165

A number of large companies are trying to deal with this problem · 68 | 169
by buying software that they use to track the sites that workers access · 73 | 174
from their computers. These companies warn all of their employees that · 78 | 179
visiting offensive sites at work can have major consequences and might · 82 | 183
even result in job loss. They tend to be a little more lenient on the time · 87 | 188
abuse issue and often treat the Internet the same way that they deal · 92 | 193
with the telephone. Limited personal use of the Internet or email is not · 96 | 198
a major problem. If the usage becomes excessive, then action is taken. · 101 | 202

3' | 1 | 2 | 3 | 4 | 5 |

Project Setting

HESS OFFICE PARK

In this project you will be preparing documents for William Wright, the attorney, who serves as the executive director of the legal department at Hess Office Park. As you work through each job, make sure you do the following:

- Use Hess Office Park letterhead and memo forms to create all letters and memos, use the current date, and the block letter style with open punctuation.

- Format the signature lines for Mr. Wright's letters as follows:
 Sincerely | William Wright, Executive Director | Hess Office Park Legal Department

63-d1

Table with Table Style

1. In a new blank document, create a 4-column, 6-row table. Key the table below; decimal-align columns B–D.

2. Add a row at the bottom of the table. Key the word **TOTAL** in cell A7. Calculate and insert the total expenses for each month. Verify the number format is the same as the other numbers in the table.

3. Add a column to the right of the table. Key **Total** in cell E1. Insert the totals for each expense in column E (change the formula to =SUM(LEFT) as needed).

4. Add a row above the table. Merge the cells in row 1 and change the row height to 0.7". Key **EXPENSES FOR LAURA PEREZ** in bold, 14-point font, all caps. Tap ENTER; then key **First Quarter, 201-** in bold, 12-point font.

5. Apply Grid Table 4 – Accent 6 style. In Table Style Options, select Total row and Last Column. Adjust column widths to display the information attractively.

6. Bold and Align Center all column heads.

7. Save and close. (*63-d1*)

Expenses	January	February	March
Rent	$1,200.00	$1,250.00	$1,250.00
Food	$275.50	$255.25	$295.00
Transportation	$260.00	$280.00	$675.00
Clothing	$395.00	$110.00	$225.00
Miscellaneous	$135.00	$170.00	$165.00

63-d2

Recalculate

1. Open *63-d1* that you saved in Apply It 63-d1. Change the February rent to **$1,375.00** and the March rent to **$1,425.00**.

2. Recalculate the totals in cell E3, C8, D8, and E8.

3. Save and close. (*63-d2*)

63-d3

Recalculate and Sort within Table

1. Open *63-d2* that you saved in Apply It 63-d2. Insert a row between Rent and Food. Key the following information in the new row: **School | $875.00 | $460.00 | $515.00**.

2. Insert the total in cell E4. Recalculate the totals in row 9.

3. Select cells A3–A8 (*Rent – Miscellaneous*). Sort column 1 in ascending order. (Sort by Column 1; Text; Ascending.)

4. Save and close. (*63-d3*)

102-d4

Email

1. Compose an email message to Mark Thompson at **mthompson@abc.com**. Inform this tenant that the lease is attached and needs both signatures.
2. Attach the Lease Agreement created in *102-d3* to the email.
3. Add the following privacy statement at the bottom of the message.
4. Send a blind copy or print screen to your instructor.

CONFIDENTIALITY STATEMENT: The documents accompanying this transmission may contain confidential information that is legally privileged. The information is intended only for the use of the individual or entity named above. The authorized recipient of this information is prohibited from disclosing this information to any other party unless required to do so by law or regulation and is required to destroy the information after its stated need has been fulfilled. If you are not the intended recipient, you are hereby notified that any disclosure, copying, distribution, or action in reliance on the contents of these documents is strictly prohibited. If you have received this information in error, please notify the sender immediately and arrange for the return or destruction of these documents.

Law Offices, Technology, and Web 2.0 Apps

Communicating Today ▶

Law offices have changed drastically with the use of technology. The time spent in law libraries researching information has declined. Attorneys utilize the Internet to obtain information about witnesses, opposing parties, and clients. Social networks, blogs, podcasts, and other Web 2.0 applications allow lawyers to keep up with current law, collaborate with colleagues, and communicate with clients and prospective clients.

Law offices utilize videoconferencing, Voice over IP, scanners, and other technologies to improve efficiency, saving time and money. As law offices embrace today's technology, they must not forget their responsibility to comply with confidentiality and privacy rules.

63-d4

Create and Format Table

1. In a new blank document, key the table below. Adjust column widths. Center columns D and E.

2. Apply Grid Table 1 Light – Accent 5 style. Center column heads and center the table horizontally.

3. Save and close. (63-d4)

Last Name	First Name	City	State	ZIP
Louie	Melinda	Seattle	WA	98101-1075
Palms	Jacob	Minneapolis	MN	55455-8415
Straus	Patricia	Omaha	NE	68105-4398
Soey	Helen	San Francisco	CA	94107-0357
Zampich	Alex	Hayden Lake	ID	83835-2735
Le	Trinh	Oxnard	CA	93033-4890
Phan	Chinh	San Francisco	CA	94107-6592
Kumar	Sanjeet	Durham	NC	27703-5283
Williams	James	New Bern	NC	28562-7963
Toyota	Janice	Del Rio	TX	78840-3122
Carpenter	Roger	Laredo	TX	78040-2361
Garcia	Pena	Bellevue	WA	98005-9407

63-d5

Sort Table and Apply Style

1. Open *63-d4* that you saved in Apply It 63-d4 and sort the table in ascending order by last name. (*Hint:* Check to see that Header row is selected.)

2. Sort the table in descending order by ZIP Code. (The Sort by entry you will see is ZIP.)

3. Apply Grid Table 4 – Accent 4 style. Center the table horizontally.

4. Save and close. (*63-d5*)

63-d6

Multiple Sort

1. Open *63-d5* that you saved in Apply It 63-d5. Sort the table in ascending order by state, then by city, and then by last name.

2. Insert a row above the table and merge the cells.

3. Key **NATIONAL TEAM LEADERS** in 14-point, bold, all caps.

4. Change the height of the row to 0.4". Align Center the text in row 1. Bold and center all column heads.

5. Save and close. (*63-d6*)

102-d2

Rental Property Table

1. In a new blank document, format the title in Heading 1 style and align at center. Tap ENTER twice.
2. Format *Assessment Key* in Heading 2 style.
3. Create a table with 5 columns and 19 rows. Use the column headings and rows below:

 Column headings: **Property Contents | Begin Lease | End of Lease | Location | Comments**

 Rows: **Doors, Windows and frames, Blinds & curtains, Floor, Carpeting, Walls, Lights and switches, Outlets, Stove, Refrigerator, Dishwasher, Garbage disposal, Sink, Cabinets and counter, Tub and shower, Toilet, Garbage & recycling containers, Other**

4. Center the column headings. Change the width of the first column to 1.65" and the last column to 2". Select columns 2–4 and change the column width to 1".
5. Apply the Grid Table 5 Dark – Accent 1.
6. Save and close. (*102-d2*)

ASSESSMENT OF RENTAL PROPERTY

Use the table below to evaluate the condition of the property at the beginning of your lease. Complete the column "Begin Lease" using the Assessment Key below. Please keep a copy for your files and provide one for your Landlord. When your lease is terminated, complete the column "End of Lease." Your Landlord will corroborate your assessment. This information will be used to determine if your security deposit will be refunded.

Assessment Key:

- G = Good Condition
- M = Missing
- D = Damaged
- R = Repairs Needed

102-d3

Lease Form

lease form

Some documents use "fill-in fields" rather than blank lines to enter variable data.

1. Open the data file *lease form*. The document will open in Read Mode. Change the mode to Print Layout.
2. Click in each Placeholder to insert the information below in each of the fill-in fields.
3. Save the document as *102-d3*. You will use this in *102-d4*.

Landlord	Wayne Marshall
Tenant	Mark and Mary Thompson
Address	534 Oak Street
City, State, ZIP Code	Memphis, TN 38111
Occupancy	From: January 1, 2018 To: December 31, 2019
Monthly Installments	850 (use again for first month's rental)
Security Deposit	1,000
Dated	Select the current date

Lesson 64 Graphics Review

Review

64b

GRAPHICS

Proper use of graphics can greatly enhance the appearance of a document, help illustrate a point, or convey important information.

PICTURES AND ONLINE PICTURES

The Pictures and Online Pictures commands are used to insert pictures and Clip Art in *Word* documents. The Pictures command enables you to insert pictures from your computer or other computers on your network. The Online Pictures command is used to access digital pictures from sources such as the Bing Image Search Box, Flickr, or your OneDrive.

To insert pictures from your computer:
Insert/Illustrations/Pictures

1. Click at the position where the picture is to be inserted; then click Pictures to display the Insert Picture dialog box.
2. Browse to locate the picture you wish to insert.
3. Double-click the picture or select it and click the Insert button at the bottom of the dialog box to insert it.

To insert Online Pictures:
Insert/Illustrations/Online Pictures

1. Click at the position where the picture is to be inserted; then click Online Pictures to display the Insert Pictures dialog box.
2. Click the Bing Image Search box, enter a search term, and then tap ENTER to find the desired image.
3. Click the image to select it, then click the Insert button to insert it.

In most cases, the illustration will need to be formatted to appropriately fit in the document.

DRILL 1 **INSERT ONLINE PICTURE** 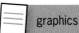 graphics

1. Open *graphics* from the data files and click the insertion point at the beginning of the document.

2. Click the Online Pictures command to display the Insert Pictures dialog box.

3. Key **orchid** in the Bing Image Search box, then tap Enter.

4. Select an image of an orchid and click Insert.

5. Save and close. (*64-drill1*)

Tenant shall take good care of the premises and all appliances, fixtures, appurtenances or equipment therein and make all repairs needed as a result of the Tenant's misuse or negligence.

Tenant shall not, without written consent from the Landlord, paint, mark, deface in any way, or make alterations or improvements in or to the premises, or any part thereof inside or out.

Tenant is responsible for insuring personal property. The Landlord shall not be liable for damage to or loss of any property by fire, theft, or otherwise.

Landlord shall have the right to enter the premises at a reasonable time for the purpose of inspecting or making any repairs that the Tenant may see fit to be made.

If the Tenant should fail to pay any installment of rent when it becomes due or fail to perform or observe any other such term or condition of this agreement, then in any such event, the Landlord may re-enter and repossess the premises without prior notice or demand, using such force as may be necessary, charge for any and all locks in the premises, all without being guilty of forcible entry or detainer, trespass, or other tort, and declare this agreement to be terminated without prejudice to the Landlord's rights to recover unpaid rent and damages.

At the end of the first year, this lease shall be automatically renewed for successive periods of one month at 125% of the monthly installment stated for the first year. Either party may terminate this lease after the first year at any time upon 30 days written notice to the other party.

It is agreed that at the termination of this lease, the Tenant shall return the premises in the same condition received; or if not so returned in the same condition, the Landlord shall be entitled to deduct the cost of restoring said property to said condition from the Tenant's security deposit. ↓ 2

Remove 3.5" left tab.——→DATED THIS _____ day of _____ 2018. ↓ 2

TENANT:

LANDLORD:

FORMAT PICTURES

Most pictures that are inserted into documents will need to be sized, cropped, and positioned in the document. The text will then need to be wrapped around the image.

To size pictures:
Picture Tools Format/Size/Height or Width Arrows

Pictures can be resized or cropped. Cropping removes unwanted portions of the picture. After a picture has been cropped, it should be compressed to reduce the size of the file.

1. To change the size of a picture, select it and use the Height or Width arrows to increase or decrease the size. -or-

2. Select the picture and position the mouse over the sizing handles. When the pointer changes to a double-headed arrow, drag to the desired size.

To crop pictures:
Picture Tools Format/Size/Crop

1. To crop one side of a picture, click Crop and drag the cropping handle on the side inward. The cropping line will illustrate what will be cut off.

2. To crop the same amount on two sides, tap CTRL while you drag the handle.

3. To finish, click outside the picture.

After a picture has been cropped, it is good practice to compress it to reduce the file size.

To compress pictures:
Picture Tools Format/Adjust/Compress Pictures

1. Select the picture and click Compress Pictures to display the Compress Pictures dialog box.

2. Note the options that are available; then click OK to accept the defaults.

To use Wrap Text:
Picture Tools Format/Arrange/Wrap Text

To move a picture with the mouse, you must first apply Wrap Text. The Wrap Text command coordinates the flow of text and pictures. By default, pictures are inserted with the In Line with Text wrapping style, which limits your ability to move the picture. Changing the wrap style to one of the other layout options allows you to freely move the picture.

The other layout options also determine how the text will flow around the picture. For example, *Square* wraps the text around all sides of the picture, forming a square. *Top and Bottom* wraps the text above and below the picture, but not on the sides. *Behind Text* places the picture in back of the text.

Lesson 102 Preparing Lease Agreements

Document Design

102b

LEASE AGREEMENTS

A real estate lease is a contractual agreement between the tenant or lessee to pay the landlord or lessor for use of property (also called premises). Many times this is also referred to as a rental agreement. A lease states the rights and responsibilities of each party. The terms of a lease agreement will vary depending upon the parties involved and the type of property. A "residential" lease refers to real estate used as the place a tenant lives, while a "commercial" lease applies to business property. A written lease should be prepared and signed whenever property is rented to reduce the likelihood of misunderstandings between the tenant and the landlord regarding the rental arrangement.

Apply It

102-d1

Residential Lease Agreement

1. Use default margins. Tap ENTER twice after the title; apply Title Style and center-align.
2. At the first blank, set these tabs: right underline at 3", left at 3.5", and a right underline at 5.5". Remove the left tab at 3.5" for the dateline near the bottom. For the blanks with dollar amounts, key 10 underlines.
3. Tap ENTER twice above and below the date line.
4. Save and close. (*102-d1*)

Rental Agreement and Lease ↓2

This lease agreement is made between:

Set tabs: right underline at 3", left at 3.5". →

_____ (Landlord) and
_____ (Tenant)

For the property on:

_____ (Address)
_____ (City, State and ZIP code)

Set right underline at 5.5". → Occupancy From: _____ To: _____

Use 10 underlines. Tenant agrees to pay in consecutive monthly installments of $_____ each month, payable on the first of each month. Receipt is hereby acknowledged of the sum of $_____ for the first month's rental, and further sum of $_____ as security deposit.

Tenant agrees to use the premises for residential purposes only and not for illegal, immoral, or hazardous purposes. Only persons who have signed this agreement and their minor children, if any, may occupy the premises.

Tenant is responsible for the electric, gas, water, and telephone service, and all other utility services used in the property during the rental period.

(continued)

 When a picture is selected, a Layout Options button displays next to the picture. You can click the button to display some of the layout options, or you can click the Wrap Text drop-list arrow to obtain a more detailed list.

To wrap text around a picture:
Picture Tools Format/Arrange/Wrap Text

1. Select the picture and click Wrap Text to display the Wrap Text options.
2. Select the desired option, such as Square or Tight. Then drag the picture to the desired position.

To position a picture:
Picture Tools Format/Arrange/Position

1. Select the picture and click Position to display the position options.
2. Click on the desired position as shown below.

| DRILL 2 | FORMAT PICTURE | Crop |

1. Open *Crop* from the data files and click to select the picture.

2. Click Picture Tools Format tab, then click Crop.

3. Crop to remove the image of the child on the right.

4. Click Compress Pictures; click OK to accept the defaults.

5. Decrease the height of the picture to 0.7".

6. Change the Wrap Text to Behind Text. Change the Wrap Text to In Front of Text. Notice how the image is displayed with each setting.

7. Click the Position down arrow and choose Position in Top Center with Square Text Wrapping. Change the position to Position in Top Left with Square Text Wrapping.

8. Save and close. (*64-drill2*)

WORDART

 WordArt is graphical text that can be used for document headings to make them more visually appealing. It is typically used in announcements, flyers, newsletters, and other casual documents.

To insert WordArt:
Insert/Text/WordArt

1. Display the WordArt gallery.
2. Preview and select the desired option.
3. Select the text in the text box that displays and replace it with your text.
4. Size and position the WordArt as desired.

101-d5 and 101-d6

1. Open document *101-d4* and key the information for each bookmark for Document 101-d5. Save and close. *(101-d5)*
2. Repeat the steps, inserting the information for Document 101-d6. Save and close. *(101-d6)*

Bookmark	Document 101-d5	Document 101-d6
DAY	25	18
MONTH	May	June
FIRST_PARTY	Jeremy Jackson	Michael Parker
SECOND_PARTY	Ryan Ray	Dennis Davis

★ **NOTE**

On the Insert tab, in the Add-ins group, you may add an Add-in into your document and use the Web to enhance your work.

! **WORKPLACE SUCCESS**

Add-ins for Office

Insert/Add-ins/Insert an Add-in

As you can insert apps on your smart phone or tablet, Office has this feature allowing you to add apps from the Office Store. Microsoft Store has a variety of categories available and many free Add-ins or Apps available. When you access the Add-ins, select All and scroll down to explore the ones available, then select Document Designer. Click the link for Document Designer. You will be taken to Microsoft Office on the web, which is also called officeatwork365, where you will see the link to download a free preview copy of Document Designer. You will need to click Trust It before using this Add-in.

After downloading the free preview copy of Document Designer, the Document Designer Welcome screen will appear in *Word*. Please view the video. At this point you may download sample documents or create your own. Document Designer now appears under My Add-ins.

WordArt can be formatted using the tools on the Drawing Tools Format tab in the WordArt Styles group.

- *WordArt Styles* applies another style.
- *Text Fill* allows you to change the interior color of the letters.
- *Text Outline* can be used to change the exterior border of the letters.
- *Text Effects* adds depth or emphasis to text.

SMARTART

SmartArt consists of predesigned diagrams that help simplify complex concepts. SmartArt layouts are grouped into nine categories: List, Process, Cycle, Hierarchy, Relationship, Matrix, Pyramid, Picture, and layouts from Office.com. You can elect to view all the layouts or the layouts in one of the categories.

To insert and add text to SmartArt:
Insert/Illustrations/SmartArt

1. Position the insertion point where the SmartArt is to be inserted. Display the Choose a SmartArt Graphic dialog box. Categories of SmartArt are listed on the left, layouts for each category display in the center, and a preview and description of the appropriate use appear in the right pane.

2. Click the category desired or scroll through all layouts and click the desired layout, and then OK to insert it.

3. Key text directly in each shape. The text size will adjust to fit the shape. -or-

4. Display the text pane shown at right (SmartArt Tools Design/Create Graphic/Text Pane) and key the text there.

Each SmartArt diagram offers a few shapes by default. If you need more shapes than the diagram offers, you can add them in the diagram. If you are keying text in the text pane, tapping ENTER after your last entry adds a new shape. Or you can add a shape at a specific location in the diagram using the SmartArt Tools Design tab.

101-d2 and 101-d3

Complete Notary Form

1. Open the document *101-d1* and key the information for each bookmark in Document *101-d2*.
2. Save and close. (*101-d2*)
3. Repeat the same steps but insert the information for Document *101-d3*.
4. Save and close. (*101-d3*)

Bookmark	Document 101-d2	Document 101-d3
COUNTY	Orange	Los Angeles
DATE	April 12, 2018	April 15, 2018
NOTARY	Robert Bayer, Vice President, Bank of Commerce	Andrew Park, Notary, Quicken Escrow Company
CLIENT	Louise Ann Kruger	Mary Lou Chan

101-d4

Land Trust

A **land trust** is an agreement whereby one party (the trustee) agrees to hold ownership of a piece of real property for the benefit of another party (the beneficiary).

1. In a new blank document, set line spacing at 1.5. Center and underline the heading. Key text in uppercase as shown. Insert a blank line before and after WITNESSETH. Key **WITNESSETH** in uppercase with a space between each letter.
2. Insert bookmarks for the items in parentheses.
3. Save and close. (*101-d4*)

<div align="center">

LAND TRUST
</div>

THIS AGREEMENT, made and entered into this (Bookmark: DAY) day of (Bookmark:MONTH), 2018 by and between (Bookmark:FIRST_PARTY), hereinafter referred to as "First Party" and (Bookmark:SECOND_PARTY) individual resident of Shelby County, Tennessee, hereinafter referred to as "Second Party"; ↓2

<div align="center">

W I T N E S S E T H ↓2
</div>

WHEREAS, First Party has heretofore conveyed or caused to be conveyed to Second Party as Trustee, the parcel or parcels of real estate located in Shelby County, Tennessee, and more specifically described on Exhibit "A" attached hereto and made a part hereof; and

WHEREAS, the parties do desire to evidence in writing certain of their agreements;

NOW, THEREFORE, and in consideration of One Dollar ($1.00) cash in hand paid this date, and other valuable considerations, each of which is hereby acknowledged, the parties do agree as included in the attachment.

To add shapes to SmartArt:
SmartArt Tools Design/Create Graphic/Add Shape

1. Click in the shape before or after another shape that will be added.
2. Click Add Shape or click the drop-list arrow and select an option from the list that displays. Repeat as needed.

DRILL 3 USE WORDART AND SMARTART

1. In a new blank document, turn on Show/Hide. Tap ENTER four times. Click the insertion point on the first ¶ marker.

2. In WordArt, choose the style Fill – Blue, Accent 1, Shadow. Key **Assessment Cycle**.

3. Click on the last ¶; then click Insert/SmartArt. In the left pane of the SmartArt Graphic box, click Cycle.

4. Select the Continuous Cycle layout in the center pane.

5. Key the text shown in the diagram.

6. Click the frame that holds the diagram. On the SmartArt Tools Format tab, click Size. Change the width to 4".

7. Click on the border of the SmartArt and position it in Middle Center.

8. Click the border of the WordArt and position it in Top Center.

9. Save and close. (64-drill3)

Apply It

64-d1

Report with Graphics

 gate fountain

1. In a new blank document, tap ENTER until the insertion point is at approximately 2.2", then key the paragraphs below.

The wrought iron gate fountain that you commissioned Carey Coles to design and craft has been completed and was delivered two weeks ago. The installation was completed this week, and the fountain is now fully operable.

The process used to prepare the setting for the new fountain is shown in the diagram below.

The process worked well, and the results were very good. The fountain was delivered on time, and the draft of the setting was approved with minor modifications. Installation was completed in a timely manner with minimal disturbance of the surrounding area. The work on the landscape began immediately and was completed on schedule.

(continued)

DRILL 1 · CREATE BOOKMARKS

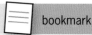 bookmark

Insert/Links/Bookmark

1. In a new blank document, turn on Show/Hide.

2. Delete the text *#1 bookmark*. Create a bookmark named **NAME**.

3. Replace *#2 bookmark* with a bookmark named **NAME_AGAIN**. Key the underscore between words. Be careful not to delete the comma; check spacing.

4. Replace *#3 bookmark* with the bookmark **ADDRESS**.

5. Replace *#4 bookmark* with the bookmark **HUSBAND_NAME**.

6. Replace *#5 bookmark* with the bookmark **HUSBAND_AGAIN**.

7. Replace the text *#6 bookmark* with a bookmark named **EXECUTOR**.

8. Save and close. (*101-drill1*)

DRILL 2 · USE BOOKMARK TO INSERT TEXT

Home/Editing/Find/Go To

1. Open the document *101-drill1*, go to each bookmark, and key the text shown at the right. Key the variable information in uppercase.

2. Save and close. (*101-drill2*)

Go To the bookmark	Key the following text
NAME	REBECCA PEREZ
NAME_AGAIN	REBECCA PEREZ
ADDRESS	One Main Street, Irvine, CA 96203-4865
HUSBAND_NAME	MATEO PEREZ
HUSBAND_AGAIN	MATEO PEREZ
EXECUTOR	GREGORY LEON

Apply It

101-d1

Notary Form

1. In a new blank document, key the notary form using default margins. Replace text in parentheses with bookmarks.

2. Tap ENTER twice, then key **Signature**. Set a right underline tab at 3.5" to create the signature line; tap TAB, then key **(SEAL)**.

3. Save and close. (*101-d1*)

State of California

County of (Bookmark:COUNTY)

On (Bookmark:DATE), before me, (Bookmark:NOTARY), personally appeared (Bookmark:CLIENT), proven to me on the basis of satisfactory evidence to be the person whose name is subscribed to the within instrument and acknowledged to me that she executed the same in her authorized capacity and that by her signature on the instrument the person, or the entity upon behalf of which the person acted, executed the instrument.

WITNESS my hand and official seal.

Signature _____ (Seal)

Ms. Coles is a gifted artist who created a beautiful work of art that will be cherished for many years. The fountain has substantially exceeded our expectations. All of the specifications were met, and the fountain fit perfectly into the area designed for it, as you will note from the picture below.

Ms. Coles requested that we notify you that the project has been completed to our satisfaction so that you will release the final payment for the work. We are delighted to convey this information to you, and we highly recommend Carey Coles for future projects.

2. Turn on Show/Hide and click the insertion point on the second ¶ marker. Using WordArt, add the heading **Fountain Installation and Setting** applying the Fill – White, Outline – Accent 2, Hard Shadow – Accent 2 style. Apply Dark Red Text Fill. Change the font size to 26 point. Change the width of the text box to 6".

3. Create the diagram shown below following the second paragraph. Use the Vertical Process layout; add shapes as needed. Key the following text in the shapes: **Fountain delivered | Prepare setting sketch | Obtain sketch approval | Begin planning | Install fountain and landscaping**

4. Size the diagram by clicking on the outer frame of the diagram, then in the Format tab, click Size and change the Height to 5".

5. Select the frame that borders the entire SmartArt, then in the SmartArt Tools Design tab, choose Change Colors. Under Accent 2, choose Colored Fill – Accent 2.

6. Insert the *gate fountain* picture at the end of the document; crop approximately 1" off the left side and compress the picture. Center the picture horizontally.

7. Number the pages at the top of the page using Plain Number 3 and Different First Page.

8. Save and close. Exit *Word*. (*64-d1*)

QUICK ✓

Check your document against the illustration below.

Sample document ©Cengage Learning. Embedded photo
©Cengage Learning courtesy of Susie VanHuss

Lesson 101 Preparing Legal Documents

New Command • Bookmark

New Command

101b

BOOKMARK

▶ Bookmark

A bookmark identifies a specific location within a document so that you can move the insertion point quickly to this location. If a document has more than one bookmark, each must have a unique name. A bookmark name may include letters, numbers, and the underscore character; do not use spaces.

In this lesson, you will use the bookmark to fill in variable information. You will use the Go To feature to move the insertion point to the specific bookmark. **Note:** As a reminder to yourself, you may want to key a bookmark name in uppercase if the replacement text will also be keyed in uppercase.

To insert a bookmark:
Insert/Links/Bookmark

1. Click the insertion point where the bookmark is to be inserted. Click Bookmark to display the Bookmark dialog box.

2. Key the name of the bookmark in the Bookmark name box. **❶** Click the Add button.
 Repeat steps 1–2 for each bookmark.

To use the bookmark:
Home/Editing/Find/Go To

1. In the Go to what pane, select Bookmark.

2. Click in Enter bookmark name box and select the name of the bookmark. Click the Go To button. Click Close.

3. The insertion point displays at the position of the bookmark. Key the information.

Lesson 65 Graphic Features

New Commands

- Page Borders
- Paragraph Borders
- Drop Cap
- Picture Styles

Warmup *Lesson 65a Warmup* lesson 65a warmup

New Commands

65b

PAGE AND PARAGRAPH BORDERS

Borders can be applied to an entire page or to paragraphs or selected text. A variety of options can be applied to borders, such as line style, color, and line width.

To apply a page border:
Design/Page Background/Page Borders

1. In the Borders and Shading dialog box, click the Page Border tab.
2. Choose the desired setting, style, color, and width.
3. In the Apply to box ❶, choose the desired option.

To apply a paragraph border:
Design/Page Background/Page Border

1. Click in the paragraph in which the border is to be applied.
2. In the Borders and Shading dialog box, click the Borders tab.
3. Choose the desired Setting option; then select line style, color, and width. The Apply to box should display Paragraph.

To apply shading:
Design/Page Background/Page Border

1. Click in the paragraph in which the shading is to be applied.
2. In the Borders and Shading dialog box, click the Shading tab.
3. Choose the desired fill and pattern, then click OK.

1	1. Any and all documents which substantiate the claim for property damage.
2	2. Any and all documents which substantiate the claim for loss of earnings.
3	3. All photographs which in any way relate to the subject matter of this action.
4	
5	
6	Dated this 1st of June, 2018.
7	
8	BARBARA M. JOHNSON
9	NEWTON & JOHNSON Attorney for Defendants
10	JONATHAN MOVERS and LAUREL DELIVERIES
11	
12	
13	
14	
15	
16	
17	
18	
19	
20	
21	
22	
23	
24	
25	
26	
27	
28	

NOTICE OF DEPOSITION AND REQUEST FOR PRODUCTION OF DOCUMENTS AT DEPOSITION - 2

Notice of Deposition and Request for Production of Documents at Deposition

DROP CAP

A drop cap is a large capital letter at the beginning of a text block. The drop cap usually extends from the top of the paragraph down two or three succeeding lines with text wrapped around it.

To create a dropped cap:
Insert/Text/Drop Cap

1. Click in the paragraph that is to begin with a dropped cap.
2. Select Drop Cap, then select Dropped or In margin.

The dropped cap can be modified by clicking on Drop Cap Options. The font style, number of lines to drop, and the distance from the text can be changed. The color of the dropped cap can be altered by selecting the dropped cap and choosing a different Font Color on the Home tab.

DRILL 1	PAGE AND PARAGRAPH BORDERS, SHADING, AND DROP CAP	architecture

1. Open *architecture* from the data files, click in the first paragraph, and apply an In margin drop cap.

2. Select the drop cap and change the color to Orange, Accent 2, Darker 25%.

3. Select the drop cap and change the style to Dropped.

4. Use Drop Cap Options to change the font style to Lucida Calligraphy.

5. Insert a box border around the second paragraph. Make the line color the same as the drop cap color.

6. Apply Orange, Accent 2, Lighter 80% shading to the second paragraph.

7. Create a Box page border with a single-style, ¾-point line, and Orange, Accent 2, Darker 25% color.

8. Save and close. (*65-drill1*)

PICTURE STYLES

The Picture Tools Format tab displays when an image is selected in your document. The Picture Styles gallery contains predesigned styles and other options in the Picture Styles group that allow you to modify a picture.

To apply a picture style:
Picture Tools Format/Picture Styles

1. Click on the picture to be formatted to display the Picture Tools Format tab.
2. Click the More button to display all the styles in the Picture Styles gallery.
3. Click the desired style to apply it to the picture.

The color and line style of the picture border can be modified by applying options in Picture Border. Special effects, such as 3-D Rotation, Shadow, Reflection, and Bevel, can be applied by using Picture Effects.

```
1   NEWTON & JOHNSON
    15 Civic Center Drive, Suite 200
2   Santa Ana, CA 92701-3821

3   Telephone: 714.55.0134

4   Attorneys for Defendants

5

6

7
                    SUPERIOR COURT OF THE STATE OF CALLIFORNIA
8
                         FOR THE COUNTY OF ORANGE
9

10
    HENRY HURT, et al.,                    Case No.: SO C 87321
11
              Plaintiff,
12
    vs.                                    NOTICE OF DEPOSITION AND REQUEST FOR
13                                         PRODUCTION OF DOCUMENTS AT DEPOSITION
    JONATHAN MOVERS, et. al.,
14
              Defendant
15

16

17

18
        TO: ALL PARTIES AND THEIR ATTORNEYS OF RECORD
19

20
            PLEASE TAKE NOTICE that defendants will take the deposition of plaintiff Henry Hurt on July
21
    7, 201-, at 2:00 p.m., at the offices of Newton & Johnson, 15 Civic Center Drive, Suite 200, Santa Ana, CA 92701 -
22
    3821, before a notary public authorized to administer oaths in the State of California. The deposition will continue
23
    from day to day, excluding Saturdays, Sundays, and holidays, until completed.
24
            PLEASE TAKE FURTHER NOTICE that plaintiff Henry Hurt is required to bring with him to the
25
    deposition the following records, documents, and things:
26
                    ///
27
                    ///
28
    NOTICE OF DEPOSITION AND REQUEST FOR PRODUCTION OF DOCUMENTS AT DEPOSITION - 1
```

Notice of Deposition and Request for Production of Documents at Deposition

ONLINE VIDEO

Word 2016's Online Video command allows you to insert a link in your Word document to an online video. The sources of the online video can be from a Bing video search, YouTube, or from a video embed code that was obtained from a website. Once the video clip has been placed in the document, you can format it using the commands on the Picture Tools Format tab.

To insert online videos:
Insert/Media/Online Video

1. Position the insertion point where the video clip is to be inserted.
2. If you are inserting a video embed code, locate the code on a website or another source and copy it to the Windows Clipboard.
3. Click Online Video to display the Insert Video dialog box.
4. Key the keywords in the Bing or YouTube search box to search for the desired video or paste the video embed code in the text box. Click the search icon.
5. Select your video, then click Insert. Format the video clip just like you would a picture. Click the arrow in the video box to play it.

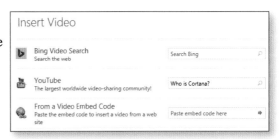

DRILL 2 **INSERT VIDEO** Cortana

1. Open *Cortana* from the data files and turn on Show/Hide. Position the insertion point on the ¶ below the last paragraph.

2. Click the Online Video command to display the Insert Video dialog box.

3. Key **Who is Cortana?** in the YouTube search box, then click the search button.

4. Select a video from the list that displays. Insert the video into the document.

5. Click the video image to select it. In the Picture Tools Format tab, change Wrap Text to Square.

6. Change the width of the image to 4"; the height will change proportionately.

7. Change the picture style to Metal Rounded Rectangle.

8. Move the video image to the right edge of the second paragraph.

9. Click the arrow in the video box to view the video.

10. Save and close. (*65-drill2*)

Who is Cortana?

Windows 10 is the newest operating system software released by Microsoft. The operating system software controls the operations of the computer and works with the application software. *Windows 10* works with *Word* in opening, printing, deleting, and saving files. It also allows you to work with photos, play music and videos, and access the Internet.

Some new features in *Windows 10* includes Cortana, a personal assistant. Cortana can assist you with finding files on your computer, manage your calendar, or chat with you. You can ask Cortana to look up information and find answers for you. Cortana will always use the Bing search engine to find the answers to your questions. Cortana will open your default web browser, even if it is Firefox or Chrome, but it will always use Bing to search for your answers.

Cortana currently works with Windows phones and on computers using the *Windows 10* operating system. Microsoft is planning on transitioning Cortana to the Android and iPhone platforms so that you can use Cortana on non-Windows smartphones as well. This will allow you to take Cortana with you everywhere.

Source: YouTube/Connected Digital World

Document Design — LEGAL DOCUMENTS

100c

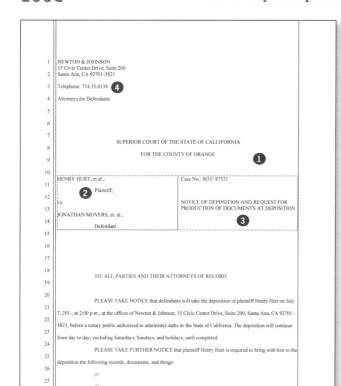

Legal documents that are presented for filing in court must follow specific guidelines and be keyed on pleading paper. Most documents today are keyed on standard 8.5" × 11" paper; some lawyers may still use legal size paper (8.5" × 14"). Legal documents contain a double ruling, from top to bottom, at the left margin; a single ruling displays at the right margin. Legal pleading forms contain line numbers in the left margin. The pleading form contains 25, 26, 28, or 32 lines per page.

Each pleading begins with a caption to identify the action. The styles of captions vary, depending on the state; however, all captions include the jurisdiction—the name of the court that has authority to rule with reference to specific persons or subject matter. The name of the county and the state in which the court is located are usually included with the jurisdiction ❶.

The pleading also contains a box, which is formed with symbols. The box shows the names of the individuals or corporations involved in the lawsuit ❷. The title of the pleading is located to the right of the box ❸.

The name, address, and telephone number of the attorney originating the paper precedes the caption ❹. In some states, this information is placed at the end of the pleading.

Apply It

100-d1

Notice of Deposition and Request for Production of Documents at Deposition

 legal pleadings 28 lines

A **deposition** is a testimony of a witness taken under oath in question-and-answer form. A deposition has the same legal effect as open court testimony.

1. Open *legal pleadings 28 lines* from the data files and key the deposition on the next two pages. Click on the bracketed text (*Placeholders*) and key the new text. Align your text with the line numbers shown in the illustration. Text shown in uppercase should be keyed in uppercase. Use the fonts of the template.

2. Center and key the placeholder for the court name.

3. Key **/ / /** on lines 27 and 28 to show that the lines were left blank by the writer.

4. To key the second page, place the insertion point on the ¶ at the end of line 28. Tap ENTER to move the insertion point to line 1 on the second page.

5. Save and close. (*100-d1*)

1. In a new blank document, tap ENTER three times, then insert *portrait* from the data files. Crop the picture 0.5″ on the right and 0.25″ on the left; compress the picture.

2. Apply Metal Oval picture style.

3. In Picture Border, choose Orange, Accent 2, Lighter 40% color.

4. In Picture Effects, choose Bevel Convex style. Also in Picture Effects, choose Glow, then Orange, 18-point glow, Accent color 2.

5. Change the width of the picture to 6″.

6. Insert WordArt and select the Fill – Gold, Accent 4, Soft Bevel style. Key **Genevieve**.

7. Select the text and change the font to Lucida Calligraphy. Change the Text Fill color to Orange, Accent 2, Lighter 40%. Change the text outline to Orange, Accent 2, Darker 25%.

8. Change the Wrap Text style to In Front of Text. Change the Zoom to One Page (View/Zoom/One Page). Move the WordArt so that it is centered attractively below the picture.

9. Save and close. (*65-drill3*)

Apply It

 65-d1

Form with Online Picture and WordArt

⭐ **TIP**

Insert the first checkbox; then key the sentence that follows. Tap ENTER to automatically insert the next checkbox.

1. In a new document, insert WordArt using the Fill – Gray-50%, Accent 3, Sharp Bevel style. Key **Adoption Agreement**. Change the width of the WordArt to 6.5". Change the Text Fill color to Orange, Accent 2, Darker 25%. Change the Text Outline color to Gold, Accent 4, Lighter 40%. Change the shape to Chevron Up (Text Effects/Transform/Chevron Up).

2. Use Bing Image Search to find a picture of a dog or cat. Insert the picture below the WordArt title. Change the Wrap Text to Square and size and position the picture attractively.

3. Key the paragraphs and checkbox items shown below. Apply a dropped cap to the paragraph; make the drop cap the same color as the title.

4. Select an appropriate checkbox from Wingding Symbols. Insert the checkbox, then press TAB and key the text. Tap ENTER three times after keying the last checkbox item.

5. Insert a signature line by setting a Right Underline tab at 6.5" (Home/Paragraph/Tabs) and then tapping TAB. Click on the ¶ marker at the end of the line and choose Remove Space After Paragraph (Home/Paragraph/Remove Space After Paragraph).

6. Key **Signature** below the line; set a left tab at 5.0" on the Ruler, tap TAB, and key **Date**.

7. Save and close. (*65-d1*)

Sample document ©Cengage Learning. Embedded image source: Openclipart.org.

Adoption of a pet can be extremely rewarding. However, it is important to remember that adoption is a privilege that requires the new owner to take appropriate care of the pet. Read the five items checked below that contain the specific requirements for the adoption of a pet. Your signature below the five checked items obligates you to follow all of these guides.

☑ I agree to take my new pet to the veterinarian within five days of adoption.

☑ I will provide appropriate food, fresh water, and shelter for my pet.

☑ I will exercise my pet daily.

☑ I will spay or neuter my pet within six months.

☑ I will not sell my pet.

Lesson 100 Legal Pleadings

Warmup *Lesson 100a Warmup*

lesson 100a warmup

Review Commands

100b

TEMPLATES

Templates are preformatted files that contain the fonts, placeholders, or locations where information is inserted each time. Legal pleading templates are available for download from Office.com. The pleading forms are preformatted to include vertical rulings, line numbers, and boxed areas.

To download the legal pleading template:
File/New

1. In the Search online templates box, key **pleadings**; tap ENTER.

2. Choose Pleading form with 28 lines.

3. Double-click on the Pleadings template to open it or click once and then click Create.

4. Once you download the template, it will be available in the template list the next time you go to File/New. In a classroom, however, you may need to save it to a flash drive or another location.

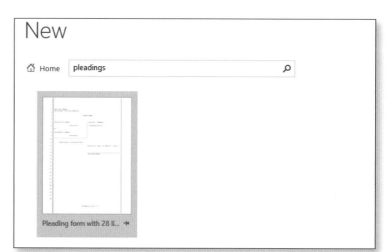

DRILL 1

DOWNLOAD LEGAL PLEADING TEMPLATE

File/New

1. Search for *Pleadings* at http://templates.office.com.

2. Download the Pleading form with 28 lines.

3. Scroll through the document; then close it without saving it.

4. Open the Pleadings template (see Use the Legal Pleadings template).

5. To save the template to a flash drive, open the template. It will appear in *Word*'s opening screen.

6. Browse to your flash drive and save as a template file with a .dotx extension, which is assigned automatically.

1. In a new blank document, use WordArt to create the main heading:
 a. Turn on Show/Hide, then tap ENTER three times.
 b. Click the insertion point on the first ¶ and insert WordArt using the Fill, White, Outline – Accent 1, Shadow style. Key **Power-Packed Foods May Save Your Life**.
 c. Change the WordArt text to 26 point so that it fits on one line.
 d. Change the Text Fill to Green, Accent 6, Darker 25%. Change the Text Outline to White, Background 1.
 e. Change the shape of the WordArt by applying the Chevron Up style on the Text Effects/Transform gallery.

2. Click on the fourth ¶ marker and key the following paragraphs.

Sample document ©Cengage Learning. Source of embedded images: Openclipart.org.

No one will dispute the fact that we must eat to stay alive. There has been much talk about whether what we eat affects how long we live and our quality of life. Some foods are packed with nutrients that, when incorporated into your diet, can help prevent future illnesses.

Check out this list of power-packed foods; including them in your diet may improve the length and quality of your life.

3. Tap ENTER twice after the last paragraph. Insert a 2-column, 5-row table. Change the width of column A to 1.55" and the width of column B to 3.75". Center the table horizontally on the page. Key the text shown below in column B; tap ENTER after each item.

4. Use Bing to search for an appropriate picture of each item in column A; size to fit in the row. Center the picture horizontally in each cell.

5. Sort the table so that the items in column B display in alphabetical order. Choose to sort by column 2, using the Text Type, and Ascending.

6. Select the table and remove all borders. Center the copy vertically on the page (Layout/Page Setup dialog box launcher/Layout/Vertical alignment/Center).

7. Save and close. Exit *Word*. (65-d2)

 TIP

Use **cereal** as the keyword to search for the oat bran picture.

Carrots are rich in beta carotene. Eating two carrots every other day will provide enough beta carotene to reduce stroke by half for men who already display symptoms of heart disease.	
Spinach contains vitamins A and C, folic acid, and magnesium. Spinach may help control cancer, reduce heart disease and stroke risk and may help prevent osteoporosis.	
Garlic may lower cholesterol and blood pressure. Garlic may also contain chemicals capable of destroying cancer cells.	
Oat bran may reduce the risk of colon cancer. Eating oat bran for breakfast will keep you from getting hungry mid-morning.	
Mangos contain bioflavonoids that can aid the immune system. Mangos are also rich in fiber.	

Enclosed you will find an envelope for returning the Certificate of Reservation of «Name» and a check for $750 to cover the processing fee.

Thank you for your attention to this matter.

Sincerely | Armando J. Reynoza | Attorney | xx | Enclosures

99-d3

Create Resolution to Dissolve Corporation

1. In a new blank document, beginning at about 2", center and underline the title. Tap ENTER five times. Remove space after all paragraphs.
2. Key the document using uppercase and bold where shown. Tap ENTER between paragraphs and between parts of the document as marked.
3. Indent the last two paragraphs 0.5" from the left margin.
4. For the signature line, set a left tab at 3" and a right underline tab at 6.5". Drag the left tab to 3.5" before keying **NAME**.
5. Save and close. (99-d3)

<u>RESOLUTION SETTING FORTH PLAN TO
DISSOLVE FAIREY FOOD SHOPS</u>

5

WHEREAS, the Board of Directors wishes to dissolve the Corporation, authorized by the Corporations' Articles of Dissolution date June 30, 2018, and

WHEREAS, the Board of Directors also deems it desirable that the Corporation dissolve its corporate form and its corporate charter in Memphis, Shelby County, Tennessee, and

WHEREAS, the Corporation is a Tennessee Corporation as that term is used and defined in the General Corporation Act of Tennessee;

3

NOW, THEREFORE, BE IT RESOLVED

That pursuant to this resolution, the shareholders and incorporators of record hereby authorize and direct that the Corporation's Articles of Dissolution be accepted and the corporation shall be dissolved.

↓6

Left tab 3"; Right underline tab 6.5" ⟶ _____
Drag tab to 3.5" ⟶ NAME

Lesson 66 Document Backgrounds

New Commands
- Watermarks
- Page Colors
- Text Box

Warmup *Lesson 66a Warmup* lesson 66a warmup

Skill Building

66b **Textbook Keying**

Key each line once;
concentrate on using
good keying techniques.

left hand

1 crazed bass averages dessert cedar badger affect braggart detects
2 beware greatest feet effects gag faster bazaar assess drawers ads
3 grease estate carafe awarded exerted get careers agrees beads ear
4 In my opinion, today anyone can play pool or monopoly with Jimmy.
5 honk million kimono pumpkin yolk poplin oil lumpy homily hoop lip
6 pill nylon million puppy uphill yoyo ninny opinion lion polio mum

right hand

7 Jimmy minimum pupil holly imply kinky monopoly pool union you ohm
8 Their neighbor's mangy dog and lame duck slept by a box of rocks.

New Commands

66c

WATERMARKS

A watermark is text or a picture that displays behind document text in a light or washed-out version. It displays in Print Layout and Full Screen Reading views and on printed documents. Watermarks are grouped in three categories: Confidential, Disclaimers, and Urgent. The logo of a business is often displayed as a watermark.

To insert a text watermark:

Design/Page Background/Watermark

1. Display the gallery of built-in watermarks.
2. Scroll down and click the desired option, such as DO NOT COPY 1, to insert it. Note that watermarks are typically positioned either horizontally or diagonally on the page.

DRILL 1 **TEXT WATERMARK** recruitment

1. Open *recruitment* from the data files and display the Watermark gallery.
2. Click DO NOT COPY 1.
3. Preview the watermark.
4. Save and close. (*66-drill1*)

Set tabs ──────► Name: «Name»

Street Address: «Street_Address»

City: «City» California ZIP Code: «ZIP_Code»

V

The corporation is authorized to issue only one class of stock; and the total number of shares, which the corporation is authorized to issue is «Amount».

↓ 2

Left tab 3"; Right underline tab 6.5" ──────► _____
Move left tab to 3.5" ──────► David M. Smith, Incorporator

99-d2

Mail Merge Letter

1. In a new blank document, use the Mail Merge Wizard to create the data source using the field names in the table below. (*99-d2data*)

	Letter 1	Letter 2
Name	LO-CARB MEALS, INC.	NEW IMAGE SURGERY CENTER
First	LO-CARB MEALS ARE US, INC.	A-1 PROFESSIONAL SURGERY CENTER
Second	LO-CARB DIETS, INC.	IDEAL SURGERY CENTER
Third	LO-CARB PASTA, INC.	A-1 LASER SURGERY CENTER

2. Key the letter (*99-d2main*) in block style with open punctuation. Center «Name». Set left tabs at 0.5" and 1.5" before inserting the merge fields in paragraph 2.

3. Merge the data source and the main document.

4. Save and close. (*99-d2*)

Current date | Secretary of State | State of California | P. O. Box 12345 | Sacramento, CA 96814-2591 | Dear Secretary

Please reserve the following name to be used by a California corporation proposed to be formed in the near future:

«Name»

If the name is not available for corporate use, the following names are listed as alternatives:

Set tabs ──────► Alternative 1: «First»

Alternative 2: «Second»

Alternative 3: «Third»

(continued)

To insert a watermark with custom text:
Design/Page Background/Watermark

1. Display the gallery of built-in watermarks.

2. Click Custom Watermark at the bottom of the gallery to display the Printed Watermark dialog box.

3. Select Text watermark and then key the desired text in the Text box. Select font and layout.

4. Click Apply and Close.

To insert a picture watermark:
Design/Page Background/Watermark

1. Display the gallery of built-in watermarks.

2. Click Custom Watermark at the bottom of the gallery to display the Printed Watermark dialog box.

3. Select Picture watermark and then click Select Picture to browse, select, and insert the desired picture.

4. Click Apply and Close.

1. Use the Mail Merge Wizard to create the Articles of Incorporation (*99-d1main*).
 Begin by creating the data source in a new blank document. Use the fields and
 data shown in the table. (*99-d1data*)

Field Name	Entry 1	Entry 2
Corporate Name	Quality Care Medical Center	Gourmet Food Shops
Profession	providing medical care	providing retail sales
Name	Andrew Wainscott	Jeannette Smith
Street Address	5561 Golden Lantern Drive	1521 Mack Avenue
City	Laguna Niguel	Orange
ZIP Code	92677-1234	92865-2214
Amount	Ten Thousand (10,000)	Five Thousand (5,000)

2. Tap ENTER five times at the top margin of the main document for the Secretary of
 State to place the filing stamp. Apply Heading 1 style to the title and center-align.

3. Key the Articles of Incorporation, inserting the fields shown. In paragraph 4, set
 left tabs at 0.5", 2", and 3.5".

4. Tap ENTER twice before keying the signature. Clear the tabs and set a left tab at
 3" and a right underline tab at 6.5". Remove spacing after the line before keying
 the name. Drag the left tab to 3.5" then key the name.

5. Merge the data source and the main document.

6. Save and close. (*99-d1*)

Articles of Incorporation ↓2

I

The name of this corporation is «Corporate_Name»

II

The purpose of the corporation is to engage in the profession of
«Profession» and any other lawful activities (other than the banking or
trust company business) not prohibited to a corporation engaging in such
profession by applicable laws and regulations.

III

The corporation is a professional corporation within the meaning of Part 4,
Division 3, Title I, California Corporation Code.

IV

The name and address in the State of California of this corporation's initial
agent for service of process are:

(continued)

PAGE COLOR

A color page background is used predominantly in Web browsers; however, the subtle use of page color, and particularly fill effects, can enhance the appearance of a document. More formal documents should be limited to page color using fill effects, such as parchment or stationery. Less formal documents may be formatted using a background with more color.

To apply page color and fill effects:
Design/Page Background/Page Color

1. To apply a color, click the desired theme or standard color. Custom colors (often used to match company brand colors) can be accessed by clicking More Colors.

2. To apply an effect, click Fill Effects to display the gallery of effects. Click the appropriate tab (Gradient, Texture, Pattern, or Picture) to display the desired effect. To display the name of the effect, click the thumbnail image.

DRILL 4 PAGE COLOR invitation

1. Open *invitation* from the data files. Apply Blue-Gray, Text 2, Lighter 90% color to the document.

2. Add a 1½-point Orange, Background 2, Darker 25% page border.

3. Save and close. (*66-drill4*)

DRILL 5 FILL EFFECTS roswell

1. Open *roswell* from the data files and display the Fill Effects dialog box.

2. Click each tab and preview the options.

3. Click the Texture tab, select Parchment (column C, row 4), and then click OK. Do not edit the body of the letter.

4. Save and close. (*66-drill5*)

Document Design

99c Legal Documents

In this module you will work with a variety of legal documents, including court, corporate, and personal legal instruments. Legal document formats vary from state to state, but they share many commonalities. Most law firms still use 12-point Times New Roman to format legal documents. Court documents format the title in uppercase, and some states underline the title. Legal files are downloadable from various courts within the state.

The Articles of Incorporation at the left contains information about the name, address, purpose of the company, and share structure. Articles of Incorporation differ for medical, nonprofit, professional, and municipal corporations. The documents in this module represent various formats, such as merge documents, fill-in forms, and templates. Follow these guidelines for keying legal documents.

- **Theme:** Use default Calibri 11-point font.
- **Margins:** Use 1" default margins unless specified.
- **Spacing:** Use default single spacing (1.08).
- **Signature lines:** Set tabs as instructed to format.
- **Main headings:** Specified in the directions.

DRILL 1 REVIEW MAIL MERGE power of attorney

Mailings/Start Mail Merge/Step by Step Mail Merge Wizard

Open *power of attorney* from the data files.

Use the Mail Merge Wizard to create the main document (*99-drill1main*) and the data source (*99-drill1data*). Customize the fields and complete the merge. For further review of mail merge, see Lesson 76.

Step 1: Select Letters.

Step 2: Select Use the current document.

Step 3: Select Type a new list; click Create.

- When the New Address List appears, click Custom Columns.
- Select each field and delete it; then click the Add button and key the three field names below. Key the data for each field from the table. Click Next.

Field Name	Recipient 1	Recipient 2
County	Orange	San Diego
Name	Rod Rodriguez	Tom Thompson
Date	June 6, 2018	June 15, 2018

Step 4: Select Write your letter. Since your document is already keyed and on screen, click More items.

- To insert the first merge code, select (Field: County) and the parentheses, click Insert, and Close.
- Repeat this process for the next two fields.

Step 5: Choose Next: Complete the Merge.

Step 6: Select Edit individual letters.

- Preview and check for correctness.
- When the Merge to New Document displays, click OK.

Step 7: Save and close. (*99-drill1*)

TEXT BOX

Text Box ▾

Text boxes enable you to position text at any location on a page. Because they can be moved around, they are often called *floating boxes*.

Two types of text boxes are used—built-in (preformatted) text boxes and text boxes that you draw and format yourself. Many of the built-in text boxes are used to format pull quotes and sidebars in newspapers, magazines, reports, brochures, or newsletters.

To insert a Built-In text box:
Insert/Text/Text Box

1. Display the gallery of Built-in text boxes.
2. Scroll through the thumbnails and click the text box you wish to insert.
3. Select the text in the placeholder and key your text, or copy and paste text in the placeholder.

DRILL 6 **TEXT BOXES**

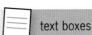 text boxes

1. Open *text boxes* from the data files and read to learn about sidebars and pull quotes. Position the insertion point at the top of the page.

2. Display the Text Box gallery. Scroll down to locate and insert the Whisp Sidebar text box.

3. Click [Sidebar Title] and key **Attractive Sidebars** in the placeholder. Click the sidebar text and key the following:

> This sidebar is used to illustrate one of the many readily available preformatted text boxes that enhance the appearance of documents and make them more interesting to read.

4. Position the insertion point on the right side of the second paragraph containing the quote. Insert the Semaphore Quote text box.

5. Select the quote in the second paragraph; copy and paste it in the placeholder. Size and position the text box as shown at the right.

6. Scroll to the bottom of the page and choose Draw Text Box from the bottom of the Text Box drop list.

7. Draw a text box at the bottom of the page that begins at approximately 2.5" and extends to 6.5". Use the Ruler as a guide.

8. Key **You can draw a text box and position it any place in the document.** Center the text.

9. Change the size of the text box to 0.3" high and 4.5" wide.

10. Save and close. (*66-drill6*)

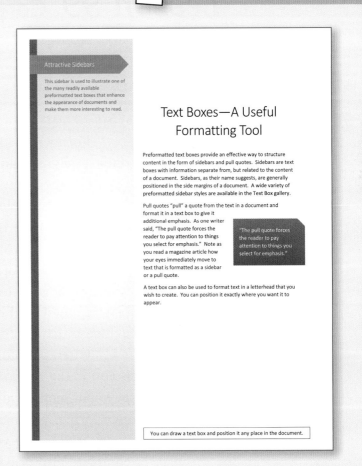

Legal Documents

LEARNING OUTCOMES

- Format legal documents.
- Format legal business documents.
- Format personal legal documents.
- Use templates to create legal documents.
- Build keyboarding skills.

Lesson 99 Corporate Legal Documents

Warmup *Lesson 99a Warmup*

lesson 99a warmup

Skill Building

99b **Timed Writing**

Key a 3' timing on all paragraphs.

	gwam	3'

Forms provide both a productive and an effective way to collect 4 | 70
data. Designing an effective form often does not happen quickly, but 9 | 75
the time spent can be justified quite easily. The time spent creating 13 | 79
a form is productive because once the form has been finished, it can 18 | 84
be used multiple times. 19 | 85

Forms provide an effective way of collecting data because they 24 | 89
add structure. Forms can be set up so that the data is organized in 28 | 94
exactly the way the designer wants to collect it. Analyzing data can 33 | 98
be simplified by the way in which the form is structured. Information 37 | 103
is also much easier to tabulate from data on a well-designed form. 42 | 107

When you complete information online, you are using a form. 45 | 111
If you make a purchase, you fill in a form with your name, address, 50 | 116
payment method and other needed information. When you create your 54 | 120
own forms, you may link to your form or embed your form in a web 59 | 124
page. Make sure you design your form so it is easy for the user to 63 | 129
complete and provides the results you need. 66 | 132

3' | 1 | 2 | 3 | 4 |

66-d1

Picture Watermark

 river camp

1. In a new document, apply landscape orientation.
2. Change the font to Baskerville Old Face 28-point.
3. Key **River Camp Experience**. Tap ENTER twice.
4. Key the remainder of the invitation, as shown below, with text centered.
5. Use WordArt for the title; format as follows:
 a. Select *River Camp Experience* and click Insert/WordArt.
 b. Choose the WordArt style Fill – White, Outline – Accent 2, Hard Shadow – Accent 2.
 c. Change the width of the WordArt box to 9".
 d. Change the font to Rockwell.
 e. Change the Text Fill color to Orange, Accent 2, Darker 25%.
 f. Apply Text Effects Transform: Chevron Up.
6. Insert the *river camp* picture watermark.
7. Apply the Center Page command (Page Layout/Page Setup/Layout/Vertical alignment/Center).
8. Save and close. (*66-d1*)

QUICK ✔

Check your document against the illustration below.

© Cengage Learning Courtesy of Susie VanHuss

Join the Leisure Travelers Club

For an exciting video report of the

River Camp Experience

Friday, March 24 at 5:30 p.m. at the Westside Center

Refreshments provided

66-d2

Financial Statement

 financial statement

1. Open *financial statement* from the data files. Use Fill Effects to add the Stationery background.
2. Add a Confidential1 watermark to the document.
3. Add a ½-point page border using the Plum, Accent 2, Darker 25% theme color.
4. Save and close. (*66-d2*)

66-d3

Draw Text Box

1. Open *65-d1* that you saved in Apply It 65-d1 in Lesson 65. Insert a footer (Insert/Footer/Blank). Click the ¶ marker below [Type here] and draw a text box that extends from left to right margin in the footer.
2. Key: **Good Samaritan Adoption Agency ◆ 5228 Hope, Shelbyville, TN 37162-0070 ◆ 800.555.2122.** Center the text. (Insert the diamond symbol from the Wingdings group.)
3. Fill the text box with the Dark Red color (Drawing Tools Format/Shape Fill). Change the text to the gold color and apply bold. Delete [Type here] but do not delete the ¶ marker after it.
4. Save and close. Exit *Word*. (*66-d3*)

QUICK ✓

Sample document ©Cengage Learning. Embedded images: Handshake and heart images courtesy of Openclipart.org. Arondale logo © Cengage Learning, courtesy of Donna Woo.

ACKNOWLEDGMENTS

Joseph Green, Mayor

Linda Rodriguez, City Council Member

Robert Smith, State Assemblyman

Accurate Results Laboratory

Arondale University Nursing Students

Austin Medical Staffing

Balfour Pharmaceuticals, Inc.

Better Meds Pharmacy

Dr. Daniel Brown, Cardiothoracic Surgeon

Crossroads Memorial Hospital

Exceptional Medical Supplies

Dr. Oscar Moore, Dermatologist

Reliance National Bank

Community Health Fair
Saturday, October 11, 201-
Many Hands Make Light Work

Thank You For Being So Kind

Sponsored by Arondale Medical Center and Hess Office Park

Sample document ©Cengage Learning. Embedded images: Microscope source: Openclipart.org. Site plan © Cengage Learning.

Seminars

Free informational seminars are offered throughout the day in the Gold Conference Room in Building B.

Cardiac Robotic Surgery 10:30 a.m.

This advanced procedure is performed through a few tiny openings instead of the foot-long incision to open the chest. This revolutionary procedure means fewer complications, less discomfort, and faster recoveries. Dr. Daniel Brown, Cardiothoracic Surgeon at Grace Trinity Hospital, is the seminar speaker.

Skin Cancer 1:30

Dr. Oscar Moore, a leading Dermatologist in the area, will discuss the dangers of sun exposure and the risk for being diagnosed with skin cancer. A variety of topics centered on skin cancer, including how skin color and type impacts your risk, why Vitamin D is important for your skin, and the various types of skin cancer.

Weight Loss Surgery 3:30 p.m.

This seminar will cover surgical procedures, expectations, recovery, and follow-up. A board-certified bariatric surgeon and bariatric nurse coordinator will share information and answer questions.

Building A: Drive-thru Flu Clinic

A drive-thru flu clinic will be administered on the north side of Reliance National Bank. This is convenient for those who do not want to park and walk to the clinic.

Building B: Seminars

Seminars will be held in the Gold Conference Room. See seminar schedule for topics and times.

Building C: Arondale Medical Center

Free health screenings and flu shots will be administered in the Arondale Medical Center.

Lesson 67 Documents with Columns and Graphics

New Commands

- Columns of Equal Width
- Columns of Unequal Width
- Position Graphics in Columns

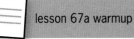
Skill Building

67b Timed Writing

1. Key a 1' timing on each paragraph; work to increase speed.
2. Key a 3' timing on all paragraphs; work for control.

	gwam	1'	3'

Eating is often the solution to any and all problems for many people. Our society has been known to use food as a tranquilizer. Many times if a child expresses unhappiness, someone will try soothing the child with cookies.

12	4	55
25	8	60
37	12	64
44	15	66

Food cravings may mean that a person is hungry. But for emotional eaters, it may mean that they need something else. For some people, it may be a sign of boredom, frustration, or loneliness. It is important to understand the reason for eating and then try confronting those issues.

11	18	69
24	23	74
38	27	78
50	31	83
55	33	84

You can control your eating by changing the way you do things. Work on a hobby during commercials rather than going to get something to eat. Special events do not need to be centered around food. Celebrate a special occasion by going dancing rather than going out for dinner.

12	37	88
24	41	92
37	46	97
50	50	101
54	51	102

```
1'  | 1 | 2 | 3 | 4 | 5 | 6 | 7 | 8 | 9 | 10 | 11 | 12 | 13 |
3'  |     1     |       2       |       3       |      4      |
```

New Commands

67c

COLUMNS OF EQUAL WIDTH

Newsletters are usually keyed in a 2- or 3-column format. Text is keyed beginning at the left column. When that column is full, the text automatically flows to the top of the next column; this is called *snaking*.

Columns are created using the Columns command. The Two and Three columns options make the columns equal width.

To format equal-width columns:
Layout/Page Setup/Columns

1. Select the text to be formatted in columns; click Columns and select the desired number of columns from the options that display.
2. To balance columns on a page, click at the end of the columns and insert a Continuous section break.

Page 2, Column 1

Seminars

Free informational seminars are offered throughout the day in the Gold Conference Room in Building B.

Cardiac Robotic Surgery 10:30 a.m.

This advanced procedure is performed through a few tiny openings instead of the foot-long incision to open the chest. This revolutionary procedure means fewer complications, less discomfort, and faster recoveries.
Dr. Daniel Brown, Cardiothoracic Surgeon at Grace Trinity Hospital, is the seminar speaker.

Skin Cancer 1:30 p.m.

Dr. Oscar Moore, a leading dermatologist in the area, will discuss the dangers of sun exposure and the risk for being diagnosed with skin cancer. A variety of topics centered on skin cancer, including how skin color and type impacts your risk, why Vitamin D is important for your skin, and the various types of skin cancer.

Weight Loss Surgery 3:30 p.m.

This seminar will cover surgical procedures, expectations, recovery, and follow-up. A board-certified bariatric surgeon and bariatric nurse coordinator will share information and answer questions.

Page 2, Column 2

(Insert site plan.tif)

Building A: Drive-thru Flu Clinic

A drive-thru flu clinic will be administered on the north side of Reliance National Bank. This is convenient for those who do not want to park and walk to the clinic.

Building B: Seminars

Seminars will be held in the Gold Conference Room. See seminar schedule for topics and times.

Building C: Arondale Medical Center

Free health screenings and flu shots will be administered in the Arondale Medical Center.

wrap text

1. Open *wrap text* from the data files, select the title, and apply WordArt Fill – Black, Text 1, Outline – Background 1, Hard Shadow – Accent 1 style.

2. Change the width of the WordArt text box to 6".

3. Select the text, click Columns, and select Three.

4. Preview the document and then revise the column structure; select the text again and click Two columns.

5. Use Bing Image Search to find an appropriate online image to be placed in the first and last paragraphs. Size them appropriately and change the text wrapping to Square.

6. Add a Continuous section break at the end of the columns to balance them (Layout/Page Setup/Breaks).

7. Save and close. (*67-drill1*)

COLUMNS OF UNEQUAL WIDTH

When newsletters include organization information, they are often formatted with that information in a narrow first column.

To format columns of unequal width:
Layout/Page Setup/Columns

1. Click More Columns at the bottom of the drop-list options to display the Columns dialog box.

2. In the Presets box, choose Left; then select the number of columns desired. The width of each column and the amount of space between columns displays. The settings can be altered by using the spin arrows.

3. Click Line between if a line is desired between columns.

POSITION GRAPHICS IN COLUMNS

Once the layout of a graphic image has been changed to any setting other than In Line with Text, the image is automatically anchored to the paragraph closest to where it was inserted. You will see an anchor symbol displayed to the left of the paragraph to which the image is anchored (the image must be selected with Show/Hide on). The image moves with the paragraph to which it is anchored.

You can keep the image at the same position regardless of where the text moves by clicking Fix Position on Page at the bottom of the Wrap Text drop list. You can place the image at a specific horizontal and/or vertical position by clicking More Layout Options and then specifying the position on the Position tab in the Layout dialog box.

 e. Copy the logo, then close the file.

 f. In a blank new document, paste the logo below the *volunteers* image.

 g. Size appropriately and change Wrap Text style to In Front of Text.

 h. Center the text in Britannic Bold, 11-point font at the bottom of the page.

5. Format page 2, column 1:

 a. Tap ENTER twice, then center **Seminars** in Britannic Bold, 18-point font.

 b. Apply Heading 1 style to the seminar names and times. Align the times by setting a right-align tab at 4.25.

 c. Search online for a picture of a microscope. Change the height of the microscope to 6.5" high, if necessary. Change the color to Washout (Picture Tools Format/Adjust/Color/Washout). Change the Wrap Text style to Behind Text.

6. Format page 2, column 2:

 a. Tap ENTER, then insert the *site plan* picture from your data files.

 b. Key the text below the picture. Apply Heading 1 style to the headings.

7. Save and close. (*98-d2*)

Page 1, Column 1 (left column)

ACKNOWLEDGMENTS

Joseph Green, Mayor

Linda Rodriguez, City Council Member

Robert Smith, State Assemblyman

Accurate Results Laboratory

Arondale University Nursing Students

Austin Medical Staffing

Balfour Pharmaceuticals, Inc.

Better Meds Pharmacy

Dr. Daniel Brown, Cardiothoracic Surgeon

Crossroads Memorial Hospital

Exceptional Medical Supplies

Dr. Oscar Moore, Dermatologist

Reliance National Bank

Page 1, Column 2

Community Health Fair

Saturday, October 11, 201-

(insert pictures)

Sponsored by Arondale Medical Center and Hess Office Park.

(continued)

To fix the position of an image:
Picture Tools Format/Arrange/Wrap Text

1. Select the image, then display the Wrap Text drop menu.

2. Choose Fix Position on Page if you need to keep the picture at the current location. Otherwise, click More Layout Options.

3. In the Layout dialog box, click the Position tab. Key the desired horizontal and vertical positions.

4. In the Options section, deselect Move object with text. Select Lock anchor to keep the image at a particular position.

DRILL 2 — POSITION GRAPHIC IN COLUMNS OF UNEQUAL WIDTH litter

1. Open *litter* from the data files and click the insertion point at the top of the document. Use the WordArt Fill – White, Outline – Accent 1, Shadow style and key **Are you a Litterbug?**

2. Change the width of the WordArt text box to 6". Select the title and apply Green, Accent 6, Darker, 25% Fill Color. Apply Gold, Accent 4, Lighter 60% Text Outline color.

3. Position the insertion point at the beginning of the line "Students Going Green" and insert a Continuous section break.

4. Display the Columns dialog box and select Left in the Presets box. Check to see that the number of columns is set for 2.

5. Check Line between and click OK.

6. Place the cursor at the beginning of the first paragraph ("Does the appearance . . .") and insert a Column break.

7. Use Bing Image Search to find a picture related to **litter** and insert it in the second paragraph. Crop the picture as needed; compress the picture. Adjust the width of the picture to 1.2".

8. Change the text wrapping to Square. Move the picture to the right edge of the second paragraph. In the Wrap Text menu, select Fix Position on Page.

9. Move the third paragraph before the second paragraph.

10. Preview the document to ensure that it fits properly on the page.

11. Save and close. (*67-drill2*)

Creating a Flyer in the 21st Century

Communicating Today ▶

Use of a QR code (Quick Response Code) in marketing materials has become a popular trend. We see them on flyers, business cards, posters, brochures, and many other types of advertising media. Some people even put QR codes on T-shirts. QR codes are scanned with an app on a smartphone, which then takes the user to a website, provides the user with a coupon, or gives information about a product or promotion. These codes can even be used to send a message.

Businesses have been quite creative in how they use QR codes, especially if they are targeting a younger market that is typically very smartphone savvy. Use a QR code to trigger an action; marketing with a QR code is most effective when you get a "Wow" or "Cool" reaction from its users.

Address Line 1	3401 Madison Avenue	501 Harbor Avenue	17 Superior Road
City	Austin	Austin	Austin
State	TX	TX	TX
ZIP Code	73301-9076	73344-1789	78701-0192

Body of Letter:

Dear «Title» «Last Name»

A Community Health Fair will be held in the main concourse at Hess Office Park on Saturday, October 11, 201-, from 10:30 a.m. to 4:00 p.m. The Community Health Fair will promote health education and wellness living to the tenants at Hess Office Park, their family and friends, as well as to the local community. City and state officials will also be in attendance.

«Company Name» has been selected to participate as a vendor at this important community event. The event will be highly promoted and publicized by Arondale Medical Center and Hess Office Park management. Your presence is welcomed; this will provide an opportunity for prominent visibility for your organization.

We would like to thank you for your interest in taking an active part in the health fair. If you would like to reserve your booth, please complete the enclosed form and return it by September 8, 201-. Please call me if you have questions or if I can be of assistance.

98-d2

Health Fair Program

volunteers site plan
arondale logo and name

 TIP

Insert a column break (Page Layout/Breaks/Column) to move insertion point to the next column.

1. In a new blank document, prepare a two-page brochure that will be printed from front and back and folded in half. Use the illustration on page 4-74 as a page layout guide.
2. Use landscape orientation; change the left and right margin to 0.5". Format the document in two columns, each with 4.5" width and 1" space between columns.
3. Format page 1, column 1 (left column):
 a. Key **ACKNOWLEDGMENTS** using Britannic Bold, 18-point font.
 b. Center the names.
 c. Search for an appropriate "handshake" image using Bing Image Search. Change the height and width to display attractively. Change the Wrap Text style to square.
4. Format page 1, column 2:
 a. Use WordArt style Fill – Black, Text 1, Outline – Background 1, Hard Shadow – Accent 1 style, 26-point font to key the title. Change the text color to Dark Red. Change Wrap Text style to In Front of Text.
 b. Key the dateline using Britannic Bold font; apply Heading 1 style. Center the text.
 c. Insert the image *volunteers* from your data files. Center and size the picture accordingly. Use Square Text Wrapping.
 d. Open the file *arondale logo and name* from the data files.

67-d1

Newsletter with Unequal Columns

 business center

★ **TIP**

Size the pictures to display attractively. The bottom margins of the two right columns should be balanced, and the newsletter should fit on one page.

1. In a new blank document, change the margins to Narrow. Tap ENTER once and key **Crown Lake News and Views**; apply 36-point Trebuchet MS font and Blue, Accent 5, Darker 50% font color. Center the title.

2. Tap ENTER once after the title. Change to Left Align, Calibri 11-point font size, and the font color to Automatic.

3. Tap ENTER and insert a Continuous section break. Begin keying on the line below the section break. Key the newsletter shown on the next page as a one-column document. Apply Heading 1 style to all headings. Remove the space after paragraph between the staff names and positions as illustrated on the next page. Key staff titles at the left margin; they will be indented later.

4. Select the text of the newsletter and format it using the Left Preset and three columns. Check Line between. Change the settings in the Columns dialog box as follows:

 Column 1 width: 1.5" | Spacing: 0.3"

 Columns 2 and 3 width: 2.7" | Spacing: 0.3"

5. Place the insertion point at the beginning of the heading *New Development Project* and insert a Column break.

6. Insert the *business center* picture from the data files; use Square Text Wrapping, size it 2.3" high, and position it as shown on the next page.

7. Click in the paragraph below the business center picture and select Add Space Before Paragraph (Home/Paragraph/Line and Paragraph Spacing).

8. Use Bing Image Search to find a picture of an eagle; use Square Text Wrapping, size it approximately 1.5" high, and position it after the Eagle Award has been mentioned.

9. Use Bing Image Search to find a picture relating to team building; use Square Text Wrapping, and size and position it in the paragraph below the New Training Program heading.

10. Select the text in the left column and set a left tab at 0.25". Tap TAB before each staff title.

11. Save and close. (*67-d1*)

67-d2

Position Graphic

1. Open *67-d1* that you saved in Apply It 67-d1. Select the picture of the eagle and click Fix Position on Page in the Wrap Text drop list.

2. Select the picture of the eagle and click Position. Choose More Layout Options. Under Horizontal, select Absolute position, then key 6.6" in the Absolute position box. Change the setting to read "to the right of Page." Click OK.

3. Select the *Lee Daye Honored* heading and the text below it (do not select *New Training Program*). Move the text before the heading *Blood Drive Reminder*. The picture of the eagle remains in the third column.

4. Save and close. (*67-d2*)

Lesson 98 Hess Office Park

Skill Building

98b Timed Writing

1. Key a 1' timing on each paragraph; work for speed.
2. Key a 3' timing on all paragraphs; work for control.

A **ALL LETTERS**

	gwam	1'	3'

Reports are one of the best means by which busy executives at 12 | 4
any level of a business can keep well informed. The pertinent data in 26 | 9
reports can be used to solve a wide variety of problems that often 39 | 13
arise, make any changes that may be required, analyze results, and 52 | 17
make precise, timely decisions. 59 | 20

The quality of the plans and decisions made on the basis of the 13 | 24
information found in reports depends in large measure on how well the 26 | 28
reports are written and produced. A good report is a thorough and 39 | 33
objective summary of all pertinent facts and figures. If reports are 53 | 37
not well produced, the firm or organization will surely suffer. 66 | 41

1' | 1 | 2 | 3 | 4 | 5 | 6 | 7 | 8 | 9 | 10 | 11 | 12 | 13 |
3' | 1 | 2 | 3 | 4 |

Project Setting

PREPARING FOR A HEALTH FAIR

Arondale Medical Center will be hosting a health fair for the community on Saturday, October 11, 201-, from 10:30 a.m. to 4:00 p.m. The fair will be held in the main concourse of Hess Office Park. Medical suppliers, pharmaceutical companies, hospitals, schools, and clinics will be invited to participate as vendors and presenters. Arondale University nursing students will be providing free flu shots and health screenings. Vendors and presenters will provide information tables and wellness seminars.

You will assist in the planning and preparation of the health fair by sending documents to vendors and presenters and designing the program for the event.

98-d1

Mail Merge Letter

 arondale letterhead

1. Open *arondale letterhead* from the data files and key the letter as a mail merge main document. Use the Mail Merge Wizard. Set up the letter using the current document. Save as *98-d1main*.
2. Key a new list of recipients using the names and addresses below. (*98-d1data*)
3. Key the letter in block style with open punctuation. Supply all necessary letter parts. The letter is from **John Navarro | Community Relations Coordinator**.
4. Merge the documents.
5. Save and close. (*98-d1*)

Recipients:

Field Name	Recipient 1	Recipient 2	Recipient 3
Title	Mr.	Ms.	Mrs.
First Name	Leon	Hillary	Lauren
Last Name	Thompson	Jens	Park
Company Name	Exceptional Medical Supplies	Balfour Pharmaceuticals, Inc.	Crossroads Memorial Hospital

(continued)

Crown Lake News and Views

Newsletter Staff

Eric Burge
 Editor

Nancy Suggs
Christopher Hess
Anne Reynolds
 Associate Editors

Wayne Martin
 Editorial Assistant

Crown Lake News and Views is a weekly newsletter compiled by the staff of the Human Resources Department, and it is sent to all employees.

New Development Project

Crown Lake won the bid to develop and construct the new multimillion-dollar Business Center adjacent to Metro Airport. Connie McClure, one of the three senior project managers, had been named as the Business Center project manager. The project is expected to take more than two years to complete.

Approximately fifty new permanent employees will be hired to work on this project. All jobs will be posted within the next two weeks. The recruiting referral program is in effect for all jobs. You can earn a $100 bonus for each individual you recommend who is hired and remains with Crown Lake for at least six months. You may pick up your recruiting referral forms in the Personnel Office.

Blood Drive Reminder

The Crown Lake quarterly blood drive is set for next Friday in the Wellness Center. The Community Blood Bank needs all types of blood to replace the supplies sent to the islands during the recent disaster caused by Hurricane Lana. Employees in all divisions are being asked to participate this quarter because of the current supply crisis. All three donation sites will be used. Several volunteers will be needed to staff the two additional sites. The regular division rotation will resume next quarter.

Lee Daye Honored

The Community Foundation honored Lee Daye of the Marketing Department with the Eagle Award for outstanding service this year. The Eagle Award is presented each year to three citizens who have made a significant impact on the lives of others. The Community Foundation recognized Lee for his work with underprivileged children, the Community Relations Task Force, the Abolish Domestic Violence Center, and the Community Transitional Housing Project. Congratulations, Lee. You made a difference in the lives of many citizens in our community. Your award was richly deserved.

New Training Program

The pilot test of the new Team Effectiveness training program was completed last month, and the results were excellent. Thanks to all of you who participated in the development and testing of the program. Your input is vital to its success. The training schedule will be announced shortly.

Start new paragraph →

Christopher does not experience an internal source of control for his actions. He expects others to control him or to punish him after the fact. He may take responsibility for aggressive episodes. He may tend to see these as "not me" and therefore minimize them. At times these events may be repressed or dissociated.

Summary and Recommendations

Personality testing suggests the use of repression and dissociation that prevent him from having to remember or relive past painful experiences. Repressed feelings of frustration may return to be acted out behaviorally. Christopher may tend to not take responsibility for his actions or may minimize them.

It may be important for the staff to assess, in an ongoing fashion, indications of the degree of personality fragmentation that Christopher experiences. Some exploration of whether or not he remembers past events that have been reported by other family members may assist with this.

Christopher needs to learn techniques of anger management. He should be taught to become aware of when he is beginning to become angry so that he can voluntarily learn to control his behavior. Christopher may have much difficulty learning to access the signs that he is beginning to become upset. He may need to practice a variety of techniques in order to control his behavior and then later resolve the problem verbally.

An additional focus should be on his relational skills. Assisting him in becoming sensitive to reading cues and the teaching of some empathy and conscious awareness would also help improve his functioning level.

Lesson 68 Hess Office Park

Skill Building

68b Timed Writing

Key two 3' timings on the entire writing.

A ALL LETTERS

	gwam	3'

Surrogate grandparents and pet therapy might not be the types 4 of terms that you would expect to find in a medical journal, but they 9 are concepts that are quite popular with senior citizens. Two of the 13 most common problems experienced by senior citizens who do not live 18 with or near a family member are loneliness and the craving to feel 22 needed and loved. 23

Senior citizens who are healthy and who are stable mentally often 28 can have a high-quality relationship with deprived children who do 32 not have grandparents of their own. They often have time to spare and 37 the desire to give these needy children extra attention and help with 41 their school work and other needs. At first, it may seem that children 46 gain the most from being with seniors. However, it soon becomes evident 51 that the surrogate grandparents tend to benefit as much or even more 55 than the children. 56

Both assisted-living and total-care residential facilities are 60 using pets to keep senior citizens from feeling alone. In those cases 65 in which a single person lives in one of the housing units, the pet 70 can help to reduce the feeling of being alone and lonely. Even patients 74 in the total-care units who do not communicate very much become 78 animated and will talk to a very gentle pet brought in on a regular basis 83 to play with the patients. 85

3' | 1 | 2 | 3 | 4 |

Project Setting

CROWN LAKE INC. AT HESS OFFICE PARK

Crown Lake Inc. is an investment firm with offices located in major cities throughout the country; Hess Office Park is one of its many locations.

Crown Lake rents the large conference room at Hess Office Park to hold information sessions for prospective investors. They utilize the services of the print and copy center to prepare handouts, signs, and mailings for the information sessions. As the administrative assistant for the Hess Office Park print and copy center, you will be working with Crown Lake to prepare for the Crown Lake SportsPlex Information Session scheduled for February 15, 201-.

1. Follow the steps in *97-d2* to create a psychological testing report for Christopher Smith.
2. Save and close. (*97-d3*)

Patient Name: Smith, Christopher **Age:** 9 **Date of Testing:** 6/28/201-

Reason for Referral

Christopher Smith was referred for psychological testing by his inpatient psychiatrist, Linda Murillo, M.D. Description of personality dynamics with projective tests was requested.

Tests Administered

The Rorschach Technique

Roberts Apperception Test

Testing Behavior

Christopher Smith was tested while he was an inpatient at the Children's Unit at Oak Ridge Hospital. He is a friendly boy with short blond hair who is moderately overweight. He related to the examiner in a friendly and cooperative way. Eye contact was good. His speech and mannerisms were normal. The patient expressed himself well and had a good vocabulary. He appeared to enjoy the testing tasks and studied each stimuli card before responding. He described his responses well. His stories were fairly lengthy and had well-developed themes.

Testing Results

Personality testing suggests that mentally Christopher is very active, but his emotions are suppressed. There are indications of underlying depression and anger. Dissociation is also a probable defensive structure. He keeps experiences or memories dissociated so that he does not have to face or deal with them. They are potentially too overwhelming for him.

Christopher cannot keep memories and feelings detached all of the time; they occasionally break through and are likely to be acted out behaviorally. There may be periods of anger or aggressive outbursts or periods of despair or depression. The problems that Christopher experiences with anger may be apparent. His depression may be less frequently seen because he withdraws to wait it out or uses fantasy to escape from it. His feelings of depression may also be translated into anger.

(continued)

Block Letter

hess letterhead

The following letter will be sent to community members and Crown Lake investors.

1. Open *hess letterhead* from the data files, then key the letter in block letter style with open punctuation.
2. Save and close. (*68-d1*)

Dear Community Member

Crown Lake, Inc. invites you to attend an information session for the opportunity to discover how you can be an investment partner in the Crown Lake SportsPlex. Many of you have invested with us in past projects that have produced high-yield returns.

The community has expressed a need to develop a sports facility that will yield long-term positive results. This project will include integration of education, athletics, campus recreation, student athlete, alumni/donor, business, and local community interests.

The information session will be held on February 15, 201- at 7:00 p.m. in the Diamond Conference Room, Hess Office Park Conference Center. Our team of sports facility and recreation center business consultants will provide expert advice on this exciting opportunity. Please call (insert your name) at 800.555.1002 by February 10, 201- to reserve a seat at the information session.

Sincerely | Robert A. Callihan, President | Board of Directors

68-d2

Report Summary

venues
events

This document will be given to the attendees at the February 15 information session. It summarizes a large, comprehensive report that will be presented at a seminar for investors on March 15. Use the illustrations in the left margin on page 3-75 as a guide for page layout and positioning of graphics and text boxes.

1. In a new blank document, tap ENTER three times to key the title **Crown Lake SportsPlex** at 1.9" and apply Title style; key the subtitle **Executive Summary** and apply Subtitle style. Center both titles and change the font color to Blue, Accent 5, Darker 25%.
2. Key the document that begins on page 3-76. Number pages using Plain Number 3 at the top of the page. Apply Different First Page. Follow instructions in the callouts.
3. Apply a dropped cap to the C in the *Concept* heading.
4. Insert a Pyramid List SmartArt graphic where indicated. Add text:
 a. Top shape: **Students and General Public**
 b. Middle shape: **Competitive Athletes**
 c. Bottom shape: **Individual and Corporate Users**

 Change the SmartArt design style to Cartoon (SmartArt Tools Design/SmartArt Styles). Change the colors to Colorful Range – Accent Colors 5 to 6.

(continued)

3. Save and close. (*97-d2*)

Patient Name: Perez, Maria **Age:** 16 **Date of Testing:** 6/25/201-

Reason for Referral

Maria Perez was referred for psychological testing by her inpatient psychiatrist, Douglas Martin, M.D. Description of personality dynamics was requested.

Tests Administered

Minnesota Multiphasic Personality Inventory (scored with adolescent norms)

Testing Behavior

Not observed

Testing Results

Test report is based solely on testing data. Profile configuration indicates a defensive attitude. This is likely to be a very ingrained defensiveness. Part of it may be an angry reaction to being in the hospital, but there is also a long-standing lack of self-awareness. She is likely to exhibit little psychological insight into herself.

She is denying feelings of depression or any kinds of physical problems. She sees herself as healthy and active. She denies problems with anger, anxiety, or depression. She may present herself as having no reason for being in the hospital or as in no need of help.

Others are likely to perceive her as defensive and very concrete and rigid in her thinking. She may be active, even hyperactive at times. She may appear easily irritable and react angrily to minor problems.

Summary and Recommendations

At the time Maria Perez took the test she appeared to be defensive and minimizing problems. On an ongoing basis, she may have a lack of insight into her difficulties. Further testing may help describe her problems in more detail. She may lower her defensiveness so that she is more open to acknowledging and working on areas of difficulty as she adapts to the Unit and begins to feel more comfortable in the environment.

Sample document ©Cengage Learning. Source of embedded image: Openclipart.org.

5. Insert a Converting Radial SmartArt graphic (in the Relationship group) at the top of page 2. Change the SmartArt design style to Cartoon and the colors to Colorful Range – Accent Colors 4 to 5. Add text:

 a. Left shape: **Aquatics Center**

 b. Center top shape: **Golf Center**

 c. Right shape: **Olympics Center**

 d. Bottom shape: **Crown Lake SportsPlex**

6. Insert the text from the *venues* data file below the *Venues* heading. Apply Heading 2 style to all headings in the data file.

7. Insert a Simple Text Box as shown in the illustration at the left; copy the second sentence under *Venues* into the text box. Apply Standard Color Blue, Shape Fill; Shape Effects/Shadow/Inner, Inside Diagonal Top Right; Shape Effects/Bevel/Circle. Size the text box 0.9" high and 2.5" wide. Format using Align Text/Bottom. Bold the text and change the color to White, Background 1.

8. Insert the *events* picture from the data files as shown in the *Golf Center* section. Crop about 0.5" from the top and 0.75" from the bottom of the picture. Compress the picture.

 Size the picture to 4.5" high and 6.5" wide as follows:

 a. Select the picture and click the Size dialog box launcher to display the Layout dialog box. Click the Size tab.

 b. Key **4.5** in the Height box; Absolute should be selected. Key **6.5** in the width box. Deselect Lock aspect ratio and Relative to original picture size.

9. Key and format the table using Grid Table 5 Dark – Accent 6 style.

 a. Merge the cells in the top row; increase row height to 0.4"; Align Center the title using bold and 16-point font. Bold and center columns B and C headings.

 b. Set a 0.25" left tab in the first column to indent the items as shown.

 c. Select column B and set a decimal tab at 1.4" in the Tabs dialog box. Repeat this procedure for column C.

 d. Use the SUM(ABOVE) formula to total the cost of each venue and place the results in the *Total* row of the *Venue Costs* column.

 1) Place the insertion point in cell B7.

 2) Use the SUM(ABOVE) feature to obtain the total. The total should include a dollar sign and two decimal places.

 3) Select the total and drag it to cell C7.

 Repeat above steps for each venue.

 e. Obtain the total costs of the three venues and position the results in the last row of the *Venue Costs* column. In the Formula box, key **=c7+c13+c18**; no spaces, then click OK.

Lesson 97 Preparing Medical Reports

Warmup *Lesson 97a Warmup*

lesson 97a warmup

Document Design

97b

MEDICAL REPORT FORMS

Formats may vary slightly at different medical facilities; however, all medical reports contain similar sections: the heading, body, and conclusion. The **heading** contains pertinent information necessary to identify the patient. The heading is keyed at the top of the report. Some headings are quite lengthy and can take up to one-third of the first page. The **body** of the report contains the observations, test results, and/or findings. The **conclusion** includes the diagnosis and recommendations.

Apply It

97-d1

Medical Report Form

arondale logo and name

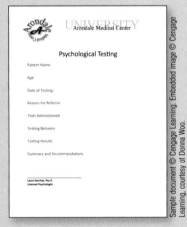

Sample document © Cengage Learning. Embedded image © Cengage Learning, courtesy of Donna Woo.

1. Open *arondale logo and name* from the data files center the heading **Psychological Testing** at approximately 2" and apply Title style. Tap ENTER twice.

2. Key the side headings at the left margin and apply Heading 1 style to each. Tap ENTER twice after each heading.

 Patient Name:

 Age:

 Date of Testing:

 Reason for Referral

 Tests Administered

 Testing Behavior

 Testing Results

 Summary and Recommendations

3. After keying the last heading, tap ENTER four times. Set a left underline tab at 3" for the physician's signature. Key the physician's name and title below the line. Apply the Strong style to the physician's name and title. Remove space after paragraph.

 Laura Sanchez, Psy.D.

 Licensed Psychologist

4. Save and close. (*97-d1*)

97-d2

Psychological Testing Report

1. Open the document *97-d1* and key the psychological testing report for Maria Perez. **Patient Name, Age,** and **Date of Testing** should be keyed on the same line as the heading. The rest of the report is keyed under the respective side heading; click the ¶ below the heading and key the text.

2. Insert a header at the top of the second page that consists of the patient's name, the page number, and the date of the testing. Format as follows:

 a. Click Insert tab/Header and Footer/Header/Blank. Key **Perez, Maria**.

 b. Tap ENTER. Key the word **Page** followed by a space.

 c. Click Insert tab/Header & Footer/Page Number. From the Page Number drop list, choose Current Position and then Plain Number.

 d. Tap ENTER and key the date of the testing. Tap ENTER and choose Different First Page.

 (continued)

10. Create three text boxes.
 a. Copy the text box that you created in the *Venues* section and paste it three times in the *Investment Opportunities* section as shown in the illustration.
 b. Replace the text in the text box with the following text. (Press SHIFT + ENTER after each level of investor.)

 Level-One Investor
 Minimum investment of $250,000 but less than $500,000.
 Level-Two Investor
 Investments larger than $500,000 but less than $1,000,000.
 Level-Three Investor
 Investments of $1,000,000 or more.

 c. Change the alignment of the text in the third text box to Middle.
11. Save and close. Exit *Word.* (68-d2)

The Crown Lake SportsPlex concept and conceptual drawing of the campus plan have been approved by its Board of Directors. The plan will be unveiled at a special seminar for potential investors on March 15.

Apply Heading 1 style ⟶ Concepts

The SportsPlex is envisioned as a three-tiered venue. The tiers match users and type of sports offered. The tier structure is based on revenue-generating potential, with the individual and corporate users expected to produce the bulk of the revenue. Students, competitive athletes, and the general public are expected to produce the highest volume of use but the lowest level of revenue.

Insert Pyramid List
SmartArt graphic here ⟶

The SportsPlex will be divided into three component venues—the Aquatics Center, the Golf Center, and the Olympics Center. Supporting facilities, restaurants, pro shops, boutiques, and family-oriented activities will be provided with each of the three venues.

Insert Converging Radial ⟶ Venues
SmartArt graphic here

Apply Heading 1 style;
Insert the venues data
file after the heading;
position the text box on
the right side of the first
paragraph under the
Venues head; copy the
second sentence and
place it in the text box.

Estimated Project Costs

Land and existing facilities, including the Crown Lake Special Events Center, have been purchased by the Crown Lake SportsPlex founders at a cost in excess of $10 million. The estimated costs of the facilities are shown in the following table.

(continued)

Disclosure Statement and Consent to Treatment

Confirmation of arrangements for the orthodontic management of:

Patient: _____

Parent responsible party: _____

Address: _____

Responsible Party Authorization

❑ All information displayed on the computer screen is accurate.

❑ I authorize Arondale Medical Center to send all information, not limited to orthodontic treatment and finances, to the provided email address. I also take responsibility for providing updates on my email address and mailing address.

❑ I authorize the staff at Arondale Medical Center to perform any necessary services during the diagnosis and treatment.

❑ I authorize Arondale Medical Center to release any information required to process insurance claims.

Financial Arrangements

The undersigned hereby agrees to the following financial arrangements:

PROFESSIONAL FEE	
Limited Treatment	$5,220.00
Phase I	$875.00
Phase II	$500.00
Full Treatment (Single Phase)	
Retainer Fee	
Retainer Visit Fee	
Finance Charge	
Total	

A service charge of 15% per month will be made on all past due balances. If it becomes necessary to send your account to collection, the undersigned agrees to pay all costs and expenses including the attorney's fee.

I hereby certify that I discussed the content of this contract with the physician and I give INFORMED CONSENT for all necessary orthodontic treatment and related services.

Patient/Responsible Party Signature: _____

Total Estimated Cost by Facility		
Venue and Facility	Facility Costs	Venue Costs
Aquatics Center		
Sailing Club	$1,375,000	
Swim Center	225,000	
Marina	165,000	
Total		
Golf Center		
Golf Course	5,350,000	
Practice Areas	250,000	
Walking Trails	195,000	
Clubhouse	1,600,000	
Total		
Olympics Center		
Courts	1,275,000	
Fields	1,325,000	
Track	890,000	
Total		
Total Costs		

The total cost is projected to be $12,650,000. Detailed costs of each facility and venue are provided in the comprehensive report. Conceptual designs are also available.

Apply Heading 1 style. Insert three text boxes to the right of the paragraphs. Key the text from the instructions on page 3-76.

Investment Opportunities

Qualified investors are being offered the opportunity to invest in the Crown Lake SportsPlex. Extensive pro formas have been prepared, and investment professionals will attend the March 15 seminar to explain the investment opportunities and offer professional opinions about the project. They will discuss the projected return on investment and other benefits associated with the project. In addition to the return on the investment, all levels of investment include private club membership benefits.

The reward provided with this investment opportunity is significant, but it is important to understand that the risk involved in this project is also significant.

This document contains confidential and proprietary information that is provided only to investors and potential investors of the Crown Lake SportsPlex. Do not copy, distribute, or share this information.

DOCUMENT 2 SOAP NOTE BODY

S	Pt complains of cough and head congestion for the past 48 hours, shortness of breath, lethargy, and low appetite.
O	Pt coughing up green sputum. Lungs clear, ears clear. Lymph nodes enlarged bilateral neck. Bilateral tonsils enlarged. CXR-WNL, PPD negative. CBC—elevated white count.
A	Acute upper respiratory infection.
P	Pt is to take Azithromycin, 250 mg. Take two tablets immediately, then take one tablet every day for the next four days. Increase fluids, increase rest. Pt is to stay home for three days. Recheck in one week or sooner, if needed.

DOCUMENT 3 SOAP NOTE BODY

S	Pt complains of pain in right knee; tripped and fell 6/17/201-.
O	Inflammation/hematoma on right anterior medial patella; decreased ROM right knee, with flexion, extension.
A	Diagnosis: Pre-patella bursitis. Treatment: R.I.C.E. on right patella anterior medial with ice pack twice a day for 4-6 weeks. Stay off right leg. ADL: rest knee; ice right anterior knee morn/night; elevate.
P	Stay off right leg. Rest; ice morn/night; elevate. Week 1: decrease pain; week 2: increase ROM.

96-d4

Disclosure and Consent to Treat Form

 arondale letterhead

1. Open *arondale letterhead* from the data files and change the bottom margin to 0.7". Key the document on the next page. Apply Heading 1 style to the title and Center; make sure a blank space is included below the title. Apply Heading 2 style to the side headings.

2. Use right underline tabs set at 6.5" for the underlines.

3. Apply Grid Table 4 – Accent 6 style to the table. Use the SUM formula to obtain the total; display the total with a dollar sign and two decimal places. Use a decimal tab to align the numbers. Key the table title in all caps, center, and bold. Center the table horizontally on the page.

4. Key a signature line below the last paragraph for **Patient/Responsible Party Signature:** and insert a line for the date below it.

5. Save and close. (96-d4)

(continued)

Lesson 69 Assessment Modules 10 and 11

Apply It

69-d1

Block letter

69-d1 letterhead

1. Open *69-d1 letterhead* from the data files. The insertion point should be at the left margin, 2.5". Key the letter using block style and open punctuation.
2. Begin the date at approximately 2". Be sure to press SHIFT + ENTER after the short lines in the letter address and closing lines to adjust spacing.
3. Create an envelope and add to the letter.
4. Proofread and correct any errors; save and close. (*69-d1*)

January 7, 201- | Ms. Margaret Kaplan | 1413 Ventura Street | Arcadia, OK 73007-8650 | Dear Ms. Kaplan

Summons for Jury Duty

This is a summons to report for jury duty on March 16, 201- at 8:00 a.m. at the Camacho County Courthouse. Parking for jurors is provided in the structure located on 75 South Magnolia Street between Broadway and Ocean Avenue. Place the enclosed Juror Parking Permit on your dashboard.

You will pass through a metal detector upon entering the building; do not carry anything that may be considered a weapon. Proceed to the Jury Assembly Room, located on the second floor of the Camacho County Courthouse; a floor plan is enclosed for your convenience.

Bring a book or magazine with you, as you may experience some wait time. Jurors are usually dismissed for lunch at 11:30 a.m. and return from lunch at 1:00 p.m. Plan on being at the Courthouse until 5:00 p.m.

We look forward to having you as a participant in our jury system.

Sincerely | Jacob Stern | Court Clerk | Enclosures: Courthouse floor plan | Parking permit

69-d2

Table with Calculations

1. In a new blank document, create the 6-column, 7-row table shown on the next page. Merge the cells in column A.
2. Key the main heading **MONTHLY DEDUCTIONS** in bold, 14-point caps. Rotate the text, Align Center, and apply White, Background 1, Darker 15% shading. Change the width of column A to 0.5".
3. Change the height of row 1 to 1". Key the column headings in bold, 12-point font, then center them vertically and horizontally in the cells; rotate the headings in columns C–F.
4. Key the table; adjust column widths, and center the table horizontally.

(continued)

96-d1

Create SOAP Note Form

arondale letterhead

1. Open *arondale letterhead* from the data files and create a table at approximately 2" for the patient's vital signs. Bold the text and change the row height to 0.4"; Align Center Left all text.

Last Name:			First Name:	
Patient No.		Age:	Allergies:	Meds:
T:		P:	R:	B/P:
C/O:			Date:	

2. Tap ENTER, then create a table for the SOAP notes. Make the letters *SOAP* 26 point and bold. Make each row height 1.25". Align Center the letters. Drag the border between columns A and B to make column A approximately 0.5" wide.

3. Select column B and change the alignment to Align Center Left; text will be centered vertically in the box when the note is keyed.

4. Modify the footer to make the tab at 3.25" a center underline tab. Place the physician's signature line in the footer.

5. Preview the document and adjust vertical placement as needed.

6. Save and close. (*96-d1*)

96-d2 and 96-d3

Create SOAP Notes

1. Open the document *96-d1* and fill in the form with the information for Document 2. **Note:** *Pt* is the abbreviation for *patient*; spell it out when keying the notes.

2. Proofread and check, then save and close. (*96-d2*)

3. Repeat the above steps for Document 3.

4. Save and close. (*96-d3*)

Sample document and Embedded Image © Cengage Learning

Field Names	Document 2	Document 3
Last Name	Jones	Pham
First Name	Sarah	Lisa
Patient No.	10680	31048
Age	20	27
Allergies	None	Bee stings
Meds	None	None
T	99.5	98.5
P	84	62
R	20	15
B/P	130/87	112/72
C/O	Cough	Pain in right knee
Date	6/9/201-	6/21/201-

(continued)

5. Insert the totals in the last row and last column. Totals should contain a comma and two decimal places. Use a decimal tab to align all numbers. Change the height of rows 2–7 to 0.25"; center text vertically in the cells.

6. Change Bennet's Disability Insurance to **55.00** and Fraser's Tax Shelter Annuity amount to **375.00**. Update the totals to reflect the changes.

7. Proofread and correct any errors; save and close. (*69-d2*)

MONTHLY DEDUCTIONS	Employee	Tax Shelter Annuity	Health Insurance	Disability Insurance	Total Deduction
	Bennet, Susan	500.00	425.00	35.00	
	Carillo, Marlan	175.00	685.00	75.00	
	Fraser, Elisol	275.00	420.00	0.00	
	Jones, Anna	325.00	475.00	55.00	
	Tanaka, Ellen	200.00	510.00	55.00	
	Total				

69-d3

Newsletter

69-d3 text

1. Open *69-d3 text* from the data files and turn on Show/Hide; then click the insertion point at the beginning of the document. Tap ENTER.

2. Move the insertion point to the ¶ marker in the first line. Key the title **Juror Information**. Apply 48-point Cambria font and Blue, Accent 1, Darker 50% color. Apply the Outer Offset Right shadow and Center.

3. Tap ENTER; change the font to Calibri 11-point, Automatic font color; remove shadow; and Align Left. Key the text shown below. Apply Heading 1 style to the side heading.

A cornerstone of the American judicial process is the right of each individual to have legal issues heard by a jury of his or her peers. Peers serve as the "judge" of the facts of a case. Individuals called to serve as jurors have an obligation to serve unless they are excused by the judge presiding over the case. Generally, individuals younger than 18 years of age and individuals who have been convicted of a crime for which they have not been pardoned are not eligible to serve on a jury. Individuals with custody of young children and who cannot arrange adequate care for the children and individuals over 65 years of age may elect to be exempt from jury duty. Individuals with schedule problems may be granted a transfer to serve on a different date.

Jury Selection

(continued)

Lesson 96 SOAP Notes and Medical Forms

Document Design

96b

SOAP NOTES

All medical offices keep recorded notes of the patient's office visit, which are commonly called SOAP notes. SOAP notes contain the patient's complaints, the physician's findings, and the physician's assessment and plan for treatment. The letters *S O A P* stand for Subjective, Objective, Assessment, and Plan.

S—SUBJECTIVE (what the patient tells the physician)

O—OBJECTIVE (the physician's findings as a result of a physical exam or evaluation)

A—ASSESSMENT (the physician's diagnosis or impression of the problem)

P—PLAN (the planned treatment for the patient)

Physician's signature line in footer

Command Review

96c

SET UNDERLINE TAB

Leader tabs can be used to create the underlines for signatures, addresses, phone numbers, and so on. Using underline tabs allows the underlines to align evenly.

To set an underline tab:
Home/Paragraph/Dialog Box Launcher/ Indents and Spacing/Tabs

1. Key the tab position in the Tab stop position box. Select the desired alignment.
2. Under Leader, select option 4. Click the Set button to display the tab setting in the Tab stop position box.

DRILL 1

SET UNDERLINE TAB

1. In a new blank document, set a left, underline tab at 2.75". Set a left tab with no leaders at 3.0". Set a right, underline tab at 6.5".

2. Turn on Show/Hide. Key **Name**, tap the Space Bar, and then tap TAB twice.

3. Key **Address** and tap the Space Bar, then tap TAB. Tap ENTER.

4. Key **Work Phone** and **Cell Phone** with an underscore following each.

5. Save and close. (*96-drill1*)

4. Select the paragraphs and place them in two columns; make the left column 1.7" wide and the right column 4.3" wide. The spacing between columns is 0.5". Insert a line between columns.

5. Click the insertion point at the beginning of the first column and insert a column break to move the text to the second column.

6. With Show/Hide displayed, click the insertion point at the beginning of the Column Break in the left column.

7. Change the Zoom setting to Whole Page (View/Zoom/Zoom). Use Draw Text Box to draw a text box in the left column. The text box should be 8" high by 1.9" wide. Change the Shape Fill color to match the title. Search for a picture of a courthouse and insert it at the top of the text box.

8. Key the following text so that it displays attractively in the text box; use the White, Background 1 color. Key the telephone number in 14-point bold font.

Camacho County Courthouse (Bold, center, 16-point font)
Jury Services Department

The Juror Services Department is available to assist you during your services. The office is located on the first floor of the Camacho County Courthouse, adjacent to the main entrance.

The office is open Monday through Friday from 8:00 to 5:00. The Jury office reporting instruction number is 405.555.1210. Juror information is available 24 hours a day, 7 days a week.

9. Insert a text box, 1.1" high by 2" wide, in the first paragraph below Jury Selection with Square Text Wrapping. Make the fill color and font the same as in the left column. Key: **Serving on a jury when called is an obligation of every qualified citizen.** Place the text in italic, bold, and 12 point font, and Align Text Middle. Apply Convex Beveling to the text box.

10. Use Bing Image Search to find a picture of the U.S. flag; insert it as a picture watermark.

11. Proofread the document. Save and close. Exit *Word*. (69-d3)

Sample document ©Cengage Learning. Source of embedded courthouse and flag images: Openclipart.org.

QUICK ✓

Heart-Healthy Checklist

DIET
✓ Limit intake of foods that are high in saturated fats, trans fatty acids, and cholesterol. Meat, dairy products, and eggs are the biggest culprits.
✓ Eat mostly fruits, a wide variety of vegetables, and whole grains.
✓ Limit eating sugar and processed carbohydrates, such as white bread, pasta, cookies, and cake.
✓ Limit salt intake.
✓ Eat a limited amount of "good" fats, such as nuts, fish, and olive oil.

EXERCISE
✓ If you live a sedentary lifestyle, you are at risk.
✓ If you are overweight, you are at risk.
✓ Exercise 60 minutes per day.
✓ Choose an exercise program that you enjoy.

LIFESTYLE
✓ Don't smoke.
✓ Do not drink more than two alcoholic beverages a day.
✓ Enjoy life, laugh, and have fun.

Take Care of Your Heart

#1

Make living a heart-healthy lifestyle a top priority!

Sample document ©Cengage Learning. Embedded apple and heart images courtesy of Openclipart.org.

According to the U. S. Department of Health and Human Services, heart disease is the leading cause of death in the United States. Death from heart attack, stroke, and other cardiovascular diseases claims one American life every 34 seconds.

The heart, like any other muscle in the body, requires preventative care in order to provide top performance. Some people are born with a congenital heart disease, but the majority of the people develop heart disease as they move through life. Lifestyle changes can lessen or eliminate many heart problems.

CONTRIBUTORS TO HEART DISEASE

- Smoking. The risk of heart disease for smokers is more than twice that of non-smokers.
- High cholesterol diet. Change your diet to eating foods made without saturated fats.
- High blood pressure. A healthy diet, losing weight, exercising regularly, and restricting sodium will help lower blood pressure.
- Diabetes. Many people who are overweight are at risk for type 2 diabetes.
- Physical inactivity. The Institute of Medicine recommends 60 minutes of moderately intense physical activity each day.
- Obesity. Change your diet to include more heart-healthy ingredients and increase your physical activity to control your weight.
- Stress. Try some stress relievers such as exercise, meditation, spending time with friends, or taking up a hobby.

MyPlate is the current nutrition guide published by the United States Department of Agriculture. The plate is divided into four sections with a glass on the side. Each of the sections and the glass represent the five food groups.

Fruits. Any fruit or 100% fruit juice counts as part of the Fruit group.

Vegetables. Any vegetable or 100% vegetable juice counts as a member of the Vegetable group.

Grains. Any food made from wheat, rice, oats, cornmeal, barley or another cereal grain is a grain product.

Protein. All foods made from meat, poultry, seafood, beans and peas, eggs, processed soy products, nuts, and seeds are considered part of the Protein group.

Dairy. All fluid milk products and many foods made from milk are considered part of the Dairy group.

Reports

LEARNING OUTCOMES

- Format two-page reports with cover pages.
- Insert page numbers in report with preliminary pages.
- Insert multilevel list.
- Create and modify table of contents.
- Create and modify table of figures.
- Use navigation tools.
- Build keyboarding skills.

Lesson 70 Review Reports

New Command

- Multilevel List

Warmup *Lesson 70a Warmup*

lesson 70a warmup

Skill Building

70b Timed Writing

1. Key a 1' timing on each paragraph; work to increase speed.
2. Key a 3' timing on all paragraphs.

ALL LETTERS

	gwam	1'	3'

Do you ever "goof off" for an hour or more with a television 12 4
program or a visit on the telephone and realize later that you haven't 26 9
actually enjoyed your leisure? Each nagging little vision of homework 40 13
or chores to be completed always seems to result in taking the edge 53 18
off your pleasure. And then you must hurriedly complete whatever you 67 22
postponed. Why do so many people end up rushing around in a frenzy, 80 27
trying to meet their deadlines? 87 29

First, do not waste time feeling guilty. Check with your friends 13 33
who always seem ready for a good time but are also ready for unexpected 27 38
quizzes. Learn their secrets to managing time. Knowing that there are 41 42
sixty seconds in every minute and sixty minutes in each hour, you can 55 47
schedule your activities into the time available. Second, learn to set 69 52
priorities. You can achieve your plans and enjoy your leisure as well. 83 56

1'	1	2	3	4	5	6	7	8	9	10	11	12
3'		1			2			3			4	

The heart, like any other muscle in the body, requires preventative care in order to provide top performance. Some people are born with a congenital heart disease, but the majority of the people develop heart disease as they move through life. Lifestyle changes can lessen or eliminate many heart problems.

CONTRIBUTORS TO HEART DISEASE

- Smoking. The risk of heart disease for smokers is more than twice that of non-smokers.
- High cholesterol diet. Change your diet to eating foods made without saturated fats.
- High blood pressure. A healthy diet, losing weight, exercising regularly, and restricting sodium will help lower blood pressure.
- Diabetes. Many people who are overweight are at risk for type 2 diabetes.
- Physical inactivity. The Institute of Medicine recommends 60 minutes of moderately intense physical activity each day.
- Obesity. Change your diet to include more heart-healthy ingredients and increase your physical activity to control your weight.
- Stress. Try some stress relievers such as exercise, meditation, spending time with friends, or taking up a hobby.

Page 2, column 2

MyPlate is the current nutrition guide published by the United States Department of Agriculture. The plate is divided into four sections with a glass on the side. Each of the sections and the glass represent the five food groups.

(Use SmartArt and Shapes to insert illustration of plate)

Fruits. Any fruit or 100% fruit juice counts as part of the Fruit group.

Vegetables. Any vegetable or 100% vegetable juice counts as a member of the Vegetable group.

Grains. Any food made from wheat, rice, oats, cornmeal, barley, or another cereal grain is a grain product.

Protein. All foods made from meat, poultry, seafood, beans and peas, eggs, processed soy products, nuts, and seeds are considered part of the Protein group.

Dairy. All fluid milk products and many foods made from milk are considered part of the Dairy group.

MULTILEVEL LIST

A multilevel list shows the list of items at different levels rather than at one level that is created when bullets and numbering commands are used.

To format items in a multilevel list:
Home/Paragraph/Multilevel List

1. Select the items to be formatted and click the Multilevel List button.
2. Use the Increase Indent button to demote items in the list or Decrease Indent button to promote in the list.

DRILL 1 MULTILEVEL LIST

1. In a new blank document, key the information shown in the left column below.

2. Select the items under Phase 1 and format them as a multilevel list, applying the numbered decimal option. Use the Increase Indent command to demote items 1.1 and 1.2. Repeat for Phase 2 items.

3. Compare your solution to the one shown in the right column.

4. Save and close. (*70-drill1*)

Click Increase Indent to Demote

Click Decrease Indent to Promote

Phase 1

Identify risks
Collect data
Analyze data
Review plan

Phase 2

Analyze risk
Evaluate costs

Solution

Phase 1

1. Identify risks
 1.1. Collect data
 1.2. Analyze data
2. Review plan

Phase 2

1. Analyze risk
2. Evaluate costs

DRILL 2 REVIEW COMMANDS

 progress report

1. Open *progress report* from the data files. Position the insertion point after the title *Technique Rating Sheet and Progress Report* and insert the following footnote. Italicize the book title. (References/Footnotes/Insert Footnote)

Technique rating sheet used with permission of Cengage Learning from the keyboarding textbook *College Keyboarding: Microsoft Word 2016 Keyboarding & Word Processing*, 20th edition.

2. Apply the Retrospect document theme. (Design/Themes)

3. Use the Page Number command to number the pages at the top right. Select the Plain Number 3 number style. Click Different First Page to suppress the page number on the first page. (Insert/Header & Footer/Page Number)

4. Save and close. (*70-drill2*)

 d. Click the Insert tab and choose Shapes. Select the oval shape and draw a circle to the right of *Grains*. Right-click the circle and choose Add Text. Key **Dairy**. If necessary, adjust the font size or the circle to accommodate the text.

8. Key the description of the food groups; bold the name of each food group as shown.

9. Save and close. (*95-d2*)

Page 1, column 1

Heart-Healthy Checklist

DIET	
✔	Limit intake of foods that are high in saturated fats, trans fatty acids, and cholesterol. Meat, dairy products, and eggs are the biggest culprits.
✔	Eat mostly fruits, a wide variety of vegetables, and whole grains.
✔	Limit eating sugar and processed carbohydrates, such as white bread, pasta, cookies, and cake.
✔	Limit salt intake.
✔	Eat a limited amount of "good" fats, such as nuts, fish, and olive oil.
EXERCISE	
✔	If you live a sedentary lifestyle, you are at risk.
✔	If you are overweight, you are at risk.
✔	Exercise 60 minutes per day.
✔	Choose an exercise program that you enjoy.
LIFESTYLE	
✔	Don't smoke.
✔	Do not drink more than two alcoholic beverages a day.
✔	Enjoy life, laugh, and have fun.

Page 1, column 2

Take Care of Your Heart

(Insert picture from data files and add #1 using WordArt)

Make living a heart-healthy lifestyle a top priority!

Page 2, column 1

According to the U.S. Department of Health and Human Services, heart disease is the leading cause of death in the United States. Death from heart attack, stroke, and other cardiovascular diseases claims one American life every 34 seconds.

(continued)

UNBOUND AND LEFTBOUND REPORTS

70d

Review the formatting guides for preparing unbound and leftbound reports that you learned previously. Study the illustration of a two-page unbound report shown below and on pages 3-84 and 3-85. In the following lessons in this module you will learn more advanced report formatting.

Margins: Use the default side margins and bottom margin in an unbound report. In a leftbound report, set the left margin at 1.5", allowing ½" for the binding.

Font size: Use the 11-point default font size.

Spacing: Use the default line spacing for all reports.

Page numbers: ❶ Insert page numbers at the top right. Suppress the page number on the first page.

Enumerated or bulleted items: ❷ Use the default 0.25" indention of bulleted and numbered items. Tap ENTER once after each item.

Content footnote: ❸ Superscript appears in report text and reference displays at the bottom of the page where the reference was cited.

Headings: Headings should reflect a hierarchy of importance.

Title: ❹ Tap ENTER three times to position title at about 2". Apply Title style. Capitalize the first letter of all main words. Shrink the font so the title fits on one line. Tap ENTER twice after the title.

Side heading: ❺ Key at the left margin; apply Heading 1 style. Capitalize the first letter of all main words. Tap ENTER once after the heading.

Paragraph heading: ❻ Key at the left margin. Capitalize the first word and follow the heading with a period. Apply Heading 2 style.

Use the Keep with Next command if necessary to keep side headings from displaying alone at the bottom of the page. (Home/Paragraph dialog box launcher/Line and Page Breaks tab)

95-d2

Brochure

 apple
heart

1. In a new blank document, prepare a two-page brochure that will be printed from front and back and folded in half. Use the illustrations on page 4-61 as a guide for page layout.

2. Use landscape orientation; change the left and right margins to 0.6". Format the document in two columns each with 4.4" width and 1" space between columns.

3. Format for page 1, column 1 (left column):

 a. Turn on Show/Hide; then tap ENTER six times. Move the insertion point to the first ¶ marker. Select WordArt style Fill – Gold, Accent 4, Soft Bevel for the title. Change the font size to 26 point and the color to Orange, Accent 2, Darker 25%.

 b. Insert the image *apple* from the data files. Change the height to 1" and Wrap Text style to Behind Text.

4. Click the insertion point below the illustration. Insert a 2-column, 15-row table. Apply Grid Table 5 Dark – Accent 2 style.

 a. Change the rows containing the headings (*Diet, Exercise, Lifestyle*) to 0.3" high. Place the headings in 14 point and bold.

 b. Insert a ✓ symbol in the left column. Change the size of the ✓ to 16 points and apply bold.

 c. Place a copy of the ✓ in each row. Center the ✓ and the text vertically in the rows as necessary.

 d. Insert a column break below the table to move the insertion point to the top of the right column.

5. Format for page 1, column 2 (front of brochure):

 a. Use 36-point, bold, Monotype Corsiva font and Dark Red color to key the title. Center all text on the front of the brochure.

 b. Insert the image *heart* from the data files. Use WordArt to place #1 as shown; change Wrap Text style to In Front of Text. Change the font color to white. Crop the left and right sides of the picture so it appears as shown on page 4-61. Change the picture to approximately 4.82" high by 4.4" wide.

 c. Key the text in 16-point font below the picture; font style and color should match the title.

6. Format for page 2, column 1:

 a. Key text using default font.

 b. Apply Heading 1 style to heading; change color to red.

 c. Key bulleted text; then select the text and remove the check mark from the "Don't add space between paragraphs of the same style" box (Home/ Paragraph/Indents and Spacing tab/Spacing After).

 d. Select the bulleted text and click Decrease Indent to move it to the left margin.

7. Format for page 2, column 2:

 a. Insert SmartArt. Choose the Basic Pie diagram in the Relationship group. Add a shape to the diagram.

 b. ❋ Click the upper-right quarter of the pie and drag it inward to form a round plate.

 c. Key the text in each shape. To insert text in the shape you just added, right-click the shape and choose Edit text. Change the color of each shape by right-clicking the shape and choosing Fill. Select the stated color.

 Fruits (red); **Grains** (orange);
 Vegetables (green); **Protein** (blue)

 (continued)

Title style
Analysis of Listening Skills Study

1"
The initial phase of a communication skills study of customer service agents at Fernwell Communications has been completed. Findings of this study showed that listening is the communication task that customer service agents spend almost 50 percent of their time doing, but they clearly have had little instruction in performing this skill effectively. The purpose of this report is to highlight major barriers to effective listening and to identify poor listening habits observed in the 50 customer service agents who participated in this study.

Heading 1 style
Communication Skills Ranked

Contrary to common belief, listening is not an easy task. Interestingly, our survey findings showed that listening is a skill that was seldom taught to the participants of this study. The table[1] below compares the rank of four communication skills in terms of amount of time used and time taught. Note that writing ranks last in time used and ranks first in amount of time taught, while listening is used the most and taught the least.

Add Space Before Paragraph to adjust spacing between table and paragraph

Comparison of Communication Skills		
	Rank in Time Used	Rank in Time Taught
Listening	1	4
Speaking	2	3
Reading	3	2
Writing	4	1

The final report will include recommendations that address the components of a listening-training program. Training objectives will address the needs of the participants as determined by this study.

Issues in Listening

Two issues in listening were considered in the observation of listening skills. Observers considered the rate that listeners can process words and common barriers to listening.

Heading 2 style
Rate. Studies show that listeners can recognize words at a rate approximately five times faster than the rate at which speakers can talk. With the mind processing information at over 1,000 words per minute, the listener is challenged to listen actively.

Listening barriers. Listeners are also confronted with other barriers to effective listening. These barriers might include assumptions already made about the topic, the speaker, the potential message, or the specific setting. All of these assumptions may lead the listener to tune out what the speaker is

Footnote
[1] Results of survey administered prior to the observation period.

Unbound Report—Page 1

9. Format the second page:

 a. Click the insertion point at the beginning of the left column on the second page. Insert a column break (you will need to do this two times); a column break code is inserted in the left column, and the text moves to the right column.

 b. Click at the beginning of the column break; if needed, change the font to Calibri 11 point and tap ENTER approximately 26 times. This inserts the line between columns on the page.

 c. Copy the logo from the banner and position it in the first column; apply In Front of Text Wrapping. Click on a ¶ marker below the logo and key **Arondale Medical Center News**. Click on the following ¶ marker and key **Page 2**. Bold the text, apply 12-point Automatic color, and Center.

10. Format the table as follows:

 a. Adjust column widths. Use a decimal tab to align numbers.

 b. Change the height of all the rows to 0.3".

 c. Apply Grid Table 5 Dark – Accent 6 style. Bold and center all column heads. Center all text vertically in cells.

11. Tap ENTER following the table and key a byline right-aligned using your name.

12. Save and close. (95-d1)

 QUICK ✔

Check your document against the illustration below.

actually saying. Another barrier may simply be fatigue—the listener is too tired, too hungry, or too busy to listen. Distractions often influence the listener's ability to be an active listener. These annoyances may include loud noises near the speaker or a room that is too cold or too warm.

Heading 1 style

Poor Listening Habits

Observers noted that poor listening habits are quite common and often unknown to listeners. The following habits were noted by the observers.

Bulleted list

- Pretending to listen by nodding, saying yes, and looking directly at the speaker fakes the customer into believing that the customer service agent is listening.
- Not looking at the customer results in poor listening as facial expressions and gestures are not communicated.
- Recording detailed notes results in poor listening or over listening.
- Making judgments about the customer or the topic is not effective.
- Rushing the customer causes the customer to think the customer service agent's time is being wasted.
- Interrupting the customer is rude and does not enhance listening.
- Showing interest in something else and allowing distractions to obtain the customer service agent's attention result in poor listening.

Summary

Understanding that listening is not easy is a first step in becoming a better listener. Identifying individual habits that do not enhance effective listening is the next step.

Unbound Report—Page 2

65 with chronic medical conditions who have not had this vaccine should also get this shot. The pneumonia vaccine prevents the most common cause of bacterial pneumonia that can result in hospitalization or death.

Disease Surveillance Update

The table below contains a summary of the surveillance data obtained from county health departments in 2016. No incidences of congenital rubella syndrome or rubella were reported in the state during the 2016 year.

Disease	Age Groups		
	0–4 Years	5–17 Years	18+ Years
Hepatitis A	123	305	534
Hepatitis B	83	215	350
Measles	25	47	13
Pertussis	305	278	153
Tetanus	17	31	43

3. Set up the columns in the newsletter:
 a. Select all the text below the Section Break (Continuous).
 b. Click Layout/Page Setup/Columns and choose More Columns.
 c. In the Columns dialog box, choose two columns. Deselect the box for Equal column width.
 d. Key 1.25" for the width of column 1. Click in the Width box for column 2; it automatically changes to 4.75".
 e. Place a check mark in the Line between box. Click OK.
4. Click the insertion point at the top of the left column; insert a column break.
5. Click the insertion point to the left of the column break code in the left column; tap ENTER. Click on the ¶ marker above the column break.
6. Insert a Simple Text Box and key **Protect Yourself Now!**
7. Format the text box as follows:
 a. Select the text box and change the text direction to Rotate all text 270° (Drawing Tools Format/Text Direction).
 b. Change the text to 48-point font. Increase the height of the text box until the text fits on one line. Change the Wrap Text to Square, if needed.
 c. Change the zoom to One Page. Move the text box so that it is attractively placed in the column.
 d. Change the color of the text to Orange, Accent 2, Darker 25%. Click Text Outline and apply the same color.
 e. Remove the outline of the text box (Drawing Tools Format/Shape Styles/Shape Outline/No Outline).
8. Insert a clip art of a clock in the second paragraph; change the Wrap Text format to Square. Size the picture appropriately.

(continued)

TIP

Use the Quick Check on page 4-57 as a guide for page layout.

1. In a new blank document, key the report on pages 3-86 and 3-87. Use default side margins. Tap ENTER three times to position the title at about 2".

2. Apply Title style to the main heading; tap ENTER twice (one blank line below heading).

3. Apply Heading 1 style to the side headings and Heading 2 to the paragraph headings.

4. Apply the Grid Table 4 – Accent 5 style to the table. Adjust column widths. Merge the cells in the first row and center the title of the table. Center Align the cells with numbers. Center the table horizontally.

5. In the paragraph below the table, apply Add Space Before Paragraph to add space below the table. (Home/Paragraph/Line and Paragraph Spacing/Add Space Before Paragraph)

6. Insert the following content footnote marked in the report.

 [1] **Results of survey administered prior to the observation period.**

7. Use the Page Number command to number the pages at the top right. Select the Plain Number 3 number style. Click Different First Page to suppress the page number on the first page.

8. Save and close. (70-d1)

Analysis of Listening Skills Study (Title style)

The initial phase of a communication skills study of customer service agents at Fernwell Communications has been completed. Findings of this study showed that listening is the communication task that customer service agents spend almost 50 percent of their time doing, but they clearly have had little instruction in performing this skill effectively. The purpose of this report is to highlight major barriers to effective listening and to identify poor listening habits observed in the 50 customer service agents who participated in this study.

Communication Skills Ranked (Heading 1 style)

Contrary to common belief, listening is not an easy task. Interestingly, our survey findings showed that listening is a skill that was seldom taught to the participants of this study. The table[1] below compares the rank of four communication skills in terms of amount of time used and time taught. Note that writing ranks last in time used and ranks first in amount of time taught, while listening is used the most and taught the least.

Comparison of Communication Skills		
	Rank in Time Used	Rank in Time Taught
Listening	1	4
Speaking	2	3
Reading	3	2
Writing	4	1

(continued)

Lesson 95 Health Promotions Documents

Apply It

 95-d1

Newsletter

 arondale banner

1. Open *arondale banner* from the data files and turn on Show/Hide.
2. Place the insertion point on the ¶ marker below the section break. Key the text below; apply Heading 1 style to side headings.

This special edition of the newsletter is published due to the rising concern among the general public of the increasing number of cases of influenza, pneumonia, and other vaccine-preventable diseases. The latest updates regarding immunization and vaccines and their availability are available at your county health department. If you have further questions on immunizations, please contact the Public Immunization Coordinator at the local health department.

Still Some Time Left

Influenza will be transmitted through the winter and into the spring. You can get your vaccination through January and still be protected. Despite the overall vaccine shortage, supplies are available for persons at high risk. Plenty of doses of preservative-free 0.25 ml doses, suitable for children 6 months through 3 years old, are on hand at local health departments.

Nasal *SprayAway* Available

Federal restrictions on the use of the nasal spray flu vaccine, *SprayAway,* have been lifted. Individuals between the ages of 5 and 49 with no chronic medical conditions and who are not pregnant can be administered *SprayAway.* It is highly recommended that individuals in the following groups get the *SprayAway* vaccine.

 Insert round bullets →

All health-care workers
Adults caring for children younger than 6 months of age
School-aged children
Those who come in contact with large numbers of people

Influenza Vaccine Promotion

Flyers promoting influenza vaccination are available in English, Spanish, Chinese, Japanese, Tagalog, and Vietnamese. These flyers can be downloaded from the Immunization Organization website at www.vaccinateyou.org.

Pneumonia Vaccine Recommended

A pneumonia shot is highly recommended for all adults 65 years of age and older who have not had this vaccine. Individuals between the ages of 2 and

(continued)

The final report will include recommendations that address the components of a listening-training program. Training objectives will address the needs of the participants as determined by this study.

Issues in Listening (Heading 1 style)

Two issues in listening were considered in the observation of listening skills. Observers considered the rate that listeners can process words and common barriers to listening.

(Heading 2 style)

Rate. Studies show that listeners can recognize words at a rate approximately five times faster than the rate at which speakers can talk. With the mind processing information at over 1,000 words per minute, the listener is challenged to listen actively.

(Heading 2 style)

Listening barriers. Listeners are also confronted with other barriers to effective listening. These barriers might include assumptions already made about the topic, the speaker, the potential message, or the specific setting. All of these assumptions may lead the listener to tune out what the speaker is actually saying. Another barrier may simply be fatigue—the listener is too tired, too hungry, or too busy to listen. Distractions often influence the listener's ability to be an active listener. These annoyances may include loud noises near the speaker or a room that is too cold or too warm.

Poor Listening Habits (Heading 1 style)

Observers noted that poor listening habits are quite common and often unknown to listeners. The following habits were noted by the observers.

- Pretending to listen by nodding, saying yes, and looking directly at the speaker fakes the customer into believing that the customer service agent is listening.
- Not looking at the customer results in poor listening as facial expressions and gestures are not communicated.
- Recording detailed notes results in poor listening or over listening.
- Making judgments about the customer or the topic is not effective.
- Rushing the customer causes the customer to think the customer service agent's time is being wasted.
- Interrupting the customer is rude and does not enhance listening.
- Showing interest in something else and allowing distractions to obtain the customer service agent's attention result in poor listening.

Summary (Heading 1 style)

Understanding that listening is not easy is a first step in becoming a better listener. Identifying individual habits that do not enhance effective listening is the next step.

Headache	Most people with colds do not have headaches.	Headaches are present in about 80% of all flu cases.
Sore Throat	A sore throat is often present with a cold.	Flu victims do not commonly complain of having a sore throat.
Sneezing	Sneezing is common with a cold.	Sneezing is not common with the flu.
Coughing	A hacking, mucus-producing cough is often present with a cold.	A dry cough (non-mucus-producing) is often present with the flu.
Stuffy Nose	A stuffy nose is commonly present with a cold.	Flu victims do not commonly have a stuffy nose.

Stop by and see me in the medical center if I can be of further assistance or call me at extension 5378 if you have questions.

94-d3

Sort Table

1. Open document *94-d2* and select the table.
2. Sort the table by Symptoms in Ascending order (Table Tools Layout/Data/Sort). Remember to indicate that your list has a header row.
3. Save and close. (*94-d3*)

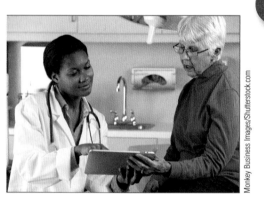

Monkey Business Images/Shutterstock.com

! WORKPLACE SUCCESS

Confidentiality

Information contained in a patient's record is confidential and should not be revealed without the patient's consent unless required by law. Confidentiality must be protected in order for patients to feel comfortable about revealing personal information. Health professionals are obligated to report findings of the following nature:

- A patient has threatened another person, and there is reason to believe that the threat may be carried out.
- Knife and gunshot wounds and injuries that may indicate child abuse must be reported.
- Communicable diseases, such as AIDS, hepatitis, and sexually transmitted diseases, must be reported.

70-d2

Edit Report

1. Open *70-d1* and apply the Slate document theme.
2. Change the left margin to 1.5" to convert this unbound report to a leftbound report.
3. Select the footnote number in the text and drag it to display after the word *survey* in the second sentence of that paragraph.
4. Double-click in the header and change the page number style to Accent Bar 2.
5. Show the navigation pane. (View/Show/Navigation Pane)
 - Click Headings and then the heading *Summary* to move to that section.
 - Click Pages and click on the miniature page 1 to move to the first page. **Note:** Use this shortcut to move quickly in reports as you complete this module.
6. Save and close. (*70-d2*)

70-d3

Multilevel List

1. In a new blank document, key an outline for the report keyed in *70-d1*. Use the multilevel list with Roman numerals (I., A., 1.). Tap ENTER three times and key the title at about 2"; tap ENTER twice; apply Title style.
2. Check your document against the illustration.
3. Save and close. (*70-d3*)

QUICK ✓

Analysis of Listening Skills Study

I. Communication Skills Ranked

II. Issues in Listening
 A. Rate
 B. Listening barriers

III. Poor Listening Habits

IV. Summary

94-d2

Two-page Memorandum with Table

arondale letterhead

Sample document and embedded table. © Cengage Learning. Arondale logo © Cengage Learning, courtesy of Donna Woo.

1. Open *arondale letterhead* from the data files and key the two-page memo shown on the next two pages. Supply all necessary memo parts.

2. Insert a table after the fourth paragraph; the table will continue on the second page. Change the width of column A to 1.6" and column B to 2". Change the height of row 1 to 0.5".

3. Apply Grid Table 5 Dark – Accent 2 style. Align Center column heads. Center the table horizontally on the page.

4. Select row 1 and click Repeat Header Rows.

5. Insert the second-page header.

6. Save and close. (*94-d2*)

TO: All Employees | FROM: Paula Jens, RN, MSN | Medical Center Coordinator | DATE: Current date | SUBJECT: Flu-like Illness

The local health board is anticipating that the number of people contracting influenza will reach record highs this winter. The medical center, in cooperation with the nursing students from Arondale University, will be offering free flu shots next week. Please call extension 5378 for an appointment.

As a safety precaution, we are asking employees with flu-like symptoms to practice self-isolation. This means staying away from work and limiting interactions with other people for at least 24 hours after fever symptoms have subsided.

We encourage hand hygiene and respiratory etiquette of people who are well and also those that have any flu-like symptoms. Wash your hands frequently with soap and water. Cover your nose and mouth with tissue when coughing or sneezing. If no tissue is available, use a shirt sleeve or elbow. Small bottles of hand sanitizer are available in the medical center free of charge.

Below is a chart describing how symptoms are manifested in a cold or flu virus.

Symptom	Cold Symptoms	Flu Symptoms
Chills	It is unusual for a patient to have chills with a cold.	Over 60% of flu cases include chills. Unexplained chills and shivering are often a sign of the flu.
Fever	A fever is rare with a cold.	A fever is present in approximately 80% of all flu cases. A flu victim usually has a fever of 100° F or higher for several days.
Aches	Mild body aches and pains are often associated with a cold.	Aches and pains are more severe with the flu.

(continued)

Lesson 71 Report with Section Breaks

New Commands
- Header and Footer
- Cover Page
- Section Breaks
- Page Number Format

 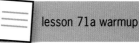
New Commands

71b

HEADERS AND FOOTERS

A header appears in the top margin of a multipage report; a footer appears in the bottom margin. The built-in gallery offers a wide variety of preformatted attractive headers and footers. The Retrospect header and footer were selected in the illustration at the left.

To insert a header or footer:

Insert/Header & Footer/Header or Footer

1. From the built-in gallery of header or footer styles, click the down arrow to browse the various styles and select the desired style.

2. If needed, click [Type the document title] and key the text for the header or select the date if included in the selected style.

3. From the Options group, click Different First Page to remove the page number from the first page if desired.

To create a custom header or footer:

Double-click in the header or footer area. Key the header or footer; add the page number if desired. Suppress the header or footer on the first page.

To remove a header or footer:

Follow the same path and click Remove Header or Remove Footer.

Insert/Header & Footer/Header or Footer

1. Open *benefits* from the data files and insert the Banded header. Click [DOCUMENT TITLE] in the header and key **Benefits: A Matter of Choice**. Click Go to Footer in the Navigation group.

2. From the Header and Footer group, insert the Banded footer, which includes the page number. Click Different First Page.

3. Save and close. (*71-drill1*)

MEDICAL CORRESPONDENCE

You will be keying medical correspondence for Arondale Medical Center. The medical center is affiliated with the Arondale University College of Medicine. The center is operated by private medical practitioners and university staff. You will be keying letters and reports to patients, other medical firms, government, and regulatory agencies. Arondale Medical Center sends informational newsletters and brochures to community members promoting health awareness and disease prevention.

Apply It

94–d1

Modified Block Letter

 arondale letterhead

1. Open *arondale letterhead* from the data files and key the letter below in modified block style with open punctuation. Supply all necessary letter parts. Key the date on line 2.4".
2. Center the address lines for Good Samaritan Medical Center and press SHIFT + ENTER for correct spacing between the address lines.
3. The letter is from **David Dostourian, M.D., President**.
4. Save and close. (*94-d1*)

Dr. Sabrina Rodriguez, M.D. | Immunization Coordinator | Quality Care Medical Center | 5252 Lamar Boulevard | Austin, TX 78704-3088

Arondale Medical Center has an agreement with the Travis County Health Department which enables us to obtain vaccinations and supplies at no cost. These include Hepatitis A and B, influenza, and pneumococcal vaccines. This agreement requires that we keep detailed and accurate paperwork pertaining to the storage and administration of the vaccine.

The vaccine is currently being stored at:

Good Samaritan Medical Center
c/o Dr. Abrahim Jordan
1560 Broadway Avenue
Austin, TX 78704-1234

The refrigerator containing the vaccine is in the infusion room. The temperature is to be measured twice a day and recorded on the form; use the thermometer in the door of the refrigerator for measuring. It is the duty of the clinic coordinator to ensure that this log is kept current. Under no circumstances should false values be added to the chart.

This agreement with Travis County Health Department provides us with an excellent opportunity to directly help the medically underserved population in the area. I am confident that you will maintain a strong relationship with the health department.

COVER PAGE

 Longer and more formal reports include a cover or title page as the first page of the report. Using the Cover Page command, the user can select from a variety of attractive cover pages.

To create a cover page:
Insert/Pages/Cover Page

1. Click the scroll arrows in the gallery to select the desired style ❶. The cover page opens as a *Word* document.

2. Select [Document title] ❷ and key the report title. Repeat for all other items located in the template. **Note:** A blank page follows the cover page for keying the report.

DRILL 2 COVER PAGE

Insert/Pages/Cover Page

1. In a new blank document, create a cover page using the Cover Page command. Select the Whisp style in the Built-In category.

2. Click [Document title] and key **Cyberspace Security Issues**.

3. Key **Review of Company Policies** as the document subtitle.

4. Click [Date], select the drop-list arrow, and select the current date. Key **Jun Yoshino** as the author name.

5. Key **Mac-Donovan Industries, Inc**. as the company name. It will be shown in All Caps.

6. Save and close. (*71-drill2*)

SECTION BREAKS

A section is part of a document that may have its own look. You might think of a section as a document within a document but with unique differences such as different margins, headers, or page number style. A section break divides a document into sections. Section breaks either can begin on a new page or you can choose to have the section break begin at the insertion point. Next Page and Continuous are the two types you will use most often; you will use Continuous breaks in this module.

The preliminary pages of a report are numbered at the bottom of the page with lowercase Roman numerals. The body of the report is usually numbered in the upper right with Arabic numerals. Page numbers are inserted as either headers or footers. These differences in page numbering are handled with a section break.

Health and Medical Documents

LEARNING OUTCOMES

- Key and format medical correspondence.
- Key and format medical newsletters and brochures.
- Key and format SOAP notes.
- Key and format medical forms.
- Key and format medical reports.

Lesson 94 Medical Correspondence

Warmup *Lesson 94a Warmup*

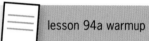 lesson 94a warmup

Skill Building

94b Timed Writing

1. Key a 3' timing on each paragraph; work to increase speed.
2. Key a 3' timing on all paragraphs; work for control.

	gwam	3'

Something that you can never escape is your attitude. It will be — 4 | 73
with you forever. However, you decide whether your attitude is an — 9 | 77
asset or a liability for you. Your attitude reflects the way you feel — 13 | 82
about the world you abide in and everything that is a part of that world. — 18 | 86
It reflects the way you feel about yourself, about your environment, — 23 | 91
and about other people who are part of your environment. Oftentimes, — 27 | 95
people with a positive attitude are people who are extremely successful. — 32 | 100

At times we all have experiences that cause us to be negative. The — 36 | 105
difference between a positive and a negative person is that the positive — 41 | 109
person rebounds very quickly from a bad experience; the negative — 45 | 114
person does not. The positive person is a person who usually looks on — 50 | 118
the bright side of things and recognizes the world as a place of promise, — 55 | 123
hope, joy, excitement, and purpose. A negative person generally has — 59 | 128
just the opposite view of the world. Remember, others want to be around — 64 | 132
those who are positive but tend to avoid those who are negative. — 68 | 137

3' | 1 | 2 | 3 | 4 |

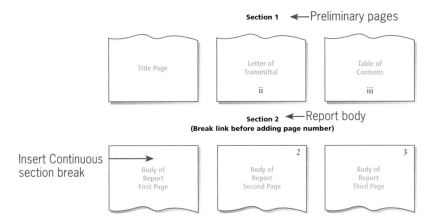

Section 1 ←—Preliminary pages

Title Page

Letter of Transmittal

ii

Table of Contents

iii

Section 2 ←—Report body
(Break link before adding page number)

Insert Continuous section break

Body of Report First Page

2

Body of Report Second Page

3

Body of Report Third Page

To use different page number formats within the same document, you insert a section break at the beginning of the report body. As a result, the title page and other preliminary pages become Section 1; the body of the report is in Section 2. *Word* continues to use the same format for page numbers in a new section until you break the link between the sections. Later in this module you will add additional preliminary pages and number the preliminary pages as well as the report page.

To enter a section break:
Layout/Page Setup/Breaks

1. From the Section Breaks category, click the desired section break ❶, and then OK.

 Next Page: Begins a new page at the point the section break is entered.

 Continuous: Begins a new section at the insertion point on the same page.

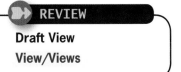

REVIEW

Draft View
View/Views

In Draft View, section breaks appear as a dotted line with the type of break indicated.

Section Break (Next Page)
Section Break (Continuous)
Section Break (Even Page)
Section Break (Odd Page)

The current section number displays on the status bar. If you do not see the section number, place the insertion point on the status bar and right-click. Select Section.

Section: 1 Page 1 of 5 At: 3.1"

To delete a section:

1. In Draft View, select the section break to be deleted.
2. Tap DELETE.

1. In a new blank document, key the following report. Use default theme, Title style, and Heading 1 style for headings. Tap ENTER twice after the title.
2. Save and close. (*93-d4*)

Guides for Selecting References

Deciding who to select as references is a very important strategic decision. Give careful thought to the individuals you select as references.

Criteria for Selection

The key is to select individuals who know you well, will provide a strong, positive recommendation, and who can support your ability to do the job for which you are applying. Employers and former employers can attest to your job performance as well as colleagues and team members. Instructors can also provide valuable insight into academic ability and share workplace attributes, such as attendance, punctuality, and ability to work with others. Friends, relatives, neighbors, or others who might be viewed as biased in your favor by the prospective employer should not be selected as references unless they are employees of the company considering you for a position.

The references selected for one position may not be as strong for a different position. Banking professors may be a better choice for a position in a bank, whereas marketing professors may be a better choice for a similar position in a public relations firm. Use references who can legitimately give you a good recommendation and who also would have credibility with the company.

Permission to Use References

Not only is it good manners to request permission to list a person as a reference; it is strategically important to do so. If a person hesitates, do not select that person as a reference. Hesitation is a sign that the person may not give you as strong a recommendation as you would like to have. Requesting permission gives you an opportunity to refresh the person's memory about you and to update him or her on recent accomplishments. You should also confirm position titles and contact information to ensure that you provide the employer with accurate information. Thank your references and update them after the job search process has been completed.

Be extremely careful about posting reference information to your website. Many references object to having their information posted on the Internet and will not serve as a reference if you post it. Posting information to an applicant tracking system on a secure company website usually is acceptable.

BREAK LINK BETWEEN SECTIONS AND INSERT PAGE NUMBERS

Word continues to use the same format for page numbers in a new section as it did in the previous section. In order for the page number format to be different between sections, you must break the link between the sections. When the link is broken, the preliminary pages can be numbered in Roman numerals and the report body in Arabic numbers.

Step 1: Break the links in Section 2:

1. Scroll to the second page of the report body. Move the insertion point to the top 0.5" ❶ and double-click to position the insertion point in the header section. Header – Section 2 label displays and the Same as Previous label displays at the right.

Header & Footer Tools Design/Navigation

2. In the Navigation group, click the Link to Previous button ❷ to break the link between the headers in Section 1 (preliminary pages) and Section 2 (body of the report). The Go to Header button is dimmed, meaning the insertion point is in the header.

3. In the Navigation group, click Go to Footer to move to the footer of Section 2. Click the Link to Previous button to break the link between the footers in Sections 1 and 2.

Note: The Link to Previous button will display in dark gray until the link is successfully broken.

Step 2: Insert page numbers in Section 2:

4. Click Go to Header to return to the header section where the page number is to be inserted.

5. In the Header & Footer group, click Page Number. Click Top of Page and select a page number style that displays numbers at the top right.

6. From the Options group, click Different First Page to select the option to suppress page numbers on the first page. **Note:** If cover page is inserted already, this option is automatically selected.

Step 3: Start number at page 1:

7. In the Header & Footer group, click Page Number and then Format Page Number. Click the Start at up arrow until 1 displays ❸.

8. Check the numbers in Section 2. No number should appear on page 1, and remaining pages should be numbered at the top right.

9:30	Call to Order John Bennett
9:35	Open Issues	
	Conflict of Interest Policy Roger Lettsworth
10:05	New Business	
	Investment Policy Jeffery Harsh
	Portfolio Performance Review Jeffery Harsh
	Investment Manager Performance Jeffery Harsh
11:00	Adjournment	

93-d2

Agenda

 changes to draft

TIP

Check to see that your name is listed in the User name box on your computer.

1. Open *changes to draft* from the data files and make the following changes to finalize the agenda:
 a. Delete the word *Draft* from the Agenda title.
 b. Make the change requested by John Bennett.
 c. Move *Investment Policy* to the position indicated by Kevin Vickers and change to his name as requested.
 d. Adjust line spacing if necessary. Then delete comments.
2. Save and close. (*93-d2*)

93-d3

Interview Checklist

1. In a new blank document, use default theme and tap ENTER three times; key **Prepare for Success** and apply Title style; then key **Develop an Interview Checklist** and apply Subtitle style.
2. Key the checklist shown below; use the customized bullet from Wingdings.
3. Save and close. (*93-d3*)

Preparation is an important key to success in job interviewing. Use this simple checklist as you prepare for a job interview. Seek the advice of experts and continue to add items to this checklist.

☑ Am I comfortable with my knowledge about the company?
☑ Am I prepared to dress professionally for the interview?
☑ How long will it take me to get to the interview at least 15 minutes early?
☑ What materials should I take to the interview?
☑ Am I prepared for questions that might be asked of me, and what are the best answers to these questions?
☑ Do I know the interviewer's name, and can I pronounce it correctly?
☑ How do I handle the handshake?
☑ When should I be seated?
☑ How important is eye contact?
☑ What does my body language tell the interviewer?
☑ What questions can I ask the interviewer?
☑ Am I comfortable with my answers to the previous questions?
☑ If not, I need to do more preparation for the interview.

Troubleshooting Tips

Save the document before you paginate it. If you have trouble with the page numbers, close the document without saving and start over; the reason for not saving it first is that *Word* seems to remember what you did previously and starts doing it automatically.

Important Points to Remember

1. Click Link to Previous before inserting the page number.
2. To suppress the page number on the first page, select the Different First Page option.

DRILL 3 — SECTIONS

 practice

1. Open *practice* from the data files and position the insertion point at the beginning of page 2 (cover page is page 1). *Hint:* Click Show/Hide and click on the first paragraph marker at the top of the page.

2. Insert a Continuous section break.

3. Check the status bar; if you do not see the section and page number, right-click the insertion point on the status bar. Select Section.

> Section: 2 Page 2 of 3 At: 1"

4. Position the insertion point in the header of page 2 of the body of Section 2 (Header – Section 2—not First Page – Header). The status bar reads *Section 2 page 3 of 3*.

 - Click Link to Previous to break the links between the headers in Sections 1 and 2. This button will not display in dark gray if the link is correctly broken.

 - Go to footer of Section of Section 2 (page 2). Break the link between the footers for both sections.

5. Go to the header of Section 2 and insert the ViewMaster header.

6. Click Go to Footer and insert the ViewMaster (Horizontal) footer. Click Date and select the current date.

7. Click Page Number and Format Page Numbers. Change the page number format to Start at page 1. The Different First Page option should already be checked to suppress the page number on the first page of the report.

8. Save and close. (*71-drill3*)

QUICK ✔

Check your document against the illustration below.

Page 1

Page 2

Page 3

Lesson 93 Assessment Modules 15 and 16

Skill Building

93b Timed Writing

Key two 3" timed writings; work on the control level.

gwam 1' | 3'

What do you think about when you hear individuals being called	12	4
student-athletes? Many people think only of the very visible football or	27	9
basketball players who attract a lot of attention and often get special	41	14
treatment on campus. Few people think about the large numbers of	54	18
young men and women who put in long hours working and training to	67	22
be the very best they can be in a wide variety of sports. These students	81	27
may never receive any type of recognition in the news media, and they	95	32
do not attract large crowds to watch them perform. They frequently	108	36
excel in both academic and athletic performance.	118	39
What does a student-athlete in one of the less visible sports with	13	44
very little opportunity to become a professional athlete gain from the	27	48
significant investment of time and effort in a sport? To be successful in	42	53
a sport, a student must be organized, be an effective time manager, and	56	58
have self-confidence. An athlete learns that teamwork, ethical conduct,	70	63
and hard work are a major part of success in any type of endeavor. The	84	67
skills do not apply just to sports; they also apply to your job and your	99	72
life. Most important of all, these individuals are doing what they really	113	77
enjoy doing.	116	78

1' | 1 | 2 | 3 | 4 | 5 | 6 | 7 | 8 | 9 | 10 | 11 | 12 | 13 | 14 |
3' | 1 | | 2 | | 3 | | 4 | | 5 |

Apply It

93-d1

Draft Agenda

1. In a new blank document, apply Metropolitan theme with default formatting style. Tap ENTER three times.
2. Key the heading **Draft Agenda | Investment Committee | Board Room | January 9, 201-, 9:30 a.m.** and format as follows:
 a. Apply Title style to first line of heading.
 b. Apply Heading 1 style to second line of heading.
 c. Apply Heading 2 style to third and fourth lines. Center all lines.
3. Tap ENTER twice; set a 1" left tab and a 6.5" right-aligned leader tab and key the body of the agenda shown on the next page.
4. Save and close. (93-d1)

(continued)

Document Design

71c

REPORT WITH HEADERS AND FOOTERS

Built-in headers and footers enhance the professional design of a report. Remember a page number must display either in the header or the footer of a multiple-page document. The page number is often suppressed on the first page.

Apply It

Report

 injuries

1. In a new blank document, key the leftbound report shown on page 3-95. Tap ENTER three times to position the title at about 2". Apply Title style to the main heading, Heading 1 to side headings, and Heading 2 to paragraph headings. Tap ENTER twice after the title.

2. Change the left margin to 1.5".

3. Apply the Retrospect document theme. Shrink title font to fit on one line.

4. Format the bulleted lists with square bullets.

5. Insert the Retrospect cover page. Key the following information:

 Document title: Refer to report title for *71-d1*. Shrink to fit on one line.

 Document subtitle: Click the subtitle text box; click the Subtitle control above the text box, and tap DELETE.

 Author: **Stephen Coleman**

 Company: **Galey Financial, LLC**

 Company address: **2901 Manhattan Road, San Jose, CA 95101-2901**

6. Insert a Continuous section break at the first paragraph marker on the first page of the report.

7. Position the insertion point in the header of page 2 of the body in Section 2 (Header – Section 2—not First Page – Header). The status bar reads *Section 2 page 3 of 3*.

 • Break the links between the headers for both sections.

 • Go to the footer of Section 2 (page 2). Break the link between the footers for both sections.

Break the link for the header and footer in Section 2 before inserting the header and footer style.

(continued)

92-d2

Job Posting

hess letterhead

1. Open the *hess letterhead* data file and key the abbreviated job description. Position title at 2" and apply Title style. Apply Heading 1 style to the two headings.
2. Save and close. (*92-d2*)

Administrative Associate Position Available

Hess Property Enterprises is seeking a talented administrative professional to join the administrative support team in Hess Office Park. The candidate will provide support services for the executive staff and for tenants. Must have excellent customer service, communication, and Microsoft Office skills. The salary is commensurate with education and experience.

Key Duties and Responsibilities

- Serve as receptionist managing telephone calls professionally.
- Prepare correspondence and reports as requested.
- Work with tenants to ensure that their needs are met effectively.
- Schedule and maintain calendars for executive team.

Qualifications

- AS degree in office or business administration or equivalent required.
- Two years of office experience preferred.
- Knowledge of Word, Excel, and PowerPoint.
- Excellent customer service and communication skills.

A complete job description is available on the Hess Property Enterprises website along with information about submitting applications.

92-d3

Compose Memo

hess memo

1. Compose a memo from Mr. Hess to tenants in Hess Office Park sending them the job posting and asking them to refer qualified applicants. He will offer them a $200 gift certificate to be used at any business in Hess Office Park for each referral they provide who submits a resume for the position. Add appropriate information that you think recipients would like to have.
2. Save and close. (*92-d3*)

8. Go to the header of Section 2 and insert the Retrospect header. Select the current date.
 - Go to the footer of Section 2 and insert the Retrospect footer.
 - Change the page number format to begin with page 1. The Different First Page option should already be checked to suppress the header and footer on the first page of the report.

9. Save and close. (*71-d1*)

Guidelines to Escape Computer-Related Injuries

Repetitive stress injuries (RSI), cumulative trauma disorder (CTD), and carpal tunnel syndrome (CTS) have mushroomed to afflict everyone from administrative assistants to executives with hurting muscles, tendons, and nerves. Hand-arm alignment is one of the causes of keyboard repetitive stress injuries. Misalignment causes muscles to become overworked, causing stress and fatigue in the hands, arms, neck, and shoulders. Improper use of the mouse causes stress injuries as well.

To avoid computer-related injuries, all computer users can benefit from understanding the basic guidelines for proper positioning at the computer and effective workstation design that are presented in this report.

Position Yourself Properly

Preventing tired wrists and hands is really a matter of taking charge of your posture and computer work environment. Awkward posture while keying and failure to change your keying or sitting position can add to wear and tear on your wrists and hands.

Hand position. Keep your wrists and hands straight. When you work with straight wrists and fingers, the nerves, muscles, and tendons stay relaxed and comfortable. Therefore, they are less likely to develop the strains and pains that are often associated with keying.

Insert file injuries; format like the rest of the report.

6. Do you tilt your neck backward to see the computer screen? (No)
7. Do you take two 5-minute breaks and one 15-minute break in the morning and afternoon? (Yes)
8. Do you vary your activities to break the repetitive motion? (Yes)
9. Do you drink plenty of water to lubricate your joints? (Yes)

For each of your responses that do not match the desired response, please accept the challenge today to correct the undesired practice and avoid computer-related stress injuries.

 REVIEW

Insert File

Insert/Text/Object down list arrow/Text from File

situation might be that you can recommend only one person for an award trip, and the selection basis you use when two people have equal qualifications.

Often interviews focus on soft skills because they are important on the job, and they are difficult to measure and document. An example might be: Who on your team, other than you, had the very best client or customer service skills? Describe three personal attributes that made that individual so successful in working with clients and customers. How would you rank yourself on those three attributes with one being your greatest strength, two being the next, and three being the lowest?

Observations

An important reason to schedule a face-to-face interview is to be able to observe the applicant's body language and other soft skills. Examples to observe include:

Professional appearance.

Handshake.

Punctuality.

Manners, mannerisms, gum chewing, or unprofessional behavior.

Way the applicant interacted with people encountered other than the interviewer.

Table manners if a meal is provided.

Respect for others.

Way the person makes judgments.

QUICK ✓ Compare the format of your document to the one shown below.

Edit Report

1. Open *71-d1* and change the cover page to Banded.
2. Double-click in the header on the second page of the report and change the header style to Facet (Odd Page).
3. Double-click in the footer and change the footer style to Ion (Dark).
4. Click in the footer of the first page of the report (First Page footer – Section 2). Insert the Ion (Dark) footer. **Note:** A header should not appear on page 1 of the report body.
5. Save and close. (*71-d2*)

QUICK ✔

Check your document against the illustration below.

Footer displays on first page

1. Open *handout* from the data files and key the notes shown below at the end of the document.

2. Apply Heading 1 style to *Interviews* and Heading 2 style to all other side headings. Add bullets to the list of thing to observe. Number pages at the top using Rounded Rectangle 3; do not show number on first page.

3. Save and close. (*92-d1*)

Interviews

Effective interviews are based on the assumption that applicants are carefully screened to ensure that they have the qualifications required to be successful on the job. However, employers often indicate that the person they envisioned from reading application documents is not the same as the person they actually talk with about the job. This explains why virtually all employers insist on interviewing an individual before hiring that individual. Thus, it is important to make sure the interview meets legal requirements and produces reliable and valid information.

Types of Interviews

Different types of interviews can be used. Examples include:

Face-to-Face Interviews: Most employers believe that in-person interviews are more effective than telephone, video, or virtual interviews. However, face-to-face interviews are more expensive. If face-to-face interviews are not used for the first interview, the final applicants are generally invited for a second in-person interview.

Structured Interviews: Most employers prepare carefully for interviews. One way to structure an interview is to develop a list of questions to be asked in the interview and to ensure that all applicants answer the same questions. Many employers like to follow up on questions, and they do not limit themselves to just the list of required questions.

Panel Interviews: Several people interview the same applicant at the same time. They may use predetermined questions, or they may vary questions.

Interview Questions

Most interviews start with easy questions that give the applicant an opportunity to talk about themselves, their interest in this particular job, and the value they think they can bring to the job. These questions serve as a warm-up and enable the applicant to get comfortable and develop confidence. These types of questions also give the interviewer an opportunity to observe the applicant and assess verbal and nonverbal skills.

Some of the most effective questions are behavioral questions. Examples are: What was the most difficult decision you made in your last job? How did you go about making it? Behavioral questions should include both positive and negative aspects of a job. On one extreme, a question might focus on how you handle conflict situations, and on the other extreme, the

(continued)

Lesson 72 Report with Preliminary Pages

New Command
• Table of Contents

Warmup *Lesson 72a Warmup*

lesson 72a warmup

New Commands

72b

TABLE OF CONTENTS

A table of contents (illustrated at the left) includes the side headings and often the paragraph headings within the report. If these headings have been formatted using styles (Heading 1 and Heading 2), a table of contents can be created automatically using the Table of Contents command. A table of contents can be modified after it has been created. Similar to a cover page, the table of contents is one of the preliminary pages of a report (see page 3-90).

In Web Layout view, the entries in the table of contents are hyperlinks. Clicking an entry moves the insertion point to the appropriate page in the document. In Print Layout view, tapping CTRL plus clicking on an entry moves the insertion point to the appropriate page in the document.

To create a table of contents:
References/Table of Contents/Table of Contents

1. Position the insertion point where the table of contents is to be created (normally on a blank page immediately before page 1 of the report).

2. Display the Built-In gallery of table of contents styles.

3. Choose the Automatic Table 2 style. The table of contents automatically displays.

4. The title *Table of Contents* generates automatically. Tap ENTER to position it at approximately 2".

To remove a table of contents, click Remove Table of Contents.

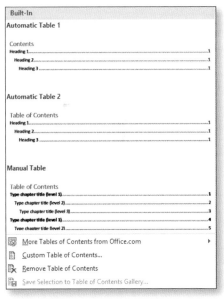

DRILL 1 TABLE OF CONTENTS

table of contents

1. Open *table of contents* from the data file and turn on Show/Hide. Position the insertion point on the blank page after the cover page at 1.9".

2. Generate a new table of contents using the Automatic Table 2 style.

3. Scroll through the document and notice if the page numbers agree with the table of contents. (You will not be able to read the body.)

4. Save and close. (*72-drill1*)

Lesson 92 Hess Office Park

Learning Outcomes

- Apply keying, formatting, and word processing skills.
- Prepare effective employment documents.
- Work independently with few specific instructions.

Warmup *Lesson 92a Warmup*

lesson 92a warmup

Skill Building

92b Timed Writing

Key two 3' timed writings.

	gwam	1'	3'
Dining etiquette is necessary as good impressions are made on		12	4
both important business clients and friends. Table manners tell so		25	8
much about a professional. Just notice as the well-orchestrated and		39	13
zealous expert makes sure that the guest has the best place at the		52	17
table and gives excellent advice on the best food items. Finally, the		66	22
napkin is placed on his or her lap to signal the beginning of the meal.		80	27
To understand a seemingly difficult table setting more easily,		12	31
think of a line down the middle of the serving plate. Then always		25	35
remember liquids are placed on the right of the line and solids are		39	40
placed on the left. Notice very carefully that glassware, cup and		52	44
saucer, knives, and spoons are positioned on the right side of the line.		66	49
Notice also that the bread and butter plate, salad plate, napkin, and		80	53
forks are positioned on the left side. Returning these items to the		93	58
same specific position after using each one will keep the table looking		108	63
very good.		110	63
Never begin eating until the host unfolds his or her napkin. Upon		13	68
this important signal, open your napkin and position it carefully on		27	72
your lap. Should you need to leave the table momentarily, position		40	76
your napkin on your chair. Remember, never move your plate away		52	81
from you when completed. Wait until the host has placed his or her		66	85
napkin on the table; then you may position yours to the right of the		79	90
dinner plate.		82	90

1'	1	2	3	4	5	6	7	8	9	10	11	12	13
3'		1			2			3			4		

Project Setting

HESS OFFICE PARK

The Human Resources staff of Hess Property Enterprises does seminars packaged in two-hour sessions, which are available to tenants of Hess Office Park at a very minimum cost. They are designed primarily for the small entrepreneurial businesses that do not have human resources staff. Parker Bradley has asked you to key the participant notes shown on the next page as a handout for the third segment of the HR seminar, which focuses on interviewing. Participant notes typically include a highlight summary of the other two segments provided by the seminar leaders and more comprehensive notes for the current session.

MODIFY TABLE OF CONTENTS

A table of contents is often modified after it has been created, because of updating changes in the headings and page numbers, choosing another format, or adding text.

To update a table of contents:

1. At the top of the generated table of contents, click Update Table ❶. The Update Table of Contents dialog box displays.

2. Select Update page numbers only or Update entire table and click OK.

To change the format:

References/Table of Contents/Table of Contents

1. Click the Table of Contents button ❷ and select another table of contents style.

 -or-

2. For additional styles, click Custom Table of Contents to display the Table of Contents dialog box.

 a. Accept the defaults to show page numbers, right-align page numbers, and use leaders; or click the arrow next to Format and select the desired format, such as Formal.

 b. Indicate the number of heading levels to be included in the table of contents in the Show Levels box (up to nine). Click OK.

To add text to the table of contents:

References/Table of Contents/Add Text

1. Select the text to be added to the table of contents.

2. Click Add Text.

3. Choose the desired level of heading.

4. Click in the table of contents and click Update Table.

Note: You may also key text directly in a table of contents. Use the Format Painter to copy the format of the entry; then key the correct page number.

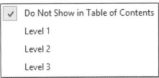

Maria J. Rex
2104 Adger Road, Columbia, SC 29204-3253
803.555.0194 | Maria.Rex@wcc.edu | http://www.linkedin.com/in/rex

Current date

Mr. Miguel Mendoza
President and CEO
Blackmon Development Corporation
548 Poplar Street
Macon, GA 31201-2752

Dear Mr. Mendoza

Begin with a buffer or neutral statement. →

Yesterday, I received your offer for a position as a management trainee at Blackmon Development Corporation. Your offer is very interesting and very competitive. I also received an offer yesterday for a position as the office manager for a consulting alliance.

Present reasons for declining tactfully. →

Although the position you offered is a very desirable one and I have considered it very carefully, it does not give me an opportunity to apply my office management knowledge and experience immediately. Therefore, I have accepted the other position because it is more directly related to my long-term career goals.

Thank the employer for considering you; end on a friendly note. →

I do appreciate Blackmon Development Corporation offering me a position and the many courtesies that were extended to me during my interview and visit to Macon. Blackmon Development Corporation is an excellent company, and I wish you much success in finding the right person for the position you have available.

Sincerely

Maria J. Rex

Job Refusal Letter

DRILL 2 UPDATE TABLE OF CONTENTS

References/Table of Contents/Table of Contents

1. Open *72-drill1* and go to the table of contents page. Click the Table of Contents button and change the style to Automatic Table 1.

2. In the body of the report, change the first subheading under Section Breaks to **Selecting Types of Section Breaks**.

3. Select the entire Section Breaks section and move after the Headers and Footers section.

4. Select the *Appendix* title on the last page of the report and click Add Text to add this text to the table of contents. Select Level 1.

5. Click the Update Table button and update the entire table.

6. Save and close. (*72-drill2*)

DRILL 3 CHANGE TOC FORMAT

1. Open *72-drill2*. Click Custom Table of Contents and change to the Formal style. Click Yes to the prompt to replace the selected table of contents.

2. Save and close. (*72-drill3*)

NUMBER PRELIMINARY PAGES

Preliminary pages are numbered with lowercase Roman numerals. Change the number format when inserting the page number in a report.

To change page number format:

Insert/Header & Footer/Page Number

1. Click Page Number Format.
2. Click the down list arrow and select the desired page number format. If necessary, set the starting page number.

DRILL 4 NUMBER PAGES listening

1. Open *listening* from the data files and position the insertion point at the top of the first page of the report (page after table of contents). Insert a Continuous section break.

2. *Number preliminary pages:* Position the insertion point in the footer of Section 1 page 2 (table of contents).

 - Insert a page number at the bottom of the page using the Plain Number 2 style. Change the page number format to lowercase Roman numerals. Change Start at to ii.

3. *Number report pages:* Click Go to Header and click Next twice to go to the header of Section 2.

 - Deselect Different First Page. Click Link to Previous to break the link.

4. Insert a page number at the top right using the Plain Number 3 style. Change the format to Arabic (1, 2, 3).

 - Change Start at to 1. If your insertion point jumps, return to the same header position.
 - Click Different First Page (check mark in box).

5. *Delete number in footer:* Click Go to Footer and click Next twice to go to Footer – Section 2.

 - Tap ENTER three times and position insertion point at 1.9" on the page after the cover page. Generate a table of contents using the Automatic Table 2 style.

6. Save and close. (*72-drill4*)

Apply It

91-d1

Social Media Profile

⭐ **OPTIONAL**

This document is listed as optional because many educational institutions block access to social media sites. It is recommended that anyone searching for a job take advantage of having an appropriate profile on a social media site. However, it may best be accomplished outside of class.

1. Determine which social media site you wish to use and make your profile public.
2. Ensure that other sites do not have unfavorable materials on it that are publically accessible.
3. Add a professional photo and then use the space below your name for your profile.
4. Transfer appropriate parts of your resume; add any additional information that may be useful.
5. Add three references who know you professionally and are willing to provide the reference.
6. Proofread and edit your site carefully. Ensure that it is free of grammar, punctuation, spelling, and word usage errors.

91-d2

Application Letter

 rex letterhead

1. Open *rex letterhead* from the data files and key the application letter to the hiring manager shown on the previous page.
2. Pay particular attention to the content of the letter and the callouts explaining the strategy used.
3. Save and close. (*91-d2*)

91-d3

My Application Letter

1. Create your own letterhead for the application letter you will prepare and save it as a Quick Part.
2. Compose an application letter to accompany your resume. Use the contact information from the job description that you printed and used to design your resume.
3. Save and close. (*91-d3*)

91-d4

Job Refusal Letter

 rex letterhead

1. Open *rex letterhead* from the data files and key the letter shown on the next page.
2. Pay particular attention to the content of the letter and the callouts explaining the strategy used.
3. Save and close. (*91-d4*)

91-d5

Compose Job Acceptance Letter

1. Use the letterhead you created for *91-d3* and compose an acceptance letter for the job you applied for in *91-d3*.
2. Confirm a starting salary that you think appropriate for the position and a starting date of one month from today.
3. Indicate your excitement about the position and how much you look forward to working with the team at your new company.
4. Save and close. (*91-d5*)

TABLE OF CONTENTS

A table of contents contains a list of the headings in a document, along with the page number on which each heading appears. Begin the title at about 2". Apply Title style and tap ENTER twice after the title.

Tap ENTER 3 times (about 2")

Table of Contents Title style

Apply It

72-d1

Report

 forms

1. Open *forms* from the data files and position the insertion point at the end of the document. Key the remainder of the report shown on the next page; apply List Table 4 – Accent 2 and center the data in column 2.

2. Apply the Integral document theme and then apply appropriate styles to the title, subtitle, and side headings of the report beginning after the Executive Summary.

3. Insert the Semaphore cover page and key the following:

 Date: Current date

 Document title: **Transition to Interactive Forms in New Workflow System**

 Subtitle: **Summary of Three-Year Implementation**

 Author: **Anna Mitchell, Forms Design Consultant**

 Company: **Mitchell Productivity Design, Inc., 78 Cottondale Street, Henderson, NV 89011-0078**

4. Position the insertion point at the top of the first page of the report and insert a Continuous section break.

5. *Number preliminary pages:* Position the insertion point in the second page (transmittal letter) of the Footer – Section 1. (Section 1 ends with the Executive Summary.)

 a. Insert a page number at the bottom of the page using the Plain Number 2 style.

 b. Change the page number format to lowercase Roman numerals and change page number to start at ii. **Note:** Different First Page is selected (check mark is in box).

6. *Number report pages:* Click Go to Header; click Next twice to go to Header – Section 2.

 a. Deselect Different First Page and click Link to Previous.

 b. Insert a page number at the top right using the Plain Number 3 style. Change the page number format to begin with page 1.

 c. Click Different First Page.

(continued)

Maria J. Rex

2104 Adger Road, Columbia, SC 29204-3253

803.555.0194 | Maria.Rex@wcc.edu | http://www.linkedin.com/in/rex

Current date

Mr. Eric Todd, President and CEO
CunCo Consulting Alliance
416 West Bay Street
Savannah, GA 31401-1115

Dear Mr. Todd

Establish a point of contact and state the job you are applying for. →

Ben Sullivan, your manager of Business Development, sent me a copy of the job description posted for the office manager position open at CunCo and suggested that I contact you. My qualifications match the requirements for the office manager you are seeking. Please consider me as an applicant for that position.

Convey key qualifications →

My education and my two years of experience managing the four-hour evening shift of two teams of trainers and one of nutrition counselors enabled me to develop the team management and the operational management skills that you require. Our teamwork resulted in a significant revenue increase and expense reduction.

State how the employer will benefit from your qualifications →

My internship in the President's Office of Wexford Community College enabled me to refine my organizational, problem-solving, and soft skills. Both my experience at Pat's Fitness and Wellness Center and in the President's office required extensive Word, Excel, and PowerPoint use and excellent communication skills. I delivered high-quality products and met very tight deadlines consistently. I understand how those skills can be of value to CunCo.

Request an interview →

After you have had an opportunity to review the enclosed resume as well as my LinkedIn Profile, I look forward to meeting with you to discuss how my qualifications and my office management career aspirations can be applied to your position at CunCo Consulting Alliance.

Sincerely

Maria J. Rex

Enclosure

Application Letter

7. *Delete number in report footer:* Click Go to Footer and click Next once to go to Footer – Section 2.

 a. Click Link to Previous.

 b. Select the page number and tap DELETE. Click Close Header and Footer.

8. Position the insertion point on the blank page left for the table of contents (not in the header section). Tap ENTER 3 times to position the heading at approximately 2". Create the table of contents using the Automatic Table 2 style. Apply Title style. Tap ENTER after the title.

9. Save and close. (*72-d1*)

Follow the directions exactly in order shown:

- Step 7: Deselect Different First Page before you break the link and insert page numbers.
- Step 8: Break the link before deleting the page number.

Final Outcomes

The goal of the system was to convert 70 to 75 percent of the paper-based and digital forms to interactive forms in the workflow system within a three-year time period. The follow-up study authorized to determine the effectiveness of the program revealed that progress has been made since the workflow system was implemented three years ago. The following table shows currently 84 percent of all forms are interactive and being routed in the workflow system. Only 10 percent are paper based and 6 percent digital forms outside workflow.

	% Paper Forms	% Digital Forms	% Forms in Workflow
Employee	2	4	27
Company	1	2	57
Vendor	3	0	0
External	4	0	0

The four forms that are currently purchased from vendors are being re-designed so that they can be made available electronically. The remaining paper-based forms are used primarily by warehouse and delivery personnel. However, the Technology Committee has recommended providing these employees with handheld computers to perform their work. As soon as this recommendation is implemented, the forms they use can be converted to electronic format.

The new workflow system has resulted in a 50 percent cost savings over the previous system. In addition, more than 90 percent of the employees indicated that the new system improved their efficiency and effectiveness.

Strategy for Application Letter

The purpose of an application letter, which serves as the cover letter for a resume, is to obtain an interview—not to get a job. Some recruiters suggest that cover letters are not necessary, and often are not read. However, most experts disagree with these recruiters. Hiring managers eventually get the cover letters and read them carefully. No downside exists for including a well-written letter, and it is a risk not to include a cover letter. These documents are used to determine that the applicant is qualified for the job. Virtually all organizations require an interview before hiring an individual. Generally, the interview is granted only to qualified applicants, and it is used to determine how the applicant would fit in with the organization and its current employees. The best strategy for an application letter is to focus on showing how your qualifications match the requirements of the available job. Your empasis should be on demonstrating that you are qualified and can add value to the company.

To write an effective application letter:

1. Establish a point of contact specifying how you learned about the company having a position available.
2. Specify the specific position you are seeking.
3. Convey your key qualificiations for that job.
4. Interpret your major qualifications in terms of how they benefit the employer.
5. Request an interview.

Strategy for Job Acceptance or Refusal Letters

Most organizations require a written acceptance for a job offer and expect a written refusal if you do not accept the offer presented. Obviously, it is much easier to write the acceptance letter than the refusal letter. Always decline a position graciously. In the future, the company may have a position you would like to accept or may even become a customer or client.

To write an effective acceptance letter:

1. Express your delight in accepting the position.
2. Confirm specific details, such as salary and starting date.
3. End on a friendly, optimistic note about your future with the company.

To write an effective refusal letter:

1. Begin with a buffer or neutral statement to cushion the bad news.
2. Present the reasons tactfully and let them lead to the decline.
3. End on a friendly note thanking the employer for considering you.

72-d2

Update Table of Contents

final report

1. Open *final report* from the data files. Move the section Workflow System Recommendation to appear below the Existing System Analysis section. Add the word *Strategies* after the heading *Implementation*.

2. On page iv, select the words *Executive Summary* and click Add Text and select Level 1 to add this preliminary section to the table of contents.

3. In the table of contents, key **Letter of Transmittal** as the first entry. Tap TAB key and then key **ii** as the page number. Use the Format Painter to copy the format.

4. Click Update Table to update the entire table of contents. Check that all changes were made.

5. Save and close. (*72-d2*)

QUICK ✔

Check your document against the illustration below.

Table of Contents

Letter of Transmittal ... ii

Executive Summary ... iv

Existing System Analysis ... 1

Workflow System Recommendation .. 1

Implementation Strategies ... 1

Final Outcomes .. 2

Writing Matters

Communicating Today ▶

It seems that everyone is blogging, tweeting, messaging, and sharing on all types of social media sites. The smartphones and tablets make communication so easy, quick, and fun for billions of users every day.

When browsing these posts, one might raise the question if grammar and spelling are still important. As a writer (bloggers and tweeters are writers), it is important to remember that assumptions (good or bad) can be easily made by the readers. Once released the written word (or text or tweet) is evaluated, and it showcases one's abilities. It is a known fact that employers are viewing social media websites to gain more information about prospective employees. The social media postings readily portray the individual's knowledge and use of proper English as well as other sought-after workplace skills, such as attitude and respect for others.

The growing popularity of social media also raises a need for increased awareness of plagiarism. With the ease of copying and pasting, online plagiarism is a common trap in which today's writers find themselves. Content similarity tools are available for checking one's text to ensure originality. Bloggers are aware of these tools and other precautions to protect their work. Enjoy the ease of communicating with friends and family, but remember it always pays to use correct and appropriate writing skills.

2. Decide which social media site you would like potential employers to access during your job search.

 a. LinkedIn is considered to be a professional network. Make your profile on the network you selected public so employers can access it easily.

 b. Use other sites such as Twitter and Facebook for networking. Make them private. Notify your contacts that you are in the job market, have updated your LinkedIn or other profile, and provide the link.

 c. Search all of the networks for companies of interest that might have job postings. Look for contacts that you might know. A job referral from a company employee or close professional associate of the employer is one of the best ways to get the job, provided you are qualified for it.

TIP

Note that the default for a Facebook profile is public. You have to change the default to make it private.

DESIGN AN EFFECTIVE PROFILE

Develop or enhance your profile on the network you select to use for the job search.

1. Include a picture.
2. Use the space directly below your name for your Professional Profile.
3. Copy and paste appropriate sections of your resume to the profile.
4. Include all of employment experience—full-time, part-time, internships, volunteer work, and projects.
5. List all educational experiences, including special training you might have had. Pages are not limited on profiles.
6. Highlight computer skills, foreign languages, and other special skills.
7. Secure at least three recommendations from people who know you professionally and will provide a good recommendation.
8. Share updates periodically. Employers may see these and check your profile.

EMPLOYMENT LETTERS

Three types of employment letters are covered specifically in this lesson: application or cover letter, job acceptance letter, and job refusal letter. Other letters are important to send during the employment process, including a thank-you letter after an interview, a request for a reference, and a thank-you letter after a reference has been provided. Good writing skills are all that you need to write these types of letters.

Design an attractive personal letterhead for your employment letter. Market yourself. Never use a company's letterhead in the search for a job. Use the same theme, colors, and style that you use for your resume. Use block letter format with open punctuation.

Lesson 73 Report Features

New Commands
- Captions
- Table of Figures

New Commands

73b

TABLE OF FIGURES

A table of figures is a list of all of the captions for tables, charts, pictures, graphics, and equations in a document. Captions can be added automatically or manually to an existing object. See the illustration below. Generally, tables are labeled above the table, and figures are labeled below the figure.

Table of Figures

To insert a caption:

References/Captions/Insert Caption

1. Select the item to be captioned. In the caption text box, space once after the number and key the caption.

2. From the Label list, click the drop-list arrow and select the desired label, e.g., Figure, Table, Equation. The Position list will populate according to the label you choose.

3. Click the Numbering button to choose the desired number format, e.g., 1, 2, 3. Click OK.

4. Click New Label to create a new label group, such as Sports Photos. Click OK.

Note: Click AutoCaption to select the objects for which you want captions created automatically, e.g., *Microsoft Word* Table.

Caption ? ✕

Caption:

| Figure 1 Sales Peak in July |

Options

Label: | Figure ▾ |

Position: | Below selected item ▾ |

☐ Exclude label from caption

[New Label...] [Delete Label] [Numbering...]

[AutoCaption...] [OK] [Cancel]

Caption Numbering ? ✕

Format: | 1, 2, 3, ... ▾ |

☐ Include chapter number

Chapter starts with style | Heading 1 ▾ |

Use separator: | - (hyphen) ▾ |

Examples: Figure II-1, Table 1-A

[OK] [Cancel]

Lesson 91 Social Media and Employment Letters

Document Design

91b

1. Review the internal and external recruiting strategies on pages 1–2 in the Employment Strategies white paper (*89-d1*) you printed in Lesson 89, on page 4-28.
2. Review the *Job Sources* section on page 4 of that document.

SOCIAL MEDIA

The *Employment Strategies* document emphasized how broadly organizations advertise positions available. Note that many sources companies use are online media. Also note in the *Job Sources* section for job seekers that companies usually post job openings internally first—that is a major part of the hidden job market and often a great source for the best jobs. Think about your contacts on social media who may be aware of job openings in their company. Companies promote themselves widely; social media gives you a free opportunity to promote yourself widely. While social media profiles are not likely to replace resumes in the near future, they can be a valuable promotion tool for a person in the job market.

Perhaps the most important thing to remember in using social media during a job search is that it often results in screening the applicant out. Both recruiters and hiring managers frequently use a search engine, such as Google, to gain information about job applicants. The search results generally include your Facebook, Twitter, LinkedIn, and other social networks. Often potential employers find offensive or unprofessional material that works against you in the job search.

GUIDELINES FOR USING SOCIAL MEDIA

The following guides are designed for individuals who are in the midst of a job search and either already have social media accounts or plan to use social media while they are searching for a job.

1. Review your social media networks from the perspective of an employer.

 a. Would it be to your advantage for a prospective employer to read the information on this network?

 Examples of a few things to look for include:

 - offensive language
 - unprofessional pictures
 - political statements
 - strong religious statements
 - poorly written communications
 - personal or intimate information
 - drug and alcohol references
 - bad reputation of contacts

 b. If not, either remove any unfavorable information from each network or make it private so that it cannot be accessed by a potential employer. Keep in mind that neither of these options is foolproof.

(continued)

To create a table of figures:
References/Captions/Insert Table of Figures

1. Position the insertion point where the table of figures is to be positioned (two lines below the Table of Figures title). Display the Table of Figures dialog box.

2. Click the down arrow beside the
 a. Tab leader box and select the leader type.
 b. Formats box and select the format.
 c. Caption label box and select the caption label, e.g., Table. Click OK.

To update a table of figures:

1. Change the caption as desired.
2. Click in the table of figures. From the Captions group, on the References tab, click Update Table. *Shortcut:* F9.
3. Select Update page numbers only or Update entire table. Click OK.

DRILL 1 **TABLE OF FIGURES** guide

1. Open *guide* from the data files. Insert captions below the figure for the first two figures in this file. Label as follows:

 Figure 1 **Caption Box**

 Figure 2 **Caption Numbering Box**

2. Create a table of figures on the first page using the Formal format and the Figure caption label. Choose the dot leaders (second option).

3. Add the word **Dialog** before the word *Box* in both figures.

4. Insert caption below the third figure and label Figure 3 as **New Label Dialog Box**

5. Update the table of figures. Reapply the format if necessary. Compare your work to the illustrations below.

6. Save and close. (*73-drill1*)

Figure 1 Caption Dialog Box

Figure 2 Caption Numbering Dialog Box

Figure 3 New Label Dialog Box

Honors and Activities

Participated in numerous volunteer and community service projects. Received awards and served as a leader in honorary and professional organizations:

- Named a Dean's Scholar.
- Received the Outstanding Business Student Award.
- Member of Student Advisory Council.
- President of the Wexford Honor Society.
- President of the Office Management Club.

90-d4

My Resume for ATS Screening

1. Review the job description you printed and the *resume worksheet* you prepared in Lesson 89.
2. Customize the resume you prepared in Apply It 90-d2 and saved as *90-d2* to enhance it for ATS screening.
3. Save and close. (*90-d4*)

Communication

90e

 word usage

1. Check the list carefully to make sure that you know how the words on the list should be used.
2. If you are not sure how all of the words should be used, review the Word Usage section of Appendix C.
3. Open the *word usage* data file and key the correct option in the first column for each sentence.
4. Save and close. (*90e*)

The following list contains sets of words that are often confused and misused.

1. accept/except
2. advice/advise
3. affect/effect
4. assure/ensure/insure
5. complement/compliment
6. farther/further
7. good/well
8. it's/its
9. principal/principle
10. their/there/they're
11. to/too/two
12. who's/whose

QUICK ✔ Check your table of figures from the illustration below.

Table of Figures

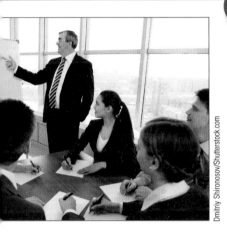

Dmitriy Shironosov/Shutterstock.com

! WORKPLACE SUCCESS

What Is Your Listening Grade?

Isn't it interesting that students are not required to complete a course in listening when 80 percent of our time each day is spent listening? To perform well in organizations, a keen listening skill is essential. Evaluate yourself on the following areas and start today working on a listening improvement plan in those areas. Search for excellent listening quizzes to assist you.

BODY LANGUAGE

Do you ... sit with your arms closed?
stand with your hand on the door as you listen to someone?
doodle while listening or play with a pen or some other object?
look at your watch while others are talking?
continue checking your email while listening to someone on the phone or someone face to face?

MINDSET

Do you ... think you already know what the speaker has to say?
think the speaker is wasting your time?
tune out anything boring? or too long?
disregard anything being said if you do not agree with it?
judge the speaker before he/she begins to speak?

RESPONSES TO THE SPEAKER

Do you ... finish the speaker's sentence because you know what he/she is going to say?
think about what you will say while the speaker is talking?
interrupt the speaker so you can start talking sooner?
look ridiculous sometimes when you respond in a manner that tells others that you were not listening?

 TIP

The length of your resume does not matter if you are entering data on a company form for an ATS. The system produces a report of matched qualifications rather than the entire resume.

Note the differences in the resume you keyed for the hiring manager and the one illustrated on the previous page for ATS matching:

- The Ion theme was changed to the default Office theme because it has a smaller but still acceptable font size.
- A bulleted list of no more than 10 core competencies (also called core strengths or keywords) is included.
 - Core competencies should be worded slightly different than the competencies included in the profile, but they are the same key requirements from the job description.
 - Different terms may be used for the heading—*Core Competencies*, *Core Strengths*, or *Keywords* are often used.
 - The list should be positioned in the middle of the resume after the major area of strength—for college students, Education.
 - Adding a bulleted list will often extend the resume to a second page. The resume should be no more than two pages.
- In the first resume you keyed, the *Honors and Activities* section was minimized to keep the resume to one page. Note that in this resume, the *Honors and Activities* section was reworded and formatted with bullets to emphasize the leadership aspect and to make it more readable.

Apply It

90-d3

Resume for ATS Screening

Open *90-d1* that you saved from Apply It 90-d1 Resume and customize the resume as follows:

1. Change the theme from Ion to the default Office theme.
2. Tap ENTER after the *Education* section and key **Core Competencies**. Use the same format for this heading as the other headings.
3. Then key and format the core competencies as follows:
 a. Apply bullets and position them at the left margin.
 b. After all competencies are keyed, select them and apply two equal-sized column format.
4. Revise the Honors and Activities as shown on the next page; then number the pages; do not show number on the first page.
5. Save and close. (*90-d3*)

- AS degree; strong business knowledge.
- Two years' relevant part-time experience.
- Excellent Microsoft Office skills.
- Excellent communication, interpersonal, social, and customer service skills.
- Effective team leader and team player.
- High level of integrity and strong work ethic.
- Motivated self-starter; work independently.
- Organized; productivity focused-- manage time and office effectively.
- Strong problem-solving skills.
- Records and project management experience.

(continued)

Apply It

73-d1

forms report

1. Open *forms report* from the data files. Add the captions shown below to the two tables. Position the caption above the table and number with Arabic numbers. Choose Table as the caption.

 Table on first page: Table 1 **Form Sources from Initial Survey**

 Table on second page: Table 2 **Form Sources from Concluding Survey**

2. Insert a blank page after the page break on the table of contents page. Remember to click Show/Hide so you can see the Page Break.

3. Create the table of figures using the default format. Key the title **Table of Figures** at approximately 2" and apply Title style. Change the font color to Turquoise, Accent 1, Darker 25%.

4. Save and close. (*73-d1*)

73-d2

Edit Table of Figures

1. Open *73-d1*. Edit both table options as follows. Update the table of figures.

 Table 1: Initial Comparison of Paper-Based and Digital Forms

 Table 2: Final Comparsion of Paper-Based, Digital, and Interactive Forms

2. Save and close. (*73-d2*)

QUICK ✔

Check your table of figures from the illustration below.

> ## Table of Figures
>

RESUME FOR ATS SCREENING

In the first section, you keyed and formatted a traditional resume (see Rex resume on page 4-33) and then you created your own resume and formatted it as a traditional resume. In this section, you will key and format a customized version of the Rex resume for ATS screening. Then you will customize your own resume and format it for ATS screening.

When you seek a job in a medium-to-large-size organization or when the job description or posting indicates that the resume should be sent to the Human Resources Department, you should assume that your resume will first be screened by an ATS. The resume you keyed in *90-d1* has been customized for an ATS screening and is shown below. Note that the previous resume already has keywords in the Qualifications Profile.

Maria J. Rex
2104 Adger Road, Columbia, SC 29204-3253
803.555.0194 | Maria.Rex@wcc.edu | http://www.linkedin.com/in/rex

Qualifications Profile for Office Manager

Highly effective, results-oriented, administrative office professional with AS degree and two years of relevant part-time work experience, including demonstrated effective supervisory, customer service, records management, time management, and project management skills. Create professional documents that enhance company image and productivity using Word, Excel, and PowerPoint. Strong written, oral, and electronic communication skills. Excellent interpersonal skills. Honest, ethical, and possess strong work ethic.

Education

AS degree in Business Administration with majors in Office Administration and Office Management from Wexford Community College, Columbia, SC, May 2015, 3.65 GPA.

High school diploma with career emphasis in English and Business, Maxwell High School, Charleston, SC, August, 2013, 3.85 GPA.

Core Competencies

- AS degree; strong business knowledge.
- Two years' relevant part-time experience.
- Excellent Microsoft Office skills.
- Excellent communication, interpersonal, social, and customer service skills.
- Effective team leader and team player.
- High level of integrity and strong work ethic.
- Motivated self-starter; work independently.
- Organized; productivity focused—manage time and office effectively.
- Strong problem-solving skills.
- Records and project management experience.

Experience

Wexford Community College, President's Office, Columbia, SC, internship, summer 2015.

- Prepared correspondence, reports, and presentations for senior administrators.
- Scheduled and coordinated special events with high-level constituents.
- Received outstanding evaluation commending my professionalism, social skills, creativity, reliability, problem-solving skills, and the excellent quality of all work.

Pat's Fitness and Wellness Center, supervisor and promoted to office manager for the 3:30 to 7:30 shift (20-25 hours per week) from June 2013 through May 2015.

- Managed two teams of trainers and one team of nutrition counselors; resolved conflicts for clients. Responsible for correspondence with referring physician, vendors, and clients.
- Managed facility, records, billing, equipment, and supplies; developed procedures.
- Increased client participation and revenue from my shift over 20 percent and reducing expenses by 12 percent.

2

Honors and Activities

Participated in a numerous volunteer and community service projects. Received awards and served as a leader in honorary and professional organizations:

- Named a Dean's Scholar.
- Received the Outstanding Business Student Award.
- Member of Student Advisory Council.
- President of the Wexford Honor Society.
- President of the Office Management Club.

Lesson 74 Productivity Tools for Reports

New Commands
- Go To
- Splitting Panes
- Document Formatting Style Set

 lesson 74a warmup

Skill Building

74b Improve Keystroking

1. Key each line, concentrating on using good techniques.
2. Repeat the drill if time permits.

b 1 bib box baboo abbey abduct babka bubbles beaux bulk bebop abdomen

r 2 rebuke roux army carry organize warrant review ajar rough explore

b/r 3 brain bridge celebrate fabric debris zebra brusque broccoli bread

b/r 4 Brett wrote rubrics for the bronze broadcast assignment at break.

n 5 nods name naive nail barn napkin conquest pound kerning neon zone

u 6 none union untie ugly ultra usher flux menu bayou justice vaguely

u/n 7 under unique unwrap nudged nuzzle nutrient account immunize nouns

u/n 8 Hunter saw a number of squirrels lug nuts to the hidden bungalow.

Communication

74c

1. Review the rules for the apostrophe, colon, italic, hyphen, and dash in Appendix C.
2. Key each sentence single-spaced, correcting punctuation errors related to the apostrophe, colon, italic, hyphen, and dash as you key. Do not key directions shown in parentheses in blue. Key the sentences as a numbered list.
3. Save and close. (74c)

1. Youre to pick up Dr. Harris gift at the registration table.
2. The three speakers credentials are included in the head coordinators information packet.
3. Concurrent sessions are scheduled for 50 while computer sessions are scheduled for 90. (Denote time in minutes.)
4. Exhibit booths measuring 10 x 20. (Denote measurements in feet.)
5. The resort amenities illustrated on the website are: two golf courses, three pools, exercise room, and activity room.
6. The layout of the condominium shows the following rooms master bedroom with bath, guest bedroom with bath, kitchen, dining room, and laundry room.
7. Registration opened at 7 30 a.m. and closed at 4 30 p.m.
8. An excellent book for an overseas trip is *International Travel Made Easy*.
9. Thirty five volunteers staffed the busy convention registration area during the three day conference.
10. The officers not the committee chairs are seated at the head table.

Apply It

90-d1

Resume

TIP

Heading styles were not used in case the resume is scanned into a Human Resources management system. Using the same Dark Red color on side headings would be acceptable.

1. In a new blank document, key the model resume on the previous page. Use the Ion theme; this theme was selected because the Century Gothic font is a very readable one.

2. Use the following formats:

 a. Apply Moderate margins.

 b. Use Century Gothic bold 14-point heading font and apply Dark Red, Accent 1, 25% Darker font color to the name. Apply 12-point heading font for all side headings.

 c. Use the 11-point body font for all other text.

 d. Apply Dark Red, Accent 1, 25% Darker font color to the vertical lines and the two hyperlinks in the address.

3. Preview and proofread the document several times; remember an error in a resume can be disastrous. Note that the resume is aligned with the sample resume worksheet prepared in *89-d2*.

4. Save and close. (*90-d1*)

90-d2

Compose Your Resume

TIP

Using the same color as the name on side headings would be acceptable.

TIP

Always edit your resume carefully, preview it, print it, and proofread it again. Avoid the risk of having an error on your resume.

1. Review the *Creating or Updating a Job Description, Recruiting New Employees,* and the *Summary* of the *Employment Strategies* (*89-d1*) documents that you prepared in the previous lesson. Keep in mind what employers are seeking and how they go about it.

2. Review the *resume worksheet* (*89-d2*) and the description of your desired job that you printed in the previous lesson. Update it if you think it is necessary.

3. Then in a new blank document, prepare the resume that you would use to apply for that job assuming that the resume would be sent directly to the hiring manager. Use the following guides:

 a. Do not use a separate keyword or core competency list in this resume.

 b. Use the format of the resume you just keyed or select a style of your preference.

 c. Ensure that the format is attractive, consistent, and looks professional.

 d. Use an appropriate theme and font.

 e. Use black and white or no more than one color in your resume. Some experts recommend finding the company's website and using the predominant color in your resume.

 f. Your qualifications profile or summary should be a minimum of four lines and a maximum of six.

 g. Limit your resume to one or at most two pages.

4. Save and close. (*90-d2*)

New Commands

GO TO

The Go To command is also used to navigate within a document. A variety of document segments can be located with the Go To command, such as pages, footnotes, tables, or headings.

TIP

Use the keyboard shortcut CTRL + G to bring up the Go To command.

To use the Go To command:
Home/Editing/Find

1. Click the drop-list arrow on the Find command; then click Go To.

2. Click on the item you wish to find, such as Page or Heading. Then key the number in the text box.

 Option: Click the Magnifying Glass button and click Go To.

DRILL 1 **GO TO** go to

1. Open *go to* from the data files and use the Go To command to go to Section 2.

2. Go to Table 1. Change *December 1* to *December 15*.

3. Go to Footnote 2. Change *displays* to *display*.

4. Go to Heading 2. Change *Ensure* to *Ensuring*. Update table of contents.

5. Go to Page 1. Save and close. (*74-drill1*)

SPLITTING PANES

To view two parts of the document at the same time, split the window into two panes.

To split panes:
View/Window/Split

Click, hold, and drag the split bar to the desired location and release it where you want it ❶. Note that you have two panes, with each having a ruler bar and scroll bars.

Maria J. Rex

2104 Adger Road, Columbia, SC 29204-3253 ◄——Shift + ENTER
803.555.0194 | Maria.Rex@wcc.edu | http://www.linkedin.com/in/rex

Qualifications Profile for Office Manager

Highly effective, results-oriented, administrative office professional with AS degree and two years of relevant part-time work experience, including demonstrated effective supervisory, customer service, records management, time management, and project management skills. Create professional documents that enhance company image and productivity using Word, Excel, and PowerPoint. Strong written, oral, and electronic communication skills. Excellent interpersonal skills. Honest, ethical, and possess strong work ethic.

Education

AS degree in Business Administration with majors in Office Administration and Office Management from Wexford Community College, Columbia, SC, May 2012, 3.65 GPA.

High school diploma with career emphasis in English and Business, Maxwell High School, Charleston, SC, August, 2013, 3.85 GPA.

Experience

Wexford Community College, President's Office, Columbia, SC, internship, summer 2015.

- Prepared correspondence, reports, and presentations for senior administrators.
- Scheduled and coordinated special events with high-level constituents.
- Received outstanding evaluation, commending my professionalism, social skills, creativity, reliability, problem-solving skills, and the excellent quality of all work.

Pat's Fitness and Wellness Center, supervisor and promoted to office manager for the 3:30 to 7:30 shift (20-25 hours per week) from June 2013 through May 2015.

- Managed two teams of trainers and one team of nutrition counselors; resolved conflicts for clients. Responsible for correspondence with referring physicians, vendors, and clients.
- Managed facility, records, billing, equipment, and supplies; developed procedures.
- Increased client participation and revenue from my shift over 20 percent while reducing expenses by 12 percent.

Honors and Activities

Named a Dean's Scholar; received the Outstanding Business Student Award. Member of Student Advisory Council, president of the Wexford Honor Society, and president of the Office Management Club.

Resume

View/Window/Split

1. Open *top 10* from the data files. Click Split to divide window into two panes. Drag the split bar and drop just before #3.

2. In the bottom pane, scroll to #9.

3. In the top pane select the second numbered item (accept, except and examples). Do not select the automatic number 2.

4. Drag the selection across the split bar. Drop to the left of the word *fewer* (Item #9). The entry for *accept/except* will now be #8. **Note:** If you did not drop the text correctly, you may have to make minor spacing and numbering adjustments.

5. Double-click the split bar to remove it.

6. Save and close. (*74-drill2*)

Apply It

74-d1

Review Report

 review

❋ **Discover**

Document Formatting Style

Design/Document Formatting

Select one of the document formatting styles sets. Note the change in appearance of the Title, Heading 1, and Heading 2 styles in this report using the Centered document formatting style set.

 TIP

Follow the directions exactly in order shown. You must:

- Step 6: Deselect Different First Page before you break the link and insert page numbers.

- Step 7: Break the link before deleting the page number.

1. Open *review* from the data files. Change the left margin to 1.5".

❋ 2. Apply the Retrospect document theme with Centered document formatting style set. On page 1, shrink the main heading to fit on one line.

3. Insert the Retrospect cover page and shrink the title to fit on one line.
 Document title: **Marketing Analysis Report**
 Subtitle: **Administrative Skills Assessment**
 Author: **Anna Mitchell, Forms Design Consultant**
 Company: **Mitchell Productivity Design, Inc.** | **78 Cottondale Street, Henderson, NV 89011-0078**

4. Position the insertion point at the top of the first page of the report and insert a Continuous section break.

5. *Number preliminary pages:* In the table of contents page, insert a page number at the bottom of the page using the Plain Number 2 style. Change the page number format to lowercase Roman numerals and change page number to start at ii.

6. *Add header to report pages:*
 - Click Go to Header; click Next twice to position the insertion point in the Header – Section 2.
 - Click Different First Page (deletes checkmark); click Link to Previous to break link. Insert the Banded header.
 - Click Different First Page (adds checkmark) to suppress the header on the first page of the report.

7. *Delete number in footer and insert page number:*
 - Click Go to Footer and click Next to move to Footer – Section 2.
 - Click Link to Previous to break link and then select the page number in the footer and tap DELETE.
 - Insert the Retrospect footer. Change the page number format to begin with page 1.

8. On the First Page Footer – Section 2 (first page of the body of the report), insert Retrospect footer to display on page 1. The footer and page number will display. This design is attractive with the footer on all pages of the body.

9. Position the insertion point on the blank page for the table of contents (not in the header section). Generate the table of contents using the Automatic Table 2 style. Position the heading at approximately 2" and apply Title style. Tap ENTER once after the title.

10. Change the left margin in Section 1 to 1.5".

11. Save and close. (*74-d1*)

RESUME DESIGN

The resume on this page illustrates side headings, common terminology, and one way of formatting a resume. Another alternative is to use a 2-column table with the headings in the first narrow (1.5") column. Use of one color is acceptable. The font should be standard and very readable (minimum 11 point). The overall appearance should be that of a professionally designed document. List items with dates in reverse chronological order. Present strengths first—usually education for recent graduates. Use formats consistently. Ensure that the document is error free and information is factual.

Identification: Include your name, address, telephone number, email, and a LinkedIn, other social network URL, or your website if desired.

Qualifications Profile or Professional Profile: Experienced applicants tend to use *professional*; less experienced use *qualifications*. Focus on your greatest strengths and results. Make sure the things you include match the qualifications listed in the job description.

Education: List the degree, major, educational institution, location, and date of degree. If it is to your advantage, list your GPA (generally 3.0 or higher). If you have not yet received the degree, indicate the expected or completion date. Listing high school is optional for experienced applicants—usually better for college students to emphasize educational strengths. You may want to emphasize computer skills more than shown in this illustration.

Experience: List all work experience unless you have many years of it; then list for past few years and summarize other experience. Use active verbs and focus on results not just activities. Show that your experience prepared you for the qualifications listed in the job description. Include internships and volunteer work if you have limited experience.

Honors and Activities: Select specific examples of leadership potential and commitment.

Maria J. Rex
2104 Adger Road, Columbia, SC 29204-3253
803.555.0194 | Maria.Rex@wcc.edu | http://www.linkedin.com/in/rex

Qualifications Profile for Office Manager

Highly effective, results-oriented, administrative office professional with AS degree and two years of relevant part-time work experience, including demonstrated effective supervisory, customer service, records management, time management, and project management skills. Create professional documents that enhance company image and productivity using Word, Excel, and PowerPoint. Strong written, oral, and electronic communication skills. Excellent interpersonal skills. Honest, ethical, and possess strong work ethic.

Education

AS degree in Business Administration with majors in Office Administration and Office Management from Wexford Community College, Columbia, SC, May 2012, 3.65 GPA.

High school diploma with career emphasis in English and Business, Maxwell High School, Charleston, SC, August, 2013, 3.85 GPA.

Experience

Wexford Community College, President's Office, Columbia, SC, internship, summer 2015.

- Prepared correspondence, reports, and presentations for senior administrators.
- Scheduled and coordinated special events with high-level constituents.
- Received outstanding evaluation, commending my professionalism, social skills, creativity, reliability, problem-solving skills, and the excellent quality of all work.

Pat's Fitness and Wellness Center, supervisor and promoted to office manager for the 3:30 to 7:30 shift (20-25 hours per week) from June 2013 through May 2015.

- Managed two teams of trainers and one team of nutrition counselors; resolved conflicts for clients. Responsible for correspondence with referring physicians, vendors, and clients.
- Managed facility, records, billing, equipment, and supplies; developed procedures.
- Increased client participation and revenue from my shift over 20 percent while reducing expenses by 12 percent.

Honors and Activities

Named a Dean's Scholar; received the Outstanding Business Student Award. Member of Student Advisory Council, president of the Wexford Honor Society, and president of the Office Management Club.

Print the resume on high-quality white or cream paper if you are mailing it. Consider sending the same resume in both printed and electronic versions to prospective employers. The resume can be sent as a *Word* document attached to an email with a cover letter.

74-d2

Edit Report

1. Open *74-d1*. Click the Table of Contents button and then Custom Table of Contents. Change to the Distinctive style with dot leaders. Click Yes to the prompt to replace the selected table of contents.

2. Modify the report as follows and update the table of contents. Click Update entire table.

 a. Split the window into two panes. In the first pane, position so you can see the Market Analysis section on page 1 of the report. In the second pane, position so you can see the Developers section on page 2.

 b. In the top pane, select the Marketing Analysis section, drag across the split bar, and drop just before the side heading *Developers*. The Market Analysis section is now on page 2. Remove the split pane.

 c. In the paragraph heading *Small Businesses*, change *Businesses* to lowercase.

3. Select the *Appendix* title on the last page of the report and click Add Text to add this text to the table of contents. Select Level 1. Click Update Table button to update the entire contents page.

4. Verify that the page numbers were updated, the heading was changed, and the Appendix was added to the table of contents. Apply Title style to title if needed.

5. Save and close. (*74-d2*)

You can use Cut and Paste instead of drag and drop to move the text to the second pane.

QUICK ✓

Check your table of contents against the illustration below.

Lesson 90 Resumes

Skill Building

90b Master Difficult Reaches

Key each line once, concentrating on using good keying techniques.

direct reaches

1 red much brief hunt bred zany check jump decrease music many brat

2 polo excel munch brake junk swim wreck lunch curve kick dazed bed

3 Cec and Kim enjoy a great hunting trip in June after school ends.

adjacent reaches

4 were guy sad junior tree trio fast point rest joint walk gas join

5 opt crew going port backlog poster web suit few folder buy porter

6 Porter saw two important guys after we walked past Union Station.

double letters

7 bell look deed glass upper inn odd committee cabbage effect inner

8 add spell pool happy jazz mass scurry connect office fall setting

9 Debbie Desselle called a committee meeting at noon at the office.

Document Design

90c

Traditional Resume

RESUME

The resume is an employment document designed to introduce you to an organization that has a position available for which you would like to be hired. Your resume should be designed to entice the potential employer to offer you an interview. It is your opportunity to showcase your qualifications (knowledge, skills, and personal attributes) for that specific position and convince the employer that you are qualified and that you would likely be successful in the position. Always focus on the value you can provide to the company. Never post your social security number on a resume.

This lesson is divided into two sections. In the first section, you prepare resumes designed to go directly to the department and person (often called the supervisor or hiring manager) to whom you would report if you were hired. In the second section, you prepare resumes that will be screened by an ATS system.

Different formatting styles, terminology, and categories are used on resumes. Design your resume to present your qualifications in the best light possible. Many experts believe that the best way to begin your resume is to provide a qualifications or professional profile or a summary of your most important qualifications—not a job objective as was recommended in previous years.

Many companies require that you apply for a job on their website. Providing specific information in a form on the company website often replaces the opportunity to submit a resume. Having a resume makes it easier to complete the form. In some cases you can copy information from your electronic resume directly into the fields on the form. Always provide the company with a resume you created if you have the opportunity to do so. You choose what and how to present information on a resume you prepare. On a form, you are limited to what the company wants you to present.

Lesson 75 Hess Office Park

Skill Building

75b Timed Writing

1. Key a 1' timing on each paragraph; work to increase speed.
2. Key a 3' timing on all paragraphs.

A ALL LETTERS

gwam 1' | 3'

You must prepare early for an international trip. If you do not — 13 | 4
have a passport, you will need to apply for a passport well in advance — 27 | 9
of the travel date. Also, you will need to attach a recent photograph — 40 | 13
that meets passport rules. Begin reading books and browsing websites — 54 | 18
that offer details on international travel to your destination. Be sure — 68 | 23
to update your immunizations and buy digestive medicines that might — 82 | 27
be needed when exploring new foods. — 89 | 30

Frequently the time on the plane is quite long, with some — 11 | 33
international flights over ten hours in the air. Travel delays are — 25 | 38
possible, so keep a small bag with a change of clothes, toiletries, — 38 | 42
medicine, and other important items with you. Bringing your own travel — 52 | 47
pillow, a good book, and other entertainment along with that provided — 66 | 51
by the airline will make your trip an enjoyable one. — 76 | 55

When you leave the plane, you will be given a card to be presented — 13 | 59
upon entry to the country and one to present when you exit the country. — 27 | 64
Keep those cards and your passport with you at all times. When you — 41 | 68
remember these preparation guides, you are on your way to a memorable — 54 | 73
international experience. — 59 | 75

1' | 1 | 2 | 3 | 4 | 5 | 6 | 7 | 8 | 9 | 10 | 11 | 12 | 13 |
3' | 1 | 2 | 3 | 4 |

Project Setting

HESS OFFICE PARK

You are continuing your work as an assistant to Patrick J. Hess, the manager of Hess Office Park, the 500-acre office park managed by Hess Property Enterprises. Your assistance in preparing the annual report is required for this project as well as a letter to a new tenant inviting him to the Owners and Tenants Association meeting and a memo announcing the office closings for the next year.

Standard operating procedures for the project:

1. Use the Retrospect document theme for all documents.
2. Use block letter style with open punctuation and the Hess Office Park letterhead from the data files. Include an appropriate salutation and use *Sincerely* as the complimentary closing. Begin the data at approximately 2". **Use Patrick J. Hess, Manager** as the writer's name and title.
3. Create envelopes for letters only when directed, as many letters are attached to an email.
4. The data files also contain a Hess Office Park memo form.
5. Add your reference initials and other notations as appropriate.
6. Use the List Table 4 – Accent 2 table style for all tables and center tables horizontally.

89-d2

Job Search Plan

resume worksheet

★ **TIP**

The resume worksheet that you complete is essential for the resumes you will prepare in the next lesson. If you do a good, thorough job on it, you will be able to produce better resumes in much less time.

You will need the job descriptions and company information that you printed in Drill 1 before you begin this activity. Open *resume worksheet* from the data files and add or delete rows if needed.

1. The heading for a resume should contain:
 a. Your full name, address, telephone number, and email address. Some instructors recommend including both your current and permanent address if you are a student. A better approach might be to send an address change two weeks before it takes effect. Consider it an opportunity to communicate again and affirm your interest in the job.
 b. If desired, include the URL for additional information, such as the URL for a LinkedIn public profile or a website.
2. Complete your SWOT Analysis.
 a. List your key strengths (competencies, knowledge, and personal attributes) that are relevant to the job you want to obtain.
 b. List your key weaknesses—things that are important for the type of job, but that you have not developed.
 c. List opportunities—weaknesses that can be turned into strengths. For example, a degree (associate or bachelor's) is required, but you have not finished the program yet; or in-depth knowledge of *Excel*, but you are enrolled in an *Excel* course.
 d. List threats—weaknesses that in all likelihood you cannot turn into strengths in a reasonable amount of time. For example, two years of work experience is required, but you have none; threats put you at a disadvantage in getting the job.
3. Identify and list the keywords and key phrases in the job description for the desired job.
 a. Educational requirements.
 b. Experience requirements.
 c. Specific job qualifications.
 d. Personal attributes.
4. Identify a list of core competencies:
 a. Strengths relevant to the job that match keywords in the job description.
 b. Opportunities that you feel certain that you can convert to strengths prior to obtaining the job or very shortly after and that match the keywords.
5. Print this document for later use. Save and close. (*89-d2*)

Using Keywords Effectively

Communicating Today ▶

★ **TIP**

ATS stands for Applicant Tracking System.

Keywords are used by **ATS software** to match qualified applicants to the requirements listed in a specific job description. Actual phrases, sometimes called **search strings**, are used by the software. A number of experts indicate that the ATS screens out many qualified candidates; therefore, it is critical to understand how they work. It is also important to know that some ATS software is linked to social media.

To get an idea of what employers want, read a variety of job descriptions in your field and review the terminology they use for the type of job you seek. Analyze the description for the specific job you are applying for thoroughly to determine the keywords. Prepare a customized resume using the company-desired keywords several times worded in a slightly different manner. Listing core competencies is one effective way to get an additional repetition of keywords.

75-d1

Letter

hess letterhead

Key a letter to **Mr. Jackson Price, President** of **Price & Price Company**, with information about the Owners and Tenants Association and an invitation to the December meeting. The mailing address is **100 Hess Boulevard, Suite 3532, Austin, TX 78712-2196**. (Include the company name in the letter address.)

1. Open *hess letterhead* from the data files and save as *75-d1*. Date the letter **November 20, 201-**.
2. Add **Enclosures** since this letter is being mailed. Create an envelope and add to the letter.
3. Save and close. (*75-d1*)

We are pleased to welcome you as a new tenant in the Hess Office Park and invite you to the Owners and Tenants Association December meeting on Tuesday, December 2, at the offices of Schniepp Enterprises. The meeting begins at 6:30 p.m. with snacks and drinks provided by our host and offers a casual environment for meeting other owners and tenants.

The Owners and Tenants Association meets regularly on the first Monday of each month at 6:30 p.m. at the location of one of the owners and tenants. However, the December meeting was moved to Tuesday evening to accommodate the many businesses involved with the local Christmas parade. The January meeting will return to Monday evening and will be hosted by Hess Office Park at our newly renovated conference center.

To acquaint you with our association, I am enclosing the current directory and the most recent newsletters. I look forward to seeing you at the December meeting and am eager to introduce you to our fine group of owners and tenants.

75-d2

Table

REVIEW

Save Quick Part

Insert/Text/Quick Parts down arrow/Save Selection to Quick Part Gallery

Select the text to be saved and then follow the path to save it.

In a new blank document, create a two-column table showing the list of holiday closings of the Hess Office Park; make the company name the first line heading and **201- Holiday Closings** the second line.

New Year's Day: January 1; Memorial Day: May 26; Independence Day: July 4; Labor Day: September 4; Thanksgiving: November 23-24; Christmas: December 24-26

1. Create a 2-column table using the required table style. Center the text in rows 1 and 2.
2. Adjust the column spacing attractively and center the table horizontally.
3. Select the table and save as a Quick Part named **holiday closings**.
4. Save and close. (*75-d2*)

The next step for applicants is to prepare a customized resume and cover letter to apply for each specific job they have located. The type of resume prepared is determined by the size and type of company and the information listed in each job posting. Resumes prepared for recruiters must contain keywords that match the job description, or they will be rejected and not granted an interview. Recruiters typically do not focus on cover letters. They send the applicants screened in by the ATS to the hiring managers to interview, evaluate, and select appropriate applicants. Hiring managers in small companies typically evaluate both resumes and cover letters carefully to determine which applicants match the company needs most closely. Then they interview selected applicants and begin the selection process. Always bring your resume and reference list to the interview.

QUICK ✓

Did you locate the unmarked errors? Check below to see if you corrected these errors.

1. On page 1, in the second to last paragraph, replace *personel* with *personal*.
2. On page 2, in the second full paragraph, replace *frequent* with *frequently*.
3. On page 3, in the second full paragraph, replace *includes* with *include*.
4. On page 4, in the last full paragraph, replace *there* with *their*.
5. On page 5, in the first full paragraph, replace *applicant* with *applicants*.

If you did not locate all of the errors, remember that on a resume or cover letter, errors such as these could cause your application to be rejected.

! WORKPLACE SUCCESS

Applicant Tracking Systems

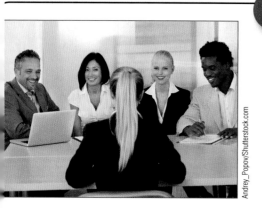

Andrey_Popov/Shutterstock.com

Understanding how companies track resumes is very important to a successful job search. Many, if not most, medium- and large-size companies manage their job recruitment process by using an applicant tracking system. They request electronic resumes or scan paper-based resumes into their system. Once a resume has become a part of an applicant tracking system, the software then determines from all resumes received which ones will be reviewed by the potential employer. Keywords are used to match the resume to the job description. The best way to format a resume depends on the software used by the company that receives it. To get the best results, check the company's website for information about submitting a resume.

Report

dan rivera

Follow the steps for 74-d1 if you need additional help with the steps.

Mr. Hess has drafted the fourth-quarter report he will present to the Owners and Tenants Association meeting in January. In a new blank document, key a report using the leftbound report format and the Retrospect theme. Shrink the title to fit on one line.

1. Use this information for the cover page. Obtain other information from the letterhead.

 Title: **Hess Office Park Fourth Quarter Activity Report**
 Subtitle: **October – December, 201-**

2. Apply styles to the title and side headings. Adjust space after each table.

3. Insert the data file *dan rivera* as the picture of the new staff person at the beginning of the paragraph. Use square wrapping and size attractively.

4. Leave a blank page after the cover page for the table of contents. Number the table of contents page with small Roman numerals and the report with Arabic numbers. Remember to insert a section break at the top of the first page of the report.

5. Use the Retrospect header and footer style. The style will populate the content automatically. Display the page number in the footer on all pages of the report body.

6. Create a table of contents at 2" using the default template format; apply Title style.

7. Save and close. (75-d3)

Title Hess Office Park Fourth Quarter Activity Report

Subtitle Quarter Ended December 31, 201-

The Hess Office Park Fourth Quarter Activity Report is prepared for the Owners and Tenants Association and is presented at the January meeting of the Association. The staff of Hess Office Park is pleased to report the following activities during the fourth quarter, ending December 31, 201-. Activities include work accomplished in the community as well as achievements in the office park.

New Owners and Tenants

One new owner and three new tenants have joined Hess Office Park in the fourth quarter. One tenant vacated space as of December 1. The table below outlines the changes in detail.

Space Changes in Fourth Quarter				
	Type of Lease			
	Owner	Tenant	Change	Suites Assigned
1		Ayesha Liem	Add	311
2		Ethan Madison	Add	323-325
3	Riley Grant		Add	410-412
4		Jackson Price	Add	422-423
5		Paula Bowen	Terminate	521-525

(continued)

Apply It

89-d1

White Paper

 employment process

★ **TIP**

Ensuring that employment documents are error free is critical. Errors in an employment document often result in a rejection of the application.

1. Open the *employment process* data file; locate and correct the five unmarked errors in it.
2. Format the document.
 a. Use the Office theme with the default formatting style; use standard unbound report style.
 b. Format the headings using the directions in parentheses for heading styles: (Title), (Subtitle), (H1), and (H2); then delete the directions shown in parentheses after each heading.
3. Key the summary at the bottom of the report.
4. Number the report pages using the Facet (odd page) header; do not show the header on the first page.
5. Proofread the entire document carefully and print it. Save the printed copy; you will use it as a reference throughout Module 16.
6. Save and close. (*89-d1*)

Summary (H1)

Employers begin the job process by developing a job description, then posting and advertising the position described in numerous outlets. In large organizations, recruiters began to search actively for job applicants using all of the search resources available including social networks, other online media, print media, employment agencies, placement offices, and personal contacts. They typically manage the search using an applicant tracking system (ATS), which screens resumes provided by applicants and refers applicants passing the screen to the hiring manager, who is responsible for the interviews, evaluation, and selection of employees. In small organizations, supervisors or hiring managers are typically responsible for searching for appropriate applicants, evaluating them, and selecting the best applicants that meet the needs of the organization.

Applicants begin the job process by analyzing their strengths and weaknesses to determine the types of jobs in which they could be successful. Then effective applicants begin a broad-based search using all of the resources that employers use to post and advertise positions to locate available positions and job descriptions for which they believe they are qualified. Networking is one of the most effective search tools. Some applicants prepare a generic resume and send it to numerous companies listing their strengths and the type of job they are seeking. This approach is generally not very productive. A targeted search identifying available positions that match the applicants' qualifications is a more productive approach.

(continued)

These changes represent an increase of 5 percent over last year's fourth quarter and a gain of 20 percent this year. This past year Patrick Hess, manager of Hess Office Park, has added the following recruitment activities:

- Joined the Chamber of Commerce and five civic organizations.
- Accepted office of vice president for one civic organization.
- Accepted leadership role in securing funding for college scholarships for area students.

These networks are producing excellent connections and resulted in one added owner and two additional tenants to Hess Office Park.

5K Scholarship Fun Run

Hess Office Park is the site for the 5K Scholarship Fun Run sponsored by the East Central Education Foundation (ECEF) to be held on April 10, 201-. Scholarship monies are awarded to freshmen students entering college in the fall semester.

Mr. Robert Kaczynski, president of ECEF, is the contact person and has signed the official agreement with our office. Hess Office Park will designate spaces in the south parking lot on Friday afternoon and all day on Saturday. Tables and chairs will be set up along the race route for volunteers to distribute drinks and snacks to the runners/walkers. Security and police assistance will be provided at the main intersection of Hess Boulevard and Elm Street. Space will also be provided for vendors near the entrance of the office park.

Staff Updates

We are pleased to welcome Dan Rivera, who joined our staff on October 1 as an accountant. Dan holds a master's degree in accounting and has worked as an auditor for seven years and three years as a forensic accountant. Dan and his wife, Marilyn, recently moved to Austin from San Antonio. They have two sons. Danny is 3 and Sam is 1. We look forward to Dan's contributions to our office.

Holiday Closings

Holiday closings are approved annually by the Board of Directors. The table below lists the six approved closings.

REVIEW

Insert Quick Part

Insert/Text/Quick Parts

Select the saved Quick Part.

Insert holiday closings Quick Part created in *75-d2*.

In case of emergency, tenants and owners are to contact Colton Blake at 512.555.0100.

(continued)

Document Design

EFFECTIVE EMPLOYMENT STRATEGIES

Before you can design effective documents to be used in search for a job, you need to understand how an organization goes about determining that it needs a new employee, specifying what it wants the employee to do, determining the skills and personal attributes needed to be effective in the job, and selecting the best person to hire.

This lesson includes a drill and two activities:

1. Key the summary and format a white paper (specialized report) designed to help you understand the employment process.

2. Create a plan for writing your resume and a cover letter for a specific job that prepares you to do the remaining jobs in this module and to plan and execute a successful search for a job.

To create a job search plan:

1. Think seriously about:
 a. Your educational and work experiences, if any.
 b. Your personal attributes and soft skills that would enhance your job success.
 c. The type of job that you would like to obtain.
 d. Your preference in company size and type.
 e. The geographic area in which you would like to work.

2. Select the broad job title—such as administrative assistant, office manager, customer service representative, accounting associate, marketing associate, events coordinator, graphics designer, etc.—for the job you want to obtain.

3. Obtain one or more job descriptions for the position.
 a. Use the keywords *most popular job websites* to locate job sites online and search at least two of them, such as Indeed, CareerBuilder, Monster, or any other sites listed.
 b. To search the site, provide the job title you selected and the city and/or state in which you would like to work.
 c. Find the option for full job descriptions. Most sites provide this option.
 d. Note the companies that provided the description. Most job websites provide the option to learn more about the company. If not, search the Internet for information using the company name. Note the size, the presence or absence of a Human Resources Department, and the location of the company.

DRILL 1 RESUME WRITING PLAN INFORMATION

1. Search a job website to find information about the job you would like to have.

2. Read several job descriptions. Print one or two that appeal to you most.

3. Access information about the company that provided the job description and make notes or print it.

4. Keep the information from this drill to use in *89-d2* and to write resumes in Lesson 90.

Summary

The fourth quarter has shown positive growth, and preliminary data indicates additional growth for the first quarter of next year. Additional information is available on our website at www.hesspropertyenterprises.com.

Compose Memo

 hess memo

Mr. Hess asks you to compose a memo for him to send to the **Owners and Tenants Association** informing the members of the dates the Hess Office Park office will be closed for the upcoming year.

1. Open *hess memo* from the data files and save as *75-d4*. In the first paragraph, explain that the Board of Directors have approved the holiday closings for Hess Office Park and indicate the list is shown in the table below.

2. After the first paragraph, insert the table saved as a Quick Part in *75-d2*.

3. In the last paragraph, give the name of **Colton Blake** as the contact to call in case of emergency. Colton's number is **512.555.0100**.

4. Date the memo **November 20, 201-**. Supply an appropriate subject line.

5. Save and close. (*75-d4*)

Employment Documents

Lesson 89 Job Search Strategies
Lesson 90 Resumes
Lesson 91 Social Media and Employment Letters
Lesson 92 Hess Office Park
Lesson 93 Assessment Modules 15 and 16

LEARNING OUTCOMES

- Develop a plan for a successful employment search.
- Prepare traditional and specialized resumes.
- Compose and format employment documents.
- Build keyboarding skills.

Lesson 89 Job Search Strategies

Warmup *Lesson 89a Warmup*

lesson 89a warmup

Skill Building

89b Timed Writing

1. Key a 1' timed writing on each paragraph; work to increase speed.
2. Key a 3' timed writing on both paragraphs.

	gwam	1'	3'

An effective job search requires very careful planning and a lot of hard work. Major decisions must be made about the type of job, the size and the type of business, and the geographic area. Once all of these basic decisions have been made, then the complex task of locating the ideal job can begin. Some jobs are listed in what is known as the open job market. These positions are listed with placement offices of schools, placement agencies, and they are advertised in newspapers or journals.

13 | 4
26 | 9
39 | 13
52 | 17
65 | 22
80 | 27
93 | 31
97 | 32

The open market is not the only source of jobs, however. Some experts believe that almost two-thirds of all jobs are in what is sometimes called the hidden job market. Networking is the primary way to learn about jobs in the hidden job market. Employees of a company, instructors, and members of professional associations are some of the best contacts to tap the hidden job market. Much time and effort are required to tap these sources. But the hidden market often produces the best results.

12 | 37
25 | 41
38 | 45
51 | 49
64 | 54
77 | 58
91 | 63
97 | 65

1'	1	2	3	4	5	6	7	8	9	10	11	12	13
3'		1		2			3			4			

Mail Merge

LEARNING OUTCOMES

- Merge form letters.
- Merge envelopes and labels.
- Edit the data source.
- Sort and filter records.

Lesson 76 Mail Merge

New Command
- Mail Merge

Warmup *Lesson 76a Warmup*

lesson 76a warmup

Skill Building

76b Timed Writing

1. Key a 1' timed writing on each paragraph. Work to increase speed.
2. Key a 3' timing on all paragraphs.

	gwam	1'	3'

What characterizes the life of an entrepreneur? Those who have 12 | 4
never owned their own businesses may think owning a business means 26 | 9
being your own boss, setting your own hours, and making a lot of money. 40 | 13
Those who have run their own businesses are quick to report that 53 | 18
owning a business may be exciting and challenging, but it also requires 67 | 22
hard work, long hours, and personal sacrifice. A good idea is not the 81 | 27
only prerequisite for a successful business. A little luck even helps. 95 | 32

Many small businesses are operated as businesses from the initial 13 | 36
stages. However, some small businesses that turn out to be successful 27 | 40
are just hobbies in the early stages. The entrepreneur has a job and 40 | 45
uses the income from it to support the hobby. When the hobby begins 54 | 49
to require more and more time, the entrepreneur has to choose between 68 | 54
the job and the hobby. The decision is usually based on finances. If 81 | 59
enough money can be made from the hobby or can be obtained from 94 | 63
another source, the hobby is turned into a business. 104 | 66

1'	1	2	3	4	5	6	7	8	9	10	11	12
3'		1			2			3			4	

Row 5: 10:05 a.m. Depart (DFW) at 10:05 a.m. on Executive West Flight
 1357 and arrive at Oklahoma City Will Rogers Airport
 (OKC) at 11:15 a.m. Taxi to Oakie Inn, 3 Park Avenue;
 Confirmation #384930C.

Row 6: 2:00 p.m. Meet with Elizabeth Glenn and various staff members
 at GameDay Wi-Fi Inc., 401 Couch Drive. Return to
 hotel at 5:30.

Row 7: 7:30 p.m. Picked up by Connor Bass for dinner at the Southwest
 Country Club.

Row 9: Wednesday, January 29 Oklahoma City to Austin

Row 10: 8:15 a.m. Depart OKC at 8:15 a.m. on Executive West Flight 1459
 and arrive at DFW at 9:10 a.m.

Row 11: 10:25 a.m. Depart DFW at 10:25 on Executive West Flight 1234
 and arrive at AUS at 11:35.

88-d6

Compose

hess news release
form

Hess Office Park uses
the same style for news
releases as the one
illustrated on page 4-20.

Use the *hess news release form* and compose a one- or two-paragraph news release
for Hess Office Park to announce that Elizabeth Glenn signed a 10-year contract
to move her rapidly growing high-tech company, GameDay Wi-Fi Inc., to the
Technology Quad of our office park.

She told Daniel and Patrick that our office park matched the type of environment
she wanted for her company perfectly. She said that she already has numerous
contracts with both collegiate and professional organizations in Texas to enhance
the GameDay experience for their fans. She works with all types of sports—football,
baseball, hockey, soccer, basketball, and others.

When asked why she picked Texas, she said Texas and Austin in particular had
excellent educational institutions, a passion for sports, and a reputation for
embracing technology—all of which are critical for the success of her company.
She has 125 employees now and expects to expand the operations soon.

After you have composed the news release, check to ensure that you have included all of
the necessary information, then proofread the document. Save and close. (88-d6)

MAIL MERGE

Creating personal form letters, printing labels, and addressing envelopes to a large number of individuals are tasks done easily using the Mail Merge feature. Mail merge is creating a new (merged) document by combining information from two other documents—the main document and the data source.

The **main document** contains the text and graphics that remain the same for each version of the merged document. Within the main document, **merge fields** are inserted as placeholders in locations where you want to merge names, addresses, and other variable information that comes from the data source file.

The **data source** is a file that contains the names, addresses, and other variables to be merged with the main document. All the variables for one individual are called a **record**. The separate variables for each record are called **fields**.

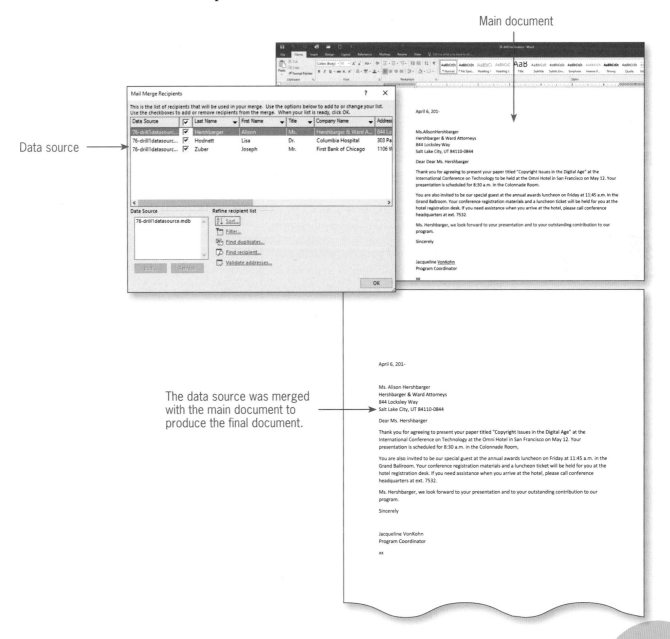

Main document

Data source

The data source was merged with the main document to produce the final document.

2. Continue to offer the discounted rate for short-term office and conference room use to nonprofit organizations. Make sure our staff realizes that these organizations provide valuable support to our community and that we want to work closely with them. These organizations are more than willing to use the conference rooms with movable tables configured appropriately to meet their needs.

3. Add six new conference rooms to our current building plans. Building 4 still has an entire floor unallocated. It could easily handle a quad layout with four conference rooms, an open lobby area with registration space, and a food service setup area. Restrooms are already provided on each floor. Two of the conference rooms on this floor would have the large fixed conference table, and the other two would have movable tables that could be configured to meet different needs. Two conference rooms could be added to the Conference Center. The space on the second floor that was previously used by Wexford QCT Trainers has been vacated. Both of these rooms would have fixed furniture with seating for 36. All of the support services are already in place on that floor of the Conference Center.

88-d5

Itinerary

Daniel Forde asked Patrick Hess if he would make a quick development trip with him to Oklahoma City. An executive in a high-tech company is considering moving her company headquarters from Oklahoma City to Austin. Her company, GameDay Wi-Fi Inc., specializes in installing Wi-Fi systems around college and professional stadiums and other venues to enhance the game day experience. Prepare the itinerary for Patrick and Daniel.

1. In a new blank document, tap ENTER three times and insert a 2-column, 11-row table. Apply List Table 4 – Accent 1 table style.

2. Adjust the first column to 2" width. Apply 0.4" row height to the first row and 0.3" to the other rows. Apply Orange, Accent 1 theme color, bold, and Align Center Left to the rows listing the dates and locations. Increase the font size in the first row to 14 points.

3. Add space before paragraph for each entry with text in the second column to make it easier to read. Leave a blank line between the entries for the two dates.

4. Key the information shown below for the itinerary.

5. Save and close. (88-d5)

Row 1: Itinerary for Patrick Hess and Daniel Forde

Row 2: Austin to Oklahoma City January 28-29, 201- (right align date)

Row 3: Tuesday, January 28 Austin to Oklahoma City

Row 4: 8:04 a.m. Depart Austin Bergstrom International Airport (AUS) on Executive West Flight 1202 at 8:04 a.m. and arrive at Dallas/Ft. Worth (DFW) at 8:58 a.m.

(continued)

MAIL MERGE WIZARD

The Mail Merge Wizard is a straightforward way to produce a merged document such as the form letters you will create in this lesson. The Mail Merge task pane displays in the far right of the screen and is used to navigate through the six steps of the Wizard.

To start the Mail Merge Wizard:

Mailings/Start Mail Merge/Start Mail Merge

1. In a new document, follow the path above to display a list of mail merge options.
2. Click Step-by-Step Mail Merge Wizard ❶.

📄	Letters
✉	E-mail Messages
▣	Envelopes...
▣	Labels...
▤	Directory
W	Normal Word Document
▨	Step-by-Step Mail Merge Wizard... ❶

DRILL 1 MAIL MERGE WIZARD

1. Begin a new blank document and save as *76-drill1main*. Follow the path above to display a list of mail merge options. Click Step-by-Step Mail Merge Wizard.

2. Follow the six steps of the Mail Merge Wizard explained below and on the next few pages. To move from one step to the next, click Next located at the bottom of the pane. This drill will lead you through the steps for using the Mail Merge Wizard.

Step 1: Select document type

- Choose Letters ❶.
- Click Next: Starting document to go to step 2 of the Wizard.

Step 2: Select starting document

- Click Use the current document ❷ to create a new form letter in the active window.
- Click Next: Select recipients. (**Note:** You may click Previous: Select document type to return to the previous step.)

Step 3: Select recipients

- Click Type a new list ❸.
- Under Type a new list, click Create ❹ to display the New Address List dialog box.

88-d2

Compose Memo

 hess memo

Hess Office Park has recently established a Director's Extranet. All Board Meeting documents and supplementary materials should be posted on the extranet once they have been finalized. Draft documents should be distributed by email after Mr. Hess reviews them.

1. Send a memo to Board members and meeting participants from you dated January 9.
2. Remind them of the meeting date, time, and location; ask them to confirm their attendance at the meeting.
3. Ask everyone to review the Agenda for the Board meeting and send you any recommended changes or additions to the agenda. Remind them that supplementary meeting materials should be posted on the Director's Extranet at least one week prior to the meeting.
4. Edit and proofread your memo carefully.
5. Save and close. (88-d2)

88-d3

Final Agenda

 agenda with changes

Mr. Hess asked you to finalize the agenda so that it could be posted to the Director's Extranet.

1. Open *agenda with changes* from the data files and check to see that Track Changes are turned on and All Markup displays the changes.
2. Mr. Hess indicated that all of the changes recommended were appropriate and asked you to implement them.
3. Make the required changes and finalize the document (by deleting the comments).
4. Check spacing and formatting carefully to ensure that no errors exist.
5. Save and close. (88-d3)

88-d4

Minutes

 minutes 1-21-201-

Open *minutes 1-21-201-* from the data files and use the instructions and information below to finalize the minutes of the January 21 meeting of the Hess Office Park Board.

1. Make sure your name and initials are in the User and Initials boxes.
2. Add a second-page header using Blank (three columns). Insert the Board name in the first column, the page number using Current Position in the second column, and the meeting date in the third column.
3. Review carefully the changes and the comments from each reviewer; then make the following changes:
 a. Add the information in Marcia and Mike's comments to the document.
 b. Accept the insertions and deletions indicated in the document.
 c. Key the recommendations for Hess Property Enterprises Board shown below.
4. Finalize the document; check to ensure that you have followed the SOPs.
5. Save and close. (88-d4)

> The Hess Office Park Board approved the following recommendations to be presented to the Hess Property Enterprises Board:
>
> 1. Approve the budget changes required to increase the energy efficiency rating of the buildings, including the pet center, identified by the Energy Efficiency Evaluation Team. The detailed plan and cost analysis is posted on the Director's Extranet.

(continued)

- Click Customize Columns ❺ to edit the default field names.

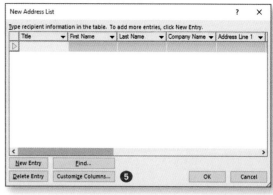

a. To delete a field name: Select the field and click Delete ❻. Click Yes to confirm the deletion. For this drill, delete Address Line 2, Country or Region, Home Phone, Work Phone, and E-mail Address.

b. To add a field name: Select it and click Add ❼. Add three fields: Speech, Room, and Time.

c. To position the new fields correctly, select the field to be moved. Click Move Up or Move Down as appropriate. Move the field names so they are positioned as shown at the right. Click OK.

- Key the variables for Record 1 in the New Address List dialog box. Tab to the next field. Click New Entry to begin a new record, and key the variables for Record 2. Repeat for Record 3. Click OK after keying all of the records.

Field names	Record 1	Record 2	Record 3
Title	Ms.	Dr.	Mr.
First Name	Alison	Lisa	Joseph
Last Name	Hershbarger	Hodnett	Zuber
Company Name	Hershbarger & Ward Attorneys	Columbia Hospital	First Bank of Chicago
Address Line 1	844 Locksley Way	303 Park Circle Road	1106 Whispering Pines Road
City	Salt Lake City	Milwaukee	Chicago
State	UT	WI	IL
ZIP Code	84110-0844	53221-0303	60650-1106
Time	8:30 a.m.	9:30 a.m.	10:30 a.m.
Room	Colonnade Room	Diplomat Room	Laurel Suite
Speech	"Copyright Issues in the Digital Age"	"Creating Interactive Presentations"	"Using Social Media to Market Your Organization"

Standard operating procedures for the project:

1. Use the *hess memo* and *news release* forms provided in the data files. Note that they have the Retrospect theme already applied. Follow the SOPs you applied in Module 10, page 3-32.

2. Apply Retrospect theme to each document you prepare.

3. Use the same heading and format for all meeting, travel, and news documents that you prepare for Patrick Hess, manager of Hess Office Park. Just change the name of the document such as *Agenda* or *Minutes*. See the illustration below. To create the heading, apply Title style to the document name and Heading 2 to the Board name, location, date, and time lines. Insert an en dash with space before and after between the times in the last line. Update the information as appropriate. Save it as a Quick Part to simplify document preparation.

4. On Agendas, Patrick prefers to list the beginning and ending time of meetings and not list the time allocated for each item on the agenda.

5. Draft documents are sent to appropriate individuals for review. Mr. Hess reviews the recommended changes and comments and provides instructions on how to handle the changes. After making the recommended changes on documents, be sure to delete all comments. Note that first names are used frequently in these internal documents.

6. Hess Office Park uses action-style minutes. Include all action taken and a brief summary of the discussion of key items.

88-d1

Draft Agenda

1. In a new blank document, prepare the draft agenda for the January 21 Quarterly Board meeting.
2. Use the standard heading and set a dot leader tab at the right margin.
3. Key the items shown below.
4. Save and close. (*88-d1*)

Welcome and Call to Order	Patrick Hess
Quarterly Financial Report	Carolyn Hess
Report on Energy Efficiency Evaluation	Inga Kock
Large Conference Rooms Needs Assessment	Mike Burge
Recommendations for Hess Property Enterprises Board	Patrick Hess
Review of Hess Office Park Facilities	Michael White
Business Development Update	Daniel Forde
Executive Session	Patrick Hess
Adjournment	

- The Save Address List dialog box displays. Key a filename (**76-drill1datasource**) in the File name box and click Save. In the Save box, choose the appropriate folder for saving this file.

- The Mail Merge Recipients dialog box now displays and shows the variables in table format. Click OK.

- **Note:** To move within the Mail Merge Recipients dialog box, click the desired row. Use the scroll bar to navigate in the record. With a long recipient list, click Find recipient to search for the desired recipient ❽.

- Click Next: Write your letter from the Mail Merge task pane.

Step 4: Write your letter

- Begin keying the main document at approximately 2". In this drill, key **April 6, 201-** as the date. Often the Date command is inserted with an option selected to update automatically. Tap ENTER two times.

- Insert the merge fields for the letter address:

 a. From the right pane, click More items ❾.

 b. Select Title, click Insert, and then click Close. Tap Space Bar.

 c. Repeat step b to add First_Name and Last_Name. Press SHIFT + ENTER to remove extra spacing between lines of the letter address.

 d. Continue inserting the merge fields for the remaining lines of the letter address.

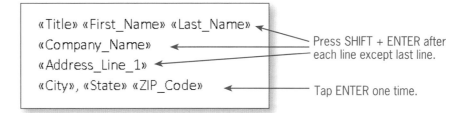

«Title» «First_Name» «Last_Name»

«Company_Name»

«Address_Line_1»

«City», «State» «ZIP_Code»

Press SHIFT + ENTER after each line except last line.

Tap ENTER one time.

Lesson 88 Hess Office Park

Learning Outcomes

- Apply keying, formatting, and word processing skills.
- Prepare documents with columns and graphics.
- Work independently with few specific instructions.

Warmup *Lesson 88a Warmup*

 lesson 88a warmup

Skill Building

88b Timed Writing

Key two 3' timed writings.

	gwam	3'
Employees who work together as a team are more effective than	4	64
those who work solo. This concept is known as synergy. Synergy simply	9	69
means that the joint action exceeds the sum of individual actions. The	13	73
results are not just in the quantity of work; major increases in quality	18	78
result when people work together as a team. Teamwork is critical for	23	83
success.	23	83
What characterizes an excellent team member? An excellent team	27	87
member understands the goals of the team and will place team values	32	92
above her or his individual objectives. An excellent team member helps	36	96
to determine the most effective way to reach the goals that were set by	41	101
the group and will help to make each decision that affects the group.	46	106
Above all, an excellent team member will support a decision made by	50	110
the team. Each member must understand his or her role and respect	55	115
the roles of others. Every member of a team must share in both victory	59	119
and defeat.	60	120

3' | 1 | 2 | 3 | 4 |

Project Setting

HESS PROPERTY ENTERPRISES

In this project, you continue to work for Hess Property Enterprises and the management team of the Hess Office Park. Your work in this project focuses on helping Patrick J. Hess, manager of Hess Office Park, prepare documents related to the upcoming quarterly Board meeting of the Hess Office Park. This Board is a subset of the Hess Property Enterprises Board and deals strictly with Hess Office Park needs and issues. You will draft documents for Board review and then incorporate recommended changes and finalize documents. You will also assist Mr. Hess with the preparation of other documents.

Review the standard operating procedures (SOPs) on the next page. Use them as a check list when you proofread each document and again after you have completed all documents.

- From the Mail Merge task pane (at far right), click Greeting Line. Click the down arrow to the right of the comma and select none. Click OK. Tap ENTER one time and continue keying the letter until the Speech merge code.

- Insert the merge field for Speech. Continue keying the letter shown below. Insert the merge fields for *Time* and *Room* at the appropriate places.
- When finished keying the letter, click Save to update the changes made in the main document. (*76-drill1main*)
- Click Next: Preview your letters.

Insert Merge Field ▾

April 6, 201- (ENTER 2 times)

«AddressBlock» (ENTER 1 time)

«GreetingLine» (ENTER 1 time)

Thank you for agreeing to present your paper titled «Speech» at the International Conference on Technology to be held at the Omni Hotel in San Francisco on May 12. Your presentation is scheduled for «Time» in the «Room».

You are also invited to be our special guest at the annual awards luncheon on Friday at 11:45 a.m. in the Grand Ballroom. Your conference registration materials and a luncheon ticket will be held for you at the hotel registration desk. If you need assistance when you arrive at the hotel, please call conference headquarters at ext. 7532.

«Title» «Last_Name», we look forward to your presentation and to your outstanding contribution to our program.

Sincerely (ENTER 2 times) | Jacqueline VonKohn | Program Coordinator | xx

TIP

Press SHIFT + ENTER after name to remove extra spacing between writer's name and title.

Sun Property and Casualty Insurance Company

1592 S. Plaza Way, Flagstaff, AZ 86011-0136
Phone: 928.555.0174 | Solana.Rodriquez@apic.com | Fax: 928.555.0136

News Release

Contact Person: Solana Rodriquez

Current date

For Release: Immediately

SUN RECEIVES NATIONAL AWARD

FLAGSTAFF, AZ—The Sun Property and Casualty Insurance Company announced today that it received the *American Family-Friendly Work Environment Award* presented by the American Council on Insurance. Only one award is given each year to an insurance company for a unique contribution to improving the work environment for families.

Sun was cited for the unique partnership it established with Century Medical University and Sunbelt Child Development Centers to create a state-of-the-art Sun Child Development and Research Center. The center is in its first year of operation. The first floor of the center provides facilities for approximately two hundred children, and the second floor research center focuses on health and development issues impacting preschool children. Children receive medical screenings, and special isolated facilities are available for sick children at the center. Sun provides partial scholarships to employees and to low-income families.

Sun is the only insurance company to ever receive this prestigious award more than once. Five years ago, Sun received the award for its creative *Surrogate Grandparents Mentoring Program* in partnership with Central Academy to mentor children from low-income families after school. That program is still in effect today and is very successful. More than forty "grandparents" mentor over a hundred students each year.

Sun has offices throughout the Southwest and has 1,274 employees—430 of whom are in the Flagstaff area.

###

News Release

Step 5: Preview your letters

1. When previewing letters, select the lines of the letter address except the last one and remove the extra spacing after the paragraph. Click the navigation buttons to preview and proofread each of your letters. *Tip:* To edit variables, click Edit recipient list and make the necessary changes to the data source file.

2. Click Next: Complete the merge.

Step 6: Complete the merge

1. Click Edit individual letters ➓. Click All; then OK. The merge letters will *not* appear on the screen. You will see the message: *Mail merge is done and document is generated. Click OK.*

2. Check. The merged letters will appear on the screen as the checked document. Save the merged letters and close. (*76-drill1*)

EDIT MAIL MERGE DOCUMENT

Mailings/Start Mail Merge/Start Mail Merge/Step-by-Step Mail Merge Wizard

Often it is necessary to edit the main document. Perhaps the user did not finish the job before closing the document, or perhaps changes are now needed in the main document.

With the main document open, follow the path above and open the Mail Merge Wizard. Click the Next or Previous button until you locate the desired step to be edited. Make the desired changes or continue creating the main document.

Troubleshooting Tips

1. When you open the main document, you will be prompted that data from your database will be placed in the document. Click Yes to accept the data if the desired data source is connected to the main document. If you wish to use another data source, click No and select the new data source.

2. When in the *Write your letter* step of the Wizard, the merge field codes will display; but when in the *Preview your letters* step of the Wizard, actual data from the data source will display. Click Next or Previous to move to the correct step.

Lesson 87 News Release

Warmup Lesson 87a Warmup

lesson 87a warmup

Document Design

87b

NEWS RELEASE

A news release provides information that an organization wishes to publish. Typically, it is sent to reporters and news professionals at newspapers, radio and television stations, and other media outlets. The news often gets published if the release is newsworthy, well written, and easy to publish. Always design the release with the important information first because many outlets will publish only a portion of it.

Note in the illustration on the next page that a heading is included in addition to the letterhead. It typically includes the release date, the contact person, and a title that could serve as a news headline. Usually, ### or -30- is used to indicate the end of the article. If the news release goes to a second page, the word *more* is centered in a footer. The second page should have a short heading (often called a slug line) and the page number.

Many experts agree that traditional news releases do not work well on social media, especially media such as Facebook. If you are going to post a release on a professional network, such as LinkedIn, make it shorter, more visual, and conversational. A better alternative is to use a blog, but again keep it more visual and conversational.

Apply It

87-d1

News Release

sun news release

1. Open *sun news release* from your data files and key the news release shown on the next page. Pay particular attention to the heading information and the way it is formatted. Key an em dash (two dashes) after the state in paragraph 1.
2. Save and close. (*87-d1*)

87-d2

News Release

sun news release
sun ceo

1. Open *sun news release* from your data files and insert the current date. The news will be released immediately. Key the first paragraph shown below.
2. Insert the data file *sun ceo* after the first paragraph.
3. Then key the following closing paragraph: **Ledbetter is married to Kirk T. Parham, a nationally known pediatrician. They have two teenage children—a son, Joseph, and a daughter, Caitlyn.**
4. Save and close. (*87-d2*)

SUN NAMES NEW PRESIDENT AND CHIEF EXECUTIVE OFFICER

FLAGSTAFF, AZ—The Sun Property and Casualty Insurance Company announced today that its Board of Directors unanimously approved Amy T. Ledbetter as its new chief executive officer. Ledbetter replaces Mark R. Daff, who served as chief executive officer for the past eight years.

Apply It

76-d1

Mail Merge

1. Begin a new blank document and save as *76-d1main*. Create the data source. Customize the address list to include the fields below.

2. Key the following data for each of the three records. (*76-d1datasource*)

Field names	Record 1	Record 2	Record 3
Title	Mrs.	Mr.	Ms.
First Name	Jessica	Allen	Paje
Last Name	Quarrels	Bouchillon	Vang
Company Name	Hendrix Plastics	Magnolia Chemicals	Faulkner Florists
Address Line 1	5689 Old Vinton Road	538 Hill Street	885 North Third Street
City	Starkville	Columbus	West Point
State	MS	MS	MS
ZIP Code	39759-5689	39701-0538	39773-0885
County	Oktibbeha	Lowndes	Clay

3. Key the main document that follows and insert the merge fields in the main document. Use open punctuation. Insert the date to update automatically. Save the changes to the main document.

4. Merge the data source and the main document.

5. Save the merged letters and close. (*76-d1*)

TIP

Press SHIFT + ENTER after each line of the letter address except the last one.

<<Title>> <<First_Name>> <<Last_Name>>

<<Company Name>>

<<Address_Line_1>>

<<City>>, <<State>> <<ZIP_Code>>

<<GreetingLine>>

Thank you for submitting your proposal for enacting a more culturally diverse employment program for city workers to the American Studies Association.

The American Studies Association continually strives to work with city governments in three area counties to provide work environments that value diversity. The goal, of course, is to employ persons who reflect differences in age, gender, and interests. Different people solve problems differently, and having diverse groups leads to better decisions.

You may be contacted, <<Title>> <<Last_Name>>, to represent <<County>> County on the special Council for Managing Diversity that is being established in our three-county region. Again, thank you for letting us know what you are doing to ensure diversity at <<Company_Name>>.

Sincerely | Hunter Nyiri, Director | xx

LESSON 76 MAIL MERGE MODULE 13 **3-123**

1. In a new blank document, tap ENTER and key the itinerary using a 2-column table with default theme and margins. Insert an en dash between the dates in the heading and add a space before and after the en dash. Adjust the width of the first column to 2".

2. Apply List Table 4 – Accent 5. Deselect First Column in the Table Style Options.

3. Use 1" row height for the first row; apply 16-point Calibri Light and Align Center to the title.

4. Bold the information in the three rows with the dates. Adjust row height to 0.4" and apply Align Center Left to those rows. Add a blank row before days 2 and 3.

5. Compare the Heading style of this itinerary to the previous one you keyed.

6. Save and close. (86-d3)

Itinerary for Laurie Hammer July 14 – 16, 201-	
Wednesday, July 14	**Columbia to Cincinnati**
4:40 p.m.	Leave Columbia on non-stop Cincola Flight 5173 and arrive in Cincinnati at 5:55 p.m.; Metro Rental Car (Confirmation #67540912); Riverside Hotel (Confirmation #34898732)
8:15 p.m.	Picked up at hotel by Dave Calhoun and Jack Shaut; dinner at Royal Mason
Thursday, July 15	**Cincinnati**
8:00 a.m.	Leave for Natorp Publishing Center; 6319 Natorp Boulevard, Mason, Ohio
9:00 a.m.	Meet with President and Editor-in-Chief; President's office, Suite 600
9:45 a.m.	Meet with the Editorial Team, Fifth Floor Conference Room
11:45 a.m.	Break
12:00 noon	Working lunch, Fifth Floor Conference Room
2:00 p.m.	Meet with book designers, Fifth Floor Conference Room
2:30 p.m.	Break
3:00 p.m.	Meet with the Production Team, Fifth Floor Conference Room
5:30 p.m.	Return to hotel
7:30 p.m.	Meet Project Team for dinner; Chez Ruby; 644 Walnut Street; map in Travel folder
Friday, July 16	**Cincinnati to Columbia**
7:45 a.m.	Return rental car; Cincola Flight 6754 departs at 9:20 a.m. and arrives in Columbia at 10:40 a.m.

76-d2

Compose Mail Merge

1. Decide on a form letter that would be useful to you personally or to your class. Secure the names and addresses of the recipients of the form letter.

2. Begin a new blank document and save as *76-d2main*. Create the data source (*76-d2datasource*).

3. Compose the main document and insert the merge fields in it.

4. Merge the data source and the main document. Save the main document.

5. Save the merged document and close. (*76-d2*)

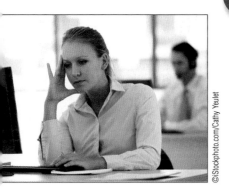

! WORKPLACE SUCCESS

Managing Information Overload

Business employees are under siege with the volume of information that is coming at them from all sides—text messages, voice mail, email, the Internet, television, radio, fax, magazines, news feeds, and many others. Interestingly, much of the data that business employees review is not relevant to their jobs. Because managing information overload is a critical skill needed by today's business employees, please consider the following technology and behavior suggestions.

Technology—Use email information filters to screen messages that do not demand your attention. Use delegation features to allow an assistant to respond to email when possible. Delete participation in list servers not desired. Take advantage of RSS feeds to compile data from the Internet and to allow the review of one set of data. Locate reputable blogs in the area of your research to decrease search time on the Internet and provide views of many individuals.

Behavior change—Maintain responsibility in email use; do not copy to another person just in case he or she may need it. Limit the control information has on your life and set the hours you will work per week. Set limits on when you check emails and use the cell phone, including vacation time.

Itinerary for Landon Winn

Chicago to Atlanta	October 9-11, 201-
Wednesday, October 9	Chicago to Atlanta
8:45 a.m.	Leave Chicago Midway Airport (MDW) on Southern Express Flight 1387 and arrive at Atlanta Hartsfield (ATL) at 11:20 a.m.; take MARTA to Buckhead Station (N-7). Taxi to Buckhead Inn (Confirmation #204857) 260 Pharr Road, NE. (45 minutes)
2:30 p.m.	Meeting with Rhett Brown, Joyce Downy, and Hudson Davis in Conference Room A of the Buckhead Inn. Refreshments ordered.
Thursday, October 10	Atlanta
9:45 a.m.	Picked up at the hotel by Michael Jones; drive to Dunwoody Conference Center. Full-day meeting with Pearce Sports Equipment Company.
7:15 p.m.	Dinner with Michael Jones, Kevin Pearce, and Trinity Jenkins. Restaurant to be determined by hosts. Return to hotel by 10:15 p.m.
Friday, October 11	Atlanta to Chicago
8:30 a.m.	Breakfast at hotel with Trey Meyer, Travis Smoak, and Drew Dyson.
9:45 a.m.	Leave for Atlanta Airport (ATL) with Trey Meyer. Southern Express Flight 1436 departs at 11:35 a.m. and arrives at Chicago (MDW) at 1:10 p.m.

Itinerary

Lesson 77 Edit the Data Source

New Commands

- Edit Data Source
- Sort Data Records
- Filter Data Records

Skill Building

77b Improve Keystroking

Key each line once.

i 1 sit in said did dirk city did fin its lit iris wit hit ilk simmer

e 2 gem ewe men eke ever me le hen cede key led fen eye be pen leader

i/e 3 pie lei piece feign mein feint neigh lie reign die veil vein diem

i/e 4 Either Marie or Liem tried to receive eight pieces of cookie pie.

w 5 new jaw awe win we was awe away hew saw flaw law wan pew wit wavy

o 6 to onto rot job coho sox box oboe wok roe out oil dot tote oriole

w/o 7 ow wows how won worn now woe wool mow row work cow woke flows low

w/o 8 Women won't want to work now; we are worn out after woeful worry.

k 9 Keep keen keg kayak keno keepsake kerchief kennel kernel kerosene

d 10 drag mind ride made ahead drove trade proud riddle riding discuss

k/d 11 dark kind dock katydid drink awkward grandkids padlock jackknifed

k/d 12 Dozens of ducks dunked up and down in a murky pool at the bridge.

Communication

77c

1. Review the Subject/Verb section of Appendix C.
2. Key each sentence single-spaced, selecting the correct verb that is shown in parentheses. Use automatic numbering.
3. Save and close. (77c)

SUBJECT/VERB AGREEMENT

1. Dr. Waites (recommend/recommends), "When you are a guest in a new country, experience the culinary differences by dining at authentic restaurants."
2. The lyrics for the song (was/were) written by a music student.
3. Either Jim or his team members (is/are) prepared to present the team findings.
4. Either the children or the parent (is/are) eligible for entry.
5. All of the candidates (participate/participates) in the debate.
6. Each of the high school seniors (invite/invites) a guest to the banquet.
7. The group (discuss/discusses) the procedure for election of group chair.
8. The firemen and the paramedics (protect/protects) the community each day.

Document Design — ITINERARY

86d

An itinerary is a detailed plan for a trip. Itineraries for work-related trips provide details about the business activities and the travel information. Typically, an itinerary includes the following information.

- Heading with name and dates of trip.
- Transportation information—maps and route information for driving trips; or airline flight numbers and times, ticket information, passport or other identification, visa requirements, rental car or ground transportation for air travel.
- Hotel information—name and address, confirmation number, special requests made.
- Restaurant information—name and address, reservation information, participants.
- Meetings or appointments—individual and company names, times, addresses, and transportation information if needed.
- Leisure-time information.

Generally, itineraries are prepared using a table. Review the document shown on the next page; pay particular attention to the way the content is presented. Also review the format.

Apply It

86-d1
Itinerary

1. In a new document, tap ENTER three times and apply Retrospect theme.
2. Insert a table with 2 columns and 13 rows. Change the design to Grid Table 1 Light – Accent 1. In the Table Style Options group, deselect the check mark for First Column.
3. Key the table shown on the next page. Leave a blank row between days of the trip.
4. Merge cells in row 1, and apply Heading 1 style and Align Center.
5. In row 2, apply Heading 2 style and Bold; apply Align Center Left to column A and Align Center Right to column B.
6. Apply Heading 3 style and Bold to the rows containing the day and date.
7. Change the height of the remaining rows to 0.3". Adjust the width of the columns to utilize the space well.
8. Apply Add Space Before Paragraph to each row without a heading to enhance reading.
9. Save and close. (*86-d1*)

86-d2
Modified Itinerary

1. Open *86-d1* that you saved in Apply It in 86-d1 Itinerary and turn Track Changes on. Make sure your name is in the User name box.
2. Make the following changes in the itinerary:
 a. On Wednesday, October 9, add:

 7:00 p.m. | Dinner at Pat's Buckhead Café with Rhett Brown, Joyce Downy, and Hudson Davis.

 b. Change the time on the return flight to Chicago to **11:40 a.m.** with arrival at **1:15 p.m.**
 c. Click at the end of the entry and insert the comment: **Southern Express Airlines called with the flight schedule change.**
3. Review in All Markup and Simple Markup views.
4. Save and close. (*86-d2*)

USE MERGE COMMANDS ON MAILINGS TAB

77d

An alternate method for creating and editing a mail merge document is to access the merge commands on the Mailing tab.

Use the Address Block ❶, the Greeting Line ❷, and Insert Merge Field ❸ buttons to create the placeholders for the merge fields in the main document. The Edit Recipient List ❹ button is used to edit the data source, while the Finish & Merge button ❺ is used to complete the merge.

EDIT DATA SOURCE

Sometimes you will need to edit the data source (list of variables) by changing individual records or revising the fields for all records.

★ TIP

Check for Errors

When using the Check for Errors command, you (1) simulate the merge and report errors in a new document; (2) complete the merge, pausing to report each error; or (3) complete the merge without pausing and report the errors in a new document.

To edit records:

Mailings/Start Mail Merge/Edit Recipient List

1. In the Data Source box, click the data source, e.g., *76-drill1datasource* ❶. Click Edit.
2. Click the desired entry ❷ or click Find ❸ to locate a record quickly.
3. Make the desired changes.
4. Click New Entry to add a new record, or click Delete Entry to delete a record. Click OK.

Review/Tracking/Dialog Box Launcher

1. Open the *track changes options* data file and turn on Track Changes; check to see that you are listed in the User name box; if not, change to your name and initials. *Nursing Partnerships* should remain in Title style.

2. Change all side headings in the document to Heading 1 style; then make the changes in Section 1.

3. Lynn West asked you to make the changes Section 2 for her. Change the name and initials in the User name box from your name to **Lynn West** and **lw**. Check the box: Always use these values regardless of sign in to Office, which is located below the Initials box.

4. Make the changes in Section 2 starting with the paragraph after the heading *Hospitals* to the end of the document.

5. Save and close. (*86-drill1*)

Section 1—Make changes in this section with your name in the User box.

Nursing Partnerships

Demand for Nurses Exceeds Supply

As we all know, the demand for nurses far exceeds the supply of nurses in this *the entire* *central* region of the state. Local colleges *educational institutions* are unable to prepare an adequate supply of nurses to meet this growing demand. *The result is that healthcare facilities are unable to meet workforce demand.*

Partnership Proposed

five The four local hospitals, the local technical college, and the local university in *central have* the region has developed a strong comprehensive and viable plan to increase the supply of both licensed practical nurses and registered nurses. *over the next ten years*

Hospitals

Five Four area hospitals will contribute $1,000,000 each to the Nursing Partnership this year. Of the $4,000,000, the university will be allocated $3,000,000, and the technical college will be allocated $1,000,000. In addition, the hospitals each pledged to invest $50,000 a year in the Nursing Partnership for the next five years. These annual funds will be split 50/50 *equally* between the technical college and the university.

Section 2—Make changes in this section with Lynn West's name in the User box.

The attached table summarizes the five-year funding plan for the hospitals and the five-year spending plan for the educational institutions.

Program Implementation

The agreement will be finalized and signed within three weeks, and the funds will be made available within three months. Other potential partners are being contacted to determine their willingness to participate in the program.

Changes to fields are made by editing the data source. Once the change is made, all of the records are revised.

To edit fields:

Mailings/Start Mail Merge/Edit Recipient List

1. In the Edit Data Source dialog box, click the Customize Columns button.
2. Edit as follows:
 a. *Add new field:* Click the Add button; key the field name. Use the move buttons to position correctly. (**Reminder:** Be sure to update the main document by inserting the new merge field.)
 b. *Delete field:* Select the field to be deleted. Click the Delete button.
 c. *Rename field:* Select the field to be renamed. Click the Rename button. Key new name.
3. Save your main document to update your data source.

DRILL 1 EDIT RECORDS AND FIELDS

1. Open *76-drill1main*. Add **Fax Number** as a new field after the ZIP Code field.

2. Update the records with the following fax numbers:

 Ms. Hershbarger **217.555.0181**

 Dr. Hodnett **414.555.0194**

 Mr. Zuber **708.555.0192**

3. Change Ms. Hershbarger's address to **206 Fourth Avenue, Springfield, IL 62701-0206**. Save the main document.

4. Merge the data source and the main document. Save and close. (*77-drill1*)

5. Close the main document, *76-drill1main*.

EDHAR/Shutterstock.com

! WORKPLACE SUCCESS

Multicultural Skills

What is your multicultural quotient? Companies are seeking employees who have multicultural awareness, knowledge, and skills. These valuable employees are aware that their attitudes, beliefs, assumptions, etc., do affect how they work with others who are of different cultures. These employees are very knowledgeable of the many aspects of these cultures, including history, practices, and values. They also have developed skills that are needed to interact effectively with those of different cultures. One skill might be learning the language of that culture.

Spend some time in this module increasing your own multicultural literacy. Develop an awareness, knowledge, and skills in another culture.

New Commands

86c

TIP

Previously you changed the user name using *Word* options. If you are working using Track Changes, you have the option to use the Change User Name command in the tracking options.

TRACKING OPTIONS

Track Changes Options provide a convenient way to change the user name, and they also provide advanced options to display the default Track Changes Options or to change the tracking options. The Track Changes Options defaults meet the needs of most users, and they do not change them. View the options so that you will be aware of the way changes made in a document with Track Changes display.

To change the user name and initials:
Review/Tracking/Dialog Box Launcher

1. Display the Track Changes Options
 dialog box and click Change User Name ❶.
2. Key the appropriate name and initials and click OK.

To view the Track Changes Options dialog box:

1. Click Advanced Options ❷ and note:
 a. How insertions, deletions, and comments display.
 b. How changes in repositioned text (moves) display.
 c. How color is used to show cells inserted, deleted, merged, or split.
 d. How track formatting controls whether or not formatting is tracked and how options are displayed.
 e. Size and position of balloons and how the way they display can be changed.
2. Click OK without changing the defaults.

SORT DATA RECORDS

Sorting records determines the order in which the records are merged. You might sort records in ZIP Code order, Last Name order, or City order. Occasionally, a multiple sort is needed to sort first by one field and then a second field, and so forth. For example, merged name badges or registration letters might be sorted first by state, then by city, and then by last name. Records are sorted either in ascending order (A to Z or 1, 2 …) or descending order (Z to A or 100, 99, …).

To sort records by one field:

Mailings/Start Mail Merge/Edit Recipient List

1. Open the main document and display the Mail Merge Recipients dialog box.

2. Click the column heading of the field to be sorted to display the data (such as Last Name) in ascending order ❶.

 Click again to display in descending order. Click OK.

 Note: You may also click the drop-list arrow by each field ❷ and select Sort Ascending or Sort Descending.

3. To merge, in the Finish group, click the Finish & Merge button. Click one of the merge options.

To sort records by multiple fields:

Mailings/Start Mail Merge/Edit Recipient List

1. Open the main document and display the Mail Merge Recipients dialog box.

2. From the Refine Recipient List, click Sort.

3. From the Filter and Sort dialog box, select the Sort Records tab ❶.

4. Click the Sort by ❷ drop-list arrow and select the first field to be sorted in the multiple sort.

5. Click the arrow for Then by ❸ and select the second field, and so forth. Click OK.

Lesson 86 Itinerary

New Commands
- Change User Name
- View Track Change Options

Warmup *Lesson 86a Warmup*

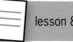 lesson 86a warmup

Skill Building

86b **Improve Techniques**

Key each line once, concentrating on using good keying techniques.

1st row
1 Zack and Max became exercise advocates, but they ate many pizzas.
2 Max Mizel verbalized his excessive love for throwing curve balls.

home row
3 Ada Hall's class was at a lake in Dallas; Kala Klass had a salad.
4 Sally's glass flask was full of salt; Sal also saw a glass flask.

3rd row
5 Terry or Peter saw Perry at the polo tryout; you were there, too.
6 Trey, a poet, wrote the quote for Peter; we were there with Trey.

4th row
7 10487 24680 31579 90642 35179 86210 38764 21430 79538 24680 97315
8 63829 87321 90543 28645 80902 21354 87654 23890 27480 46572 89340

balanced hand
9 pens turn fur slam pay rifle worn pan duck ham lap slap burn girl
10 Andy Clancy, a neighbor, may visit at the lake and at the island.

one hand
11 read ploy create kiln crate plum were pony cats jump severe hump
12 Phillip, as you are aware, was a reader on deferred estate cases.

combination
13 did you we spent pony street busy jump held severe pant exert due
14 Were profits better when we were on Main Street than Duck Street?

Monkey Business Images/Shutterstock.com

! WORKPLACE SUCCESS

Fear of Failure

Many employees—particularly young employees—limit their success because they have an unfounded fear of failure. They often confuse failing with being a failure. If they take on a project and it fails, they think of themselves as failures and avoid taking on similar projects. This type of behavior is often referred to as a self-fulfilling prophecy. If you think you can do something, you are likely to, but if you do not think you can do something, you are not likely to do it. The attitude that leads to success is to view failed projects as something that did not work, to try to learn why, and to move to something that might work. The owner and chef of a great restaurant had a total failure with his first restaurant, then took a job as a chef and was fired; his next venture was a resounding success—arguably the leading restaurant in the country. Baseball home-run kings often also have high strikeout numbers. Successful people are persistent—when something does not work, they try alternatives and learn from each trial until they reach success.

DRILL 2 — SORT IN ASCENDING ORDER

1. Open *76-drill1main*. Sort by ZIP Code in ascending order and merge to a new document.

2. Save the merged letters and close. (*77-drill2*)

3. Close *76-drill1main* without saving.

DRILL 3 — SORT IN DESCENDING ORDER

1. Open *76-drill1main*. Sort by ZIP Code in descending order and merge to a new document.

2. Save the merged letters and close. (*77-drill3*)

3. Close *76-drill1main* without saving.

DRILL 4 — MULTIPLE SORT

1. Open *76-drill1main*. Sort in ascending order first by State, then by City, and then by Last Name.

2. Merge to a new document.

3. Save the merged letters and close. (*77-drill4*)

4. Close *76-drill1main* without saving.

FILTER RECORDS

Filtering records before merging the main document and the data source allows you to select a specific set of records to merge. For example, you can create a target mailing to individuals in a specific state or ZIP Code area.

To filter data records:

Mailings/Start Mail Merge/Edit Recipient List

1. Open the main document and display the Mail Merge Recipients dialog box.

2. From the Refine Recipient List, click Filter.

3. From the Filter and Sort dialog box, select the Filter Records tab ❶.

4. Choose the appropriate data field ❷ (e.g., State); click a comparison phrase ❸ (e.g., Equal to); and key the text or data you will use for the comparison ❹ (e.g., IL). Click OK. (**Note:** Click the down arrow for comparison and note the comparison phrases.)

5. Note the records displaying in the Mail Merge Recipients dialog box to determine if you have filtered correctly. Click OK.

(**Reminder:** In the Filter and Sort dialog box, click the Clear All button to remove filters before using the main document again to ensure all records will merge.)

Terms

Bentley Burns presented the changes reflecting the additional $1,000,000 committed by the fifth area hospital. The hospital also committed to the $50,000 annual contribution. The Board decided to use the same distribution formula for the funds contributed by the other hospitals. Mary Freeman was asked to revise the final agreement to reflect the additional funds, and she agreed to finalize all documents within one week.

Hospital Perspective
Tyler Walker presented the attached funding plan submitted by the hospitals. The Board approved the plan.

Technical College Perspective
Jane Metze presented the attached fund usage plan submitted by the technical college. The Board approved the plan.

University Perspective
Lester Caldwell presented the attached fund usage plan submitted by the university. The Board approved the plan.

Approval
After considerable discussion of how plans would be implemented, the Board approved the entire project.

Adjournment
The meeting adjourned at 12:05 p.m.

85-d2

Minutes with Track Changes

 draft minutes

1. Open *draft minutes* from the data files, turn Track Changes on, and select All Markup view. Check that your name and initials are in the User name and Initials boxes. (File/Options/General)
2. Delete the first sentence in paragraph 1.
3. Add a second-page header using Blank (three columns). In the first column, key **Minutes—Nursing Partnership Board**; in the second column, insert the page number using Current Position, and key the meeting date **January 15, 201-.**
4. Insert a new heading, **Next Meeting**, before *Adjournment* and key: **The Chair reminded the group that the next Nursing Partnership Board Meeting is scheduled for February 8 at 10:30 in the Hospital Atrium.** Apply Heading 2 style to the heading.
5. Save the document as *85-d2 draft*. Leave it open.
6. Review the summary in the Reviewing Pane. Then review changes by each reviewer separately. Remember to check the reviewer's name that you wish to review and deselect the other reviewers. Accept all changes shown for each reviewer.
7. View your changes and accept all changes in the document.
8. Save and close. (*85-d2*)

DRILL 5 FILTER DATA RECORDS

1. Open *76-drill1main*. Filter as follows:

 Field: State

 Comparison Phrase: Equal to

 Compare to: Illinois (IL)

2. Merge to a new document.

3. Save the merged letters and close. (*77-drill5*)

4. Close *76-drill1main* without saving.

DRILL 6 FILTER DATA RECORDS

1. Open *76-drill1main*. Clear filters used in Drill 5.

2. Filter to select records of speakers who live in Illinois and are scheduled to speak at 8:30 a.m. (*Hint:* Because both conditions must be met, select *and*; then key the requirements for the second condition.)

3. Merge to a new document.

4. Save the merged letters and close. (*77-drill6*)

5. Close *76-drill1main* without saving.

Personalize Form Letters

Communicating Today ▶

A personal letter is always preferred to a form letter; however, a form letter can be personalized by remembering these tips:

1. Format the letter with all the letter parts of a personal letter, such as letter address and personal salutation. Avoid using *To Whom It May Concern*.

2. Be sure the salutation is coded with the correct merge fields. A form letter is a dead giveaway if the greeting is *Dear Smith* instead of *Dear Mr. Smith*.

3. Use merge fields in the body of the letter to make it personal. Using a robust data source with complete variables for each record allows the writer to personalize each letter very specifically. A data source may be created in *Word*, but an *Excel* or *Access* database can also be used as the data source.

4. Proofread the variables carefully to ensure accuracy when the data source is merged with the main document. Proofread the spacing between the merge field and the main document text. These spacing errors can be another signal to the reader that this is a form letter.

Apply It

(77-d1)

Edit Data Source

1. Open *76-d1main*. Edit data source as follows:
 - Mr. Bouchillon now works for **Prestage Technology Company**.
 - Ms. Vang's new address is **983 Old Cedar Place**; ZIP Code is **39704-0983**.

2. Add two new records:

Ms. Brenda Andres	**Mr. Juan Seuffer**
Gifts and More	**Kubly and Ross Associates**
1456 West 18th Street	**356 Airline Road**
Starkville, MS 39759-1456	**West Point, MS 39773-0356**
Oktibbeha County	**Clay County**

3. Add **Representative** as a new field.

(continued)

Minutes

Nursing Partnership Board
Hospital Atrium
January 15, 201-, 10:30 a.m.

The Nursing Partnership Board met on January 15, 201- at 10:30 a.m. in the Hospital Atrium. Board members present were Lester Caldwell, chair; Mary Freeman, meeting facilitator; Jane Metze, technical college representative; Wanda Stewart, project coordinator; Bentley Burns, project assistant; and Tyler Walker, hospital representative.

Proposal

Mary Freeman presented the agreement with the markup showing all changes in it. She pointed out that these changes were made in the last meeting. The Board agreed that the revised version reflected the discussion of the previous meeting. Mary Freeman was asked to revise the final agreement with the changes noted.

Terms

Bentley Burns presented the changes reflecting the additional $1,000,000 committed by the fifth area hospital. The hospital also committed to the $50,000 annual contribution. The Board decided to use the same distribution formula for the funds contributed by the other hospitals. Mary Freeman was asked to revise the final agreement to reflect the additional funds, and she agreed to finalize all documents within one week.

Hospital Perspective

Tyler Walker presented the attached funding plan submitted by the hospitals. The Board approved the plan.

Technical College Perspective

Jane Metze presented the attached fund usage plan submitted by the technical college. The Board approved the plan.

University Perspective

Lester Caldwell presented the attached fund usage plan submitted by the university. The Board approved the plan.

Approval

After considerable discussion of how plans would be implemented, the Board approved the entire project.

Adjournment

The meeting adjourned at 12:05 p.m.

4. Edit the records with the following data:

Record	Representative
Quarrels	**Beth Stevens**
Bouchillon	**Kelly Cancienne**
Vang	**Patrick Konscak**
Andres	**Wade Sanford**
Seuffer	**Jennifer Fleming**

5. Edit the writer's name and title in the closing lines. Delete *Hunter Nyiri, Director* and insert the merge field *Representative*. Add the word **Representative** as the writer's title.

6. Sort by Last Name in ascending order and merge to a new document.

7. Save and close. (*77-d1*). (**Reminder:** Save the main document, *76-d1main*, and close.)

77-d2

Filter Data Source

1. Open *76-d1main*. Filter the data source to select records in Oktibbeha County.
2. Merge to a new document.
3. Save the merged document and close. (*77-d2*)
4. Save and close the main document, *76-d1main*.

77-d3

Directory

 77-d3datasource

1. In a new blank document, prepare the main document and data source for a membership directory. Choose Directory as the document type. Name the main document *77-d3directory*.

2. Use the existing data source *77-d3datasource* from the data file. Add information for three people in your personal address book.

3. Arrange the directory as follows. Set left tabs at 2.5" and 5.5". Bold Last Name.

 Last Name, First Name Email Address Cell Phone

4. Sort by Last Name and then First Name in ascending order and merge to a new document.

5. Apply the document theme Celestial with Basic (Elegant) document formatting style set.

6. Add the title **Membership Directory** at the top of document; apply the Title style and center.

7. Save and close. (*77-d3*)

8. Save and close the main document, *77-d3directory*.

 QUICK ✔ Check your document format against the illustration below (solutions will vary).

MEMBERSHIP DIRECTORY

Forde, Connie cforde@ck.com 662.555.0133
VanHuss, Susie svanhuss@ck.com 803.555.0145

Document Design

85d

TIP

For minutes that are more than one page long, include an appropriate header on all pages except the first one. Generally, the header would include the meeting name and the page number. Many organizations also include the date.

MINUTES

Minutes provide a record of what occurred in a meeting. Typically, minutes are prepared relatively soon after a meeting and distributed to all participants. Minutes may vary significantly depending on the type of meeting. In some cases, only a brief summary of the action taken is recorded. In other cases, a verbatim transcript of everything said in a meeting is recorded. Most organizations prefer to record only the essential or very important information that needs to be preserved for future reference. These minutes are usually called *action minutes* because they capture the decisions that are made and the actions that take place. Some minutes are very formal; others are very informal, using first names and a casual writing style.

Typically, minutes contain the following information:

1. Heading information—*Minutes*, meeting name, date, time, and location.
2. Name of presiding officer or meeting leader and names of attendees.
3. Introduction of topics or outcomes expected.
4. Summary of decisions and actions.
5. Handouts and meeting materials may be attached to be part of the record.

Apply It

85-d1

Draft Minutes

1. Apply Organic theme to a new document. Tap ENTER three times and insert the *NPB Agenda Heading* from the Quick Part Gallery (created in *84-d1*). Select *Agenda* and replace it with **Minutes**. Save the selection as a Quick Part. Use the *NPB Minutes Heading* for the name and description.
2. Review the *Minutes* model document on the next page. Then key the minutes shown below and on page 4-12, using normal margins.
3. Apply Heading 2 to all headings.
4. Save and close. (*85-d1*)

The Nursing Partnership Board met on January 15, 201- at 10:30 a.m. in the Hospital Atrium. Board members present were Lester Caldwell, chair; Mary Freeman, meeting facilitator; Jane Metze, technical college representative; Wanda Stewart, project coordinator; Bentley Burns, project assistant; and Tyler Walker, hospital representative.

Proposal

Mary Freeman presented the agreement with the markup showing all changes in it. She pointed out that these changes were made in the last meeting. The Board agreed that the revised version reflected the discussion of the previous meeting. Mary Freeman was asked to revise the final agreement with the changes noted.

(continued on page 4-12)

Lesson 78 Merge with Envelopes and Labels

New Commands
- Merge Envelopes
- Merge Labels

New Commands

78b

TIP

Open a new document and save it as the main document with an appropriate name, e.g., *78-drill1envelope*. Remember to resave; then the main document is complete.

MERGE ENVELOPES

Envelopes can be merged from the data source. When printing envelopes, you will need to know the type of envelope feeder your printer uses. In this lesson, you will create #10 landscape envelopes (standard business envelope).

To create envelopes:

Mailings/Start Mail Merge/Start Mail Merge

1. Open a new blank document and save it with an appropriate name, e.g., *78-drill1envelope*.
2. Follow the path above and click Step-by-Step Merge Wizard to display the Mail Merge pane at the right of the screen.
3. Under Select document type, select Envelopes. Click Next: Starting document.
4. Under Select starting document, check that Change document layout is selected.
5. Under Change document layout, click Envelope options. The Envelope Options dialog box displays. The Size 10 envelope is default. Click OK, then Next: Select recipients.
6. Under Select recipients, click Use an existing list. Click Browse. From the appropriate disk drive, select *76-drill1datasource*, the data source created in Lesson 76. The Mail Merge Recipients dialog box displays the records. Click OK. Click Next: Arrange your envelopes.
7. Under Arrange your envelope, position the insertion point in the letter address area. Click Address Block to insert as a merge field. Click Next: Preview your envelopes.
8. Under Preview your envelopes, click the navigation buttons to preview envelopes. Click Edit Recipient List to edit the data source. Click Next: Complete the merge.
9. Under Complete the merge, click Edit individual envelopes and select the records to merge (all).
10. Save the main document again (for Drill 1, save it as *78-drill1envelope*).

DRILL 1 PREPARE ENVELOPES

1. In a new blank document, follow the directions in 78b to prepare envelopes for the data source *76-drill1datasource*.

2. Merge the main document and the data source.

3. Save and close. (*78-drill1*) (**Reminder:** Resave the main document *78-drill1envelope* after you insert the merge fields but before you preview your document.)

DRILL 3 REVIEW CHANGES

Review/Tracking/Reviewing Pane

1. Open *85-drill1* that you saved in Drill 1 Display for Review and display the Reviewing Pane vertically.

2. Accept each change in sequence until you get to the comment. Select the text in the comment, and copy and paste it before the last sentence in the document; then delete the comment.

3. Click All Changes in Document to accept the remainder of the changes.

4. Save and close. (*85-drill3*)

Communication

85c

 pronoun agreement

1. Review the guides at the right and the pronoun agreement guides in Appendix C.

2. Open the data file *pronoun agreement* and follow the specific directions provided.

3. Save and close. (*85c*)

PRONOUN-ANTECEDENT AGREEMENT

1. The antecedent is the word in the sentence to which the pronoun refers. In the examples, the antecedent is bold and the pronoun is in italic.

 Players must show *their* birth certificates.

 The **boy** lost *his* wallet.

2. The antecedent must agree with the pronoun in **person** (first, second, third).

 I am pleased that *my* project placed first. (Both are first person.)

 You must stand by *your* display at the science fair. (Both are second person.)

 He has lost *his* watch. (Both are third person.)

3. The antecedent must agree with the pronoun in **gender** (neuter when gender of antecedent is unknown).

 Gail said that *she* preferred the duplex apartment.

 The adjustable **chair** sits firmly on *its* five-leg base.

 The **dog** looked for *its* master for days.

4. The antecedent must agree with the pronoun in **number**. If the antecedent of a pronoun is singular, use a singular pronoun. If the antecedent is plural, use a plural pronoun.

 All **members** of the class paid *their* dues.

 Each of the Girl Scouts brought **her** sleeping bag.

Team Collaboration on Documents

Communicating Today ▶

Too often team members leave the final writing and editing of the reports of their team projects to one person. Team members have equal responsibility for the quality of the final reports and other documents they produce in their team projects. Comments and track changes are useful editing tools that enhance collaboration. Documents with track changes can be shared in a number of ways—through email, a company intranet, or on OneDrive. With *Word 2016*, real-time co-authoring (two or more individuals working on the same document at the same time) makes it easier for teams to work together to enhance the quality of their documents.

LESSON 85 **MINUTES WITH TRACK CHANGES** MODULE 15 **4-9**

DRILL 2 PREPARE ENVELOPES

1. Begin a new blank document and save as *78-drill2envelope*. Prepare envelopes for the records stored in data source *76-d1datasource*. From the More items list, select the following merge fields and arrange as shown here:

Title First Name Last Name

Company Name

Address Line 1

City, State ZIP Code

2. Sort by ZIP Code in ascending order. Complete the merge.

3. Save the merged envelopes and close. (*78-drill2*)

MERGE LABELS

Labels designed for printers are available in all sizes and for many purposes, including file folder labels, mailing labels, name badges, and business cards. The data source is often used for merging letters, registration forms, envelopes, and numerous types of labels. Merging labels is very similar to merging envelopes.

To create labels:

Mailings/Start Mail Merge/Start Mail Merge/Step-by-Step Mail Merge Wizard

1. Open a new blank document and save with an appropriate file name. (For Drill 3, save it as *78-drill3labels*.)
2. Follow the path above and click Step-by-Step Merge Wizard.
3. Under Select document type, select Labels. Click Next: Starting document.
4. Under Select starting document, be sure Change document layout is selected.

5. Under Change document layout, click Label options. Choose Avery US Letter from the label vendor list and 5160 from the product number list. Click OK. Click Next: Select recipients.
6. Under Select recipients, click Use an existing list. Under Use an existing list, click Browse. From the appropriate disk drive, select *76-drill1datasource*. The Mail Merge Recipients dialog box displays the records. Click OK and Next: Arrange your labels.
7. Under Arrange your labels, click Address Block and click OK. Click Remove Space Before Paragraph to remove the extra spacing between the address lines. (Click More items to select the merge fields individually for the Address Block.)
8. Under Replicate labels, click Update all labels to replicate the Address Block merge field on each label on the page. Save the main document again. Click Next: Preview your labels.
9. From Preview your labels, click the navigation buttons if needed. (If changes in the data source are needed, click Edit recipient list.) Click Next: Complete the merge.
10. From Complete the merge, click Edit individual labels. Click All, then OK. The merged labels will appear on the screen.
11. Resave the main document.

★ **TIP**

Remove Space After Paragraph

Home/Paragraph/Line and Paragraph Spacing/ Remove Space After Paragraph

Review/Tracking/Track Changes

1. Open *onsite meeting* from the data files and turn Track Changes on and make the changes shown below.

2. Review the document by checking All Markup, then Simple Markup, and No Markup.

3. Save and close. (*85-drill2*)

The first on site meeting is scheduled for November 10. We plan to meet at the main entrance at 10:30 o'clock *a.m.* to tour the property and review the procedures that NatureLink plans to use in redesigning the trails close to *near* the Red-cockaded Woodpecker (RCW) habitat. Since the RCW is an endangered species, we want to balance the wishes of ecotourists to observe these birds and the need to preserve *protect* them.

REVIEWING PANE

The Reviewing Pane provides a summary of the tracked changes and comments in a document. The Vertical pane displays at the left side, and the Horizontal pane displays at the bottom of the screen.

To view a summary of tracked changes and comments:
Review/Tracking/Reviewing Pane

- Click Reviewing Pane and select either Reviewing Pane Vertical or Reviewing Pane Horizontal.

REVIEW CHANGES AND COMMENTS

Changes and comments can be reviewed in sequence, and each change can be accepted or rejected. Comments should be marked done or deleted after they have been read and action has been taken. Changes can also be accepted or rejected at once.

To accept or reject changes:
Review/Changes/Previous or Next

1. Click Previous or Next to move to a change.
2. To accept a change, click Accept and Move to Next; to reject a change, click Reject and Move to Next.
3. To accept all changes at once, click Accept All Changes. To reject all changes at once, click Reject All Changes.

DRILL 3 MERGE LABELS

1. In a new blank document, follow the directions provided on the previous page to prepare address labels for the data source file *76-drill1datasource*. *Hint:* Click Remove Space Before Paragraph after inserting the Address Block.

2. Click Update all labels.

3. Save the merged labels and close. (*78-drill3*)

Apply It

78-d1

Mail Merge

The Holland Eye Center is hosting two seminars to inform its patients about laser vision correction. Prepare the form letters for the records shown below.

1. Begin a new blank document and save as *78-d1main*. Create the data source (*78-d1datasource*).

Field names	Record 1	Record 2	Record 3
Title	Dr.	Mr.	Ms.
First Name	Karen	Angelo	Mary
Last Name	Wiseman	Seay	Wiseman
Address Line 1	137 Sonoma Drive	P.O. Box 88	539 Swoope Avenue
City	Omak	Tonasket	Tonasket
State	WA	WA	WA
ZIP Code	98841-0174	98855-3918	98855-8096
Date	January 31	January 31	February 25

2. Key the main document and insert the merge fields in it. Use block letter style with open punctuation. Save the changes. (**Note:** The date should update automatically.)

<<AddressBlock>>

<<GreetingLine>>

Do you ever imagine being able to see the alarm clock when you wake up? Do you ever imagine no more hassles of daily contact lens maintenance? Perhaps you may have imagined playing your favorite sport with complete peripheral vision—no fogging or slipping glasses. Millions of people across the world have chosen laser vision correction as an alternative to glasses and contact lenses. They now are enjoying these freedoms that you have only imagined.

The Holland Eye Center invites you to attend a special seminar sponsored for our patients who are potential candidates for laser vision correction. This seminar held at our clinic on <<Date>> at 7 p.m. will feature a panel of doctors and patients and a live laser vision correction procedure. A question/answer period will also provide an opportunity to have all your questions answered by these laser vision correction experts. You'll also have an

(continued)

TIP

When previewing letters at the end of the merge job, select the first two lines of the letter address and remove the extra spacing after paragraph.

DISPLAY FOR REVIEW

Documents with tracked changes can be viewed from four different perspectives.

❶ **Simple Markup:** Shows comments and the document as it would look if all changes are accepted. Lines on left indicate corrections.

❷ **All Markup:** Shows the document with all proposed changes included.

❸ **No Markup:** Shows the document as it would look with all changes accepted.

❹ **Original:** Shows the document before changes were made.

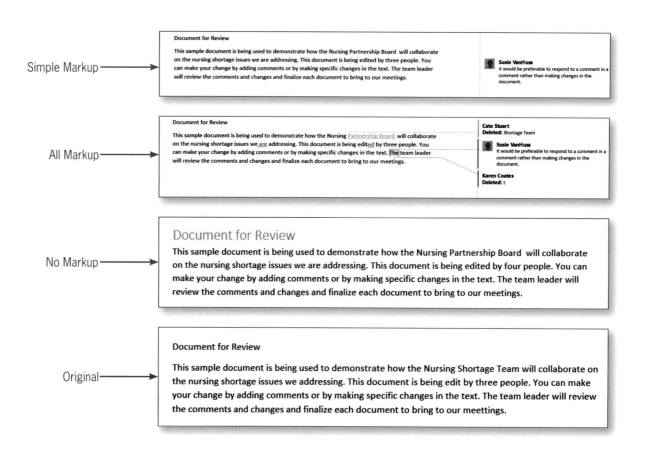

| DRILL 1 | DISPLAY FOR REVIEW | document for review |

Review/Tracking/Show Markup

1. Open *document for review* from the data files and note that the open document is in Simple Markup view. Click the line on the left and hover the mouse above each change and review the information provided.

2. Apply Heading 1 format to the title.

3. View the document in each of the four options for review.

4. Check to see that your name is listed as a reviewer in All Markup. Then turn Track Changes off.

5. Save and close. (*85-drill1*)

opportunity to enter your name in a drawing for a complimentary laser vision correction procedure to be presented at the close of the seminar.

Would you like to join the millions of people who have chosen laser vision correction and be free of the daily hassles of glasses and contact lenses? Get started today by completing the enclosed reservation card indicating you will attend the seminar on <<Date>> and learn for yourself the details of laser vision correction.

Sincerely | Edward S. Vickery, M.D. | xx | Enclosure

3. Sort by Last Name in ascending order and then First Name in ascending order. Merge the data source and the main document.

4. Save and close. (78-d1) Close the main document.

78-d2
Edit Data Source

1. Open *78-d1main* and edit the data source as follows.
 - Invite Dr. Karen Wiseman to the February 25 seminar.
 - Ms. Mary Wiseman's new address is **235 North Fifth Street, Omak, WA 98841-3592**.

2. Add two new records for the February 25 seminar.

Mrs. Darlene Chism	**Mr. James Lee**
830 Yorkville Street	**332 Matilda Road**
Tonasket, WA 98855-1251	**Omak, WA 98841-2028**

3. Filter to select records of patients invited to the February 25 seminar. Preview and proofread.

4. Complete the merge; save the merged letters and close. (78-d2)

78-d3
Envelopes

Prepare envelopes for all the patients invited to the February 25 laser vision correction seminar.

1. Begin a new blank document and save as *78-d3envelopes*. Prepare envelopes for the records stored in the data source *78-d1datasource*.

2. Filter appropriately and sort by Last Name and then First Name.

3. Proofread, complete the merge, save the merged envelopes, and close. (78-d3)

78-d4
Name Badges

1. Begin a new blank document and save as *78-d4labels*. Prepare name badges (Avery 5095) for the records stored in the data source *78-d1datasource*. Include the First Name and Last Name fields on the name badge. Sort by Last Name and First Name in ascending order. Change font to Arial 14-point and center.

2. Click Update all labels.

3. Proofread, complete the merge, save the merged labels, and close. (78-d4)

Lesson 85 Minutes with Track Changes

New Commands

- Track Changes
- Show Markup
- Review Changes
- Reviewing Pane
- Accept/Reject Changes

New Commands

85b

TIP

Use Show/Hide with Track Changes.

TRACK CHANGES

Off On

Track changes show suggested revisions or changes in a document in the form of insertions, deletions, and formats without the document itself changing. Each change can be viewed and accepted or rejected. Once changes are accepted, the document actually changes. Comments differ from tracked changes in that suggestions are offered, but they cannot be accepted and made a part of the document. Comment text must be copied or keyed to be integrated in the text.

To turn Track Changes on or off:
Review/Tracking/Track Changes

1. Click Track Changes to turn tracking on; the button turns blue.
2. To turn tracking off, click the blue Track Changes button.

MARKUP

Markup provides options for viewing changes that have been tracked. Some reviewers prefer to focus on insertions and deletions and deal with other revisions separately. Others prefer to review the suggestions of one reviewer at a time.

❶ **Display for Review:** Choose how to review proposed changes in the document.

❷ **Show Markup:** Choose the type of markup to show in the document.

❸ **Reviewing Pane:** Show revisions in a vertical or horizontal pane.

❶ Simple Markup
❷ Show Markup ▾
❸ Reviewing Pane ▾

TIP

Colors will vary on different computers. However, each author should have a different color.

To show markup:
Review/Tracking/Show Markup

1. Display the markup options.
2. Check options that you wish to display and deselect options that you do not wish to display.

Lesson 79 Hess Office Park

Skill Building

79b Timed Writing

1. Key a 1' timing on each paragraph; work to increase speed.
2. Key a 3' timing on all paragraphs.

gwam 1' | 3'

Still a major trend in the workplace today is telecommuting. In 13 | 4
fact, millions of workers own home-based businesses or work for a 26 | 9
business from home. This number of workers grows each year with 38 | 13
companies of all sizes hiring workers who will work from home offices. 52 | 17

Why do workers choose to telecommute? Reasons include reducing 65 | 22
stress of rush hour traffic, being flexible to balance family and work 79 | 26
time, and being able to work when they work best. Workers often find 92 | 31
an increase in work done because of fewer stops to answer the telephone 106 | 35
or talk to another person. 112 | 37

Working successfully from home requires new considerations. Of 12 | 41
course, it is obvious that technology needs must be in place in the 26 | 46
home office. Yes, the worker must have a home office, one that is 39 | 50
separate from the rest of the house. He or she must set a daily routine 53 | 55
and request that family respects the new freedom and knows the work 66 | 59
performance that is expected to be achieved. 75 | 62

Project Setting

HESS OFFICE PARK

You are continuing your work as an assistant to Patrick J. Hess, the manager of Hess Office Park, the 500-acre office park managed by Hess Property Enterprises.

You will use mail merge to create a form letter and envelopes to the short-term renters of Hess Office Park. Updating the short-term renters' database is another important responsibility that you are assigned.

Use November 15, 201- as the date for all documents in this project.

Standard operating procedures for the project:

1. Use the Retrospect document theme for all documents.
2. Use block letter style with open punctuation and the Hess Office Park letterhead from the data files. Include an appropriate salutation and use **Sincerely** as the complimentary closing. Begin the data at approximately 2". Use **Patrick J. Hess, Manager** as the writer's name and title.
3. The data files also contain a Hess Office Park memo form. Use an appropriate subject line if a subject line is not provided.
4. Add your reference initials and other notations as appropriate.
5. Use the List Table 4 – Accent 2 table style for all tables and center tables horizontally.
6. Use mail merge to create form letters and envelopes.

Apply It

84-d1

Agenda with Comments

1. In a new blank document, prepare the agenda illustrated on the previous page, formatting it as indicated below.
2. Tap ENTER three times and apply Organic theme.
3. Key the heading and apply the following styles: line 1 Title; line 2 Heading 1, and lines 3 and 4 Heading 2. Then center all four lines.
4. Set a left tab at 1" and a right-aligned dot leader tab at the right margin (6.5).
5. Add and edit the following comments to the agenda:
 a. Select *Call to Order* and add Comment 1: **Please confirm your attendance.**
 b. Select *Proposal* and add Comment 2: **Copies will be delivered at least three days prior to the meeting.**
 c. Select *Approval* and add Comment 3: **If the Board is not ready to finalize the decision, another meeting will be scheduled.**
 d. Edit Comment 1 as follows: **Please confirm your attendance and indicate any additional agenda items desired.**
6. Select the heading and save it for future use as a Quick Part with the name and description **NPB Agenda Heading**.
7. Save and close. (*84-d1*)

84-d2

Revised Agenda

1. Open *84-d1* that you saved in Apply It 84-d1 Agenda with Comments and make the following revisions to the preliminary agenda.
2. **Approval of Minutes** needs to be added. Mary Freeman does not require additional time for that item. Position after Call to Order and do not list a time.
3. The three speakers giving their perspective on the proposal indicated that 10 minutes would be adequate for their comments. Reduce their times to 10 minutes each and add the 15 minutes saved to the discussion time.
4. Delete all comments.
5. Save and close. (*84-d2*)

84-d3

Agenda Formatted in Table

 training agenda

1. Open *training* agenda from the data files and select the date and replace it with **5/14/201-**.
2. Key the response to Comment 2 made by Lee West: **I agree. The Bradford, Eastman, and McAlexander proposals should be reviewed separately.**
3. Select *Discussion* and add a new comment: **I think we should allow 10 minutes for each proposal and 20 minutes for discussion.**
4. Save and close. (*84-d3*)

84-d4

Revised Agenda

1. Open *84-d3* that you saved in Apply It 84-d3 Agenda Formatted in Table and make the following revisions to the agenda.
2. Add two rows below row 4 (2:50 time slot). Add the following information:

Row 5:	**3:00**	**Review of Eastman Proposal**	**Carolyn Mayes**
Row 6:	**3:10**	**Review of McAlexander Proposal**	**Student's Name**

3. In row 4, modify the text in column B to **Review of Bradford Proposal**.
4. Change times: Discussion **3:20**; Recommendations **3:40**; and Adjournment **4:00**.
5. Delete all comments.
6. Save and close. (*84-d4*)

79-d1

Form Letter

hess letterhead

The first assignment is to send a form letter to four short-term renters informing them of an increase in their rent. Send a copy to **Jayden Mason**.

1. Open *hess letterhead* from the data files and save as *79-d1main*. Prepare the main document (*79-d1main*) and key the following information in the data source (*79-d1datasource*).

Field names	Record 1	Record 2	Record 3
Title	Ms.	Mr.	Ms.
First Name	Maryanne	Tim	Chan
Last Name	Fair	Drechsler	Chao
Company Name	Zisusu Company	Voxihi, LLC	Rivcu Company
Address Line 1	100 Hess Boulevard, Suite 3105	100 Hess Boulevard, Suite 2619	100 Hess Boulevard, Suite 2061
City	Austin	Austin	Austin
State	TX	TX	TX
ZIP Code	78712-2149	78712-3893	78712-8333
Current rent	3,000	4,000	6,000
New rent	3,500	4,500	6,750

2. Sort by Last Name in ascending order.
3. Proofread, complete the merge, save, and close. (*79-d1*)

We are very appreciative of the fine short-term renters who have chosen to be a part of Hess Office Park, and our goal is to provide the best services possible to our tenants. We are very fortunate to be located in a beautiful 5,000-acre wooded area that is a perfect backdrop for our businesses. The large conference center, day care center, pet center, and copy center are nice amenities that make the office park one of the best in the region.

After careful financial analysis, our Board of Directors has determined a slight rent increase is necessary to offset increases in energy and maintenance costs of the property. Beginning January 1, it will be necessary to adjust your rent from the current rate of $<<Current rent>> to a new rate of $<<New Rent>>. However, as a way of showing our appreciation of your business, Hess Office Park is extending two new benefits as part of the new rental agreement.

First, you will have a two-day complimentary access per month to the beautiful conference room located in the Hess Office Park conference center. This room includes a large conference table that accommodates 20 people and a spacious adjoining kitchen for preparing breaks and meal functions. Reservations should be requested at least one month in advance. Second, you will receive up to 1,000 complimentary black and white copies per month at our copy center in the Hess Office Park suite.

(continued)

An agenda is a plan for conducting a meeting. Prior to the meeting, participants are asked to review the agenda and respond with additional items. Then the final agenda is distributed to participants prior to the meeting so that they can prepare appropriately for it. Agendas normally contain five types of information:

1. A heading with the general topic of the meeting, the date, the time, and the location.

2. A list of specific topics to be discussed in the meeting.

3. The individual or group responsible for leading the discussion on each topic.

4. Time allocated for the discussion of each topic, -or- the beginning and ending time of the meeting. Time allocation depends on company philosophy.

5. Attachments that provide information about some of the discussion topics. In some cases, this information is distributed separately from the agenda.

Agendas may be prepared using a traditional format, a template, a table, or building blocks. The heading format varies widely among companies. The theme and style set often determine the most appropriate way to design the document. Meeting documents generally follow report format guides. Unless the meeting is very long, agendas typically fit on one page even if the margin spacing at the top of the first page has to be reduced.

Agenda

Nursing Partnership Board
Hospital Atrium
January 15, 201-, 10:30 a.m. ↓ 2

10:30	Call to Order	Mary Freeman
10:35	Proposal	Mary Freeman
10:45	Terms of the Agreement	Student's Name
11:00	Hospital Perspective	Tyler Walker
11:15	Technical College Perspective	Jane Metze
11:30	University Perspective	Lester Caldwell
11:45	Discussion and Approval	All
12:00	Adjournment	

We ask you to please sign the enclosed rent agreement and return it by December 15. Please let me know if you have questions concerning the new agreement. We look forward to continuing to serve you in the first-rate manner that you have come to enjoy.

79-d2

Envelopes

1. Open a new blank document and save as *79-d2envelopes*. Create the envelopes for the form letters created in *79-d1*. Sort by Last Name in ascending order.
2. Proofread, complete the merge, save, and close. (*79-d2*)

79-d3

Edit Form Letter

Mr. Hess just added another person to the list of short-term renters receiving rent increases beginning January 1. You must add a new record to the data source (*79-d1datasource*) and create the form letter for this one company.

Mr. James Garcia

Iotasecond, Limited

100 Hess Boulevard, Suite 2199

Austin, TX 78712-3111

Current rent: **5,500**

New rent: **6,000**

1. Open *79-d1main* and add the new record.
2. Filter the data source and merge to generate the one new letter.
3. Add an envelope to the letter generated.
4. Proofread, complete the merge, save, and close. (*79-d3*)

79-d4

Compose Memo

 hess memo

Open *hess memo* from the data files and save as *79-d4*. Compose a memo to the Conference Room Reservation Staff and Hess Office Park Copy Center Director informing them of the new complimentary services being provided to the four short-term renters.

1. Explain that the Board of Directors approved the new services to the short-term renters effective January 1, 201-.
2. Include the specific services that will be complimentary to these renters. Refer to the letter in *79-d1* for details.
3. In a table, list the company name and contact person of the four short-term renters approved. List in alphabetical order by company name.
4. Proofread the document. Save and close. (*79-d4*)

New Commands

84c

COMMENTS

Comments enable multiple reviewers to critique a document and insert remarks or annotations. Comments are generally displayed in balloons positioned in the right margin.

To insert/edit a comment:
Review/Comments/New Comment

1. Select the text or click at the end of the text on which you wish to comment, and click New Comment to display the Comment balloon.

2. Key the comment you wish to make.

3. To edit a comment, click in the balloon of the comment you want to edit and key the changes you want to make.

TIP

Before you enter comments, check to see that your name and initials are in the User name and Initials boxes on your computer.

File/Options/General

To reply to a comment:

1. Click Reply in the top right corner of the balloon ❶.

2. Key your response below your name in the balloon that displays.

❄ **Discover**

To navigate from one comment to another, click Next to jump to the next comment or Previous to jump back to a comment.

To mark a comment done:

1. Right-click the balloon containing the comment you want to mark done.

2. Click Mark Comment Done. The comment is dimmed.

To delete a comment:
Review/Comments/Delete

1. Click in the balloon containing the comment you want to delete.

2. Click Delete. -or-

1. Right-click the balloon containing the comment you want to delete.

2. Click Delete Comment.

DRILL 1 COMMENTS comments

1. Open *comments* from the data files and review each comment that is attached to text in the document.

2. Select *Comments* in the first line of the document and add the new comment: **Adding a new comment is very easy to do.**

3. Click the Reply icon in the first Jan A. Hawkins comment and key the following response: **Will most people include pictures?**

4. Click in the comment attached to Delete Comments and read it; then delete it.

❄ 5. Use the Previous command to navigate to the comment you added at the beginning of the document. Mark the comment done.

6. Save and close. (*84-drill1*)

Lesson 80 Assessment Modules 12 and 13

Apply It

80-d1

Leftbound Report

★ TIP

Remember to proofread and preview each document for placement before you move to the next one.

1. Key the report that starts below and continues to page 3-140. Format the report as a leftbound report. Apply the Berlin document theme and apply appropriate styles to the title and headings.

2. Insert the Ion (Dark) cover page and add the following information:

 Document title: See report title below; shrink font so title fits on one line

 Subtitle: **Three Market Regions**

 Author: **Livia Baresi**

 Company: **Marcus Employment Services**

 Address: **39 East Ridgewater Nook, Destin, FL 32541-3933**

3. Insert the following content footnote at the end of the second paragraph.

 [1] **Employment statistics provided by Phil Tidwell**.

4. Insert a blank page after the cover page for the table of contents you will generate in step 10.

5. Position the insertion point at the top of the first page of the report and insert a Continuous section break.

6. Click in the footer of the second page of Section 1 and insert a page number at the bottom of the page using the Plain Number 2 page number style. Change the page number format to lowercase Roman numerals. Start number at ii.

7. Click Go to Header and click Next twice to position the insertion point in the header of Section 2. Deselect Different First Page if it is selected. Break the links between the headers for both sections. Go to the footer of Section 2. Break the link between the footers for both sections. Delete the page number in the Section 2 footer.

8. Go to header of Section 2 and number the pages of the report at the top right using the Banded header style.

9. Go to footer of Section 2 and insert the Retrospect footer style. Change the page number format to begin with page 1. Click Different First Page to suppress the header and footer on the first page of the report.

10. Position the insertion point on the blank page left for the table of contents (not in the header section). Generate the table of contents using the Automatic Table 2 style. Position the heading at approximately 2" and apply Title style. Click ENTER after the TOC title to leave a blank line.

11. Add **Prediction** to the *Job Growth* heading. Update the table of contents.

12. Continue to the next document. (*80-d1*)

Regional Employment Analysis

The Executive Committee of Marcus Employment Services requested an analysis of the labor market in three service regions. Previous studies show that these three regions are representative of the total market Marcus serves.

(continued)

Meeting, Travel, and News Documents

Lesson 84 *Agenda with Comments*
Lesson 85 *Minutes with Track Changes*
Lesson 86 *Itinerary*
Lesson 87 *News Release*
Lesson 88 *Hess Office Park*

LEARNING OUTCOMES

- View, insert, respond, mark done, and delete comments.
- Track changes, show markup, review changes, and accept or reject changes.
- Design and format meeting, travel, and news documents.
- Enhance communication skills.
- Build keyboarding skills.

Lesson 84 Agenda with Comments

New Commands
- New Comment
- Delete Comment
- Previous Comment
- Next Comment
- Respond to Comment
- Mark Comment Done

Warmup *Lesson 84a Warmup*

lesson 84a warmup

Skill Building

84b Timed Writing

1. Key a 1' timed writing on each paragraph; work to increase speed.
2. Key a 3' timed writing on all paragraphs.

gwam 1' | 3'

	1'	3'
Americans tend to have a different view of vacation than citizens | 13 | 4 |
of many other countries. In this country, companies usually provide | 26 | 9 |
employees with a maximum of two or three weeks of vacation each year. | 40 | 13 |
Many companies wait to award the second week of vacation until | 53 | 18 |
employees have five years of tenure with them. Those who earn more | 66 | 22 |
than three weeks of vacation typically do so by staying with the same | 80 | 27 |
company for many years. | 84 | 28 |
In many other countries, the case is quite different. Employees | 13 | 32 |
typically receive four to six weeks of vacation each year. It is also | 26 | 37 |
awarded much earlier in their tenure with the company. Vacation is | 40 | 41 |
thought of as just another benefit that has value to the company | 52 | 46 |
as well as to the employee. Employees often spend a whole month on | 66 | 50 |
holiday as they call vacation time. | 73 | 52 |
While some individuals think how wonderful and luxurious it would | 13 | 57 |
be to have extra days or weeks of vacation, the fact is that a large | 27 | 61 |
percentage of Americans do not take the vacation time they are allotted | 41 | 66 |
by their companies. The American culture is such that many employees | 54 | 70 |
feel they cannot be away from their positions for more than two weeks | 68 | 75 |
at one time. | 71 | 76 |

A ALL LETTERS

1' | 1 | 2 | 3 | 4 | 5 | 6 | 7 | 8 | 9 | 10 | 11 | 12 | 13 |
3' | 1 | 2 | 3 | 4 | 5 |

Economic Conditions

Similar economic conditions exist in the three market regions. Leading economic indicators in all three regions support the conclusion that the economy is growing slowly and at a sustainable rate. The unemployment rate in the three areas ranges from 4.1% to 4.4%, explaining the gradual increase in wages in all three areas. Demand for temporary services remains strong. Demand may even increase as employers hesitate to fill permanent positions until the economy improves significantly. Unemployment is predicted to remain under 5% for the next six to twelve months. ← Insert footnote

Wage Survey

The wage survey focused on the three broad categories of jobs that Marcus specializes in providing temporary workers—computer specialists, office assistants, and healthcare services. Approximately fifty separate job titles were analyzed as part of this study. Complete data for all of the specific jobs that were analyzed can be accessed from the detailed report that is available on the human resources website. The standard access restrictions apply to these data.

Careful analysis of the data is needed to determine if the rates Marcus charges employers need to be adjusted in any of the specific job categories. Virtually all of the office assistant and legal assistant positions required knowledge of word processing, spreadsheet, presentation, database, and personal information management software. The few positions that did not list this requirement had significantly lower pay rates.

Job Growth

The predicted growth of jobs in many positions in which Marcus supplies employees is much higher than previously estimated. The current plan for hiring workers will not meet the predicted demand in any of the three market areas. Further analysis of the data collected is warranted before making any adjustments in the hiring plan. Although the data collection design matches the design used in the previous surveys, the changing market situation may require some modification in the data collection methodology to verify these high growth rates.

Conclusions

Market conditions make it feasible to raise the hourly rates Marcus charges employers in many categories. However, it is also evident that Marcus will have to increase the wages paid to its staff of temporary workers in order to retain the quality of worker required to meet market demand.

If further analysis supports the job growth data presented, significant changes must be made in the strategic plan for all regions. The current strategic plan for Marcus is based on a much lower growth rate than this study shows.

Documents for Specialized Fields

Learning Outcomes

Document Design Skills

+ Apply effective designs to a variety of complex documents.

+ Organize content effectively with graphics.

+ Improve document quality using review and collaboration tools.

+ Design documents in administrative and specialized areas, including meeting, travel, news, employment, legal, and medical documents.

Word Processing Skills

+ Learn and apply word processing commands to create and format specialized documents.

Communication Skills

+ Review and improve basic communication skills.

+ Produce error-free documents and apply language arts skills.

Keyboarding

+ Improve keyboarding speed and accuracy.

Prepare the main document and data source for a form letter to participants of a summer workshop. You will need to edit your data source after you create it.

1. Begin a new blank document and save as *80-d2main*. Create the data source as shown below (*80-d2datasource*).

Field names	Record 1	Record 2	Record 3
Title	Mr.	Ms.	Ms.
First Name	Phillip	Anele	Anna
Last Name	Lancaster	Nyiri	Skelton
Address Line 1	35 Wallace Circle	16060 Aspen Road	1355 Palomino Drive
City	Norfolk	Richmond	Richmond
State	VA	VA	VA
ZIP Code	23501-3849	27173-5721	27173-0616
Date	June 15-16	June 23-24	June 23-24
Room	204	205	205

2. Move Ms. Skelton to the June 15–16 workshop. Change Mr. Lancaster's address to **89 Castle Road**.

3. Key the main document (block style with open punctuation style) and insert the merge fields. Key the date as **May 1, 201-**. (Do not update date automatically.) Add notations as needed. Save the changes.

4. Sort by ZIP Code in ascending order. Filter to select only the participants attending the June 15–16 workshop. For the Address Block, remove space after paragraphs when the letters are previewed.

5. Preview, proofread, and complete the merge.

6. Save and close. (*80-d2*)

<<AddressBlock>>

Dear <<First_Name>>

I am delighted you will be attending the Community Development Partnership Workshop on <<Date>> at Braswell Community College. Please arrive at Room <<Room>> of the Harper-Kock Union Building at 8 a.m. for registration and a brief orientation.

Directions to Hathorn Hall, the residence hall designated for summer workshop participants, are enclosed. You may check in at Hathorn from 8 a.m. to 10 p.m. Housing payment can be made at the residence hall.

<<First_Name>>, should you have any questions about the workshop, please call me at 540.555.0123. I look forward to your being a part of our workshop series.

Sincerely | Jane D. Gunter | Workshop Coordinator

 QUICK ✓ Compare your report to the one shown below.

Hess Pet Center
Business Plan

PRELIMINARY DATA
SUSIE H. VANHUSS

Table of Contents

Hess Pet Center Business Plan

Preliminary Data

The Hess Pet Center is a new venture that integrates an existing successful veterinary clinic, Faulk Pet Care, with a full-service luxury pet boarding, grooming, day camp, and boutique center and moves to a new location—Hess Office Park. The joint venture has been branded as Hess Pet Center to capitalize on the popularity of its new location.

Revenue Projections
The purpose of this study is to analyze the revenue-generating potential of each segment of the center and project the contribution each segment can be expected to make during the first year of operation. Accurate revenue projections are needed to complete the business plan.

Historical and Market Data
Hess Pet Center has historical data only for Faulk Pet Care, the veterinary clinic, which has been operated by Dr. Erin Faulk for more than five years. Sources of data for the luxury boarding segment, the day camp, the grooming and spa facility, and the boutique are based on surveys of clients of the veterinary clinic, industry data, and on market research in the Austin area. Focus groups were held with representatives of the companies located in Hess Office Park and surrounding upscale neighborhoods.

Revenue Potential Analyzed
Both qualitative and quantitative data were analyzed to determine the revenue potential for each market segment. A conservative approach was used in the analysis because the negative consequences of projections on the high side were much more significant than projections on the low side.

Veterinary Clinic
The new clinic, formerly known as Faulk Pet Care, is located near a very high-income residential and office park area. Most clients are owned by affluent families. The clinic also has a relationship with the managers of the Hess Office Park. Because of lack of space, boarding has been limited to pets with medical conditions being treated at the clinic and to selected clients.

Growth of the veterinary business has been flat for the past two years because the facilities were fully utilized. Very few new clients were accepted because the center was operating at full capacity. Growth for the first year has been projected at 30 percent.

New board-certified veterinarians and trained technicians are being phased in during the year. Completion of the new surgical facilities including the installation of the new technology and reorganization of the operation is scheduled within three months. Major growth is expected in the second year of operation when all facilities are fully utilized. The revenue projection for this segment is $1,860,300.

Luxury Suite Boarding
Both standard units and luxury suites are included in this segment. A number of kennels and boarding facilities operate in the Austin area. Several are upscale facilities, but they do not offer true luxury suites for discriminating clientele who want their pets pampered. Even the Hess Pet Center standard units are more upscale than the typical "luxury" suites of other facilities. Industry data show that luxury suites are in high demand in high-income residential and in upscale office parks.

Clients bringing pets in for medical treatment were surveyed to determine how frequently they would use boarding facilities and the type of facilities desired. Clients clearly indicated a strong preference both for using the Hess Pet Center and for luxury accommodations for their pets. Local market data showed that upscale facilities were more profitable than moderately priced facilities. The revenue projection for this segment is $673,480.

Doggie Day Camp
Historically, this segment of the industry accounted for a very small part of the market. However, during the past three years, this area has grown dramatically. Information we collected shows that growth in the use of Doggie Day Camp facilities has grown more than 40 percent nationally. Day camp facilities in the Austin area appear to be in high demand with local residents who do not have fulltime help at home and with employees who can drop off pets at the beginning of the workday and pick them up after work. Focus groups with managers of Hess Office Park companies confirmed the need for day camp facilities. Projected revenue for this segment is $480,840.

Pet Grooming and Spa
The primary source of data for this segment was the surveys of clients who brought their pets in for medical treatment. A major requisite for success in this area is one-stop shopping. Clients indicated in the interviews that they want to have grooming and spa treatments done while pets are receiving other services such as medical attention or are being kept in day camp or in the overnight boarding facility. Both national industry data and local market data were analyzed. The revenue projected for this segment is $360,720.

Boutique
Success of the retail operation is more difficult to predict than other segments of the business. The one-stop shopping phenomenon is critical in this area. Having an attractive display of items that appeal to pet owners promotes impulse shopping, which is important in a high-income area. Having premium pet food in the boutique that is generally not available in other outlets is also important. The pharmacy can be operated out of either

the veterinary clinic or the boutique. Current plans are to locate the pharmacy in the boutique to increase the traffic flowing through the retail area. It was very difficult to obtain reliable data in this area, but the analysis team believes that the projections will be met because they are so conservative. Revenue projections for the first year are $240,480.

Total Revenue Projections
Revenue projections for all of the segments are provided on a monthly and an annual basis. The monthly revenue figures are averages. Averages were used because data were not available to determine the seasonal impact. Figure 1 summarizes the revenue projections for the first year of operation.

Hess Pet Center	Monthly Revenue	Annual Revenue	Percentage
Veterinary Clinic	$155,025	$1,860,300	51
Pet Boarding	56,290	673,480	19
Doggie Day Camp	40,070	480,840	13
Grooming and Spa	30,060	360,720	10
Boutique	20,040	240,480	7
Total Revenue	$301,485	$3,617,820	100

The projections for revenues for the first year of operation are significantly higher than originally anticipated.

Figure 2 shows the percentage of revenue contributed by each of the five segments of Hess Pet Center.

Note from Figure 1 that the veterinary clinic and the pet boarding segments are projected to produce more than two-thirds of the total revenue for the first year of operation.

Comparison to Pro Formas
The initial pro formas, prepared when the joint venture was formed, projected revenue for the first year of operation to be $3,017,820. The initial pro formas assumed that the new surgical facilities would not be completed during the first year of operation and only the standard units would be available. Completion of both the surgical facilities and the luxury suites is scheduled within three months and can be fully utilized within six months. Therefore, the current revenue projections are $600,000 higher than the initial projections. These projections are conservative and are based on solid data.

Hess Pet Center Profitability
The expense projections need to be updated to reflect the additional variable costs that result from the availability of the surgical facilities and the luxury suites during the last six months of the first year of operation. Virtually all of the fixed costs have already been accounted for; therefore, most of the additional revenue projected will go directly to the bottom line. Profitability for the first year of operation has been enhanced significantly.

Hess Pet Center I

Lessons 81–83 *Hess Pet Center I*

LEARNING OUTCOMES

- Apply keying, formatting, and word processing skills.
- Work independently with few instructions.

Warmup *Lesson 81a Warmup*

lesson 81a warmup

Skill Building

81b Timed Writing

Key two 3' timed writings.
Strive for control.

A ALL LETTERS

	gwam 1'	3'	
You have most likely heard it said that people would rather die	13	4	54
than speak before a group. To assist in overcoming this fear, many	26	9	59
experts recommend preparation. Spending a large amount of time	38	13	63
preparing will result in big dividends. Select a topic you like and	52	17	67
research it completely, know your audience, and practice before a	65	22	72
mirror and in front of a group of friends.	73	24	74
Finally, presenting with ease requires an excellent knowledge of	13	29	79
technology. Come to the room early to open the show and to practice	26	33	83
in the presentation room. Determine which key to press to jump to the	40	38	88
next slide or to move to a previous position. Know how to move to an	54	42	92
exact position in the show. Practice these success skills and prepare	67	47	97
your next presentation with zeal and confidence.	77	50	100

```
1'  | 1 | 2 | 3 | 4 | 5 | 6 | 7 | 8 | 9 | 10 | 11 | 12 | 13 |
3'       1            2            3            4
```

Project Setting

HESS PET CENTER

Hess Pet Center
186 Hess Boulevard, Austin, TX 78712-2149
Phone 512.555.PETS (7387) | Fax 512.555.7378
www.hesspetcenter.com

© Cengage Learning/
courtesy of Susie VanHuss

Welcome to Hess Pet Center—a new joint venture between a veterinarian, Dr. Erin A. Faulk, and an entrepreneur, Mr. Douglas C. Schmidt. Dr. Faulk owns Faulk Pet Care, which offers a wide range of services to dog owners. Mr. Schmidt owns a 10-acre outparcel adjacent to Hess Office Park and is investing in Hess Pet Center.

The leased building has adequate facilities for the offices, boutique, grooming area, and most of the Veterinary Clinic. Mr. Schmidt has an agreement with Hess Office Park to expand the space for the Clinic and to use the outparcel to build boarding and pet day camp facilities that will not be disruptive to other tenants of Hess Office Park. The agreement allows Hess Pet Center to use the Hess Office Park logo.

(continued)

14-d10

Business Plan

business plan

Dr. Faulk and Mr. Schmidt asked you to work with a small team of analysts to put together the preliminary data needed to update and complete the Hess Pet Center Business Plan. You will prepare a professional unbound report that will be distributed electronically.

1. Open *business plan* from the data files and apply Title and Subtitle styles. Select all text below the subtitle and apply Justify.

2. Apply Heading 1 style to all headings except for the five market segment headings after the *Revenue Potential Analyzed* heading; apply Heading 2 style to those five headings.

3. Format the table as follows:

 a. Apply Grid Table 4 – Accent 1.

 b. Apply 0.3" row height to all rows.

 c. Apply Align Center to all headings in row 1 and Align Center Left to the remainder of the table.

 d. Set a decimal tab at the center of each column with numerical data.

 e. Use the *Annual Revenue* column to sort the data in descending order.

 f. Sum the columns with numerical data. Apply Number format #,##0; add a dollar sign ($) in the bottom row of columns B and C.

4. Change the design of the SmartArt from a Radial Cycle to a Radial Cluster. Select the Doggie Day Camp shape and click Move Up so that the percentages will be in descending order to match the table.

✻ Discover

When a document is created from scratch, your name should appear automatically as the Author Name from the User box on your computer.

5. Insert the Ion (Light) cover page. Select the Year and key the title and subtitle of the report. ✻ Key your name as the Author Name. Add a blank page after the cover page for the table of contents.

6. Position the insertion point at the top of the blank page after the cover page and create a table of contents. Apply Automatic Table 2 style.

7. Format page numbers as follows:

 a. Insert a Continuous section break at the top of the first page of the report. Go to the header of Section 2 and click Link to Previous to break the link between the sections. Do the same for the footer.

 b. Go to the Footer on the second page of Section 1 and insert a Plain Number 2 and format it in lowercase roman numerals. Check Different First Page.

 c. Go to the Header of the first page of the report (Section 2), and click Format Page Numbers and Start at page 1.

 d. Go to the second page of Section 2 and insert the Facet (Odd Page) header. Make sure Different First Page is checked. Select the page number at the bottom of the page and delete it.

8. Add a 1-point Dark Red, Accent 1, Darker 25% page border to the whole document.

9. Preview the document to ensure that the preliminary pages and the body of the report are numbered and formatted correctly. Compare your report to the Quick Check shown on the next page.

10. Save and close. (*14-d10*)

The primary goals are to maintain the current clients of Faulk Pet Care and to develop new business from the numerous employees in Hess Office Park and the surrounding upscale residential neighborhoods.

Legal and financial consultants have finalized the formal documents for the new joint-venture business. Dr. Faulk and Mr. Schmidt hired you as a part-time intern to help with the office work.

STANDARD OPERATING PROCEDURES (SOPs)

Dr. Faulk has talked with you about setting up and following standard operating procedures, which are important in creating a consistent image and establishing the corporate brand. SOPs can enhance productivity and provide employees with access to information needed to work independently.

TIP

Use these procedures as a checklist for each document you prepare.

1. Preview and proofread each document you prepare.
2. Use the Hess Pet Center letterhead and memo form from the data files for letters and memos. Do not prepare envelopes. In this office, most documents are distributed as attachments to email.
3. Apply the Ion theme with Casual document formatting style to all documents. The letterhead and memo form already have this style applied.
4. Use the current date for all documents requiring a date unless directed otherwise; position it at 2.5" or two blank lines below the letterhead.
5. Use block letter format with open punctuation as the standard style.
6. Use *Dear* + the title and last name as the salutation unless directed otherwise. The partners use first names for individuals they know well.
7. Use the following closing lines spaced appropriately:

TIP

Save the formatted closing lines and your reference initials as a Quick Part to save keying time and increase productivity.

Sincerely
Douglas C. Schmidt, Managing Partner
Retail and Service Operations

Sincerely
Erin A. Faulk, DVM, Manager Partner
Veterinary Operations

8. Use first names on memos you prepare for Mr. Schmidt and Dr. Faulk.
9. Save all documents as *14-d* + the document number.
10. As a shortcut, employees often use *hpc* for Hess Pet Center; always spell it out in documents.

14-d1

Memo

 hpc memo form

1. Prepare a memo from you to **Dr. Lynn F. Hudson**.
2. Use the subject: **Request for Internship Credit**.
3. Key the memo on the next page.
4. Save and close. (*14-d1*)

TIP

Do not add your initials to the memo since you are preparing it for yourself.

(continued)

This newsletter summarizes all of our services that are currently available for both dogs and cats. The veterinary clinic is more than 50 percent larger than our previous clinic and offers the highest level of pet care available. The new facility has state-of-the-art technology. The number of luxury units available for boarding has been increased and the boutique features many more items.

We look forward to seeing you at the *hpc* soon.

QUICK ✓

Check your documents against the illustrations below.

14-d9

Labels

1. Use the Mail Merge Wizard to create address labels for the recipients of the form letter prepared in *14-d8*.
2. Use Avery US Letter 5162 labels. (*14-d9*)

Business Plan—Effective Communication Tool

Communicating Today ▶

A business plan is not only an excellent tool for managing a business; it is also a key tool for communicating with potential and current investors, bankers, suppliers, and clients. Individuals and organizations that invest in a company want to have enough reliable information about a company to be able to make a good decision before risking the investment. A business plan provides information about the strategic direction of the company and how it plans to reach its goals. It shows that the company understands the market and competition and has access to the financial resources needed to make the business successful.

This week I was offered and accepted an internship at the newly created Hess Pet Center, which is a joint venture between Dr. Erin Faulk, owner of Hess Pet Care, a veterinary clinic, and Mr. Douglas Schmidt, an entrepreneur. The new business integrates the veterinary clinic with a full-service luxury pet boarding, grooming, and boutique center.

This position offers me a great opportunity to work in an environment that I have learned about in my Small Business Management and Financial courses, while applying the word processing and document formatting skills I learned in your class. I will work with Dr. Faulk and Mr. Schmidt to develop standard operating procedures and to standardize the formats for letters, memos, reports, and table styles for documents that are specifically related to the business. They both have indicated to me that they expect me to take full responsibility for my position and to expect very little direct supervision.

I have agreed to work for a minimum of six months for at least 10 hours per week, but I have the option to work as many as 25 hours a week. My plan is to average 20 hours per week. The type of position and the number of hours worked meet and exceed all of the requirements for receiving academic credit for my internship. Dr. Faulk and Mr. Schmidt have agreed to evaluate my work and complete the required forms for the internship. Therefore, I respectfully request that you approve this internship for academic credit.

Please let me know if you need additional information.

14-d2

Letter

 hpc letterhead

Mr. Schmidt asked you to prepare the following letter to **Mr. Patrick J. Hess, Manager | Hess Office Park | 100 Hess Boulevard | Austin, TX 78712-2149** with a copy to Dr. Faulk. Use only the DVM title after her name for copies.

All of the information you need to prepare the letter is contained in the SOPs. After you have completed the document, save and close it. (*14-d2*)

This letter confirms that Erin Faulk and I have finalized our joint venture, Hess Pet Center, and will begin our operations today. We especially appreciate being able to use the Hess name as part of our brand. It gives us instant credibility and name recognition, especially with all of the employees in companies located in Hess Office Park and with residents of the surrounding neighborhoods.

Signing a long-term lease provided us with the security and the incentive that we needed to invest heavily in this venture. Our architect is reviewing the plans you submitted for the expansion of the veterinary clinic. He is

(continued)

14-d8

Mail Merge

hpc letterhead
maggie and gracie
andy & bentley
rolfi

Prepare a form letter that will be sent to the owners of pets that will be featured in the next newsletter.

1. Open the *hpc letterhead* from the data files and save it as *14-d8 main*. In the open document, insert the current date at 2.2"; check update automatically.

2. Create the data source using the records shown in the table below. Customize the field names to include those shown in the first column. (*14-d8 data*)

Field Names	Record 1	Record 2	Record 3
Title	Mr. and Mrs.	Mr. and Mrs.	Mr. and Mrs.
First Name	Tommy	Pat	Ernie
Last Name	Suggs	VanHuss	Csiszar
Address Line 1	823 Harris Avenue	3106 Duval Street	4105 Avenue G
City	Austin	Austin	Austin
State	TX	TX	TX
ZIP Code	78705-2540	78705-3089	78751-4707
Pets	Maggie and Gracie are	Andy and Bentley are	Rolfi is

3. Key the main document shown below and insert the merge fields in it.

4. For the closing lines, use your name and title (**Intern**).
 Insert the three pictures across the bottom of the page. Size them 2" high. Position Maggie and Gracie at Bottom Left with Square Wrapping, Andy and Bentley at Bottom Center with Square Wrapping, and Rolfi at Bottom Right with Square Wrapping. Adjust pictures horizontally to eliminate overlapping.

5. Sort by ZIP Code in ascending order. Preview and proofread the document.

6. Merge the data source and the main document.

7. Compare your letter to the Quick Check on the next page.

8. Save and close. (*14-d8*)

TIP

Remember to remove the space after paragraph in the address block and between the name and title in the closing lines when you preview and check the letters.

«AddressBlock»

«GreetingLine»

We are currently preparing a new newsletter that will be sent to all of our current clients and the employees of Hess Office Park. When you receive the newsletter, you will note that «Pets» featured in it. The pictures of all pets in the newsletter are shown at the bottom of this letter. We hope you enjoy reading it.

(continued)

also finalizing our plans for the boarding and day camp facilities to be built on the property that has now officially been annexed into Hess Office Park. As we agreed, we will move our grooming operation to that facility as soon as it is ready for occupancy. Doing so will provide a significant part of the extra space needed for the veterinary clinic. Our contractor tells us the type of facility needed can be constructed within a month.

Erin and I look forward to our meeting with you on Friday so that all of these details can be finalized. We also would like to spend some time with your marketing and business development staff to talk about ways we can promote Hess Pet Center to the many potential clients who are part of Hess Office Park.

14-d3

Announcement

 hpc logo

Drag the WordArt text box to the right of the logo and expand it to the right margin. The title will appear on two lines.

Mr. Schmidt asked you to key the Open House announcement, shown below, for all Hess Office Park employees. It will be distributed electronically.

1. In a new blank document, tap ENTER once and insert the *hpc* logo.
2. Insert WordArt, Fill – Black, Text 1, Outline – Background 1, Hard Shadow – Accent 1 WordArt. Apply Dark Red, Accent 1, Darker 50% font color. Position it on the right side of the logo and key the title.
3. Tap ENTER four times after the logo. Change font size to 14 point and Justify text.
4. Apply square bullets with Dark Red, Accent 1, Darker 50% font color to the five items *hpc* offers. Add a 1-point page border the same color as the bullets.
5. Review the Quick Check on the next page.
6. Save and close. (*14-d3*)

Hess Pet Center | Open House

All employees of the companies in Hess Office Park are cordially invited to join us any day Monday through Thursday, January 14-17, from 5:00 p.m. to 6:30 p.m. for refreshments and a tour of our new business in Hess Office Park. You will also have an opportunity to view our new plans to expand the veterinary clinic and to build additional boarding and day camp facilities.

Hess Pet Center offers:

Complete veterinary services | Hess Pet Boutique | Pet grooming and spa | Pet boarding | Doggy day camp

We will custom tailor our hours to meet the needs of Hess Office Park employees. In addition, all Hess Office Park employees will have an opportunity to sign up for a special Hess discount card to receive a 10 percent discount on all purchases at the Hess Pet Boutique, and for all grooming, boarding, and day camp services this year.

You are welcome to bring family and friends with you to the Open House. We look forward to meeting all of our neighbors in Hess Office Park.

(continued)

Hess Pet Center now provides full-service luxury pet care to dog owners. Recently, we have been inundated with requests from current clients and from employees in Hess Office Park to expand our services to cat owners. Providing services to cat owners has always been part of our long-range business plan; therefore, we decided to survey all of our clients and Hess Office Park employees.

Survey Results

First, we asked our current clients if they had any objections to adding cats to the facilities. We are happy to report that there were no objections. More than 20 percent of our current clients have both dogs and cats. Approximately 25 percent of Hess Office Park employees indicated that they needed services for cats.

What was even more surprising were responses from clients who only have dogs, but who suggested many of their friends would like to use our services for their cats. Several sent pictures of their friends' cats. They all indicated we could publish their names and pictures in our newsletter. Sadie, shown above, is one that would likely be a frequent boarder at Hess Pet Center.

Some of our clients even sent pictures of their dogs with cats that belonged to their friends who want to use our services. Andy is pictured below with his friend Choo.

Action Plan

We will begin immediately with a pilot project that will include three types of services for cats:

- Total professional care provided by board-certified veterinarians and highly trained technicians.
- Luxury boarding.
- Boutique that provides one-stop shopping to meet your cat's needs and desires.

The architects and construction team met and agreed that we could finish an expansion area of the new addition and have a nice area to meet the demand for accommodating cats. This expansion will not impact the construction completion dates. Space in the veterinary clinic and the boutique is already available.

Compare your announcement to the one shown below.

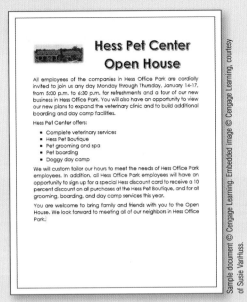

Hess Pet Center
Open House

All employees of the companies in Hess Office Park are cordially invited to join us any day Monday through Thursday, January 14-17, from 5:00 p.m. to 6:30 p.m. for refreshments and a tour of our new business in Hess Office Park. You will also have an opportunity to view our new plans to expand the veterinary clinic and to build additional boarding and day camp facilities.

Hess Pet Center offers:

- Complete veterinary services
- Hess Pet Boutique
- Pet grooming and spa
- Pet boarding
- Doggy day camp

We will custom tailor our hours to meet the needs of Hess Office Park employees. In addition, all Hess Office Park employees will have an opportunity to sign up for a special Hess discount card to receive a 10 percent discount on all purchases at the Hess Pet Boutique, and for all grooming, boarding, and day camp services this year.

You are welcome to bring family and friends with you to the Open House. We look forward to meeting all of our neighbors in Hess Office Park.

Sample document © Cengage Learning. Embedded image © Cengage Learning, courtesy of Susie VanHuss.

14-d4

Compose Memo

hpc memo form

Mr. Hess indicated to Mr. Schmidt and Dr. Faulk that March Walker, from his office, would be happy to email an announcement to all of the Hess Office Park employees for *hpc*. Compose the memo to her from you. The announcement will be attached.

1. Use the subject: **Please Distribute**; use **January 7, 201-** as the date.
2. Refer to the offer Mr. Hess made for March to assist with the distribution.
3. Indicate that the announcement is attached and to whom it should be distributed.
4. Show appreciation for her assistance and indicate that you hope she will attend.
5. Save and close. (*14-d4*)

! WORKPLACE SUCCESS

Click Fraud

Nicolas Sutcliffe/Shutterstock.com

Buyer or user beware is an appropriate term to remember anytime you use the Internet. Many companies advertise on the Internet and agree to pay the host an advertising fee based on the number of clicks or hits on their ad. To increase advertising fees and to make buyers believe the advertising is being viewed by numerous visitors, many unscrupulous hosts pay individuals to do nothing but click on the ad as quickly as they can. Some individuals are in foreign countries, and some sites even have robots to click on the ads. The scam could have a very serious effect on the future of advertising on the Internet. Most buyers are willing to pay for legitimate prospects to view their ad, but not for scams.

14-d7

Newsletter

sadie
andy and choo

✳ Discover

Rotate

Picture Tools Format/
Arrange/Rotate Objects

1. Click the drop-list arrow on Rotate Objects to display rotate options.

2. Click Flip Horizontal.

1. In a new blank document, apply Moderate margins and tap ENTER twice.

2. Key the information shown on the next page. Apply Heading 1 style to both headings.

3. Apply Dark Red, Accent 1, Darker 25% square bullets and position at the left edge of the column.

4. Select the text and apply two-column layout with equal-width format.

5. Insert the picture *sadie* from the data files and position it after the first line of the paragraph in which she is mentioned. Format it as follows:

 a. Crop the picture so that only the cat is shown. Size the picture 2.3" high.

 b. ✳ Rotate the picture horizontally and compress it.

 c. Apply Square Text Wrapping and position the picture at the left side of the column.

6. Insert the picture *andy and choo* immediately below the paragraph in which they are mentioned. Size the picture 2.4" high and compress it.

7. In the space at the top of the page above the Section Break (Continuous) line, key **Hess Pet Center News and Views** and format as follows:

 a. Apply 26-point font and Fill – Black 1, Text 1, Outline – Background 1, Hard Shadow – Background 1 Text Effects.

 b. Dark Red, Accent 1, Darker 25% theme color and center the text horizontally.

 c. Add a 1-point, Dark Red, Accent 1, Darker 25% page border.

8. See the illustration on the next page.

9. Save and close. (14-d7)

(continued)

14-d5

Table

hpc logo

Design a table for pet boarding fees.

1. In a new blank document, apply Landscape orientation. Insert the *hpc* logo at the top line and apply Square Text Wrapping. Tap TAB and key the title, *hpc*; apply Title style and Dark Red, Accent 1, Darker 25% font color.

2. Tap ENTER three times and create a 4-column, 8-row table and key the information shown in the table on the next page.

3. Change the text direction of the *Daily* and *Weekly Costs* headings to vertical; Align Bottom Center.

4. Sort the data in the *Daily Cost* column in ascending order.

5. Delete the *Doggie Day Camp* column.

6. Insert one column to the left of the *Weekly Cost* column and one to the right of it; change the text direction back to horizontal and key **Multiple Pets in Same Unit** for both column heads.

7. Adjust the width of columns A, C, and E to 2.3" and the width of columns B and D to 1".

8. In the first three rows under the *Multiple Pets in the Same Unit* headings (columns C and E), split the rows into two columns; key the following information:

 a. In the Standard Units row, key **Two** in the first split column and **Three** in the second. Do the same for the second split column.

 b. In the Small and Medium pet rows, key **45** and **50** for the daily costs for two pets and **50** and **55** for three pets.

 c. In the Small and Medium pet rows, key **225** and **250** for the weekly costs for two pets and **250** and **275** for three pets.

 d. In the *Large* row under both *Multiple Pets in Same Unit* columns, key **Not available**.

 e. In the three remaining rows under the *Multiple Pets in the Same Unit* columns, key **No extra charge**.

9. Add a row at the top of the table, merge the cells, and key **PET BOARDING FEES**.

10. Apply Grid Table 4 – Accent 1 table style. Apply Align Center and 16-point font to the heading.

11. Apply the following formats to the table:

 a. Deselect First Column in the Table Style Options group.

 b. Bold all headings in rows 2 and 3.

 c. In row 2, apply Align Center Left to the heading in column A, Align Center to columns C and E, and Align Bottom Center to columns B and D.

 d. Set row height at 0.8" for rows 1 and 2.

12. In rows 3–9, increase the row height to 0.3" and apply Align Center Left to the first column and Align Center to all other columns.

13. Compare your table to the Quick Check on the next page.

14. Save and close. (*14-d5*)

(continued)

Unit Type and Pet Size	Daily Cost	Weekly Cost	Doggie Day Camp
Standard Units			20
Luxury suites	75	325	NA
Junior suites	70	300	NA
Luxury units	60	275	30
Small: <35 pounds	35	175	
Medium: 35-75 pounds	40	200	
Large: >75 pounds	45	225	

 QUICK ✔

Compare your table to the one shown below.

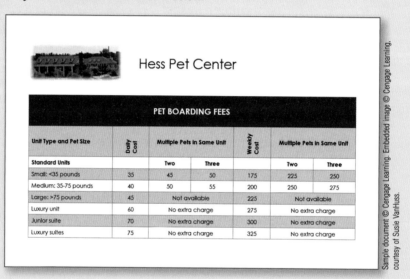

Sample document © Cengage Learning. Embedded image © Cengage Learning. courtesy of Susie VanHuss.

<table>
<tr><td colspan="8" align="center">Hess Pet Center</td></tr>
<tr><td colspan="8" align="center">PET BOARDING FEES</td></tr>
<tr><td rowspan="2">Unit Type and Pet Size</td><td rowspan="2">Daily Cost</td><td colspan="2">Multiple Pets in Same Unit</td><td rowspan="2">Weekly Cost</td><td colspan="2">Multiple Pets in Same Unit</td></tr>
<tr><td>Two</td><td>Three</td><td>Two</td><td>Three</td></tr>
<tr><td>Standard Units</td><td></td><td></td><td></td><td></td><td></td><td></td></tr>
<tr><td>Small: <35 pounds</td><td>35</td><td>45</td><td>50</td><td>175</td><td>225</td><td>250</td></tr>
<tr><td>Medium: 35-75 pounds</td><td>40</td><td>50</td><td>55</td><td>200</td><td>250</td><td>275</td></tr>
<tr><td>Large: >75 pounds</td><td>45</td><td colspan="2">Not available</td><td>225</td><td colspan="2">Not available</td></tr>
<tr><td>Luxury unit</td><td>60</td><td colspan="2">No extra charge</td><td>275</td><td colspan="2">No extra charge</td></tr>
<tr><td>Junior suite</td><td>70</td><td colspan="2">No extra charge</td><td>300</td><td colspan="2">No extra charge</td></tr>
<tr><td>Luxury suites</td><td>75</td><td colspan="2">No extra charge</td><td>325</td><td colspan="2">No extra charge</td></tr>
</table>

14-d6

Organization Chart

1. In a new blank document, prepare the organization chart for the Retail and Service Operations, shown on the next page, using the Name and Title Organization Chart from the Hierarchy category of SmartArt diagrams.
2. Use Landscape orientation and Narrow margins.
3. Add your name to the chart.
4. Size the chart 7" high and 10" wide.
5. Use the following font sizes:
 a. Use 20-point font for all names; use SHIFT + ENTER to remove space after the paragraph to key the second line.
 b. Use 16-point for the second line in each shape and for all titles.
6. Select the shape for each manager and click Add Shape/Add Shape Below to insert additional shapes. Key the names and titles of the assistant managers.
7. Save and close. (14-d6)

(continued)

Appendices

Appendix A Windows 10

START
WINDOWS 10

Windows 10 is the newest operating system software released by Microsoft. The operating system software controls the operations of the computer and works with the application software. *Windows 10* works with *Word* in opening, printing, deleting, and saving files. It also allows you to work with photos, play music and videos, and access the Internet.

Some new features in *Windows 10* include Cortana, a personal assistant. Cortana can assist you with finding files on your computer, manage your calendar, or chat with you. *Microsoft* introduced a new web browser, *Microsoft Edge*. This new default browser is faster and more secure than *Internet Explorer*. *OneDrive*, formerly called *Sky Drive*, is the online storage service that is easily accessible from *Windows 10*.

When you turn on your computer, the *Windows 10 Lock* screen displays. Tap any key to display the *Windows 10 Sign-in* screen. Key your password and tap ENTER to display the *Windows 10 Desktop*.

Windows 10 Lock screen

11:06
Sunday, July 19

Windows 10 Sign-in screen

WINDOWS 10
DESKTOP

The *Windows 10* desktop displays once the sign-in procedure is competed. The *Windows* desktop, similar to the actual top of a desk, will be the surface on which you work. You can open files and folders and place them on the desktop. When you open *Microsoft Word*, it will display on the desktop. To display the desktop from any location, press ⊞ + D. The Windows key (⊞) is located to the left of the Space Bar; it is often referred to as the WinKey. *Microsoft* provides keyboard shortcuts that make it easy for you to interface with *Windows 10*. Pressing WinKey + D is a shortcut because it quickly displays the *Windows* desktop. WinKey + E is another shortcut that opens *File Explorer*.

Refer to the illustration on the following page to familiarize yourself with the basic screen elements.

Icon

Desktop

Taskbar ❶

Windows 10 Desktop

- *Taskbar* ❶. The taskbar displays across the bottom of the window. Use the mouse to point to each item in the taskbar. Look for the ScreenTip that displays identifying each element.
 - *Start button* ❷. Click the Start button to display the Start menu. The Start menu provides access to the recently used apps, commonly used settings, and live tiles.
 - *Search box* ❸. The search box allows searches of files and folders on the computer and online.
 - *Apps and file buttons*. Buttons display for the apps that are open or pinned to the taskbar and allow you to switch between them easily. The *Task View* ❹ icon shows all open applications. The *Microsoft Edge* ❺ icon is displayed to provide quick access to the Internet. The *File Explorer* ❻ icon provides quick access to your files. The *App Store* ❼ leads to the Windows Store and access to purchase digital content including apps, games, and media.
 - *Notification Area* ❽. The notification area provides helpful information, such as the date and time and the status of the computer. When you plug in a USB drive, Windows displays an icon in the notification area letting you know that the hardware is connected.
- *Icons and Shortcuts*. Icons, small pictures representing certain items, may be displayed on the desktop. The Recycle Bin, shown as a wastepaper basket, displays when Windows is installed. Other icons and shortcuts may be added.
- *Desktop*. This is the work area where you will be working on your documents and apps.

SHUT DOWN COMPUTER

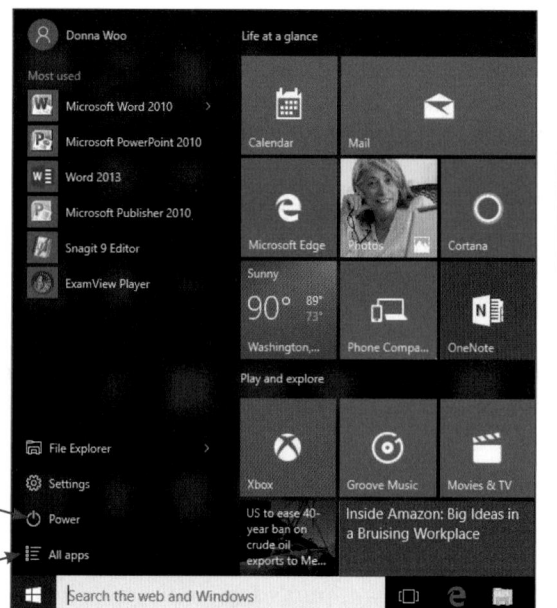

Start menu

Power

All apps

Shut down menu

1. Move your mouse pointer to the lower left of the Desktop and click Start, or tap the WinKey on your keyboard to open the Start menu. The right side of the Start menu displays application tiles. The left side of the menu displays the recently accessed apps and programs, as well as frequently accessed places on the PC. Your Start menu probably does not look identical to the illustration.

2. Click Power to display the Power options.

3. Click Shut down.

DRILL 1 START WINDOWS

1. Sign in to *Windows 10*.

2. Click the Start button to display the Start menu.

3. Click All apps to display an alphabetical list of installed apps. Use the vertical scroll bar to scroll down to find the Get Started tile.

4. Click Get Started; the *Get Started* app opens.

5. Click *Cortana* from the list on the left, then click What is *Cortana*? Read about *Cortana*, using the scroll bar to view all the information.

6. Click *Microsoft Edge* from the list on the left, then click Get to know *Microsoft Edge*. Use the scroll bar to view all the information. Close the window.

7. Click the WinKey to display the Start menu.

8. Click Power, then Shut down.

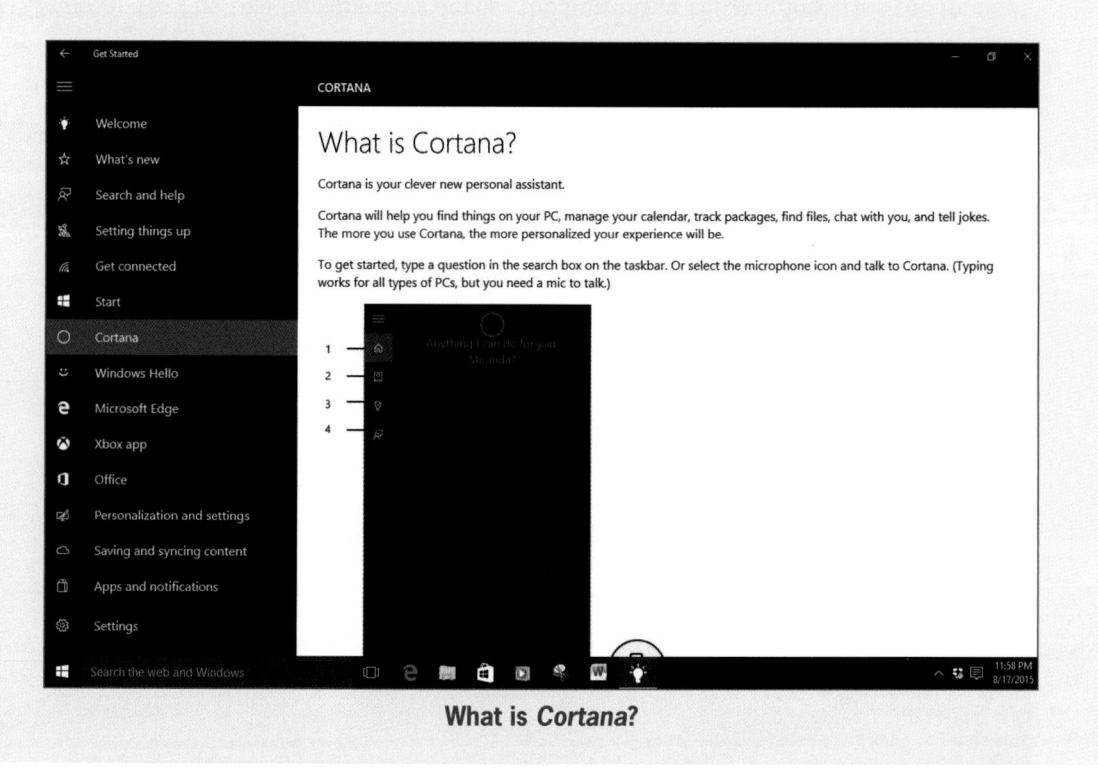

What is *Cortana*?

WINDOWS 10 HELP

The *Windows 10 Help and Support* feature contains documentation on how to use *Windows 10*; this feature is stored online. You must be connected to the Internet to access online help.

You can access Help by keying your question in the Search box located in the taskbar area. You can also access Help by tapping F1 from within Windows or any desktop program. A list of topics will display; click the link to display the information.

Windows 10 **Search box**

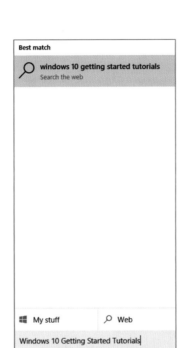

Windows 10 Getting Started Tutorials

Windows search results

DRILL 2	USING WINDOWS HELP AND SEARCH

1. Sign in to *Windows 10*.

2. Key **Windows 10 getting started tutorials** in the *Windows 10* Search box, then tap ENTER.

3. A list of related topics displays. Click on one of the icons below **Videos of Windows 10 getting started tutorials** to view the video.

4. When you finish viewing the video, click the close button ☒ in the upper right to close the window, then return to the Desktop.

5. Click the *File Explorer* icon in the Taskbar.

6. With the application open, tap the F1 key to display the help topics relating to *File Explorer*.

7. After viewing, close the window and return to your desktop.

Appendix B File Management

FILE EXPLORER

Expand and collapse icons may not display until the mouse moves into the left Navigation page.

Data is stored in files on the computer. To use the files, you need to know the name of the file and the location in which it is saved. *Windows 10* stores related files in folders. Folders can also be stored within folders, called subfolders. *File Explorer* provides the interface for you to manage the file system. Click the File Explorer icon on the taskbar to display the *File Explorer* window.

The left pane is the Navigation pane, which shows the drives on the computer and the files stored on each drive. If an expand icon > displays to the left of the folder or drive, that means the folder or drive contains subfolders. You can expand the list to view the subfolders by clicking the > icon. Once the list is expanded, the expand icon changes to a collapse icon; clicking the collapse icon V will hide the subfolders.

The Contents pane lists the contents of the folders. Click on a folder in the Navigation pane to display the contents of the folder in the Contents pane. If you want to get a preview of what a file looks like, click the View tab; then in the Panes group, click Preview pane to display an additional pane that shows a preview of your file.

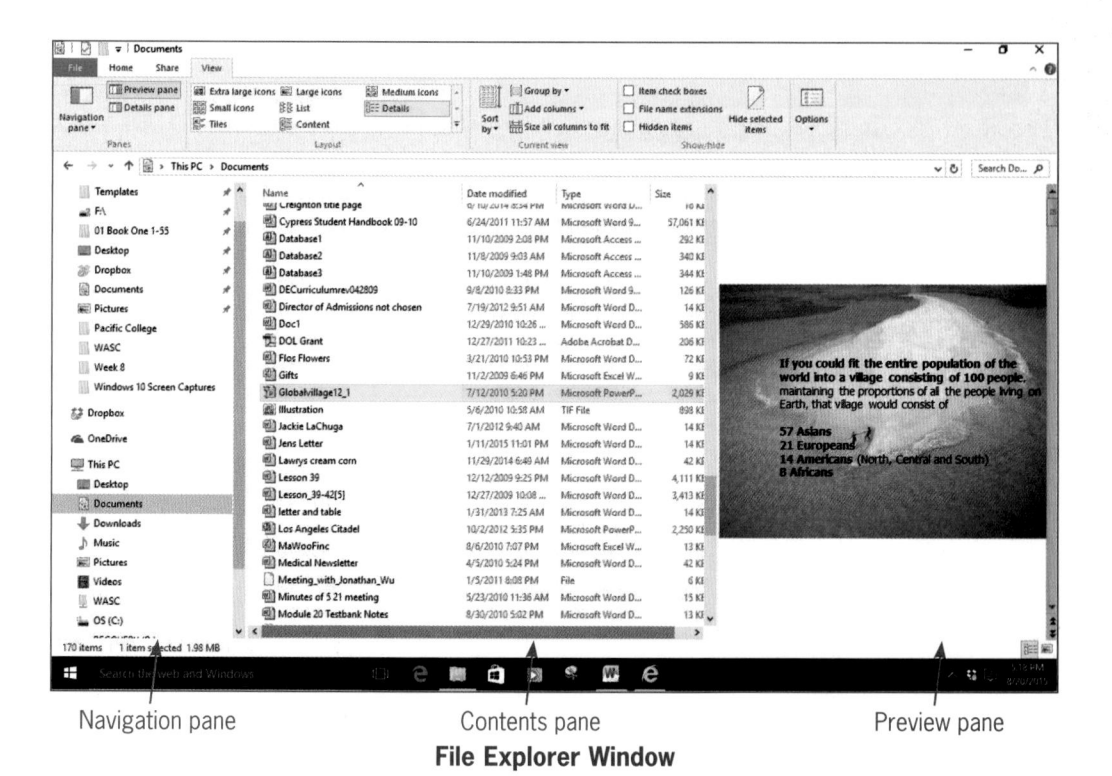

Navigation pane Contents pane Preview pane

File Explorer Window

When you open *File Explorer*, it displays six Quick Access areas—Desktop, Downloads, Documents, Music, Pictures, and Videos. Documents, by default, save in the Documents folder. To view the Documents folder, move the mouse over Documents in the left pane, then click the expand icon. Click the expand icon to the left of the Documents folder to display its contents.

Files can be stored in various locations or drives on the computer. To view the drives on your computer, click This PC in the Navigation pane. The drives display in the right pane. They are labeled with letters followed by a colon (C:, D:, E:). The local disk, which stores the software, is usually labeled as drive (C:). If you are using a USB drive to save your files, it is often designated as drive E: or F:.

This PC

FILE ADDRESSES

The address bar, located above the Navigation and Contents pane, shows the location or address of the file. Each level of the file hierarchy is separated with a > symbol; the highest level displays at the left of the address bar. The > symbol indicates the next lower level. The illustration below shows that the selected file, How To Earn A's ❶, is located in the Success subfolder ❷, which is located in the Documents folder ❸.

Address Bar Path

You can move up the hierarchy by clicking on the higher level in the address bar or by clicking on a higher level in the Navigation pane. You can also display the contents of the folder by clicking on the folder name in the address bar.

WORK WITH FILES AND FOLDERS

Folders are extremely important in organizing files. You will create and manage folders and the files within them so that you can easily locate them. A folder can store files, or it may contain subfolders that store files. The use of folders and subfolders helps to reduce clutter so that you can find, navigate, and manage your files, folders, and disks with greater speed.

NAMING FILES

Good file organization begins with giving your folders and files names that are logical and easy to understand. A filename should be meaningful and reflect the contents of the file. Filenames can be up to 255 characters long, but in practice you will not use filenames that long. In addition, the following symbols cannot be used in a filename: \ / : * ? " , . . The descriptive name is followed by a period (.), which is used to separate the descriptive name from the file extension. The file extension is three or four letters that follow the period. When renaming a file, do not delete or change file extensions as this may cause problems opening the file.

Drive Specifier File Extension

Descriptive Name

FILE EXPLORER HOME TAB

Commands that are commonly used are located on the Home tab. The Ribbon is divided into groups, similar to those of other *Microsoft Office* products. The commands to create new folders and to rename files and folders are located on the Home tab.

Home tab on the Ribbon

To create a file folder:
Home/New/New folder

1. In the left pane of *File Explorer*, double-click the drive or folder that is to contain the new folder ①.

2. Click the New folder command. A yellow folder icon displays in the right pane with the words *New folder* highlighted ②.

3. Key the new folder name and tap ENTER.

New Folder Creation

To rename a file or folder:
Home/Organize/Rename

1. Access *File Explorer* and display the contents of your removable storage drive (or the location where you have been instructed to save your document files or folders).
2. Click the file or folder icon to be renamed.
3. Click Rename on the Ribbon.
4. Key the new name and tap ENTER.

COPY, MOVE, OR DELETE FILES OR FOLDERS

You can use the commands in the Organize group on the Home tab to move, copy, or delete files and folders.

To move a file or folder:
Home/Organize/Move to

Organize Group

1. Select the file or folder to be moved.
2. Click the Move to drop-down arrow; a list of folders on your computer displays.
3. Select a location from the Move to drop-down list, *or*
4. Click Choose location to display the Move items dialog box. Select the destination and click Move.

Move to drop-down list

Move Items dialog box

To copy a file or folder:
Home/Organize/Copy to

1. Select the file or folder to be copied.
2. Click the Copy to drop-down arrow to display the Copy to drop-down list.
3. Select a location from the Copy to drop-down list or click Choose location to display the Copy items dialog box. Select the location for the copy to be placed and click Copy.

To delete a file or folder:
Home/Organize/Delete

1. Select the file or folder to be deleted.
2. Click Delete.

When you delete a file or folder from the hard drive, it is not removed from storage immediately. It moves to the Recycle Bin and remains there until the Recycle Bin is emptied. This gives you the opportunity to restore the file to its original location if you discover that it should not have been deleted.

ONEDRIVE APP

Microsoft made OneDrive an integral part of the *Windows 10* operating system by including the *OneDrive* app as part of the *File Explorer* navigation. OneDrive is a service that allows you to store documents, photos, videos, and audio files on the Microsoft servers. A benefit of storing files on OneDrive is the ability to access the files from any computer or *Windows* phone. The files can be shared with family and friends. Coworkers can collaboratively work on *Microsoft Office* documents. You need to have a Microsoft account to access OneDrive.

To access OneDrive: *(Internet connection and a Microsoft account needed.)*

1. From the *Windows 10* Desktop, open the Start menu, click All apps, and find the *OneDrive* app. Alternatively, you may access OneDrive using the navigation menu of *File Explorer*.

2. If this is the first use of OneDrive on the computer, you may be prompted to sign in with your Microsoft account. Folders and files located on OneDrive will display; you may use these files as if they were on your computer, and changes made will synchronize to OneDrive.

3. OneDrive can be used in the same way a file or folder on your computer is used.

TIP
Updates are continually made to OneDrive. Read your screen carefully as its appearance and steps may vary over time.

Welcome to OneDrive

Your most important files are with you wherever you go, on any device.

Welcome to OneDrive

Appendix C Reference Guide

Pronoun Case Agreement

1. Use the nominative case when the pronoun is the subject of a verb.

 She enjoys reading before going to sleep.

2. Use the nominative case for a predicate pronoun following a linking verb.

 It is **she** who made the motion to adjourn.

3. Use the objective case when the pronoun is the object of a preposition.

 This information must be kept between you and **me**.

4. Use the objective case when the pronoun is a direct or an indirect object.

 He told **her** to take the subway. (direct object)
 Please send **me** Joe's address. (indirect object)

5. Use *who* in the nominative form as a subject of the sentence; use *whom* in the objective form as a direct object.

 Who is knocking at the door?
 To **whom** do I write my check?

6. Use the possessive case to show ownership.

 My sister is moving to Paris for **her** internship.

Pronoun Agreement (Person, Gender, Number)

1. A personal pronoun agrees in person, gender, and number with the noun or pronoun it represents.

 The **students** worked to pay **their** tuition.
 You worked in the summer to pay **your** tuition.

2. Indefinite pronouns such as *each, every, everyone, everything, somebody, anybody, either,* and *neither* are singular. The indefinite pronouns such as *many, both, few,* and *several* are plural.

 Each of the honorees worked to pay **his/her** tuition.
 All of the honorees had guests for **their** banquet.

3. A personal pronoun that represents a collective noun may be singular or plural, depending on the meaning of the collective noun.

 The **team** voted unanimously to keep Coach Johnson as **its** head coach. (individual action)
 The **family** are debating on **their** vacation destination this summer. (separate actions)

Subject/Verb Agreement

1. Use a singular verb with a singular subject. Use a plural verb with a plural subject.

 The **granddaughter is** loved by her grandparents.
 The **honorees are** seated at the head table.

2. Use a singular verb with singular indefinite pronouns. Use a plural verb with plural pronouns.

 Each of the honorees **works** to pay his/her tuition.
 All of the winners **work** to pay their bills. (plural)

3. Use a plural verb with a compound subject joined by *and*.

 The **students** and the **faculty attend** the meeting.

4. For subjects joined by words like *or* or *nor*, use a singular verb if the subject closer to the verb is singular and plural if the subject closer to the verb is plural.

 Neither Susie nor **I is** available today.
 Either Pat or his team **members are** available.

5. Use a singular verb with a collective noun when the group acts as a unit. Use a plural verb when the members act individually.

 The **team votes** unanimously today. (singular)
 The **family are** debating their vacation. (plural)

Abbreviations

1. With a few exceptions, do not use abbreviations in general writing.

2. Spell out an abbreviation for the first use and key the abbreviation in parenthesis. For future uses of the word, use the abbreviation.

 First time: National Science Foundation (NSF)
 Second and subsequent times: NSF

3. Abbreviate the names of well-known organizations and agencies with capitals and no periods.

 NSF NATO

4. Abbreviate professional designations and academic degrees after a name.

 CPA PhD

5. Add *s* to make most abbreviations plural. Generally, to make them plural possessive, add an apostrophe.

 CPAs

6. Spell out standard units of measure in general writing; elsewhere, use abbreviations for space or readability.

 He weighs 200 pounds and is 5 feet 10 inches tall.

Punctuation

Use an apostrophe

1. To make most singular nouns and indefinite pronouns possessive (add **apostrophe** and **s**).

 anyone's one's somebody's

 computer + 's = computer's Jess + 's = Jess's

2. To make a plural noun that does not end in s possessive (add **apostrophe** and **s**).

 women + 's = women's men + 's = men's

 deer + 's = deer's children + 's = children's

3. To make a plural noun that ends in s possessive. Add only the **apostrophe**.

 boys + ' = boys' managers + ' = managers'

4. To make a compound noun possessive or to show joint possession. Add **apostrophe** and **s** to the last part of the hyphenated noun.

 son-in-law's Rob and Gen's game

5. To form the plural of numbers and isolated lowercase letters and the capital letters A, I, M, and U, add **apostrophe** and **s**. To show omission of letters or figures, add an **apostrophe** in place of the missing items.

 7's A's p's and q's it's '70s

Use a colon

1. To introduce a listing.

 The candidate's strengths were obvious: experience, community involvement, and forthrightness.

2. To introduce an explanatory statement.

 Then I knew we were in trouble: The item had not been scheduled.

Use a comma

1. After an introductory phrase or dependent clause.

 After much deliberation, the jury reached its decision.

 If you have good skills, you will find a job.

2. After words or phrases in a series.

 Mike is taking Greek, Latin III, and Chemistry II.

3. To set off nonessential or interrupting elements.

 Troy, the new man in MIS, will install the hard drive.

 He cannot get to the job, however, until next Friday.

4. To set off the date from the year and the city from the state.

 John, will you please reserve the center in Billings, Montana, for January 10, 2018.

5. To separate two or more parallel adjectives (adjectives could be separated by and instead of a comma).

 The loud, whining guitar could be heard above the rest.

6. Before the conjunction in a compound sentence. The comma may be omitted in a very short sentence.

 You must leave immediately, or you will miss your flight. We tested the software and they loved it.

7. Set off appositives and words of direct address.

 Karen, our team leader, represented us at the conference.

 Paul, have you ordered the ten dozen red roses?

Use a hyphen

1. In two-word adjectives before a noun.

 two-car family

2. In compound numbers between twenty-one and ninety-nine.

3. In fractions and some proper nouns with prefixes/suffixes.

 two-thirds ex-Governor all-American

Use italic

1. With titles of complete literary works.

 College Keyboarding *Hunt for Red October*

2. To emphasize special words or phrases.

 What does *professional* mean?

Use a semicolon

1. To separate independent clauses in a compound sentence when the conjunction is omitted.

 Please review the information; give me a report by Tuesday.

2. To separate independent clauses when they are joined by conjunctive adverbs (*however, nevertheless, consequently, etc.*).

 The traffic was heavy; consequently, I was late.

3. To separate a series of elements that contain commas.

 The new officers are Fran Pena, president; Harry Wong, treasurer; and Muriel Williams, secretary.

Use a dash

1. To show an abrupt change of thought.

 Invoice 76A—which is ten days overdue—is for $670.

2. After a series to indicate a summarizing statement.

 Noisy fuel pump, worn rods, and failing brakes—for all these reasons I'm trading the car.

Use an exclamation point

After emphatic interjections or exclamatory sentences.

 Terrific! Hold it! You bet! What a great surprise!

Capitalization

Capitalize:

1. First word of a sentence and of a direct quotation.

 We were tolerating instead of managing diversity. The speaker said, "We must value diversity, not merely recognize it."

2. Names of proper nouns—specific persons, places, or things.

 Common nouns: continent, river, car, street
 Proper nouns: Asia, Ohio, Buick, State Street

3. Derivatives of proper nouns and geographical names.

American history	English accent
German food	Ohio Valley
Tampa, Florida	Mount Rushmore

4. A personal or professional title when it precedes the name or a title of high distinction without a name.

Lieutenant Kahn	Mayor Walsh
Doctor Welby	Mr. Ty Brooks
Dr. Frank Collins	Miss Tate
the President of the United States	

5. Days of the week, months of the year, holidays, periods of history, and historic events.

 Monday, June 8 Labor Day Renaissance

6. Specific parts of the country but not compass points that show direction.

 Midwest the South northwest of town

7. Family relationships when used with a person's name.

 Aunt Helen my dad Uncle John

8. Noun preceding a figure except for common nouns such as *line*, *page*, and *sentence*.

 Unit 1 Section 2 page 2 line 2

9. First and main words of side headings, titles of books, and works of art. Do not capitalize words of four or fewer letters that are conjunctions, prepositions, or articles.

 Computers in the News Raiders of the Lost Ark

10. Names of organizations and specific departments within the writer's organization.

 Girl Scouts our Sales Department

Number Expression

General guidelines

1. Use **words** for numbers *one* through *ten* unless the numbers are in a category with related larger numbers that are expressed as figures.

 He bought three acres of land. She took two acres. She wrote 12 stories and 2 plays in 13 years.

2. Use **words** for approximate numbers or large round numbers that can be expressed as one or two words. Use **numbers** for round numbers in millions or higher with their word modifier.

 We sent out about three hundred invitations. She contributed $3 million dollars.

3. Use **words** for numbers that begin a sentence.

 Six players were cut from the ten-member team.

4. Use **figures** for the larger of two adjacent numbers.

 We shipped six 24-ton engines.

Times and dates

5. Use **words** for numbers that precede *o'clock* (stated or implied).

 We shall meet from two until five o'clock.

6. Use **figures** for times with *a.m.* or *p.m.* and days when they follow the month.

 Her appointment is for 2:15 p.m. on July 26.

7. Use **ordinals** for the day when it precedes the month.

 The 12th of October is my anniversary.

Money, percentages, and fractions

8. Use **figures** for money amounts and percentages. Spell out *cents* and *percent* except in statistical copy.

 The 16 percent discount saved me $145; Bill, 95 cents.

9. Use **words** for fractions unless the fractions appear in combination with whole numbers.

 one-half of her lesson 5 1/2 18 3/4

Addresses

10. Use **words** for street names First through Tenth and **figures** or ordinals for streets above Tenth. Use **figures** for house numbers other than number **one**. (If street name is a number, separate it from house number with a dash.)

One Lytle Place	Second Avenue
142—53rd Street	

Spelling Rules

1. To make most nouns plural, add s.

boy	boys
chair	chairs
parent	parents

2. Add es to nouns ending in s, x, z, ch, or sh.

Jones	Jones
tax	taxes
buzz	buzzes
church	churches
wish	wishes

3. If a noun ends in a consonant plus y, change the y to i and add es.

puppy	puppies
fly	flies

4. Add es to some nouns ending in a consonant plus o.

potato	potatoes

BUT not pianos

5. For some nouns ending in f or fe, change the f or fe to ves.

half	halves
wolf	wolves

6. Memorize or look up irregular nouns.

child	children
woman	women

7. Keep a silent e before a suffix that begins with a consonant. Drop it before a suffix that begins with a vowel.

excite	excitement
excite	exciting

8. When adding a suffix that begins with a vowel to a word that ends with a vowel and consonant, double the consonant.

commit	commitment
shop	shopping

9. When you add a prefix, the spelling does not change.

wash	prewash
view	preview

10. Put i before e except after c or when the letters sound like a, as in neighbor and weigh.

receive	believe
neighbor	weigh

Composition

Most careers require good writing skills. You can learn to be an effective writer with practice. Writing at the keyboard facilitates editing and is easier and more effective than handwriting documents. Editing requires complete focus on each of the following areas:

Content accuracy—Determine what needs to be included in a message and then check to see that necessary information is included and that all information is accurate.

Organization—Check sentence structure to see that ideas are presented logically and flow smoothly.

Writing style—Ensure that the message is clear, crisp, concise, and written at an appropriate level.

Mechanical correctness—Check for errors in grammar, spelling, punctuation, capitalization, number usage, and word usage.

Composition Guides

1. Begin with short, easy sentences and paragraphs on topics in which you have knowledge. Then work on putting the sentences and paragraphs together for complete messages.
2. Key your thoughts first and then edit them carefully. It is very difficult to write perfect copy when you begin keying.
3. Use familiar words and a simple, straightforward writing style.
4. Edit to ensure that sentences are carefully arranged, clear, and grammatically correct.
5. Structure paragraphs carefully, making sure that all sentences in the paragraphs relate to the same topic and that they flow logically.
6. Edit and proofread carefully.

★ TIP

Editing and proofreading usually make the difference between high-quality and mediocre writing.

Proofreading

Often the difference between high-quality and mediocre documents is in how carefully they are proofread. Careful proofreading ensures the accuracy of the final document.

Proofreading requires complete focus on each of the following areas:

Overall appearance of a document—check for appropriate stationery, attractive placement, and correct and consistent format.

Content accuracy—check for accuracy and completeness, such as making sure dates are correct and times are not left off.

Mechanical correctness—check for keying errors, as well as mistakes in spelling, grammar, punctuation, capitalization, word usage, and number usage. Review basic guides if you are not comfortable with your knowledge level in each of the areas listed.

Proofreading Guides

1. Check the document using the Spelling and Grammar commands.

2. Proofread the document on the screen slowly, on a word-by-word basis. Focus on words that may be spelled correctly but are misused, such as *you/your, is/in, if/it, there/their, two/to/too, then/than,* and *principle/principal.*

3. Check specifically for capitalization, punctuation, and number usage.

4. Check to see that the document is complete, ensuring that enclosure or copy notations are not left off.

5. Verify that each number is correct. The only way to ensure that a number is correct is to check it against the source from which it was keyed.

6. Preview the document on screen to ensure that placement is appropriate.

7. Print the document and proofread it again. It is helpful to use a guide (ruler, large envelope, or folded sheet of paper). Move it down line by line as you read. Mark the corrections using proofreaders' marks. Refer to a list of common proofreaders' marks found in the right column of this page.

★ TIP

Learn to proofread on the screen first and then, as a last check, proofread the printed document again.

Proofreading Statistical Copy

Statistical copy requires special attention. It is very easy to make errors in keying numbers, and it is very difficult to determine if a number keyed is correct.

The same thing is true for a date or time.

1. Verify numbers against the original source, verify dates against the calendar, and check computations with a calculator.

2. Read numbers in groups. For example, the telephone number 618.555.0123 can be read in three parts: *six-one-eight, five-five-five, zero-one-two-three.*

3. Read numbers aloud and preferably with a partner checking against the original copy.

★ TIP

An error in a number could have significant negative consequences; for example, keying $300,000 rather than $400,000 in quoting a price or authorizing a loan at 7% when the correct percentage is 8% could prove to be very costly.

Proofreaders' Marks

Mark	Meaning	Mark	Meaning
#	Add horizontal space	/ or *lc*	Lowercase
‖	Align	⌐	Move left
∼	Bold	¬	Move right
Cap or ≡	Capitalize	⌐	Move up
[]	Center	⌐	Move down
‿	Close up	¶	Paragraph
ℓ	Delete	*sp*	Spell out
∧	Insert	∼ or *tr*	Transpose
⌄ ⌄	Insert quotation marks	___ italic or ⟨ital⟩	
. . . or *stet*	Let it stand; ignore correction	*wf*	Wrong font

Word Usage

Accept/Except
Accept—to receive something
Except—to exclude
She **accepts** the compliment with grace.
All outfits were appropriate **except** the jeans and polo shirt.

Advice/Advise
Advice—noun that means a recommendation
Advise—verb that means to recommend
The student appreciated the **advice** her teacher gave her.
Please **advise** the students to seek safety.

Affect/Effect
Affect—a verb that means to change or influence something
Effect—a noun that means something that happens is due to a cause
Number of absences **affects** a student's academic success.
Research shows that the **effect** of excessive absences is poor grades and can lead to a decline in the graduation rate.

Assure/Ensure/Insure
Assure—a verb that means to make a promise
Ensure—a verb that means to make certain
Insure—a verb that means to protect against financial loss
I **assure** you I will submit the bid before the deadline.
To **ensure** a fragile item is safe, wrap it in bubble wrap.
He will **insure** the package for $100.

Complement/Compliment
Complement—a verb that means to make complete or perfect
Compliment—a verb that means to praise
The maroon scarf **complemented** her suit.
The teacher **complimented** the students on their hard work.

Farther/Further
Farther—an adjective meaning a greater distance.
Further—a verb that means to help move forward, an adverb that means to a greater extent, or an adjective that means additional.
She drives **farther** to work than her husband.
Her plans are to **further** her education by completing a master's degree. (verb)
I become more excited the **further** we advance on this project. (adverb)
Further specifics will be forthcoming. (adjective)

Good/Well
Good—an adjective that means of fair quality.
Well—an adverb that describes an action as satisfactory or an adjective that means fit or healthy.
They enjoyed a very **good** meal at the new restaurant.
The students performed very **well** on the final exam.
When asked how he felt, the patient responded, "Very **well**."

It's/Its
It's—a contraction of it is
Its—a possessive form of the pronoun it
It's his first opportunity to sail his new boat.
Given **its** size and location, the house was perfect for the couple with three children.

Principal/Principle
Principal—a noun that refers to a chief or head or something of chief importance and an adjective that means highest or main importance.
Principle—a noun that means a basic truth or belief
The **principal** announced school will dismiss at noon.
The **principal** of the loan is $10,000.
The parents taught their children the **principle** of giving with a generous heart.

Their/There/They're
Their—the possessive form of the pronoun they
There—an adverb that shows where and a pronoun that introduces a sentence or clause
They're—the contraction of they are
There are three popular wedding venues for wedding receptions in **their** small town.
Do you want to put your books **there** on the desk?
They're both working this summer as a lifeguard.

To/Too/Two
To—a preposition to show direction toward
Too—an adverb that means also or to a great extent
Two—a noun that refers to a number
The **two** girls often go **to** the library after school and **to** the donut shop **too**.

Who's/Whose
Who's—a contraction of who is
Whose—possessive form of the pronoun who
Who's the sponsor of coffee break for the conference?
Whose turn is to bring snacks for the study group?

Letters with Special Parts

Letters and memos longer than one page require a header on the second and subsequent pages. Appropriate placement of the following special letter parts are illustrated below: mailing notation, attention line, subject line, copy notation, blind copy notation, and reference line.

Subject line

Two-page header

Copy notation

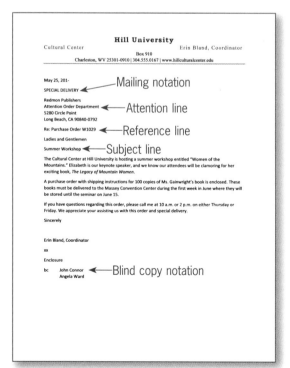

Mailing notation

Attention line

Reference line

Subject line

Blind copy notation

Attention Line, Reference Line, Subject Line, and Blind Copy Notation

Newsletter

Business Reports

Margins: Tap ENTER three times to begin first page of report at 2"; default 1" top margin for succeeding pages; default 1" for bottom margin.

Unbound report: Side margins 1"

Leftbound report: Side margins 1.5"

Titles: Title style. Main words capitalized.

Side headings: Heading 1 style. Main words capitalized.

Page numbers: Second and subsequent pages are numbered at top right of the page. One blank line follows the page number.

Spacing: Default line spacing; paragraphs blocked. Tap ENTER once between paragraphs.

Unbound Report, Page 1

Tap ENTER 3 times (about 2")

Title style → Essentials for Writing Success: Revise, Revise and Use Technology to Create Attractive and Correct Style

Being able to communicate effectively in a clear, concise, and logical manner continues to be one of the most demanded work skills. Employees who practice effective revision skills are far ahead of their counterparts who have had the mind-set that the first draft is the final draft. This report details excellent procedures for revising a report draft, explaining effective technology tools that make the process easier. The result is a more professional and accurate final product.

Heading 1 style → Revising the Draft
After a first draft of a report is completed, the writer is ready to refine or polish the report. The writer must be objective when revising the report draft and cultivate an attitude for improving the report by always considering the draft as a process.

First, read the draft for content. This might mean inserting sections of the report or adding information to areas that appear weak in this review. In this evaluation review, the writer may realize that one section would be more logically after another section.

When the writer is satisfied with the content, it is time to verify that all style rules have been followed. For example, check all headings to ensure they are "talking" headings. Do the headings describe the content of the section? Also, be sure all headings are parallel. If the writer chooses side heading Know Your Audience, other side headings must also begin with a verb. Note that the side headings in this report are parallel, with both beginning with a gerund.

Ensuring Correct and Attractive Formats
The effective writer understands the importance of using technology to create an attractive document that adheres to correct style rules. Here are a few examples of how to use technology to create a professional final document.

Bulleted list → • Select attractive headers and footers from the built-in design galleries to provide page numbers and other helpful information to the reader.
• Suppress headers, footers, and page numbering on the title page and on the first page of the report.

Unbound Report, Page 2 (Plain Number 3 Style)

Page Number 0.5"

• Invoke the Widow/Orphan control feature to ensure that no lines display alone at the bottom or top of a page. Use the Keep with next command to keep side headings from appearing alone at the bottom of the page.
• Take advantage of automatic features, such as a table of contents and citations.
• Use styles to format tables and charts.
• Be sure to use the online thesaurus, spelling, and grammar features of the word processing software.
• Bookmark widely accepted online desk references and style manuals for easy use.
• Use the ShowHide command to show the ¶ marks and other hidden formatting symbols.

These simple steps will assist you in your goal to create well-written and attractive reports. The next step is to practice, practice, and practice.

Leftbound Report with Footnote, Page 1

Tap ENTER 3 times (about 2")

Title style → Polish Communication Skills for Career Success

Probably no successful enterprise exists that does not rely upon its ability of its members to communicate with each other and with third parties for its success. The role that effective communication plays in business success cannot be stressed too strongly; it is essential that strict attention be paid to the application, implementation, and administration of communication within a business venture.

1.5" → Business communication falls into two main categories: written and verbal. More time is spent by most business firms studying and perfecting their written communication. It is verbal communication, however, that makes up a major portion of all communication and deserves more attention than is typically the case.

President Schaefer's writes, "Make no mistake, both written and verbal communication are the stuff upon which success is built. Both forms deserve careful study by any business that wants to grow. Successful businesspeople must read, write, speak, and listen with skill."[1]

Heading 1 style → Written Communication
Written communication confirms facts and intentions, and any important verbal conversation should be confirmed in writing. Written communication also constitutes proof; a letter signature can have the same effect as a contract signature. Further, written communication can be retained for later reference, and being as close as a hard copy in a file folder or an electronic file on a computer server. Written communication avoids some of the natural barriers of verbal communication. Shyness, speech problems, and other distractions are not found in a written document. Types of written communication include but are not limited to the following:

Bulleted list → • Memos
• Letters
• Reports
• Email
• Fact sheets
• News release

[1] Excerpt from President Schaefer's report to the Board of Directors.

← Explanatory Footnote

Leftbound Report, Page 2 (Page Number Style)

Page Number 0.5" · Page | 2

Verbal Communication
Since verbal communication often involves encounters on a one-on-one basis, it can bring quicker results. Misunderstandings are avoided, questions are answered. It is usually less formal and friendlier; moods, attitudes, and emotions are more easily handled. Verbal communication is augmented with facial expressions and pictures, assuring greater clarity of the message. Words and phrases can be given special emphasis not possible in a written message, where emphasis is given by the receiver, not the sender.

Application
Specific practice activities are outlined in the practice session that follows the discussion session. Participants should download and review these materials prior to the practice session.

Report with Preliminary Pages

Cover Page

Hess Office Park Fourth Quarter Activity Report

OCTOBER – DECEMBER 201-

Patrick J. Hess
HESS OFFICE PARK | 100 HESS BOULEVARD, AUSTIN, TX 78712-2149

Table of Contents

ii

Table of Contents

Hess Office Park Fourth Quarter Activity Report
Quarter Ended December 31, 201-

The Hess Office Park Fourth Quarter Activity Report is prepared for the Owners and Tenants Association and is presented at the January meeting of the Association. The staff of Hess Office Park is pleased to report the following activities during the fourth quarter, ending December 31, 201-. Activities include work accomplished in the community as well as achievements in the office park.

New Owners and Tenants
One new owner and three new tenants have joined Hess Office Park in the fourth quarter. One tenant vacated space as of December 1. The table below outlines the changes in detail.

Space Changes in Fourth Quarter			
& Type of Lease			
& Owner	Tenant	Change	Suites Assigned
3&	Ayesha Liem	Add	311
4&	Ethan Madison	Add	323-325
5& Riley Grant			410-412
6&	Jackson Price	Add	422-423
7&	Paula Bowen	Terminate	521-525

These changes represent an increase of 5 percent over last year's fourth quarter and a gain of 20 percent this year. This past year Patrick Hess, manager of Hess Office Park, has added the following recruitment activities:

- Joined the Chamber of Commerce and five civic organizations.
- Accepted office of vice president for one civic organization.
- Accepted leadership role in securing funding for college scholarships for area students.

These networks are producing excellent connections and resulted in one added owner and two additional tenants to Hess Office Park.

5K Scholarship Fun Run
Hess Office Park is the site for the 5K Scholarship Fun Run sponsored by the East Central Education Foundation (ECEF) to be held on April 10, 201-. Scholarship monies are awarded to freshmen students entering college in the fall semester.

PATRICK J. HESS 1

Leftbound Report with Footer, Page 1

FOURTH QUARTER ACTIVITY REPORT 09/14/2017

Mr. Robert Kaczynski, president of ECEF, is the contact person and has signed the official agreement with our office. Hess Office Park will designate spaces in the south parking lot on Friday afternoon and all day on Saturday. Tables and chairs will be set up along the race route for volunteers to distribute drinks and snacks to the runners/walkers. Security and police assistance will be provided at the main intersection of Hess Boulevard and Elm Street. Space will also be provided for vendors near the entrance of the office park.

Staff Updates
We are pleased to welcome Dan Rivera, who joined our staff on October 1 as an accountant. Dan holds a master's degree in accounting and has worked as an auditor for seven years and three years as a forensic accountant. Dan and his wife, Marilyn, recently moved to Austin from San Antonio. They have two sons. Danny is 3 and Sam is 1. We look forward to Dan's contributions to our office.

Holiday Closings
Holiday closings are approved annually by the Board of Directors. The table below lists the six approved closings.

Hess Office Park	
201- Holiday Closings	
New Year's Day	January 1
Memorial Day	May 26
Independence Day	July 4
Labor Day	September 4
Thanksgiving	November 23-24
Christmas	December 24-26

In case of emergency, tenants and owners are to contact Colton Blake at 512.555.0100.

Summary
The fourth quarter has shown positive growth, and preliminary data indicates additional growth for the first quarter of next year. Additional information is available on our website at www.hesspropertyenterprises.com.

PATRICK J. HESS 2

Page 2 with Header and Footer

Personal Business Letter

Maria J. Rex
2104 Adger Road, Columbia, SC 29204-3253
803.555.0194 | Maria.Rex@wcc.edu | http://www.linkedin.com/in/rex

Current date

Mr. Eric Todd, President and CEO
CunCo Consulting Alliance
416 West Bay Street
Savannah, GA 31401-1115

Dear Mr. Todd

Ben Sullivan, your manager of Business Development, sent me a copy of the job description posted for the office manager position open at CunCo and suggested that I contact you. My qualifications match the requirements for the office manager you are seeking. Please consider me as an applicant for that position.

My education and my two years of experience managing the four-hour evening shift of two teams of trainers and one of nutrition counselors enabled me to develop the team management and the operational management skills that you require. Our teamwork resulted in a significant revenue increase and expense reduction.

My internship in the President's Office of Wexford Community College enabled me to refine my organizational, problem-solving, and soft skills. Both my experience at Pat's Fitness and Wellness Center and in the President's office required extensive Word, Excel, and PowerPoint use and excellent communication skills. I delivered high-quality products and met very tight deadlines consistently. I understand how those skills can be of value to CunCo.

After you have had an opportunity to review the enclosed resume as well as my LinkedIn Profile, I look forward to meeting with you to discuss how my qualifications and my office management career aspirations can be applied to your position at CunCo Consulting Alliance.

Sincerely

Maria J. Rex

Enclosure

Resume

Maria J. Rex
2104 Adger Road, Columbia, SC 29204-3253
803.555.0194 | Maria.Rex@wcc.edu | http://www.linkedin.com/in/rex

Qualifications Profile for Office Manager

Highly effective, results-oriented, administrative office professional with AS degree and two years of relevant part-time work experience, including demonstrated effective supervisory, customer service, records management, time management, and project management skills. Create professional documents that enhance company image and productivity using Word, Excel, and PowerPoint. Strong written, oral, and electronic communication skills. Excellent interpersonal skills. Honest, ethical, and possess strong work ethic.

Education

AS degree in Business Administration with majors in Office Administration and Office Management from Wexford Community College, Columbia, SC. May 2016. 3.65 GPA.

High school diploma with career emphasis in English and business. Maxwell High School, Charleston, SC. August, 2014. 3.85 GPA.

Experience

Wexford Community College, President's Office, Columbia, SC. Internship, summer 2016.
• Prepared correspondence, reports, and presentations for senior administrators.
• Scheduled and coordinated special events with high-level constituents.
• Received outstanding evaluation, commending my professionalism, social skills, creativity, reliability, problem-solving skills, and the excellent quality of all work.

Pat's Fitness and Wellness Center, supervisor and promoted to office manager for the 3:30 to 7:30 shift (20-25 hours per week) from June 2014 through May 2016.
• Managed two teams of trainers and one team of nutrition counselors; resolved conflicts for clients. Responsible for correspondence with referring physicians, vendors, and clients.
• Managed facility, records, billing, equipment, and supplies; developed procedures.
• Increased client participation and revenue from my shift over 20 percent while reducing expenses by 12 percent.

Honors and Activities

Named a Dean's Scholar; received the Outstanding Business Student Award. Member of Student Advisory Council, president of the Wexford Honor Society, and president of the Office Management Club.

Memo

Tap ENTER 3 times (about 2")

Tab (1" from left margin) →

TO:	Emily Welch, Brian McKenzie, Olivia von Staden
FROM:	Michael Holcomb
DATE:	July 18, 2018
SUBJECT:	Video Conference Call Scheduled Friday, July 26

The final video conference call to select the contractor for the Keystone Community Project will be held on Friday, July 26, from 3:30 to 5:00 p.m. EST. To join the video conference, follow these steps:

1. Call 601.555.0168 and enter the passcode 8103622 when prompted.
2. Go to www.conferences.com/holcomb/PDS/ and join the meeting.

Please review the proposals carefully and be prepared to make a recommendation at the meeting. If you have questions about the proposals, please call me at 601.555.0193 or email me at mholcomb@sydco.com.

xx

Table (formatted with Table Style)

REGENTS MEMORIAL MEDICAL CENTER		
February Seminars		
Seminar Title	**Description**	**Registration**
Surgical Weight Loss	Methods of losing weight, including healthy diet, exercise and medication, will be discussed in detail. Surgical weight loss is an option for those who are motivated and willing to commit to lifestyle changes.	Classes will be held at the Outpatient Surgery Center 75 Pacific Crest Laguna Niguel, CA 92677-5773. Call 949.555.0111 to register.
Life in Motion with Osteoarthritis	Osteoarthritis no longer means that you need to live with a painful disability. Modern medicine, diet, exercise, and surgery can help you enjoy life more fully. Intricate surgical procedures including joint replacement and spinal fusion will be covered.	Register online at www.regents.org/calendar. Materials fee $10.00.
Experts' Cancer Updates	The cancer experts of Regents Medical Center will unveil the results of the latest cancer studies. New breakthrough treatments will be discussed. They will explain what you should know about cancer screenings. Tips on preventing various types of cancers will be provided.	Call 949.555.0100 or register online at www.regents.org/calendar.

Sun Property and Casualty Insurance Company
1592 S. Plaza Way, Flagstaff, AZ 86011-0136
Phone: 928.555.0174 | Solana.Rodriquez@apic.com | Fax: 928.555.0136

News Release Contact Person: Solana Rodriquez

Current date

For Release: Immediately

SUN NAMES NEW PRESIDENT AND CHIEF EXECUTIVE OFFICER

FLAGSTAFF, AZ—The Sun Property and Casualty Insurance Company announced today that its Board of Directors unanimously approved Amy T. Ledbetter as its new chief executive officer. Ledbetter replaces Mark R. Daff, who served as chief executive officer for the past eight years.

Ledbetter had served as senior vice president and chief financial officer for the past five years. Her first experience with Sun came as an intern when she was an accounting student at Meadowfield University. After she completed her accounting degree, she worked two years as a public accountant and earned her Certified Public Accountant (CPA) license. After completing her MBA degree at Eastwell International Graduate School of Business, she joined Sun as an accountant in the Corporate Finance Department.

Ledbetter is married to Kirk T. Parham, a nationally known pediatrician. They have two teenage children—a son, Joseph, and a daughter, Caitlyn.

###

News Release

Sample document ©Cengage Learning. Embedded image courtesy of Openclipart.org

Itinerary for Laurie Hammer July 14 – 16, 201-	
Wednesday, July 14	**Columbia to Cincinnati**
4:40 p.m.	Leave Columbia on non-stop Cincola Flight 5173 and arrive in Cincinnati at 5:55 p.m.; Metro Rental Car (Confirmation #67540912); Riverside Hotel (Confirmation #34898732)
8:15 p.m.	Picked up at hotel by Dave Calhoun and Jack Shaut; dinner at Royal Mason
Thursday, July 15	**Cincinnati**
8:00 a.m.	Leave for Natorp Publishing Center; 6319 Natorp Boulevard, Mason, Ohio
9:00 a.m.	Meet with President and Editor-in-chief; President's office—Suite 600
9:45 a.m.	Meet with the Editorial Team, Fifth Floor Conference Room
11:45 a.m.	Break
12:00 noon	Working lunch, Fifth Floor Conference Room
2:00 p.m.	Meet with book designers, Fifth Floor Conference Room
2:30 p.m.	Break
3:00 p.m.	Meet with the Production Team, Fifth Floor Conference Room
5:30 p.m.	Return to hotel
7:30 p.m.	Meet Project Team for dinner; Chez Ruby; 644 Walnut Street; map in Travel folder.
Friday, July 16	**Cincinnati to Columbia**
7:45 a.m.	Return rental car: Cincola Flight 6754 departs at 9:20 a.m. and arrives in Columbia at 10:40 a.m.

Itinerary

Minutes

Nursing Partnership Board
Hospital Atrium
January 15, 201-, 10:30 a.m.

Board members present were Lester Caldwell, chair and university representative; Mary Freeman, meeting facilitator; Jane Metze, technical college representative; Wanda Stewart, project coordinator; Bentley Burns, project assistant; and Tyler Walker, hospital representative.

Proposal
Mary Freeman presented the original agreement with the markup showing all of the changes in it. She pointed out that these changes were recommended at the last meeting. The Board agreed that the revised version accurately reflected the discussion of the previous meeting. Mary Freeman was asked to revise the final agreement with the changes noted.

Terms
Bentley Burns presented the changes reflecting the additional $1,000,000 committed by the fifth area hospital. The hospital also committed to the $50,000 annual contribution for the next five years. The Board discussed several alternatives for distributing the additional funds and then agreed that the best approach was to use the same distribution formula as it previously agreed to use for the funds contributed by the other four hospitals. Mary Freeman was asked to revise the final agreement to reflect the additional funds and the distribution formula. She agreed to finalize all documents within one week.

Hospital Perspective
Tyler Walker presented the attached funding plan submitted by the five hospitals. The Board reviewed and approved the plan.

Technical College Perspective
Jane Metze presented the attached fund usage plan submitted by the technical college. The Board reviewed and approved the plan.

University perspective
Lester Caldwell presented the attached fund usage plan submitted by the university. The Board reviewed and approved the plan.

Project Approval
Lester Caldwell thanked the members of the Board for all the hard work and the effective collaboration that resulted in approval of the plans presented by the hospitals, the technical college, and the university. He indicated that the next big hurdle is to ensure that the plans are implemented effectively. After considerable discussion of how plans would be implemented, the Board approved the entire project.

Minutes (Page 1)

Minutes—Nursing Partnership Board 2 January 15, 201-

Next meeting
The chair reminded the group that the next Nursing Partnership Board meeting is scheduled for February 8 at 10:30 in the Hospital Atrium.

Adjournment
The meeting adjourned at 12:05 p.m.

Minutes (Page 2)

Appendix D Command Summary

Command	Location	Button/Image
Align Text	Home/Paragraph/Click desired alignment (Align Text Left, Center, Align Text Right or Justify)	
Blank Page	Inert/Pages/Blank Page	
Page Break	Insert/Pages/Page Break	Blank Page / Page Break
Bookmark	Insert/Links/Bookmark	Bookmark
Breaks	Page Layout/Page Setup/Breaks	Breaks
Bullets or Numbering	Home/Paragraph/Bullets or Numbering	
Captions	References/Captions/Insert Caption	Insert Caption
Center Page	Layout/Page Setup/Dialog Box Launcher/ Layout tab/Vertical alignment/Center	Page Setup dialog
Change User Name	File/Options/General or Review/Options/Dialog Box Launcher	Personalize your copy of Microsoft Office; User name: Student Name; Initials: us; Track Changes Options

Close Document	File/Close or Close button at top right of screen	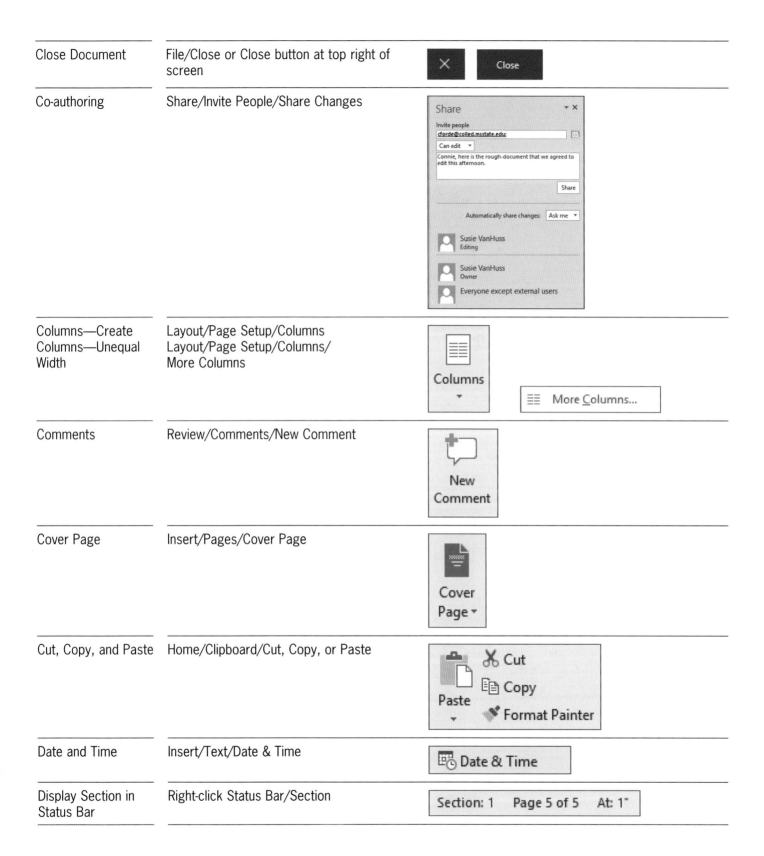
Co-authoring	Share/Invite People/Share Changes	
Columns—Create Columns—Unequal Width	Layout/Page Setup/Columns Layout/Page Setup/Columns/ More Columns	
Comments	Review/Comments/New Comment	
Cover Page	Insert/Pages/Cover Page	
Cut, Copy, and Paste	Home/Clipboard/Cut, Copy, or Paste	
Date and Time	Insert/Text/Date & Time	
Display Section in Status Bar	Right-click Status Bar/Section	

Document Formatting Style Set	Design/Document Formatting/Style Set Gallery	
Document Themes	Design/Document Formatting/Themes	
Drop Cap	Insert/Text/Drop Cap	
Envelopes and Labels	Mailings/Create/Envelopes or Labels	
Find, Replace, and Select	Home/Editing/Find, Replace, or Select	
Font Commands—Bold, Italic, Underline, Font Color, Font, Font Size, etc.	Home/Font/Command	
Footnotes	References/Footnotes/Insert Footnote	
Format Painter	Home/Clipboard/Format Painter	
Formulas in Table	Table Tools Layout/Data/Formula	
Graphics—Layout Options	Select graphic/Layout options displays	
Hanging indent	Ruler/Indent Markers	

Header and Footer	Insert/Header & Footer/Header or Footer	
Increase/ Decrease Indent	Home/Paragraph/Increase Indent or Decrease Indent	
Indent Marker	Ruler/Indent Markers	
Insert File	Insert/Text/Object/Text from File	
Insert Merge Field Address Block Greeting Line	Mailings/Write & Insert Fields/Insert Merge Field, Address Block, or Greeting Line	
Line and Page Breaks	Home/Paragraph/Dialog Box Launcher/ Line and Page Breaks tab	
Line Spacing	Home/Paragraph/Line and Paragraph Spacing	
Mail Merge Select Recipients Edit Recipient List	Mailings/Start Mail Merge/Start Mail Merge/Step-by-Step Mail Merge Wizard/Select Recipients or Edit Recipient List	
Margins	Layout/Page Setup/Margins	

Mini toolbar	Appears when text is selected	
Multilevel list	Home/Paragraph/Multilevel List	
Navigation Pane	View/Show/Navigation Pane	
New Document	File/New	
Online Pictures	Insert/Illustrations/Online Pictures	
Online Video	Insert/Media/Online Video	
Open Existing Document	File/Open	
Open in Word	Word Online Ribbon/OPEN IN WORD	
Page Borders	Design/Page Background/Page Borders	

Page Break	Insert/Pages/Page Break	
Page Numbers—Insert	Insert/Header & Footer/Page Number	
Page Orientation	Layout/Page Setup/Orientation	
Paste Options	Home/Clipboard/Paste/Click a Paste Option	
Pictures—Crop	Picture Tools Format/Size/Crop	
Picture—Format	Picture Tools Format	
Picture—Insert	Insert/Illustrations/Pictures/Locate and select picture/Insert	
Picture—Size	Picture Tools Format/Size/Height or Width Arrows	
Pictures—Styles	Picture Tools Format/Picture Styles	

Command	Path / Instructions	Button
Add Text to Shapes	Insert/Illustrations/Shapes Right-click and click Add Text; key the text	Shapes
Shapes—Format	Drawing Tools Format	Drawing Tools Format
Section Breaks	Layout/Page Setup/Breaks; Select the desired section break from the list	Breaks
Save and Save As (to OneDrive or This PC)	File/Save or Save As/OneDrive or File/Save As/This PC	Save As (Info, New, Open, Save, Save As, Print, Share, Export; OneDrive - VanHuss Susie.VanHuss@VanHuss.onmicrosoft.c...; Sites - VanHuss Susie.VanHuss@VanHuss.onmicrosoft.c...; OneDrive; This PC)
Ruler—View	View/Show/Ruler	Show (Ruler, Gridlines, Navigation Pane)
Remove Space After Paragraph	SHIFT + ENTER or Home/Paragraph/Line and Paragraph Spacing	Add Space Before Paragraph / Remove Space After Paragraph
Quick Parts	Insert/Text/Quick Parts	Quick Parts
Quick Access Toolbar	Upper-left corner of screen/Use down arrow to customize	[toolbar]
Print	File/Print	Print

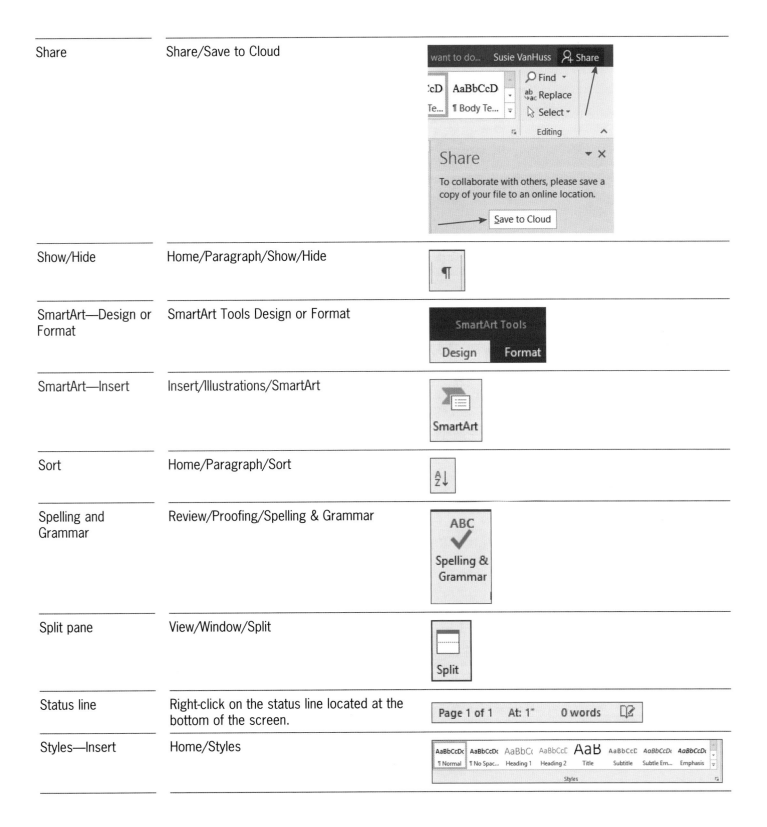

Share	Share/Save to Cloud
Show/Hide	Home/Paragraph/Show/Hide
SmartArt—Design or Format	SmartArt Tools Design or Format
SmartArt—Insert	Insert/Illustrations/SmartArt
Sort	Home/Paragraph/Sort
Spelling and Grammar	Review/Proofing/Spelling & Grammar
Split pane	View/Window/Split
Status line	Right-click on the status line located at the bottom of the screen.
Styles—Insert	Home/Styles

Symbols and Special Characters	Insert/Symbols/Symbol Insert/Symbols/Symbol/More Symbols/ Special Characters tab	
Table of Contents	References/Table of Contents/Table of Contents	
Table of Contents—Update	References/Table of Contents/Update Table	
Table of Figures	References/Captions/Insert Table of Figures	
Tables	Insert/Table	
Tables—Adjust Column Width Using the Ruler	Ruler/Column Marker/Drag to appropriate position	
Tables—AutoFit	Table Tools Layout/Cell Size/AutoFit	
Table Tools—Design or Layout	Table Tools Design or Layout	
Tables—Change Cell Height and Width	Table Tools Layout/Cell Size	
Tables—Change Text Alignment	Table Tools Layout/Alignment	

Tables—Delete Rows & Columns	Table Tools Layout/Rows & Columns/Delete	
Tables—Insert using the Insert Table Command	Insert/Tables/Table/Insert Table	
Tables—Insert Rows & Columns	Table Tools Layout/Rows & Columns	
Tables—Insert using the Table Grid	Insert/Tables/Table/Drag to select number of rows and columns	
Tables—Merge or Split Cells	Table Tools Layout/Merge/Merge or Split Cells	
Tables—Properties	Table Tools Layout/Table/Properties	

Text Box	Insert/Text/Text Box	
Templates	File/New	
Tell me what you want to do	Click *Tell me what you want to do* or key keywords in the *Search the web and Windows* box at the bottom left of screen	
Tabs—Modify Tabs using the Tabs dialog box	Home/Paragraph/Dialog Box Launcher/Tabs	
Tabs—Modify Tabs using Horizontal Ruler	Select desired tab; Click and drag the tab to the desired location on the ruler.	
Tabs—Left, Center, Right, Decimal, and Bar	View Ruler/Tab Alignment Button/Click on Horizontal Ruler	
Tables—Styles and Shading	Table Tools Design/Table Styles/Shading	
Tables—Repeat Header Rows	Table Tools Layout/Data/Repeat Header Rows	

Thesaurus	Review/Proofing/Thesaurus	
Track Changes	Review/Tracking/Track Changes	
Track Change Options	Review/Tracking/Dialog Box Launcher	
Track Changes—Review Changes	Review/Changes/Accept, Reject, Previous or Next	
Vertical Page Position	To turn on: Right-click status bar/Click Vertical Page Position	
Views—Document	View/Views/Read Mode or other views	
Views—View Buttons	Select view buttons on status bar	
Watermark	Design/Page Background/Watermark	
WordArt—Insert	Insert/Text/WordArt	

Word Count/ Pages/Characters/ Paragraphs/Lines	Review/Proofing/Word Count	ABC 123 Word Count
Zoom	View/Zoom/Zoom or Page Options	Zoom 100% One Page Multiple Pages Page Width Zoom
Zoom in or out	Click Zoom/Move left or right to zoom in or out	– ┃ +

Path to Workplace Success...Develop Critical Skills

SKILLS REQUIRED FOR CAREER SUCCESS

The earlier you start planning and preparing for your career, the more likely you are to be successful.

The skills required for specific jobs vary significantly depending on your field of interest, the organization that hires you, the type of job, and the level of the job. Regardless of these factors, a common base of knowledge and a common set of skills are required for virtually every job. These skills can be grouped into three categories:

- Technical skills
- Soft skills
- Conceptual skills

Technical Skills

Technical skills are especially important for entry-level positions. You will develop technical skills in the courses you take.

These skills include:

- Knowledge
- Expertise
- Ability to do the job

Examples of universal technical skills would be keyboarding skill and the ability to use applications such as *Word*, *Excel*, *Outlook*, and *PowerPoint*. The specific knowledge varies depending on the field, such as manager, medical professional, or architect.

Soft Skills

Softs skills are critical at every level. The remainder of this section focuses on soft skills.

Soft skills are personal attributes, interpersonal skills, and emotional intelligence. Soft skills relate to the way you interact with other employees. Examples of soft skills that are required in most jobs include:

- Communication skills
- Creativity
- Critical thinking and decision making
- Ethics, honesty, and integrity
- Accountability and responsibility
- Teamwork and collaboration
- Time management and productivity
- Work ethic

Conceptual Skills

You will learn conceptual skills in advanced courses and on the job. Conceptual skills are required for advancement in your position.

Conceptual skills are the ability to see the big picture and how things fit together. Conceptual skills enable you to understand how your job fits into the overall business strategy of your organization.

Path to Workplace Success...Develop Soft Skills

CRITICAL THINKING AND DECISION MAKING

The ability to think critically helps you to make wise decisions that impact your work and your everyday life. Follow these five basic steps to make effective decisions.

1. **Identify the decision and collect facts.** Analyze objectively the situation requiring the decision. Get all the facts. Avoid making assumptions colored by stereotypes and preconceptions.

2. **Determine the options available.** Be creative in generating as many options as possible. In some cases options are predetermined.

3. **Analyze options carefully.** Try to view the situation from the perspective of everybody involved and that of the organization. Examine consequences for each person and for the organization.

4. **Select the best option and implement it.** Evaluate all of the options and get more facts if needed. Also consider what is necessary for the option to be successful. The way a decision is implemented often determines its success.

5. **Evaluate the effectiveness of the decision implemented.** Did it produce the desired results? Can it be improved?

For each of the scenarios below, key the following information in a Word document.

1. List the decision that must be made and the key facts to be considered. Add other things you think should be considered.

2. List the options available and the pros and cons of each.

3. Select the option and explain why it is best.

Scenario 1

Situation: Assume you live at home and have saved enough money that you could (1) buy a small car so that you will have your own transportation, (2) use it to pay your tuition and other costs and avoid having to take out another substantial student loan, or (3) live in an apartment next year.

Facts: Family members lend you a car frequently when you need it. Most days you ride to classes with family or friends, but you would prefer to have your own car. Public transportation to your college is available and inexpensive. Your family provides free living and tries to help you, but they are not in a position to pay your tuition. You already have heavy student debt that you will have to begin paying as soon as you complete your program.

Decision: What decision is in your best interest? Why?

Scenario 2

Situation: You have been looking for a part-time job, and you have two opportunities: One is for the Foundation, which raises money for and supports your college. The other is a night job (6:00–11:00 p.m., four or five rotating nights a week) as the desk clerk at a local inn that is relatively inexpensive. With both jobs, you could work 20 to 30 hours per week. With the Foundation, you could work around your class schedule.

Facts: The Foundation duties include many that you are or will be studying—marketing, finance, accounting, management, and office technology. You would be able to interact with donors and board members who generally are business executives. The inn job duties include customer service skills, telephone skills, and basic office skills. The inn job pays $1 more per hour than the Foundation job. Before you make your decision, search for information about desk clerk jobs in hotels and inns and about jobs in educational-type foundations.

Decision: Which job would be in your best interest? Why? What other information do you need to make a good decision?

Path to Workplace Success...Develop Soft Skills

COMMUNICATION—MAKING A FIRST IMPRESSION

Building a strong network of professionals is essential on the path to success. Presenting yourself in a confident and energetic manner forms a positive first impression that opens the door to professional friendships. These five tips are highly recommended by communication experts.

1. **Initiate a conversation**. It's hard to build a network without starting a conversation, and often you are the one who must initiate the conversation. It's okay if you are shy—get over it.

2. **Give a firm handshake.** Show your interest and enthusiasm by giving a firm handshake—touching web to web. Please look at the person while shaking hands, and do smile.

3. **Maintain direct eye contact.** Look at the person while talking and avoid the nervous tendency to look away. You do not want to give the impression you are nervous or bored.

4. **Present good posture.** Stand tall and do not slouch. Lean forward as you are talking to indicate interest in the other person.

5. **Dress appropriately**. Attention to one's dress conveys interest in the person you are meeting for perhaps the first time. This first impression can determine the potential impact you may have on that person.

For each of the scenarios below, you will practice one of these essential communication skills. In a *Word* document, key a short explanation of what you learned in the practice activity.

Scenario 1

Situation: You have just been hired in an entry-level position, and you begin work in one week. You understand how important making a positive impression is—especially on the first day on the job. A proper handshake is the first skill you have decided to practice.

Think/Discuss/Research: What are the characteristics of a proper handshake for making a positive and powerful first impression? What are some poor techniques?

Apply: Pair with someone and practice shaking hands. For comparison, discuss and practice both effective and ineffective techniques.

Write: Describe the characteristics of a powerful handshake that you have learned are important for the first day on the job and every day.

Scenario 2

Situation: You are doing well in your position, but you know today will be important as you are sharing an idea at a team meeting. You know you must project confidence and have effective eye contact while in conversation with the team members.

Think/Discuss/Research: Why is eye contact important when sharing your ideas with your team or supervisor? What impression are you making?

Apply: With a group of at least three people, share an idea that you have. Topics might include (1) a suggestion you have for an improvement in your community or school, (2) how a person's dress has impacted your first impression of that person, or (3) time management strategies that have helped you in the past. Or you can choose a topic with which you are comfortable. Your goal is to have eye contact with each person in the group by the conclusion of the conversation.

Write: Describe your experience. Did the topic make a difference in the quality of eye contact? Did you feel uncomfortable looking at your team while you talked? Did you receive any feedback from your team by looking at them? Did you feel nervous and feel the need to look away from your team? How can you improve your next conversation?

Path to Workplace Success...Develop Soft Skills

ACCOUNTABILITY

Accepting a position in the workplace indicates agreement and commitment to fulfilling the duties and responsibilities of the position and the expectations of the manager. The organization prospers when each team member consistently meets and exceeds the position's requirements and the expected goals. A few fundamental accountability practices are essential to be successful.

1. **Arrive on time.** Punctuality is an outward sign that the job is important to the employee, and arriving early to be ready to begin work at the starting time shows commitment to excellence.

2. **Stay on task.** With today's social media and cell phones, an employee is easily tempted to lose focus on tasks at hand to quickly check for messages or play a game. The expectation is for employees to complete work tasks on company time.

3. **Commit to quality work.** An excellent employee sets high standards beyond the minimum requirements and commits to excellence in all areas. Doing mediocre work is not an option.

4. **Hone organizational skills.** Prioritizing projects and meeting deadlines are critical to fulfilling job responsibilities. Acquiring organizational skills is essential.

5. **Devote time to professional development.** Growing in the job is also an outward sign of accountability. During performance review meetings, the employee and manager agree on areas of development that will assist the employee and the company.

For each of the scenarios below, you will complete an activity related to accountability. In a *Word* document, key a short explanation of what you have learned.

Scenario 1

Situation: You have a major report due in two weeks. Your team depends on your leadership and organizational skills to produce a quality product and to meet the deadline. You have a tendency to procrastinate.

Research: Locate at least four time management suggestions recommended by time management experts.

Apply: Select at least two strategies you will use to ensure this deadline is met with a quality product. What technology will you choose to assist you?

Write: Describe the two strategies you will use and identify the selected technology tool. Explain how these strategies will assist you in avoiding procrastination and meeting your deadline.

Scenario 2

Situation: Your manager is completing a task analysis for each employee to determine the needs of the organization. If you are a full-time student and not employed, keep the log for all your activities.

Research: Keep a log for one day (if you are a part-time employee, use the hours you work) and list all activities completed. Start at 8 a.m. and list every activity for each 30-minute increment until 5 p.m.

Apply: Analyze the log. Did you use time wisely? If not, how was time wasted? Could you rearrange work activities to achieve better results? Did you arrive on time? Did you begin work promptly?

Write: Describe at least two areas that you think were effective in your daily log. Explain at least two things you could have done differently that would have allowed you to be more productive.

Path to Workplace Success...Capstone Project

SOFT SKILLS INTERVIEW WITH FOLLOW-UP ACTIVITIES

This project can be completed by a team or by each student individually. The team approach is recommended.

1. Your instructor will determine whether this is a team (three or four members) or an individual activity and will provide a timeline for you to complete the activities.
2. Obtain contact information for team members if appropriate.

Part I – 15-Minute Face-to-Face Interview (Required of Each Student)

1. Each student must select an individual who hires, supervises, or manages employees in a career area of interest. The person may be in a company in which you or a family member is employed or someone from your neighborhood, your church, or another group with which you are affiliated.
2. Contact the individual and request an appointment for a face-to-face 15-minute interview. Explain that you are studying the importance of developing soft skills as part of your career preparation. Describe one or two soft skills you explored in this activity.
3. In a *Word* document, key the five questions in item 4 below, leaving space after each question to take brief notes on the answers.
4. Conduct the interview and take brief hand-written notes.
 a. What soft skills are your strengths that helped you most to get your job and progress in your career?
 b. What soft skills do the people you manage need most?
 c. When you are hiring, how do you determine if a candidate has the required soft skills?
 d. How do you help your employees improve their soft skills?
 e. What advice would you give me about developing good soft skills?

Part II – Edit and Share Notes (Required for Both Teams and Individuals)

1. Edit and key your notes using complete sentences.
2. Share your notes with each team member **or**, if you are working individually, share your notes with your instructor.

Part III – Selection of Five Most Important Soft Skills

Part III contains two options for students to determine what they believe are the five most important soft skills for workplace success based on interview data and their joint views or their individual views plus research data.

Option 1 is to be completed by students who are working in teams to make the decision.

Option 2 is to be completed by students who are working individually to make the decision.

Part III, Option 1 – Team Meeting and Discussion (Team Option)

1. Meet with your team and discuss the answers each of you obtained. If you are in the same location, use a face-to-face team meeting. If you are doing distance education students meeting in different locations, use a chat or discussion option.

2. List all soft skills recommended by the individuals interviewed.

3. Reach a consensus on what the team thinks are the five most important soft skills recommended by the individuals interviewed. (Do not vote—discuss until you agree on the important soft skills.)

★ TIP

If you have a work schedule conflict, ask your instructor to approve your participation by telephone. All members must participate in the discussion.

Part III, Option 2 – Research Soft Skills (Individual Option)

1. Locate and find three current articles on soft skills needed most by employees. Make sure they come from reliable sources. Key the names and source information for the articles. Write a sentence or two on why you believe each source is reliable.

2. Compare the soft skills from your interview notes to those recommended in the three articles.

3. Prepare a list of at least ten important soft skills from your interview and the articles.

4. Review them carefully and list the five soft skills that you think are most important for your career.

Part IV – Soft Skills Assessment (Required for Both Teams and Individuals)

1. Use a 1 to 5 scale with 5 being the highest (your strengths) and 1 being the lowest (your weaknesses) to evaluate yourself honestly on the five most important soft skills listed in Part III, Option 1 or 2.

2. List things that you can do to improve on the two skills that were rated lowest in item 1 above. Use the Internet to research this topic if necessary.

Part V – Team Assessment (Team Requirement)

1. Rate each member of your team and yourself on the following points using the same 1 to 5 scale that you used in Part IV. Key the team member's name and the rating on each of the five following evaluation questions:

 a. Did the team member share good interview notes from his or her interview?

 b. Did the team member meet the timeline provided by your instructor?

 c. Did the team member participate effectively in the discussion?

 d. Did the team member respect the opinions of others and encourage all to share their thoughts?

 e. Did the team member do his or her fair share of the work?

2. For each team member, list the soft skills that were used most effectively during this activity.

3. In industry, leaders usually assess the results or outcomes produced by the whole team—not what each team member did. Would you be comfortable if the same standard were applied to your team— that is, the same grade would be given to all team members? Why or why not?

Index